THE
CLOSEST OF
STRANGERS

THE
CLOSEST OF
STRANGERS

Liberalism and the Politics of Race in New York

JIM SLEEPER

W·W·NORTON & COMPANY

New York   London

Printed in the United States of America.

The text of this book is composed in Times Roman,
with the display set in Serif Gothic Heavy.
Composition and manufacturing by the Haddon Craftsmen, Inc.
Book design by Jacques Chazaud.

First published as a Norton paperback 1991

Library of Congress Cataloging-in-Publication Data

Sleeper, Jim.
    The closest of strangers : liberalism and the politics of race in
New York / Jim Sleeper.
        p.   cm.
    1. New York (N.Y.)—Race relations. 2. New York (N.Y.)—Politics
and government—1951– 3. Liberalism—New York (N.Y.)—History—20th
century. I. Title.
F128.9.N4S54   1990
305.8′0097471—dc20   90-38676

ISBN 0–393–30799–9

W.W. Norton & Company, Inc., 500 Fifth Avenue, New York, N.Y. 10110
W.W. Norton & Company, Ltd., 10 Coptic Street, London WC1A 1PU

2 3 4 5 6 7 8 9 0

The Negroes of this country may never be able to rise to power, but they are very well placed indeed to precipitate chaos and ring down the curtain on the American dream.

—JAMES BALDWIN, *The Fire Next Time*

He was grave and silent, and then he said sombrely, I have one great fear in my heart, that one day when [whites] are turned to loving, they will find that we are turned to hating.

—ALAN PATON, *Cry, the Beloved Country*

How doth the city sit solitary, that was full of people! How is she become as a widow! She that was great among the nations, and princess among the provinces, how is she become tributary! She weepeth sore in the night, and her tears are on her cheeks; among all her lovers she hath none to comfort her; all her friends have dealt treacherously with her, they are become her enemies.

—The Book of Lamentations

Contents

Dedication and Acknowledgments

I dedicate this book to the children of New York City and to all New Yorkers who manage every day to overcome the obstacles discussed here—without the benefit of this type of discussion. Much of what's best and much of what's most painful about race relations in New York is unspoken or spoken sideways, with a wink, a nod, a shrug. That is not as it should be; there are too many things we need to tell one another and our children in order to help the city find a clearer voice in the years ahead. I hope this book will contribute something to such an effort.

Some of my material was gathered originally with the steady encouragement and inspiration of Irving Howe, who, as editor of *Dissent* magazine, has published a dozen of my essays on New York City politics and race relations since 1980, culminating in a special fall 1987 issue of *Dissent,* which I edited, "In Search of New York," republished by Transaction Books. When Peter Steinfels was editor of *Commonweal,* he, too, gave me invaluable opportunities to develop my ideas in print.

A Charles Revson Fellowship at Columbia University in 1982–83 let me read some New York City history, and I am grateful to Eli Evans, a historian and president of the foundation, and Eli Ginzberg, a distinguished economist and director of the fellows program, for their support. The immediate impetus for this book came from a discussion with Nicholas Von Hoffman, who helped me sharpen my ideas in conversation and encouraged me to hammer out a proposal.

My colleagues at *New York Newsday* have given me a wonderful community and a treasure trove of lore and understanding of the city. My editors, Anthony Marro, Jim Klurfeld, Tom Plate (now editorial-page editor of the *Los Angeles Times*), and Ben Gerson made possible a three-month leave in the midst of a very busy year; as editor of the New York Viewpoints section of the paper, Ben has been a brilliant and gracious interlocutor in our many workaday conversations as we've edited opinion essays touching the subject of this book. Special thanks, too, to my *Newsday* colleagues Christine Baird, Nina Bernstein, Joe Dolman, Jim Dwyer, Merle English, Josh Friedman, Mitch Gelman, Rita Giordano, Ron Howell, Leonard Levitt, Bob Liff, Michael Powell, Manuel Perez-Rivas, Sydney Schanberg, Ernest Tollerson, and Karen Van Rossem for their thoughts, their encouragement, and their help.

Other mentors and friends whose inspiration and interest in my work were more critical than they know are Jim Chapin, Charles Morris, Claudia Morgan, George Scialabba, Fred Siegel, and Shelby Steele. Brian Morton helped me immeasurably with research and was a constant source of insight. Tim O'Malley compensated for my underwhelming mastery of computers.

Many of the people who gave of their time and archives are quoted or credited in the book itself; those who appear briefly or not at all but to whom I feel a special debt include Frank Arricale, Charles Bagli, Andrew Cooper, Mario Cuomo, Robert Fitch, Eric Foner, Mike Gecan, Lou Gordon, Roger Green, Cheryl Greenberg, Jerry Hudson, David R. Jones, Francine Justa, Martin Kilson, William Kornblum, Irving Levine, Amanda McMurray, Deborah Meier, Nicolaus Mills, Jim Miskiewicz, Joshua Muravchik, Mark Naison, Morris Renek, Jonathan Rieder, Jim Rooney, Gasper Signorelli, Roger Starr, David Trager, Mildred Tudy, Gus Tyler, David Unger, the Reverend Johnny Ray Youngblood, and Jitu Weusi.

These people and many others I spoke with showed me that growing always means stumbling toward truths intuited but unproven and that dignity, especially in encounters across race lines, has something to do with how you handle yourself without adequate information, analysis—and protection. Naturally, then, while I couldn't have written this book without them, they aren't going to stand with me in everything I say. The risk, like the debt, is mine.

Finally, I thank my wife, Rachel Gorlin, and my editor at W. W. Norton & Company, Gerald Howard, two children of the city who, in their different ways, have been the anchors of my life and work.

THE
CLOSEST OF
STRANGERS

Introduction

Into the Abyss

One of the more candid observations by a public official about life in New York at the end of the 1980s came not from Mayor Edward Koch but from the city's often less than candid comptroller, Harrison J. Goldin, during a televised Democratic mayoral primary debate in August 1989. Maybe Goldin's abysmally low standing in the polls and the prospect of imminent retirement from politics had loosened his tongue; or maybe he couldn't resist the chance to score a quick point off his nemesis, Koch. Whatever the reason, when the mayor remarked, "Almost everyone wants to come to New York . . . to visit, but more likely to live," Goldin departed from the campaign norm to say something that rang absolutely if leadenly true:

Ed, I think that we're not going to save New York until we get a mayor who recognizes that there are an awful lot of people who want to leave here, who would leave here if they could. We need a mayor who would acknowledge that, because that's what it's going to take to begin to improve the quality of life. That's why businesses aren't coming to New York. That's why businesses are leaving New York. Because of the crime situation. Because of the public schools' deterioration. Because you can't find an affordable apartment. . . .

On its face, Goldin's evocation of a city in which many feel trapped and others are held only by slender threads that are snapping one by one each day offered nothing new. New York has always been a crowded, messy conduit, a place people pass through as immigrants on their way to the rest of America or as aspirants to nationwide celebrity and clout that transcend the city itself. Since its founding in 1625 as a Dutch-run, polyglot port, millions of its residents have been transients bearing burdens self-imposed by migration, idealism, or pathology—conditions that, for a while, at least, wouldn't let them live anywhere else. With always inadequate assistance from New York's public and private institutions and plenty of discrimination from those who ran them, each wave of newcomers has gotten its feet on ground, learned American rules, and won a brief ascendancy in the city's civic, commercial, and cultural life. Then it has spread out across the country and the world, bearing athletes, impresarios, engineers, political leaders—new Americans.

The only thing constant in the city itself has been this relentless churning of populations, of real estate, of public and private endeavors of every kind, and, with it, the uniquely gritty, vibrant, and dense life that both enchants and revolts its visitors. But New Yorkers themselves couldn't sustain the shocks of their own diversity and intensity without hammering out at least some provisional folkways. These have generally included a rough but ready tolerance, indispensable to survival, and an admiration, even a thirst, for excellence, everybody's ticket out of the maelstrom. Each reigning ethnic or interest group in the city's history has tried to impress these and other, sometimes contradictory, values on new arrivals through local authorities—the neighborhood cop, teacher, politician, shopkeeper, activist, social worker—who have often been resented but just as often been decisive in molding the next generation of New Yorkers. When they have managed to teach tolerance and excellence, the city has disgorged both believers in democracy and new elites into the nation's bloodstream and the world's.

But Goldin was referring to a different sort of leave-taking—and, for those unable to leave, an ominous entrapment. For the city's processes of socialization had been breaking down since the late 1960s under the impact of powerful economic and social currents, its diversity and intensity spiraling off at times into uncontrollable urban nightmares of violence, of paranoia. Other cities, too, had experienced frightening dislocations, but New York, as always, had played them larger than life, owing to its size and its role as a center of communications and entertainment: its travails were featured on network news and embellished in movies like *The Warriors* and *Escape from New York* and in novels like Tom Wolfe's *The Bonfire of the Vanities.*

Somehow, through the 1980s, it had seemed that the New York character—tough, tart, cosmopolitan—would endure. In the middle years of that decade, Koch had drawn brilliantly on the city's enormous residual strengths and on fortuitous international developments to stoke a great boom. Its glitter had eclipsed the continuing decay of opportunity, authority, and civility for a growing number of New Yorkers and the ascendancy of force and fraud in the calculations of their everyday lives. By the time of the 1989 mayoral campaign, the boom had receded, exposing not just the perennial ethnic clashes and jockeyings of elites but also a frightening disintegration of families and neighborhood institutions amid reports of soaring child abuse and abandonment. Everywhere, it seemed, were the encroachments of the drug economy, of roaming packs of violent youths, and of the homeless and mentally helpless, human wreckage which no one knew how to repair and which, it began to dawn on many New Yorkers, would remain with them for as long as they remained in the city.

And at the center of the breakdown Goldin described—the crime, the deterioration of the schools, the crisis of affordable housing — were blacks and Puerto Ricans, the only two substantial population groups in New York's history whose members could not be said to have entered into the American experiment by choice in the first place. Dutch-run New Amsterdam had held several thousand African slaves, and many southern blacks who had subsequently chosen the city had done so not for the lamp beside its golden door but in hopes that it would be one of the least cruel of their stations of the cross. By the late 1970s, it was clear that the city had failed utterly to absorb and uplift a critical mass of these sojourners—even as it continued to "work" for more recent arrivals from Hong Kong and Cartagena. In 1989, Goldin understood and articulated the simple truth that thousands of New Yorkers, black as well as white, whose time in the city ought not yet to have run its course, were scheming to leave, embittered, unfulfilled.

None of the mayoral candidates would have denied that racism—the crippling legacies of slavery and Jim Crow, along with continuing discrimination under President Ronald Reagan—helped explain why blacks and Puerto Ricans were doing worse than earlier white immigrants and more recent newcomers of color. Nor did anyone deny that the city's loss of 600,000 blue-collar jobs in the 1970s had compounded racism's effects, undermining black and Puerto Rican prospects even as civil-rights victories enhanced opportunities to compete for such jobs. Koch, too, acknowledged these constraints, though his challengers insisted he'd reinforced Reagan's "malign neglect" locally and exacerbated racial tensions—accusations that would stick and cost him renomination. Yet these explanations couldn't account for the fact that, by the end of the 1980s, local racial disputes were turning less and less on controversies over racism in employment or housing and more and more on death—highly charged criminal-justice cases involving murderous interracial assaults, black-on-white as well as vice versa, in the streets.

The city's racial recriminations had drawn national attention in 1984, when Bernhard Goetz shot four black youths in a subway car in Manhattan, and again in the Queens neighborhood of Howard Beach in 1986, when white youths assaulted three black men, chasing one to his death on a busy parkway. Hostilities reached new depths a year later, again drawing national notice, when fifteen-year-old Tawana Brawley reported that she had been kidnapped and raped by a gang of white men, including law enforcement officers. Though Brawley lived more than an hour north of the city, the Reverend Al Sharpton and the attorneys Alton Maddox, Jr., and C. Vernon Mason, leaders of the protest strategy in the Howard Beach case, sped up the Hudson, media in tow, establishing a symbolic continuity between the Brawley story and the tragedy in Queens.

Brawley's account of her violation by white authorities brought to the surface an archetype, seared into black memory, of the most intimate, passional sort of exploitation. But in the hands of her advisers, even the discovery that her story was a hoax was made to echo an equally venerable script: for centuries, whites had falsely accused blacks of raping white women. That whites themselves would now taste victimization by lie seemed to give any number of otherwise intelligent people a certain satisfaction.

Hardly had this new low in interracial trust been reached than yet another abyss opened one spring evening in 1989, during the mayoral campaign, when a white woman jogging in Central Park was assaulted by a gang of black youths. Reports that she had been raped and bludgeoned within an inch of her death loosed a torrent of white rage that had been seething in the wake of the Brawley psychodrama. Next, Yusuf Hawkins, an innocent visitor to Brooklyn's Bensonhurst section, was murdered by a gang of white youths, an outrage deepened by the silence of dwarfs who'd witnessed the killing but lost their tongues on the witness stand. By the end of the year and the decade, the city seemed numb as Maddox told an audience on the black radio station WLIB that the Central Park rape story was itself another hoax in ancient mold: who, he asked, had been allowed to see the victim before her suspiciously "miraculous" recovery? That Maddox and a colleague had watched one defendant break down on videotape while looking at photos of the battered victim somehow didn't matter.

Those of us chronicling and commenting on these disasters in the press knew that most blacks, including many black leaders, were embarrassed by the way militant black leaders were grandstanding. We wondered why so few of them challenged the venom and the lies. Perhaps it was because Maddox, Mason, and Sharpton were seeking, through communal paroxysms like the one they whipped up in the Brawley case, a moral equivalent of the Eichmann trial—a definitive, purging conviction of a white liberal society that kept copping pleas. Many blacks agreed that there should be such a trial, even if they did not endorse the tactics of Maddox and Mason: the two attorneys were renowned for trying to thwart prosecutions of white assailants in order to prove to blacks that the criminal justice system would never serve them. Even in Howard Beach, they had tried at the last minute to undo the appointment of the state special prosecutor which they themselves had won, apparently because Charles Hynes was white, because he was a friend of Governor Mario Cuomo's, and, most of all, because he might vindicate the system too easily and too soon by actually convicting the white defendants.

Now, with the Central Park attack, even liberal whites, whose patience had worn thin, began compiling their own true grievances and sweepingly false accusations. That many of them, too, had succumbed to the politics of racial resentment was demonstrated vividly in Boston early in 1990, when Charles Stuart, a young white man who'd killed his pregnant fiancée, concocted a clever but dubious tale that sent the city's police and press on a brutal witch-hunt for black suspects that lasted for days, terrorizing and abusing the innocent. Militant blacks insisted that this was just the sort of perennial outrage they had been trying to expose all along, neglecting to acknowledge that some of their targets, like Dominick Blum, the Howard Beach motorist whose car struck and killed Michael Griffith, and the Dutchess County assistant district attorney Steven Pagones, whom they accused of raping Brawley, were innocent too.

As such utterly antithetical delusional systems went on parade in the Central Park case and people took up positions on opposite sides of a deepening racial divide, some of us had long since turned to grieving. To my mind, even the passion plays that turned on real interracial brutality lacked the dignity of tragedy because they ignored a far bloodier drama playing unheralded, if not entirely unreported, across town—a swelling tide of murders of innocent young blacks by other young blacks. Body after young body was lowered into the city's choking soil without so much as a word in public from the doctors of delusion, who managed nonetheless to rush to new barricades the minute Yusuf Hawkins was killed by a white boy. Goldin was more right than he knew; who would want to remain in such a city? Not whites, who in the mid-1980s had slipped below half of the population for the first time in New York's 350-year history; not Puerto Ricans, more of whom left the city in the 1980s than moved in; not blacks, whose proportion of the population had dropped slightly, to just 24 percent of the city's 7.5 million people on the eve of the 1990 census. Only new immigrants of every hue who didn't know any better kept arriving, at levels unprecedented since the 1920s.

In the depths of our civic night, I put some of my assumptions about racism and the politics of race through a tortuous reexamination. This book is the record of my deliberations, of what has survived them and what has not, and I have tried to write of the journey somewhat as I undertook it—not as an academic or even as a journalist, but as a citizen of a city with which I have fallen in and out of love several times since my first infatuation with it in the late 1960s. This is a conversation with fellow New Yorkers to which anyone is welcome to listen; and, though New York is unique, the discussion is bound to have some resonance for city dwellers across the Northeast and Midwest, for Atlantans surely, and perhaps for others as well.

A Personal Odyssey

I am forty-three years old, white, Jewish, middle-class, an editor at *New York Newsday,* one of the city's daily newspapers, and a resident of East Fourteenth Street in Manhattan. I moved from Boston to Brooklyn in 1977 during another mayoral campaign, the one that brought Koch to City Hall, to take a part-time job teaching freshman writing at Queens College of the City University of New York and to do some writing of my own. Knowing only that I felt unaccountably drawn to the city, I was amazed to discover upon arriving that a very large part of me felt as if I had lived in it all my life.

My first months in New York were both panoramic and particular. I took long walks from affluent Forest Hills, in Queens, to abject Bushwick, in Brooklyn, the latter ravaged yet again just before my arrival by looting and arson during the great power blackout. I foraged along stagnant canals and partially abandoned industrial areas, through a rainbow of street fairs throbbing with life and through the mysteries of a transit system whose trains and passageways seemed to slip rhythmically in and out of civil authority, like provinces in a country gripped by a guerrilla war. Because my classes at Queens were mostly remedial, I was introduced to a cross section of entering City University students, including lifelong New Yorkers who hadn't done well in school and new immigrants of every capacity and description, kids working to pay their tuition and traversing broad swaths of the city every day from home to job to class and home again in order to stake a modest claim on middle-class life.

They were very serious, trying very hard and not having much fun, falling asleep sometimes in class out of exhaustion.

My deepest fascination in those first months was with the bonds that kept their families and neighborhoods functioning under what struck me as staggering burdens of social and physical decay, especially in the parts of Brooklyn I was coming to know during the rest of my week as a reporter for the *Phoenix,* a community weekly serving several brownstone neighborhoods, which preserve the ambience and infrastructure of a Victorian city ringing the borough's downtown. A child of suburbia and of a reasonable approximation of New England town-meeting democracy, I reported with barely contained shock on the viciousness of community battles over gentrification and racist real-estate practices in my new neighborhood at the fringes of Park Slope.

I'd moved into an eight-unit brick walk-up tenanted largely by black and Hispanic families struggling along on eight or nine thousand dollars a year, their lives often touched by violence—familial, accidental, criminal. I became friendly with some of my neighbors and, through a community activist living across the street, with a number of Italian-American families who'd been on the block for many years. From those relationships, some of which continue, I learned respect for unspoken dignity born of disappointments too often invisible to those more fortunate. It has been something to keep faith with.

As editor of another small weekly serving the wounded but eerily beautiful North Brooklyn communities of Greenpoint, Williamsburg, and Bushwick, I was drawn far more deeply into the life of the inner neighborhoods of the outer boroughs of the city. North Brooklyn is a kaleidoscope of orthodox Jewish Hasidim, many escaped from the Nazis; Polish immigrants still arriving; Italian-Americans of fifty years' standing; Puerto Ricans, Dominicans, and African-Americans who came north in the great postwar migrations to work in factories and a navy yard that have long since closed.

The economy and fractious cultural life of the area will not support a newspaper, but I managed to draw some of its struggling community organizations and several of its most talented young writers, two of whom speak in these pages, into a network of support for the paper, the *North Brooklyn Mercury.* In neighborhoods like these, a good paper is like a magic mirror, giving unprecedented exposure and encouragement to people who've been struggling along in obscurity and spotlighting some of the villains whom everyone has suspected but hasn't had time to investigate and expose. Some of the latter in North Brooklyn included members of the local predatory establishment—real-estate brokers and slumlords who'd collaborated with politicians, bankers, and judges of the Brooklyn Democratic machine in milking, abandoning, and torching structurally sound buildings and then redeveloping them with public subsidies that lined their pockets at the expense of the poor. Community organizations pioneered far sounder models of housing preservation and development; we tried to embarrass the city into giving them more funds.

In Williamsburg, a rickety jumble of mercantile artifacts, crumbling tenements, and ultramodern colossi such as Woodhull Hospital and Eastern District High School, we would circulate some of our 15,000 weekly copies with the help of neighborhood kids, stuffing the papers with supermarket circulars on Saturday mornings in the community room of a local housing project, climbing the pungent stairwells and slipping them under apartment doors. In the projects' community rooms, behind caged windows and graffiti-covered metal doors, I watched youth workers help good kids with little hold on the coming century rehearse job interviews and learn to fill out applications, or try to plan rallies or marches, or confess their fear of being jumped while wearing their gangs' colors in hostile territory. I watched it dawn slowly on Golden Gloves champions, lining up with 6,000 other applicants for 2,000 summer jobs, that they might be strong and quick with their fists yet still be outmaneuvered by others quick with money and words, that they were no longer just kids among friends or tough dudes in gangs but minority adults in a large, uncomprehending, often hostile society.

It mattered little to us that most of the quarter million people in our little corner of Brooklyn couldn't have understood our paper's exposés of arrangements that left such kids ever more isolated. A newspaper alters the communication loops of a community even if it's read by just a hundred people on the local planning board and in rival organizations and establishments and by a few important people downtown. When we criticized the Brooklyn Democratic boss

Meade Esposito, his borough president, Howard Golden, was interested enough to show up at one of our fund-raisers and have a word with me outside the hall. When we described the manipulative contempt for democratic institutions exhibited by certain Hasidic developers and political operatives, they responded angrily, some of them in anonymous calls threatening to cool our advertisers. When we exposed cronyism on a community school board, one of its dissident members told us that a school official hit the bottle. We got tips of all kinds from loyal readers. Bundles of our papers were stolen. We still tell ourselves that we helped shape local history for a little while through our coverage of race, real estate, and education.

But the struggle to keep the newspaper alive drained and ultimately overwhelmed us. As it did, I was drawn into the surrounding decay and depression, the paralysis and despair of people whose thoughts are scrambled by unremitting yet at the same time capricious pressures. The experience haunts me still, and it, too, has been something to keep faith with.

When the *Mercury* finally collapsed, City Council President Carol Bellamy gave me a job and a perch, first as a liaison to Manhattan community organizations, where I became involved all over again in local struggles, this time from a City Hall vantage point, and later as her speechwriter. After two years working for Bellamy, I found opportunities, as a regular free-lancer for *Dissent* magazine and the *Village Voice,* to think and write more clearly about what I'd seen. In 1982–83, as a Charles Revson Fellow at Columbia University, I researched the life and works of the former city housing administrator and *New York Times* editorial board member Roger Starr, whose interesting career has embodied some of the city's most fateful contradictions.

I married into Fourteenth Street when I wed a lifelong New Yorker, the granddaughter of a commissioner of the Salvation Army, headquartered on West Fourteenth Street, and of Russian-Jewish immigrants to the Lower East Side, who owned the building on East Fourteenth Street we live in now as tenants. On our block, the anarchist-feminist Emma Goldman tried to sell herself in order to buy the gun Alexander Berkman used to kill Henry Clay Frick (the john took pity on her and simply gave her the money); in Woody Allen's *The Front,* blacklisted writers passed scripts in the 1950s at

Hammer's Dairy Restaurant, which stood a few doors down from ours until it closed in the 1970s, becoming since then an Indian and then a Jamaican restaurant.

For more than two years now, I have worked at *New York Newsday,* with a community of people steeped in the lore and peculiar cultures of the city's newspapers and neighborhoods; without them this book would not have been possible. I miss North Brooklyn, and often I take the L train under the East River from a station near my door to eat in the diners where I scribbled columns for the *Mercury.* For all of my thirteen years in the city, I have lived on integrated blocks and in buildings of dramatically mixed populations, at times sharing meals and confidences with working-class white ethnics, at other times so losing myself in the politics of black communities that on my occasional forays into Manhattan the density of white faces was disorienting. Sometimes, like many another immigrant to the city in this century, I have found myself speaking with fellow New Yorkers in dialects and with resonances not my own, part mimic, part deep-sea diver. In a way, this book continues those conversations; but in another way, I am speaking in voices that have by now been blended into my own.

Finally, by saying as little as I have about race in this tiny autobiography, I mean to say something important about it: I wish from the bottom of my heart that it were not what it has become in the life of New York.

I first realized how deeply I felt this as I sat at a conference on race relations several years ago, listening to a young, white civil rights lawyer challenge her liberal audience to come to terms with its "obvious fear of playing second fiddle to black leadership in this city." I listened bemusedly because my wife was at that moment in the employ of Representative Major Owens, a black congressman from Brooklyn, trying to negotiate with Alton Maddox, Jr., and others over the "shape of the table" at Michigan Representative John Conyers's upcoming hearings on police brutality in New York. Seated not far from me at the conference was a black friend of mine who knew this, a writer who'd grown up in a mixed Bronx neighborhood and done all right for himself. As the young speaker went on, I caught my friend's eye. The corner of his mouth played into the hint of an ironic smile, his eyebrows lifted just enough to suggest a rolling of eyes at ceiling—and we both burst out laughing. We agreed afterward that whole libraries could be filled with what the young conference speaker—and, I suspect, many others who've lectured us on our sins—don't know about race relations in New York.

That was when it first came to me that people like the young lawyer may have a profound stake in their selective ignorance because it makes expressing their noble impulses so much easier. As I hope to show toward the end of this book, much is going on in New York even in these benighted times that doesn't show up on black militants' and their white apologists' radar; and the fact that there is racism here, perhaps even in the hearts of prominent white New Yorkers who once shared schoolrooms with black kids, doesn't preclude the possibility that the activists and their apologists are flying blind.

As I waited for the conference speaker to finish, I began wondering what would happen if those of us who care about both racial justice and the city's transracial promise turned some left-liberal and black-militant assumptions about racism inside out, worked them over, held them up to the light of our lived history, and saw which of them work and which of them don't. Why not? Since racism exists in New York, it will still be there when we're finished; but we'll see it all the more clearly for having taken into account whatever is unique in the atmosphere of the city and so will be all the more able to attack what is wrong.

The New York Idea

Sometime in the 1970s, the neoconservative social critic Irving Kristol delivered himself of the sour little apothegm that a neoconservative is a liberal who's been mugged. But it wasn't my brushes with violent crime that plunged me into a reconsideration of some of the left-liberal pieties about race that neoconservatives so grandly disdain. It was, rather, my feelings of violation by the misleadership of those local black leaders and white apologists who made sweeping assertions—about the city's history, the attitudes of whites, and, perhaps most outrageously, the attitudes of ordinary blacks—that I knew to be untrue. I found something ruinous even in their central, operating assumption that New York may be divided almost casually into two camps: oppressed people of color and unthinking white oppressors who must constantly be confronted with the evil of their banality.

On the surface, nothing could seem more obvious; as a historical generalization, nothing more reasonable. A large body of scholarship supports the contention, with which I am in substantial agreement, that white racism, fueled by capitalist urban development, is, along with rural slavery, American politics' original sin. The evidence is overwhelming that poverty and the pathologies that attend it in our inner cities come primarily, though by no means wholly, from the effects of generations of economic injustice against blacks and from white rationalizations for that injustice. But important as it is to probe and expose the origins of a problem, doing so won't by itself produce a solution. That requires leadership and a collective will to transcend wounds ancient and fresh. When people fail at this, margins of opportunity go unseen and unexploited. They participate in and perpetuate their own victimization. That has been the case with black leaders in New York.

To be sure, white society has sent blacks mixed and confusing signals that must at times resemble a hopeless maze. Blacks in New York have caught whites playing a double game, preaching an Americanism that transcends racial and ethnic divisions while providing for themselves along carefully patrolled ethnic lines. The retaliatory parochialism of black power has forced whites to admit this truth, to acknowledge their hyphenated Americanism. But now that the challenge has been posed, the question is whether the city goes forward into some new synthesis or slides backward into balkanized fantasies of ethnic and racial destiny.

Some people argue that only by continuing to discover, expose, and attack racism and ethnic parochialism can we get beneath them to the deeper economic causes of social division. But I have become convinced that the public obsession with racism on the part of some would-be champions of social justice now blinds us to more possibilities than it opens. Some of those eclipsed possibilities are unique to New York City and its peculiar, liberal traditions. Others have come here with the deluge of new immigrants from other countries and cultures whose ideas about race and a politics based in racial identity differ markedly from those of American blacks and whites. Still others, I hope to show, are bubbling up from still-vital recesses of American civil society in and around the city. The reemergence of these possibilities will further diminish the credibility of American black leaders' claims to speak for a unified "minority agenda." So may the disintegration of white working-class family life, replete with the pathologies of violent, essentially homeless youths, which may well overshadow the problems of the black underclass in the popular mind in the years just ahead.

To say all this, one need not—one cannot—deny that racism in the city is pervasive and routine, blighting, and, yes, often explicitly cruel. One does have to be willing to ask, Do frontal assaults on racism, which black militants and white radicals define ever more broadly until, like the Red menace, it is "found" under every bed, really have any remaining purchase against blacks' suffering? If not, what are the alternatives? These are difficult questions. My answers presume that much of the rhetoric, demonstrations, and legal maneuvering against "racism" has by now fatefully scanted personal accountability to certain race-transcendent standards of public truth and civil order—an accountability we must have in leaders, but also, ultimately, in followers. Needed are some social-democratic initiatives that don't stray too far from old-fashioned notions of republican, even "bourgeois," virtue. These answers are as difficult to formulate as the questions, and I hope readers will refrain from saying too quickly, "Oh, I see where he's going, and I don't like it." Those on the left will search these pages in vain for the articles of their faith, but they may find here some essential validation of what they know they ought to be. Neoconservative readers will nod in vigorous agreement with many of my observations, but ultimately they may find themselves impaled on the conclusions I draw from what I have seen.

Because it has been so long since they've done their moral homework, both sides have in effect collaborated in a cavalier betrayal of a New York political tradition that, I believe, comprehended both the questions and the answers I have just proposed. Some black leaders and their white left and liberal apologists have cast New York as another Johannesburg or as "Up South," a northern version of early-1960s Mississippi whose implacable racism needs to be bared. To the extent that our politics has followed the descending spiral I described at the outset, it is not difficult to see why some find these comparisons apt. But I take my stand in the claim that, quite unlike Johannesburg or Mississippi, New York in the sixties did have an emerging if mightily flawed consensus in favor of interracial fair play; that that consensus was beginning to bear some fruit; that, tragically, for disparate reasons, it was undermined, practically beaten to death by people who should have known better; and that recently some of its assailants have been trying to airbrush it out of history. To understand how we have come to our current predicament, we need to know this New York tradition better.

The notion of New York as a city well on its way toward interracial fair play in the early 1960s is clouded by paradox. On the one hand, the experience of Negroes in New York had always been and in the sixties remained that, in the words of Frederick Douglass, power concedes nothing without a demand. Whether blacks were boycotting white store owners in Harlem to demand jobs in the thirties; or paying their telephone bills in pennies and turning off all the lights in Harlem on Tuesday nights in the forties to make the phone and utility companies hire them; or threatening to "tarnish our image abroad" in the fifties in order to make the restaurants near the UN serve African delegates; or picketing construction sites in the sixties, seventies, or eighties and even right now; or withholding their cooperation from the Queens DA in order to embarrass the criminal justice system into prosecuting the Howard Beach assailants in 1987, the record is very clear: racism has been a sorry fact of life throughout New York's history. Anyone who thinks otherwise will be disabused, I hope, in chapter 1; I think that neoconservatives need not so much to be shown as to be reminded.

On the other hand—and here the record will strike some readers as more ambiguous—hundreds of thousands of white New Yorkers not only had grown up with blacks but were actually pleased by blacks' individual and collective gains; many thousands of whites went further and participated in efforts to help blacks obtain better opportunities and treatment. The sway of the ethic of interracial fair play was such that even whites who did not love blacks could sometimes be called to account or at least cowed by the dictum that you give a guy a fair shot. Politically, from 1945 through the early 1960s, these people were up for grabs. They could be induced to acquiesce in many social programs they would later resist.

How could both these things be true—that discrimination was pervasive and that, at the same time, so many whites had nothing against blacks or were even supportive of them? The easiest answer is to declare the second half of the paradox untrue, to charge me with mistaking the rhetorical flourishes of a few prominent liberals and old leftists for the mood of a city. But I would advise the skeptics to be careful. Many white New Yorkers' deepest feelings about what they have given to their city and what they are entitled to expect from it are wrapped up in the answer to this question. I am thinking especially of the children of the immigrant Jews of the early twentieth century, but much of what I will say about the Jews applies to the city's other white ethnics. To ignore or dismiss their feelings, as the left, liberals, and blacks have done since the early 1960s, is to release into our politics an effluent perhaps as poisonous as any that has blighted blacks' hopes.

A more substantial resolution of the paradox begins with the understanding that every political consensus, whether or not it rides capitalism's swift, unsparing currents, as does New York's liberal tradition, is imperfect, shot through with hypocrisy; humans and their institutions emerge only slowly from history's muck and slime. One can go on about the fact that Thomas Jefferson held slaves and never gave the rights of women a thought when he wrote the Declaration of Independence; or one can take what he wrote as a text awaiting interpretation and fulfillment, as many ordinary blacks and women have done with great courage, redeeming us all. The first course all too often requires merely an embittered intelligence; the second requires vision and courage.

Much the same can be said of the New York liberal tradition. Because it kept slipping the bonds of race, it had a special way of answering the questions I've posed about how best to pursue social justice while affirming individual responsibility. The sheer diversity and fluidity of New York's population rudely scrambled ethnic distinctions and refracted our perceptions of race. While some people clung all the more tightly to racial self-definitions amid the confusion, New York's irrepressible idea was that, even as each of us is raised in some ethnic, racial, or religious community, each of us can, as an American and especially as a New Yorker, decide to transcend anything in our pasts that has made us small and contribute to a unique urban experiment that E. B. White called "cosmopolitan, mighty and unparalleled." This has been a city of insular communities, yet one of the emblematic themes of its civic culture is that of breaking with the old neighborhood and finding the world.

Our paradox has been put well by Bob Liff, a white colleague at *New York Newsday* who grew up in a racially mixed part of Brooklyn's Crown Heights and then in the Linden Houses in East New York when they were still integrated and kids there fought gang wars on the basis of what buildings they lived in, not on the basis of race: "New Yorkers' tribalism goes back to Tammany's sachems, but because there's no dominant tribe, tolerance is what makes things go. It's not so much that we're liberal as that we're tolerant." Out of its rough balance of intergroup tension and tolerance, of personal opportunity and social responsibility, of neighborhood and cosmopolis, New York City has given the rest of the country Hollywood, the Harlem Renaissance, the New Deal, Jackie Robinson and the Dodgers, and James Baldwin, and we can throw in Jackie Gleason and Carroll O'Connor, Colin Powell, Woody Allen, Ella Fitzgerald, maybe Mario Cuomo. If this balance survives, the city will send out new emissaries of cultural and political confabulations we can't even begin to imagine now. One can think of the city as a great human heart, drawing into itself a hundred immigrant and American bloodstreams, and, after working its strange alchemy upon them, pumping them out again across the country and the world, bearing new talents and strengths.

To be a true New Yorker is to be marked so indelibly by the rigors and ironies of this difficult passage that one can never be quite comfortable in one's old tribe or parochial faith. David Dinkins, for example, has transmuted the subtle understandings of a Harlem Democratic party lawyer into the gifts of a peacemaker who radiates the rooted yet cosmopolitan élan that has helped New Yorkers survive their multiple abrasions. But, as we will see, Dinkins bears the weaknesses of his strengths, and he has come to preside over a city whose great heart is faltering, owing to political and structural developments which we will examine and which I will sketch broadly here.

The Violation of New York

The urgency of the plight of blacks who arrived in the city with the huge postwar migration of the late 1940s prompted well-intentioned whites to launch a variety of initiatives for social justice, some of them self-important and self-indulgent, many of them insensitive to the city's political ecology. To say that they should have been more astute is not to say that they should have "gone slow." It is to point to blind spots and strategic blunders.

White liberals, for example, fresh from forays in a South where federal law enforced by arms was often the only instrument capable of prying open closed, racist arrangements, moved quickly upon returning to New York to outstrip the antidiscrimination measures that had already gathered moral legitimacy and political steam in the city's life. They embraced instead social engineering schemes for white-ethnic and middle-class neighborhoods, symbolically potent experiments in forced busing and scatter-site, low-income housing backed by court orders and bureaucratic mandates. Because they did not live in these neighborhoods and had no idea what roles they played in the lives of people who did or how they could be maintained or destroyed by the machinations of real-estate investors, liberals stumbled into unwitting alliances with racist slumlords and speculators, who were already busily "integrating" those areas in calculated efforts to destroy them for quick profits.

That prompted working- and middle-class white New Yorkers who hadn't given race much thought to see resistance to integration as a physical and economic necessity. The decay of the city's white-ethnic idiom in the late 1960s was partly just a bigoted reaction to the city's darkening complexion. But hatred of blacks and Puerto Ricans was deepened and accelerated by the calculated channeling of impoverished, desperate minorities into many white neighborhoods, destroying them in order to ghettoize an expanding black population. The decay in white-ethnic politics also reflected a profound moral grievance felt by many decent whites, not so much against blacks' material demands as against the flouting of any spirit of social reciprocity in the way the demands were made and against black leaders' and liberals' endless, enraging rationalizations for violent crime.

Stunned by the ferocity of white-ethnic resistance to the new integration schemes, liberals reacted with self-righteous indignation, redoubling their efforts as if to punish the white working class for its intransigence. To this day, few of them comprehend their contributions to the specter of rapid-fire neighborhood decay that haunts the politics of the outer boroughs. Nor, as embittered white ethnics continue to leave the city for the suburbs or descend to violent rage, are liberals likely to feel compelled, morally or politically, to come to terms with their own mistakes.

Many on the left, meanwhile, wary of the white working class after its support for McCarthyism in the early 1950s and the Vietnam War fifteen years later, took refuge in anticipatory flutterings over every real or imagined stirring in the supposedly revolutionary consciousness of blacks. If the old left had sometimes exhibited an unwitting condescension toward blacks in the service of an interacial, "Popular Front" Americanism, the new left too often worshiped blacks as the avatars of a heroic but in the end equally fatuous anti-Americanism. Not surprisingly, the champions of this "politics of turmoil" elucidated the lesson that romantic polarization leads not to a higher synthesis but to more polarization.

Guilt-ridden white elites, preoccupied with liberating themselves from unearned privileges and concomitant repressions, formed liaisons with ghetto hustlers whose interests meshed perversely with theirs. That spelled disaster for socially conservative, low-income blacks, who needed a great deal of support for their practical moral decency in order to survive. Liberal elites mistook the vertigo of young blacks whose families and communities had been shattered for the freedom they themselves sought from upbringings and responsibilities they found too stable and confining. Leonard Bernstein's famous "radical chic" cocktail party for the Black Panthers is emblematic of these debased encounters, in which whites of all stripes conflated cultural clowns like Eldridge Cleaver with communities of the working and welfare-dependent poor, whose evanescent moral capital the hustlers appropriated for their own use.

All these spectacles of white self-indulgence in relations with blacks alienated principled black radicals and politically moderate black churchgoers, hastening their withdrawal from a civic culture that seemed scarcely worth joining except to hustle it for all it was worth. What the New York liberal tradition seemed to be offering them, after all the white gyrations of the 1960s, was little more than a foot on the bottom rung of the ladder which white-ethnic groups had been climbing for more than a century, always stepping on blacks and knocking them off. New York's belated invitation to follow in those bruising footsteps must have seemed not quite believable and at the same time deeply insulting to blacks with a sense of the city's history—and perhaps even more insulting to those, more recently arrived, without any sense of history and hence without respect for what had been accomplished and at what cost. But much of the black leadership that arose from this maelstrom only made things worse, which in turn reinforced now disillusioned whites in their conviction that the failures were all blacks' fault. Nor has a new group of what I call "professional blacks" (not to be confused with black professionals), who've developed a predictable stake in expanding the boundaries of racism in pursuit of moral and practical exemptions from social obligation, done much to restore faith.

And yet to untangle these destructive developments and reconsider the roads we have taken is to begin to appreciate some of the strengths remaining in New York and its battered liberal tradition. In a city whose black voters make up only a quarter of the electorate, David Dinkins did win, with around 30 percent of the white vote—which means that 34 percent of his voters were whites. Blacks generally become mayors in two kinds of city: those, like Newark, Atlanta, Detroit, Chicago, and Philadelphia, with clear black majorities or near-majorities; or those, like Los Angeles or Seattle, with such a small proportion of blacks, 20 percent or less, that white voters don't feel remotely threatened and so can say what many in New York still do: "Hey, give the guy a shot." How quickly we forget the special promise of this town.

Even before Dinkins was sworn in, however, he began to confront, in the form of a yawning budget deficit, a number of structural constraints upon politics and racial comity in New York. One of them is that the rest of the nation doesn't know enough to lavish on New York's great heart a tenth of what the French spend on Paris or the Italians on Rome. Another is that the city rises and falls on what Daniel Bell called the cultural contradictions of capitalism, which, even as it produces tremendous vitality and wealth, corrodes the fabric of community life, reducing social relations to extensions of the market. With each passing year, the city becomes more and more a battlefield whose only conventions are those of tribal warfare or a mad rationalism of legal rights, the contractual sorts of protection to which people resort when cutthroat competition has undermined gentler intimations of society.

Then there is the question of what value a city has as a center for work and culture when increasingly fluid market forces move capital and leadership cadres worldwide at whim. While New York has always been a conduit for such forces and populations, even the maintenance of a conduit requires some political consensus, some way for cities to influence or make claims upon new configurations of technology, investment, employment, consumption, demographics. There will be no such consensus as long as those who ought to care about the whole city are fighting one another along racial or ethnic battle lines. The only sure way to shed racism and tribalism is for New Yorkers to address together those larger problems that imperil the city and sow the seeds of racism itself. Would that offended working-class whites and offended working-class blacks talked to one another, away from the ministrations of elite liberals, the trust-fund left, and, for that matter, right-wing talk-show hosts.

Fortunately, in a few settings I will describe, they already are. And there are some signs that, for the first time in perhaps twenty-five years, black-activist ministers and political leaders are experiencing a sea change in their attitudes about racism, which "white" society still uses psychologically but can no longer afford economically. Even as some black leaders spiral off into ever deeper delusions, others are pulling back and reassessing their assumptions and tactics. I cite some such developments in this book.

Violence, Leadership, and Morality

As we have seen, at this stage in the city's history, violent crime is a powerful accelerant of racial hostilities that debase public discourse and distort understandings of personal responsibility. But those black leaders and their left-liberal apologists who would excuse almost every sort of misbehavior as a political statement or antidote to bourgeois repression have not been the only deceivers. Even as neoconservative whites rightly demand that perpetrators be held personally responsible for their actions, many of them do implicitly charge all blacks with a kind of collective complicity. What is happening to the bottom third of the city's black population is so monstrous, so unbelievable, that blacks cannot possibly be responsible for it all by themselves. I think the neoconservative attitude is largely an exasperated reaction to the fact that so many leaders on the other side have responded defensively and disingenuously to the simple reality of black crime, elaborating ever more baroque theories of white genocidal conspiracy instead of acknowledging that lines of personal responsibility do have to be drawn.

Such misleadership is indeed a tragedy. The rescue of New York requires not only more law enforcement (which inevitably brings abuses that generate more protests), and not only economic opportunity, but also the assiduous cultivation, in neighborhoods and religious and cultural communities, of the utterly conventional decencies that keep people from eating one another alive. The 1960s demonstrated that economic expansion alone does not guarantee social health. The neoconservatives' sermons are powerless here because they refuse to acknowledge capitalism's capricious, often brutal effects on communities. At the same time, those on the left who can discuss crime only in the "context" of oppression must acknowledge that in many neighborhoods disorganized crime itself has become the context that forecloses every political and economic initiative, reformist or revolutionary: at this pass in the city's history, crime creates poverty almost as much as poverty creates crime.

Violent crime is only the most obvious source of many whites' growing conviction that a disproportionate number of blacks are unwilling or unable to join the larger society, to share in a common endeavor. Revolted by the utterly helpless and homeless people who are reeling in shame and confusion, and by certain coldly hostile affirmative action elites who are expanding the definition of racism beyond all plausibility, white ethnics and neoconservatives increasingly perceive blacks as obstructing not just business as usual but also every potential social solution whose implementation requires an elusive but indispensable interracial trust.

It is one thing to say, as activists do, that blacks cannot be expected to join on its own terms a civic culture that for so many years has degraded them; some blacks may indeed have to withdraw at least provisionally into communal and personal inner journeys in order to reclaim themselves and redefine their terms of entry. But it is something else again to say that those terms can be anything black leaders say they should be and that all institutions must be wholly reconfigured to eliminate an allegedly "Eurocentric" bias. Social institutions in New York have not been standing still, and the "biases" that now permeate them—corporate, universal, sometimes even Japanese—discomfit many whites, as well. Blacks who ascribe all of their own unease to racism and who seek security in special racial prerogatives condemn themselves to deepening isolation and impotence, here and around the world.

That returns us to the questions I raised earlier about the value of frontal assaults upon racism and about what the alternatives to such assaults might be. In the course of the capsule history of the postwar city I have just presented, two dilemmas keep recurring. First, how much and to what end should activists try to rub raw a society's ingrained and often unacknowledged racial inequities and strip bare its economic contradictions and legal hypocrisies? Second, what kinds of hard work and moral discipline may people who envision a democratic and just society demand even of the poorest and most oppressed; what, indeed, would it be condescending and worse not to demand of "the least among us"? And how can it plausibly be demanded?

The only answers remotely compatible with American political culture are those developed by participants in the early civil rights movement, some of them New Yorkers, black and white. They knew that they faced deeply immoral, cynical arrangements that wouldn't budge without confrontation by organized, countervailing power. Yet they insisted that people who would disrupt custom and law in order to expose hypocrisy and injustice must prove the depth of their commitment to the society they are trying to awaken by accepting punishment under the very strictures they consider unjust. What this means, particularly when the law itself is not at issue, is something basic: you cannot build a movement for social justice on lies, grandiose distortions, vilification of innocent parties, intimidation of independents who may have legitimate differences of opinion, and dehumanization of your opponents. There are transracial standards of public truth.

To the question about the moral responsibilities of the oppressed, leaders of the civil rights movement responded that it is precisely our belief in their irreducible dignity that prohibits us from lowering our expectations of them, even in the teeth of adversity. The more confrontational, even radical a movement, the more critical is such moral discipline to its success; from Malcolm X to Nelson Mandela, the most revolutionary of black leaders, no less than the most socially conservative of churchgoers in the community, have embodied and insisted upon rectitude and self-discipline. Contrary to what some people think, that does not preclude aid and compassion. It makes them possible.

Citing the bad faith of conservatives who invoke discipline but deny aid, too many putative leaders of struggles for racial and economic justice argue that the time is never quite right to raise these questions about confrontation and personal responsibility. They note that readying any insurgency to take the brunt of the established power's wrath, "firing up" people for risks and sacrifices, often means relying on what Reinhold Niebuhr called "potent oversimplifications." Revolutionaries and soldiers don't risk their skins, nor do civilian populations endure prolonged hardships, without mythically heroic justifications. But, as Niebuhr warned, justifications can all too quickly become lies, and at times it is the obligation of wise leadership to curb them. When leaders who have painted the world in black and white in order to mobilize followers cling to their vivid portraits, they only doom themselves and their followers to miscalculation, defeat, and despair. That has certainly been the fate of too much black politics in an America which blacks can never dominate and from which they can never secede—a predicament which alone discredits facile analogies between New York City and Johannesburg.

So liberals and people on the left who cheer on insurgencies need to reexamine the limits they have set upon personal responsibility and the ways in which they have pulled the moral rug out from under the socially conservative working poor. Black radicals need to ask how much of what their people endure is attributable to racism; how much to economic injustices that hurt whites, too; and how much to that old conservative standby—the human condition. For their part, neoconservatives need to own up to the enormous systemic dispossessions and little cruelties that grind people down; they need to recall that the fallen have stories. Listening well to such stories is an acknowledgment of their bearers' dignity, and that is the only credible basis from which to appeal to their moral obligation. Those who are gratified by the collapse of Marxist movements must give us other social visions powerful enough to counteract racial and ethnic retribalization; the old left's Popular Front may have seemed forced, at times phony; but its residue was, until recently, a strong solvent of racism in the city's life. What will replace it in the 1990s?

As academics and activists of all persuasions develop their critiques of capitalism, racism, and rebellion—and this is one of the few growth industries in New York—ordinary men and women, living in whatever remnants of family or community they can find, must decide to act responsibly in conventional terms and to enforce responsibility upon one another. This side of "liberation"—indeed, in order to organize themselves to bring liberation about—they really have no choice but to help one another stay in school or find a steady job; refrain from parenting children they are unable or unwilling to raise; honor the community and obey the law. And they have to raise up new leaders who can help them do this, since no one else can: "The concept of historic reparation grows out of man's need to impose a degree of justice on the world that simply does not exist," writes the black essayist Shelby Steele. "Suffering can be endured and overcome; it cannot be repaid." Ironically, unfairly, some of the most important solutions always lie with the victims. At certain critical moments in any struggle, only they have the power to close the circle of redemption.

My explorations would have brought me to despair had they not introduced me to others who've blazed trails far ahead of mine and pioneered an interracial politics that encompasses and improves on the New York tradition. At several points in the book, I allude to the work of several powerful community-based organizations trained by the Industrial Areas Foundation (IAF), which has adapted the principles of community organizing hammered out by the late activist

Saul Alinsky to build moderate income "Nehemiah" housing in neighborhoods long thought drained of political and economic clout. Precisely because it reweaves the fabric of society among political moderates in their families, churches, and community centers, the IAF model, though sometimes brusque and formulaic, is dialectical in a way ideologues with all the answers can never be. More effectively than most black nationalists and activists on the left (I will present some happy exceptions), the IAF groups have brought tens of thousands of New Yorkers from apathy to constructive, confrontational engagement with elected officials, including Dinkins.

So doing, these predominantly black but doggedly interracial organizations have challenged two styles of black electoral politics, that of Dinkins's Harlem elite and that of Brooklyn-based insurgents. They have confirmed an unvarying rule in electoral politics which militant nationalists refuse to learn: black voters always and everywhere give stronger support to black candidates who are doing well with white voters than they do to black candidates running on appeals to racial solidarity alone. But as we will see, these church-based groups make clear that the transcending of racial parochialism is only the beginning of a truly democratic politics.

The IAF groups are not unique to New York. They began in Chicago and have stormed across the hardscrabble ground of Texas and up through the stoops and alleys of Baltimore. What does it say about New York's liberal tradition that some of the most promising politics in the city has been imported? But then, it always has been: the interracial militancy of the Transit Workers' Union, from the left wing of the Irish Republican Army; the socialism of garment workers, from the Pale of Jewish settlement in Poland and Lithuania; the "Bread and Roses" spirit of the Hospital Workers' Union, Local 1199, from the black churches and the civil rights movement of the South and from people's movements in Puerto Rico. What IAF brings is something New York especially needs right now, something quintessentially American, a theory and practice of republican virtue that taps and replenishes the wellsprings of our precious civil society. With luck, in combination with the most vital of New York's other community-based activism, it will rejuvenate what is best in the city's liberal traditions.

The city will cook these notions in its own ethnic stew, test their strength, and serve them up in its own special way. "New York is the most fatally fascinating thing in America," wrote the black essayist James Weldon Johnson in 1909; "she sits like a witch at the gate of the country." She still does. An embodiment of our worst fears about ourselves, but also of our deepest strengths, New York offers abundant instruction to a nation becoming as diverse and interdependent as the city herself. Merely coming to know her better would constitute a fine return on the investment all of us ought to make in her future.

Chapters 1 through 3 begin that investment with a historical overview of the politics of race in New York. Chapter 1 surveys the black odyssey in New York City from colonial times, examining some of the peculiar contours of racism here and the development of sophisticated, often conflicted black political responses. Chapter 2 describes the ascendancy and travails of a predominantly Jewish postwar liberalism and its attempts to end racial discrimination and promote integration. Chapter 3 traces the confluence of diverse radical currents that submerged that liberal tradition and tried but failed to replace it with a larger social vision.

Chapters 4 and 5 retrace the postwar period from the perspective of white ethnics whose neighborhoods, the central, organizing frameworks of their lives, succumbed to real-estate machinations that fanned racial fears and promoted insecurity, pathology, and criminality among poor blacks. That juggernaut of exploitation and violence, which remains one of the most powerful specters haunting the politics of New York City, merits our close examination.

Chapters 6 through 9 suspend the chronology of the first half of the book to examine thematically several other important dimensions of the politics of race in New York. Chapter 6 explores unresolved tensions between rights and responsibilities in legal responses to crime, workplace discrimination, and residential segregation. Drawing on the lessons of that exploration, chapter 7 examines the premises and politics which some black militants have developed in response to the city's notorious recent racially charged criminal cases, assessing their politics by transracial standards of honesty, accountability, and trust. Chapter 8 explores recent attempts by black cultural nationalists to reconfigure the public schools as centers of struggle against racism. Chapter 9 describes the white left's efforts to interpret black activists' initiatives to liberals, thereby bridging black and white but also creating problems for the civic culture.

Chapters 10 and 11 resume the public historical narrative of the first three chapters by following developments in electoral politics from the early 1980s through Dinkins's first months in office. These chapters and the epilogue attempt to integrate some of the most important themes of the book in order to pose challenges to the politics of race in the city in the years ahead.

1

The Black Political Odyssey in New York

Racism, New York Style

From the establishment of what James Weldon Johnson called a "comparatively mild" form of slavery in New Amsterdam under the Dutch, blacks in New York have been victims of whites' opportunism and indifference more often than of their overt hatred and outright physical violence. In today's charged racial climate, that may be difficult to believe. The signal flashes of brutality in the city's history the infamous Civil War draft riots, the seemingly relentless police brutality, the worst humiliations of segregation, the emblematic killings of the 1980s—naturally dominate docudramas, popular histories, and protest lore. But for many individual blacks, and perhaps for most blacks during certain interludes in New York's history, racism was more routinized and conventional, unremarked because enmeshed in a web of social distinctions that harshly divided whites from one another, too. Much of the exploitation of people of color in New York never approached the perverse intimacies of the master-slave relationship in the old South.

As the late historian and editor of the *Nation* Carey McWilliams once noted in a broader context, slavery itself was a variant of a much larger system of economic exploitation that degraded countless whites; think of Charles Dickens's England and the early history of the Irish in America. Monstrous though it was, slavery originated in those same exploitative calculations; it antedated actual hatred of blacks, not vice versa. Were this not so, there could be no hope of undoing slavery's bitter legacy; and because some blacks do not believe it to be so, they have, in effect, no hope. Yet New York's history does hold some promise.

There were perhaps 12,000 slaves in the city at the time of the revolutionary war; there had been slave rebellions, most notably in 1712, and the typically panicky and gratuitously brutal white reactions. But gradual manumission and tolerance emerged under the Dutch and among the Quakers and were given greater impetus by the Revolution. Toward the end of the colonial period in New York, free Negroes "moved with freedom and complacent importance about the intimate fringe of the city's active life," asserted the historian A. J. Northrup in 1900. "These Negroes were barbers, caterers, bakers, restaurateurs, coachmen," all working in highly elaborate service positions. Samuel Fraunces, prosperous owner of the landmark, namesake tavern where Washington met with other revolutionary leaders, was black. Veterans of the two colored New York regiments in the war for independence were liberated by an act of the legislature, and all slaves in the state would be freed in 1827.

In 1797, though, President John Adams's wife, Abigail, wrote him that their servant James had been expelled from an evening school where he'd been sent to learn ciphering, because some white students objected to studying with a black man. "Oh, it is not my boys, but some others" who objected, a neighbor named Faxon assured Mrs. Adams—the first recorded instance of disingenuous white buck-passing and guilt over racism in the city.

As the numbers of freeholders increased, a model African Free School drew the plaudits of visiting educators who observed the youths learning to be sailmakers, shoemakers, tin workers, tailors, carpenters, and blacksmiths. But "in almost every instance, difficulties have attended [the graduates] on account of their color," one visitor reported. They slipped down the occupational ladder to work as cooks, waiters, coachmen, and servants; many went to sea as stewards.

By the 1830s, according to the historian Herman Bloch, blacks in the city had been pushed out of their service positions into menial labor, and their status further deteriorated in the 1840s and 1850s as white immigrants, substantially Irish and German, came to constitute fully one-half of the city's population of 350,000 and drove blacks out of even those jobs. Irishmen took over carpentering and Irishwomen domestic service; Irish, German, and Slavic immigrants would drive blacks almost wholly out of construction (and have largely kept them out to this day). Shortly before the Civil War, a group of Irish longshoremen told their employer they would tie up the port if all black dockhands were not summarily dismissed. "There is not a foundry, machine shop, shipyard or carpenter shop where Negroes can enter," reported Henry Ward Beecher, minister of the Plymouth Church of the Pilgrims in Brooklyn Heights.

Nowhere in the North were ordinary people more hostile to the abolitionists than in preindustrial New York, where white immigrants' port-related jobs were intimately linked to the southern slave economy. When poor and working-class whites were conscripted to fight for the Union under a law that permitted the wealthy to buy their way out of service, they took their resentment out upon blacks in the draft riots of July 1863, lynching dozens and leaving thousands of the city's 13,000 blacks homeless by fire. White elites, unnerved and conscience-stricken by the destruction, suspended the provisions for buying one's way out of service, substituted black for Irish domestics, and raised funds to outfit a Negro fighting unit (the leading citizens marched down Fifth Avenue with that unit as it left for the front, perhaps the first such "march" against racism in at least one form).

Here began another familiar pattern, that of periodic upper-middle-class "discovery" of the plight of the Negro. It would make New York a relatively hospitable base of operations for extraordinary black leaders like Frederick Douglass and W. E. B. Dubois, even after Reconstruction's brief hopes had been dashed in the South. But northern elites had been complicit, for economic reasons, in the South's "Bourbon Restoration"; even in New York, the genteel elites' periodic rediscovery of black dignity was necessary because they didn't routinely visit the docks, factories, and hiring halls to acquaint themselves with the methods by which blacks were systematically and brutally excluded. It was as easy as it was self-serving to believe that blacks were porters, whitewashers, and bootblacks because they were somehow "suited" to menial work.

Polite society's casual condescension toward blacks wasn't consciously intended to justify white immigrants' brutality toward them. But as elites turned to commercial and industrial ventures amid westward expansion and the conquest of the Indian tribes after the Civil War, solicitude toward blacks inexorably wore thin. Despite heroic efforts by settlement-house reformers like Mary White Ovington to educate and employ blacks in the city, liberal racial policies had all but disintegrated by the turn of the century. New, work-hungry Italian, Greek, and other white immigrants took over street paving and brickmaking from the upwardly mobile Irish and Germans and shoved blacks out of their remaining skilled occupations; Italians pushed blacks wholly out of barbering for whites, for example. A police and mob riot against the black community of Manhattan's Tenderloin area one hot August in 1900, sparked by a minor incident, went wholly unpunished despite vigorous black petitions for redress. By the beginning of World War I, the city's 90,000 blacks had been excluded from skilled trades for the better part of a century and so continued to be seen as "unfit" for advancement in the eyes of most whites—a self-fulfilling prophecy, another pattern.

But in 1915 the Great War virtually shut off white immigration, and America's entry two years later sent recent arrivals off to the front, creating huge labor shortages at home. Blacks were able briefly to move back up the occupational ladder; news of their good fortune in New York and other northern cities drew more than a million Negroes off the land, where the exploitative sharecropping system that had replaced slavery was eroding. Between 1910 and 1930, the black population of New York City would more than triple, to 328,-000, while the white population would increase by a smaller but substantial 41 percent, to more than 5.5 million.

When the troops returned in 1919, however, blacks were pushed back into menial work and, for the first time, given their rising numbers, into widespread unemployment. Overbuilding by white speculators in Harlem created a glut of well-built but suddenly inexpensive housing that first lured and then imprisoned blacks, whose rents could be raised with impunity owing to a deepening segregation. That forced newcomers from the South, especially, to double up and take on strangers as lodgers in barbarically subdivided apartments.

With the entrenchment by the mid-1920s of segregated real-estate exploitation and black unemployment—that is, of high rents and low wages—the great cancer of urban-slum racism was spawned. It would metastasize with the Depression, when whites wrested even the most menial jobs from blacks, throwing them onto the New Deal's relief programs en masse. The homicide rate in Depression Harlem ran 73 percent ahead of the rest of the city's; the historian Cheryl Greenberg cites the community's high infant mortality rate— close to 70 children per thousand, compared with a white rate of 40—as "mute testimony to the effects of poverty, ignorance and congestion." Policing by white ethnics, primarily Irish, was capricious: brutality abounded, but so did indifference to black-on-black crime, which left Harlem's decent residents pathetically vulnerable to its predators.

New York's Liberal Tradition Emerges

With the white proletarian majority intransigent on the labor front and the state assuming a greater role in black survival, impoverished Harlem's only recourse in the Depression was protest politics, punctuated by rioting. Overburdened church networks and other community institutions for mutual aid were drawn into the fray and politicized. In March 1935, a rumor swept the community that Lino Rivera, a young Puerto Rican boy, had been killed for shoplifting in a Kress department store. Rivera had been sent home unharmed, but, in what would become yet another familiar pattern in the city's race relations, understandable black suspicion—fanned by a misleading leaflet put out by the Young Communist League—drew angry crowds into the streets. As bottles flew and windows were smashed, police descended and violence escalated. Three people were killed and many wounded, and there was extensive looting of black as well as white stores.

The city's new maverick Republican mayor, Fiorello LaGuardia, appointed a commission whose extensive and impressive research, conducted by the respected black sociologist E. Franklin Frazier, drew a compelling portrait of the legacy of racism and economic destitution in the Negro community. Reaction to the commission's report brought the first sustained government funding and regulation to bear upon the plight of blacks. LaGuardia responded viscerally, as a champion of the underdog, and politically, as a nominal Republican at a time when the city's swelling black community was abandoning the party of Lincoln en masse for Roosevelt and the Democrats. And because the mayor was an ally of Roosevelt's across party lines, the New Deal administration itself responded with regulations, sometimes poorly enforced, prohibiting discrimination in the provision of relief.

LaGuardia was responding, as well, to the influence of the left, which, its riot agitprop aside, understood that dividing black have-nots from white-ethnic have-littles would only deepen everyone's misery. Rejecting both black separatism and white-ethnic racism, Communists mounted a devastatingly accurate analysis of poverty in Harlem and citywide, influencing the thinking of the mayor's commission, which noted that the rioters had been "poor and property-less and therefore defenseless." The left's answer to both black and white tribalism was the Popular Front, an artificially cohesive cultural and political vision of a classless America, attractive to many for whom the country's free-market promises had been broken. It was certainly attractive to blacks, the more so because, in its Popular Front mode, the left championed the Scottsboro Boys, a group of black southern youths accused of raping a white woman in 1932, and campaigned to break the color bar in organized sports. The left thus became an indispensable leaven in the rise of the liberal consensus on race under LaGuardia.

After the riot, as Greenberg recounts, Communist party organizers in Harlem honed their techniques for wresting more equitable treatment for blacks from New Deal agencies. And they helped black supporters of Harlem's "Don't Buy Where You Can't Work" campaign achieve a counterintuitive but critical insight as they picketed white stores along 125th Street, demanding employment. Although white workers had been displacing black workers from desperately needed jobs all over the city during the Depression, leftists in the "Don't Buy" campaign argued that it was essential to demand that no white workers be displaced by stores hiring blacks as a result of the boycott.

Why? Because it was important to persuade the white unions representing those workers to bargain with store owners for antidiscrimination provisions in their contracts, lest the merchants hire blacks at non-union, near-starvation wages, reversing everyone's gains. Blacks who took such an inclusionary approach were demonstrating the political maturity to make a shrewd, perhaps poignant, concession: uniquely searing though their own suffering had been, they were not society's only victims. Indeed, their own victimization was predicated on the exploitation of whites who were easily turned against blacks precisely because they were themselves so vulnerable, so desperate to defend what little they had.

There was another consideration, impressed upon black boycott leaders by the left: demanding all-black hiring on 125th Street would confirm other communities in their determination to hire only whites. Separatism would only further legitimize segregation. Of course, segregation was already entrenched and really needed no new justifications; the rhetoric of some of the campaign's black organizers reflected their skepticism that angry black self-assertion could possibly make conditions any worse. Not surprisingly, a separatist demagogue from Chicago named Sufi-Abdul Hamed, known as Harlem's Hitler for his anti-Semitic rantings against the store owners, broke the campaign's interracial strategy with a protection racket, shaking down some employers for lower-wage jobs with which to reward his followers. At the same time, he preached black economic self-determination, his ultimate goal being to drive the white merchants out of the community.

Such nationalist militancy had pragmatic as well as romantic attractions. For one, Hamed's men kept the boycott going when court orders against picketing gave clergy and women's groups pause. For another, merchants in the black bourgeoisie opportunistically supported Hamed's efforts to transmute the "Don't Buy Where You Can't Work" campaign into a "Buy Black" campaign. That such a course would only deepen black isolation was in their interest, delivering a captive market for their goods. This, too, would become a familiar pattern in the years ahead, as black businessmen, politicians, and others whose fortunes depended on the preservation of densely compacted black districts indulged separatist demagoguery.

Fortunately, as Greenberg notes, those less blinded and corrupted by such traffic in black anguish understood that racism on 125th Street could be broken only by a united front in which integration made bedrock sense to whites as well as blacks. "For anyone to strive to build a nationalist movement in America among Negroes is to commit racial suicide," declared a young minister and rising Harlem leader, Adam Clayton Powell, Jr. The majority of the picketers held firm, Hamed was discredited, and Powell's political career was launched amid a burst of black political organizing and activism.

Emblematic of the dubious rewards blacks reaped for such political maturity was the response of white transportation workers, who in 1941 struck the city's private bus lines with enthusiastic support from Powell and other black "Don't Buy" veterans. Despite black support through a boycott during the strike, white workers opposed the hiring of black drivers afterward, forcing blacks to threaten to resume the boycott. The white resistance embarrassed both the Communist party, which had helped organize the TWU, and Mike Quill, the union's new leader. Under combined black and Red pressure, with a push, too, from LaGuardia, who controlled the subways, Quill began to promote integration on the still-private bus lines as well as on the public rails.

Blacks' experience with the rest of the labor movement was not so encouraging. The Congress of Industrial Organizations, representing millions of unskilled workers, understood the importance of embracing blacks to prevent their use as scabs, but it was not prominent in New York, which had little heavy industry. The American Federation of Labor, too, was on record against racism, but many of its skilled workers in craft unions, who actually controlled the hiring at shifting job sites, were unapologetically out for themselves. The anti-Communist International Brotherhood of Electrical Workers posed problems; an editorial in the union's paper declared, "We do not want the Negro in the IBEW, but we think that they should organize in locals of their own, affiliated with the AFL, as that organization knows no creed or color." So continued the buck-passing that "neighbor Faxon" had first shown Abigail Adams in 1797.

Black labor leaders like A. Philip Randolph, founder of the Brotherhood of Sleeping Car Porters, were caught in a bind. Convinced of the necessity of union organizing yet rejected by white workers, they built their own unions, only to be accused by disingenuous whites of championing separatism and segregation. That was untrue, of course; Randolph was following DuBois and Booker T. Washington, who, in their different ways, had tried since before the turn of the century to prepare the way for blacks' eventual inclusion in white society. But with the rise of the nationalist Marcus Garvey in the 1920s and many lesser imitators like Hamed, more than a few blacks expressed a genuine ambivalence about "joining" a society whose brutality and hypocrisy they'd experienced. The tragedy of black separatism—a tragedy because it was at once inevitable and hopeless—would bedevil later efforts to dismantle structural racism.

In the depths of the Depression, in any case, black demands for inclusion in "white" society through employment were a matter of physical survival and would not be deferred. Organizers turned their attention to the utilities and the public sector, eventually winning the first nonmenial jobs for blacks at the telephone and electric companies and in the building of the Eighth Avenue subway. Other developments also nourished New York's growing liberal consensus about race. Italy invaded Ethiopia and Hitler snubbed the black American athlete Jesse Owens at the 1936 Olympics in Berlin, reinforcing the belief, already prevalent in New York's large Jewish community, that racism was for fascists, not Americans. For reasons both socialistic and parochial, Jews became champions of racial justice—a subject of the next chapter—and other Americans began to reassess their attitudes toward race. As Roosevelt maneuvered the United States into the antifascist camp, racism at home became a mounting embarrassment to the "arsenal of democracy."

In April 1941, Randolph and other black leaders, meeting in a New York hotel, threatened a march on Washington to demand jobs and justice if Roosevelt did not forbid discrimination in the armed forces and emerging defense industries. After LaGuardia convinced the president that the black leaders meant business, Roosevelt escaped the confrontation by signing an executive order, under emergency powers granted him by Congress as war convulsed Europe, establishing the Fair Employment Practices Commission, which dramatically increased black hiring in defense industries.

Typical of the rising spirit in the city was the stand taken by a young Yale graduate and future city housing administrator named Roger Starr, who in 1941 was pictured in the left-leaning daily news-

paper *PM* over the headline "Park Avenue Youth Ready to Fight
... If They'll Put Him in a Negro Unit." Starr was convinced, he told
PM, "that Negro segregation in the armed forces and the anti-Negro
policies of many of our defense manufacturers question the sincerity
of our talk of democracy and threaten the efficiency of our entire
defense effort."

In Brooklyn's Brownsville section, activist Jews demanded and
won some of the first racially integrated public housing in the city.
Years later, some of them would tell the sociologist Jonathan Rieder
of their refusal to vacate the rear of public buses while on basic
training in the South because, as one of them recalled saying, "We're
from New York, and we don't know from Negroes in the back of the
bus." LaGuardia made a number of significant Negro appointments
and, with cooperation from regional New Deal administrators and
the Roosevelt brain truster Harold Ickes, pressed hard against discrimination in relief and public works programs, responding to continued black and Red pressure.

But the scarcity of defense work in New York, combined with
white labor's intransigence, consigned blacks to Depression conditions well into the war; high mortality rates, widespread dependence
on relief, and the degradations and pathologies attendant upon segregation persisted. Meanwhile, under Moscow's direction, the Communist party officially abandoned active struggles against racism in
order not to divert energies from the antifascist struggle. Black misery now contrasted gallingly with the expectations raised by La-
Guardia, the New Deal, the left, and war propaganda itself. Harlem
street-corner speakers mocked the war effort and opined that the
Axis must have its good points.

Frustrations exploded in 1943, when a black serviceman in uni-
form was shot by a white cop in Harlem. This time, the riot was
explicitly racial; white stores were plundered, black stores spared.
The Reverend Adam Clayton Powell, Sr., while emphasizing the
injustices underlying the riots, denounced the looters themselves as
vandals; an editorial in the *Nation,* an organ of the left, countered
that they were "protesting in their own way." White merchants,
noting the racial character of the protests, promised reforms in pric-
ing and hiring but warned that further violence would drive them out
of the area, causing a "loss of jobs for Negroes." So saying, of course,

they disingenuously touted the same black economic gains they had resisted during the "Don't Buy" campaign—a familiar white opportunism of the sort that characterized neoconservative responses to black protest later on.

The Harlem Machine

Although hundreds of thousands of blacks had served in the armed forces, "hate strikes" by returning white veterans again pushed blacks who hadn't served out of jobs they'd taken during the war in New York and other cities. But the white backlash against modest black gains, which occurred nationwide in the immediate postwar years and included lynchings in the South, sparked an unprecedented liberal surge on behalf of racial justice, nowhere more so than in New York. The 1947 conviction of three men of aggravated assault on a Negro in Elizabethtown, New York, was widely reported. The verdict was delivered under a courtroom portrait of John Brown, who had settled there in 1849 to help organize a colony of fugitive slaves.

Former Vice-President Henry Wallace's leftist third-party presidential campaign of 1948 and the emergence of young politicians like Hubert Humphrey as forceful spokesmen for the liberal agenda moved Harry Truman to strengthen the Democratic party's commitment to civil rights. Truman was responding, as well, to the development of a critical black swing vote in key northern industrial states like New York, where J. Raymond Jones, later nicknamed the Harlem Fox, was building a political machine of substantial power. A few months after the 1943 riot, Benjamin Davis, a Communist party leader in Harlem who had not abandoned the fight against racism, was elected to the City Council with the support of Powell, Sr.; the latter's son, Adam, Jr., went to Congress the following year. Between the riots of 1935 and 1943, then, Harlem, like other black communities in northern cities, had begun to organize itself as a political force to be reckoned with.

Like most black men of his generation, whose abilities meant little to whites, J. Raymond Jones had worked as an elevator operator, as a porter, and at other menial jobs upon his arrival in the United States from St. Thomas during World War I, and he had experienced his share of racist harassment. Yet Jones's ideas about black empowerment were antithetical to those of both black nationalists and the left. Since the time Samuel Fraunces presided at his tavern, black society outside the South had always sustained a bourgeoisie, albeit one usually isolated from and pathetically imitative of its white counterpart. By marshaling the power of a growing black electorate in New York, Jones would accomplish something new under the sun—a "crossover" by black professionals and entrepreneurs into the liberalizing white postwar society on increasingly equal terms.

Distancing himself in the late 1940s from the Communist Davis and the flamboyant Powell, Jones assembled a cohort of natty, political lawyers and businessmen in Harlem—Percy Sutton, Fritz Alexander, Basil Paterson, Constance Baker Motley, and later Charles Rangel, David Dinkins, and H. Carl McCall—and with them built a political machine that parlayed black votes into public appointments and contracts. Jones greeted with equanimity the abolition in 1947 of the City Council proportional representation system that had permitted Benjamin Davis's election as a Communist; a new charter returned the city to geographically based elections, reinforcing a politics based in ethnicity rather than ideology. Not that the Harlem lawyers never walked picket lines or shouted into bullhorns; some of them bragged that they had, and Percy Sutton was later Malcolm X's lawyer. Rather, in aspiration if not yet in fact, they were establishment insiders, experienced brokers of whatever patronage, real-estate deals, franchises, contracts, zoning variances, and tax breaks they could wrest from the white establishment.

The incarnation of their political and entrepreneurial élan was Sutton, the Manhattan borough president of the 1970s whom Dinkins lauded this way on the night of his mayoral victory in 1989: "We have a saying up in Harlem, that everybody stands on somebody else's shoulders; tonight I stand on the shoulders of Percy Ellis Sutton." In the late 1970s, Sutton founded Inner City Broadcasting, encompassing four radio stations, including WLIB, and a cable television franchise in which Dinkins, too, invested. Like countless ethnic entrepreneurs in the city's past, like the Harlem merchants who indulged nationalist protesters during the "Don't Buy" campaign of the 1930s, Sutton made money from the ethnocentric, often militant programming of his radio stations, where to this day nationalist speakers like Jitu Weusi and Alton Maddox, Jr., are interrupted by commercials for Visa credit cards. Sutton's colleagues, too, maintained law practices and private ventures, some marginal, some quite successful, as they pursued their political careers.

The Harlem elite's success in a white establishment was a tribute to its tenacity and cosmopolitanism. Unlike Powell, who kept a foot in the left, alternately storming the citadel of white power and thumbing his nose at it, to the delight of black masses, Jones's Harlem lawyers more often finessed the white world's rebuffs to find individual whites with whom they could deal. As *New York Newsday*'s Kevin Flynn and Ellis Henican explained in a report on Dinkins's political roots, "Jones believed almost religiously that blacks were better off making deals with the white establishment than becoming, as he saw it, inward-looking. This, of course, produced leaders who were generally moderate in their political strategies."

The deals they struck could be shrewd without being purely self-serving. At the Democratic National Convention in 1960, Jones, by then the leader of the whole Democratic Tammany organization in Manhattan, sat in a hotel room with House Speaker Sam Rayburn, who was promoting his fellow Texan Lyndon Johnson's presidential bid, and won Rayburn's promise to make Representative Adam Clayton Powell, Jr., of Harlem, the chairman of the House Education and Labor Committee in exchange for the Manhattan delegation's support for Johnson on at least the first two convention ballots. Although John F. Kennedy won the nomination, Jones and Rayburn kept their bargain, and Powell became chairman. As national Democrats began courting northern blacks like Jones, southern Democrats maintained their stranglehold on the chairmanships of congressional committees for another twelve years, but their power over presidential politics was soon broken. To Harlem's political aspirants, Jones's deal with Rayburn was a model of how to get things done, a model Jones pursued with great success on the local level, too, under Mayor Robert Wagner in the 1950s and 1960s.

Jones "was an awesome figure," Charles Rangel recalls.

He had his own little air-conditioned room there [in Harlem's Carver Democratic Club] and the big shots would be called in. The rest of the people would wait out front. . . . It was something. You had judges and lawyers and professional people filing through to meet Ray. It was the country club, the place to be. If you were a young lawyer and had absolutely no interest in politics, it still made sense to join the club to meet the judges. There were people there who had problems with their landlords. There were lawyers there to serve them. . . . It was a very busy place.

You had these powerful district leaders who really controlled the public officials. When your turn came to run, they just told you. Political leaders had patronage and armies of loyal captains and could put together hand-picked slates.

Years later, bowing to public contempt for machine politics, Jones's protégés sometimes denied their origins. "I'm not a product of the clubhouse," Basil Paterson told *New York Newsday*'s Bob Liff in 1989. "I may have been in Dave [Dinkins]'s political club once or twice when J. Raymond Jones [led] it. And it's hard to think of Sutton as a clubhouse pol." But Paterson knew that black machine politics, riding New York's ascendant postwar liberalism, had effected important breakthroughs. Later in the *Newsday* interview, he added, revealingly, "In some ways, we're witnessing the demise of the democratic process in the demise of the political clubhouse. It offset the impact of money. There were once 300 or more political clubs in New York. Now even the clubs that exist are not very effective." Paterson was echoing Jones's belief that American protest movements come to nothing without help from pros versed in electoral politics and governance.

Militancy Moves to Brooklyn

The desperate density of Harlem's slums made expansion of the ghetto inevitable. Even as its borders shifted north and east during the 1930s and 1940s, the construction of the Independent subway line linking Harlem and central Brooklyn brought many Negroes to Bedford-Stuyvesant, which by 1943 was half black. (Duke Ellington's "Take the A Train" was a celebration of this exodus to Brooklyn, not, as many believe, an invitation to come uptown). Freeholding blacks had lived in Brooklyn since before the Revolution, and many of the first newcomers of the 1930s and 1940s were professionals and civil servants, homeowners and supporters of a Brooklyn black political establishment similar to Jones's in more ways than one.

Like Jones's Harlem coterie, the new Brooklyn elite were almost all of Caribbean origin. Such politicians as Shirley Chisholm, Bertram Baker, Thomas Russell Jones (no relation to Harlem's Jones), William Thompson, Ed Griffith, and Brooklyn's answer to the Harlem Fox, Wesley "Mac" Holder, were Caribbean immigrants or their children. As they or their parents had grown up in the island colonies, they had had strict, effective, Eurocentric schooling. Because their islands had been overwhelmingly black, they were accustomed to seeing blacks in high positions. Coming to New York at their own or their parents' initiative, they felt confident, entitled to speak for all blacks.

But as southern blacks in New York became increasingly politicized after World War II, the Caribbean elite came under pressure. New color lines were drawn in Manhattan and Brooklyn, foisting upon low-income blacks in the new areas of settlement the familiar high rents, subdivided apartments, unhealthy living conditions, family instability, and crime. When Brooklyn police killed two black youths in separate incidents in 1949, the NAACP denounced their "brutal inhuman practices" and distributed leaflets with pictures of the two "murdered" youths.

Making common cause with Harlem nationalists and the left, a rising group of Brooklyn insurgents, southerners by background, viewed the lawyers and entrepreneurs in Jones's network as marginal to their lives and dreams. Such Brooklyn militants as the Reverend Milton Galamison, the Reverend Herbert Daughtry, the Reverend Bill Jones, the librarian Major Owens, the teachers Albert Vann and Les Campbell (the son of a Communist party organizer, later called Jitu Weusi), the street activists Sonny Carson, Sam Pinn, and many more were intent on building grass-roots movements of the poor. They were ambivalent, at best, about the black "firsts" the Harlem elite had achieved by bargaining for public offices. They were inclined to view the wheeling and dealing of the Harlem and Brooklyn elites less as a means of advancing the race than as a cause of its impoverishment.

Between the Caribbeans and these new insurgents lay chasms of personal style as well as of culture. West Indian politicians could be formidably courtly, but they were also often cosmopolitan, breezy, and companionable, not only with blacks but also with whites, whose lash they had never felt to the degree the southern arrivals had. The latter, by contrast, carried with them the stigmata of American slavery and Jim Crow. Their political leaders, particularly, could be brooding, shy, stiff, sullen, or mercurial. Even years later, when Owens, Vann, and other Brooklyn insurgents won elective office and the southern-bred C. Vernon Mason and Alton Maddox, Jr., became Harlem lawyers as a matter of objective fact, they sometimes bore their wounds in ways that made them unattractive to the West Indian elite.

Throughout the 1950s and 1960s, Harlem's political leaders held their prerogatives so closely that, according to Andrew Cooper, publisher of the black Brooklyn weekly the *City Sun,* "even the established West Indian blacks in Brooklyn never got a sniff of patronage under Ray Jones." But if Chisholm and company felt neglected, then Owens, Vann, and other practitioners of poor people's politics might as well have been on the other side of the world, coming as they did from that broad mass of displaced agrarian workers flooding into the city. While the West Indians' politics could often be hierarchical and elitist, most of the southerners were imbued with collective and communal ideals preached by the left and, later, by Martin Luther King, Jr., and Malcolm X. They wanted to sow among their destitute, uneducated compatriots the seeds of a new black culture and politics in Brooklyn.

But the borough was vast, its black community sprawling and disorganized. Politically as well as economically, hundreds of thousands of people were uninitiated into public life and discourse, for Brooklyn's clubhouse system had nothing like the extensive network of roots into the community that Rangel recalls in the Harlem of Jones. Indeed, as Brooklyn's black population pulled ahead of Manhattan's in the 1960s, Jones's protégés were fond of saying, "Brooklyn has the numbers, but Harlem has the brains." Naturally, Brooklyn's insurgents preferred to reverse the sequence of that sentence—"Harlem has the brains, but Brooklyn has the numbers"—adding, in the idiom of a power they wished they had, that anyone capable of marshaling the borough's black masses must have brains as well.

Inspired by the charismatic, left-leaning Reverend Galamison in the 1950s and early 1960s, Vann, Campbell, Daughtry, and others tried a number of approaches, keyed at first to the antidiscrimination legislation and court rulings that had come with the growing white liberal consensus for integration, described in the next chapter. They pushed for and won experiments in school integration through busing—even though they were ambivalent about it, they now say— because integration was where the action was. Working with Sam Pinn, Major Owens, and others in Brooklyn CORE, they also pushed for integration in housing by sending out white "checkers" to apartments said to have been "rented" when black applicants had appeared. They picketed and protested at the Downstate Medical Center and other construction sites, demanding jobs for blacks. They won promises of increased government antidiscrimination efforts after they terrified politicians by threatening to tie up traffic on the opening day of the 1964 world's fair.

The insurgents challenged the hiring policies at Sealtest Dairy and other companies. With the Reverend Bill Jones, the local chairman of Operation Breadbasket, they challenged the Taystee and Continental bakeries, Robert Hall, and Coca-Cola to deposit funds in black banks. Tactics ranged from sophisticated boycotts to extortion—free-lance protesters sometimes urged small firms to hire blacks in exchange for peace—but, contrary to the common impression, it was usually associates of black Brooklyn machine loyalists who ran scams, not the admirably principled if often dogmatic insurgents. In the mid-1960s, with Mayor Wagner's acquiescence, they got a brief but important boost from the antipoverty funding of the Great Society, designed by national elites specifically to swell Democratic ranks by facilitating activists' end runs around established local white machines and their token black collaborators.

But Harlem's lawyers weren't ineffectual Toms, and Brooklyn never did have anything quite like their "brains"—that is, their sophistication and contacts. Brooklyn lacked the rootedness, compactness, and relative intimacy among social classes, the cheek-by-jowl juxtapositions of Sugar Hill, Convent Avenue, and Striver's Row with rat-infested tenement districts. Spike Lee and the rest of today's

black middle class in Bedford-Stuyvesant and Fort Greene notwithstanding, Brooklyn did not displace Harlem as the intellectual and
artistic capital of black America—unless, ironically, one was talking
about a new generation of West Indians. Nearly half of the one million immigrants from the Caribbean to the United States after 1965
crowded into Brooklyn, which now holds more people from some
island nations than do the islands themselves.

Nor could Brooklyn match Harlem's working relationships with
important whites. There was a brief intimacy with Robert Kennedy,
who, as a U.S. senator from New York in the mid-1960s, cultivated
Bedford-Stuyvesant against Jones, in part because the latter had
sided with Lyndon Johnson against his brother in 1960. But, by and
large, black Brooklyn's leaders never knew the nation's white elites
as well as Harlem's leaders did. It was a long time before any Brooklyn black cut a deal with a Speaker of the House as Jones had done
and Harlem's Rangel later did. After stewing for nearly a century in
the pressure cooker that is Manhattan, the subtleties of interracial
encounter there were richer, more various than those in Brooklyn.

For example, there were the memories, still strong among the
older generation, of whites who'd come visiting uptown through the
1940s; there was the welcome which Harlem's political and cultural
leaders found at white Democratic party reformers' functions and
other liberal civic and cultural events downtown after the 1950s, first
in the Village and on the Upper West Side and later at the fanciest
midtown hotels. By the early 1960s, as white, anti-Tammany reformers joined the North's crusades against Jim Crow in the South, some
of Jones's younger protégés, like Basil Paterson and David Dinkins,
began to forge with them personal friendships that would blossom
into political alliances. As early as 1961, Mayor Wagner sensed the
coming realignment and won his third term by breaking with the
"bosses" and campaigning as a newly minted "reformer."

J. Raymond Jones continued to support his patron Wagner, but he
remained tied to the machine's more conservative white Democrats.
His attempt to straddle both camps became untenable in 1964, when
black and white veterans of the southern civil rights movement's
"Mississippi Summer" voter registration drives returned North. At
the Democratic National Convention in Atlantic City, they demanded that the movement's integrated Mississippi Freedom Demo-

cratic party delegation be seated at the expense of the established, all-white state delegation. Jones, Bayard Rustin, and other Harlem notables accommodated Lyndon Johnson and some of the city's liberal white Democrats in pushing the MFDP to the sidelines.

That watershed event was one of the party establishment's most serious miscalculations. It enraged black and white activists who'd put their lives on the line for civil rights during Mississippi Summer. It galvanized Robert Kennedy's Senate campaign that autumn, in which he cast himself as the new champion of civil rights reformers. It shifted at least some of the black political spotlight to Brooklyn's angry insurgents, whom Kennedy courted, and to a rising new militancy in Harlem: the betrayal at Atlantic City convinced Stokely Carmichael, Julius Lester, and other New York veterans of the struggle that separatism, not integration, held the only hope. The political upheavals of the summer of 1964 coincided with Harlem's largest riot since 1943 and with the ascendancy of Malcolm X—the beginning of the eclipse of Dr. King and the rise of a fundamental challenge to Jones's type of politics.

White Reformers, Black Radicals

By the mid-1960s, some of Jones's loyalists and associates were moving beyond the confines of Harlem, and not simply by moving upward through Tammany Hall. In 1965, David Dinkins, for example, was a loyal Carver clubhouse assemblyman and, after 1967, a party district leader; but his attraction to Kennedy and the civil rights movement had led to some fast friendships with such up-and-coming white reformers as Harold Ickes, Jr., son of Roosevelt's secretary of the interior and today a counsel to Dinkins; Victor Kovner, currently Dinkins's city corporation counsel; and Barbara Juelson Fife, one of his deputy mayors. The affinities were genuine; through Rustin and Professor Kenneth Clark, Dinkins came to know and admire many white leaders of the new movement for social justice, and he sent his children to the Ethical Culture Society's Fieldston School, with children of the city's elite Jewish liberals.

John Lindsay strengthened such relations between the young Harlem lawyers and white reformers in 1966, leading them in a valiant but losing campaign to save his civilian police-review board from a referendum to abolish it. But, like Kennedy, Lindsay had reason to remember that not all blacks lived in Harlem; a Republican-Liberal, he bypassed Jones and also Brooklyn's black Democratic club-houses, reaching for the activists in the streets, making Major Owens his commissioner for antipoverty programs.

Lindsay was in some respects a perfect emblem of the white re-form–black alliance (he became a Democrat at the end of his second term). Roger Starr has written that Lindsay and his followers were comfortable only with two types of people: those who had so little money that they needed more of it just to survive, and those who had so much money that they needed to give it away. While none of the Harlem lawyers by the 1960s were poor enough to belong in the first group and few white reformers were wealthy enough to belong in the second, there is something to what Starr says. Recall that Percy Sutton was Malcolm X's lawyer and that his cohort's origins, cou-pled with the very name of Harlem, made them emblems of the oppressed to the reformers; and the reformers, who did include in their ranks such children of privilege as Carter Burden and, in time, Robert Kennedy himself, were an attraction to the Harlemites. To both groups, the broad mass in the middle, including hard hats who clubbed antiwar demonstrators, homeowners protesting new public housing, and schoolteachers terrified of black community control, were grubby and uninspiring.

But white reformers could be fickle allies when it came to support-ing blacks and Hispanics who ran for public office. Partly it was that they were terribly self-absorbed; their relatively affluent constituents could often get what they needed from government in nonelectoral ways and so could afford to elect mavericks who'd fight to change government itself. Sometimes that independence was mere eccentric-ity: in a 1969 bid for the mayoralty, Norman Mailer, then a pseudo-populist practitioner of the politics of moral posturing, consumed a lot of ink and airtime to garner only 35,000 votes—just enough, minority critics charged, to swing the Democratic mayoral nomina-tion from Bronx Borough President Herman Badillo, a mercurial but impressive exponent of liberal and minority concerns, to the white-ethnic backlash candidate Mario Procaccino, who coined the phrase "limousine liberals." To the horror of the nascent Harlem/reform coalition, he became the Democratic nominee.

Most white reformers and most blacks, including Jones, then bolted the party to support Lindsay, who, like Badillo, had lost his party's nomination to a conservative; Lindsay squeaked back into office on the Liberal line. But the reformers disappointed Harlem's political aspirants through their insistence on procedural purity in nominating processes for judgeships and other offices. That foreclosed the racial and ethnic ticket balancing that was possible when leaders like Jones could sit in a smoke-filled room and pick a Jew, an Italian, and a black to run together on a party ticket. "We'd spend hours negotiating how to weight the [nominating convention] votes of delegates from clubs of different sizes," Barbara Fife recalls. Few of the nominees who emerged from these deliberations were black.

Yet as Jones retired at the end of the 1960s and the Tammany patronage system was depleted by civil service reforms and bureaucracies distributing entitlements, astute Harlem politicians saw white reformers as the wave of the future. In 1970, Assemblyman Charles Rangel worked closely with white reformers to defeat a washed-up Adam Clayton Powell, Jr., in a Harlem congressional district that now wrapped around into the Upper West Side to include many liberal whites.

In the meantime, radicalized black and white New York veterans of the southern civil rights struggles had begun organizing a welfare-rights movement in the city. They were determined to shock and frighten (to them) contemptible but seemingly omnipotent Democratic politicians such as Johnson—he had been reelected by a landslide after the Atlantic City deal—into making major concessions to the black community. That put them on a collision course not only with the local party machines but, for the first time, with city workers who provided social services, particularly the predominantly Jewish welfare workers and, later, in the struggle over community control of the public schools, the predominantly Jewish teachers, who had supported most of the activists' earlier initiatives. The militants argued that they had no alternative, that liberal integration and assimilation had failed to deliver justice and equality.

Lyndon Johnson's own greatest failure was the Vietnam War, which, compounding blacks' and liberal whites' alienation in Atlantic City, contributed to their characterization of America as an engine of racist oppression abroad as well as at home. Not only did the war kill, maim, and rattle disproportionate numbers of young black and Hispanic men; it shook the foundations of civil authority back home in ways that dwarfed the impact of Atlantic City. Moreover, black activists' redefinition of themselves as members of a colonized Third World, a vision articulated by Malcolm X and embraced enthusiastically by Daughtry, Weusi, and other Brooklyn insurgents, pitted them against a resurgent Jewish nationalism in the wake of Israel's Six Day War in 1967, which they misunderstood as a white, imperialist victory against people of color. Events abroad became, for both sides, a giant screen onto which grievances at home were projected, seemingly larger than life.

The willful and self-indulgent miscommunications that followed are covered in the next two chapters. Suffice it to say here that, in the battles over welfare rights, community schools, and rising crime and police brutality, everything that was undeniably hypocritical in white liberalism was cited by its new opponents to eclipse achievements that, set against the longer history of race relations of New York, were real breakthroughs; everything violent and ignorant in the paroxysms of black-power activists was used by their opponents to discredit all that was noble and clean in their strivings. As in any tragedy, the protagonists invited their own destruction, which came close enough to destroying the city.

Eventually, economic dislocation and political retrenchment forced a reassessment of liberal and radical strategies. No one was quite sure what in the city's institutional liberalism could or should be rescued; and it remained unclear what white radicals and black insurgents had learned about themselves and the institutions they'd assailed. The insurgents, centered in Brooklyn, continued their work in day-care unions, church-based poor people's movements, cultural centers, independent schools, and protests against police brutality. They saw something of their grass-roots tradition carried forward in the preaching and campaigning of yet another southerner come North, the Reverend Jesse Jackson. Indeed, for a short time, they saw him bring Harlem to heel. But only in Brooklyn did the insurgents eventually carry their militancy into public office, sweeping away the West Indians and launching themselves on an uncertain journey in search of new ways to channel black anger and hope.

The fissures and tensions between the boroughs and their representative political styles ran deep and would run on. The suave Basil Paterson touched the Brooklyn insurgents briefly during an abortive mayoral campaign in 1985, but not until 1989 did a Harlem insider actually win their support in a bid for high office, and then he was one of that elite's few members of southern descent, David Dinkins. They supported him, in part, because he came bearing the imprimatur of another southerner, the irresistible Jackson; and even then, the Brooklyn militants accused Dinkins of not according enough respect and attention to the desperate needs of the black poor. And, given the "establishment" fiscal constraints he accepted, they were right.

Under Dinkins's mayoralty, then, black New York continued to endure a cold war between the two political camps: one holding that redemption can come only through the angry solidarity of the dispossessed against a racism presumed to be implacable; the other holding that redemption will never come without an astute electoral politics that embraces many liberal values and aspirations, nourishing them from the bottom up, from the streets to the suites. Peacemakers appeared, including Dinkins himself at times, urging a synthesis or, at the very least, a working alliance; they had trouble making their way, in part because disillusioned and defensive whites gave them too little credence and support. When whites thus succumb to cynicism and despair, they contribute to a misrepresentation of New York's racial history that may sink the fragile hopes it still harbors.

Not that white alienation is surprising. As we will see in the next two chapters, the militants' resistance to liberal notions of integration challenged the reigning white consensus about the felicities of "the American way of life," angering and unnerving assimilationist whites by throwing a garish light on their own furtive doubts about whether and on what terms they had become "Americans." Black power made clear for the first time to many thoughtful whites that slavery's destruction of African culture had, ironically, made blacks the quintessential Americans, being not only among the longest here but also the most dependent on the country's living up to its promises.

Remnants of African culture may run deeply through African-American life, the more so as they have been researched, revived, and celebrated in recent years. Still, as the black writer James A. McPherson put it, unlike white immigrants who brought their cultures with them, "the slave ancestors of today's thirty or so million black Americans took their ideals from the sacred documents of American life, their secular values from whatever was current, and their deepest mythologies from the Jews of the Old Testament. They were a self-created people, having very little to look back on."

The very depth of their stake in an Americanism that received only lip service from many whites exposed blacks—nowhere more so than in New York—to all that was brutal and empty in the heart of a country that had cast its fate with capitalist liberation from every folk tradition. As blacks' struggles to stake their claim on America were stymied by white resistance that mocked the country's promise, some of them turned of necessity to scabbing, hustling, and crime, articulating their resentments through such spokesmen as a former hustler and criminal, Malcolm X, whose personal redemption became a powerful emblem of black survival. His message became a running and subversive commentary on America's pretensions to be a *novus ordo seclorum,* a "new order of the ages"—a slogan appearing, appropriately enough, on the dollar bill.

The dollar also bears the motto "E pluribus unum"—"Out of many, one"—a reference to the confederation of thirteen colonies that has picked up other meanings in this racially and ethnically divided land. James Baldwin, a child of Harlem who'd done more than most to fathom the illicit intimacies of the closest of strangers in New York, departed for Paris wondering why any black would want to "integrate into a burning house" of seething, unresolved cultural yearnings. Yet the white America he railed against, particularly its New York crucible, was not one house but many, subdivided into half a dozen major ethnic camps. Blacks might be quintessentially, irreversibly American, but, for all the power of Baldwin's *The Fire Next Time* and King's eloquence at the Lincoln Memorial, there was no single "America" for them to join.

Black protest—even, in a backhanded way, black separatism— underscored the deeper truth that America, unlike more homogeneous, mythically rooted societies, has no choice but to become indeed "a new order" transcending ethnic loyalties. The country may not be a melting pot, but neither can it flourish by retreating into an uneasy truce among increasingly distinct nationalities. In cities like New York, such truces are bound to be broken. No urban future can be built on them. For blacks, then, as well as for countless white Americans who are by now generations removed from any easily recoverable religious or ethnic identity, Americanism awaits a broader, more universal definition, one that points beyond the pragmatic "tolerance" hammered out by postwar liberal pluralism. Think of New York as one of the great national stages upon which that hammering and building will proceed or, at incalculable cost, fail.

2

The Liberal Nightmare

Integrated before We Knew It

Reaching across a newsstand counter to pay for my paper at a crowded corner of Seventy-first Street and Continental Avenue in Forest Hills one gray winter morning in 1978, I am jostled rudely by a well-dressed black woman who seems to have cut in front of me in order to pay for her newspaper. She probably thinks I cut in front of her. I'm not sure who's right, but, already grouchy from a poor night's sleep, I stand my ground. She gives me a second, sharp elbowing, and as we disengage, our eyes lock into a two-way glare.

From my lips, unpremeditated, leaps a sentence I hadn't known was in me. "I didn't do it to ya, lady," I find myself breathing in a low, portentous register, shaking my head slowly from side to side. With a start, I realize that I'm referring not to the jostling but to the three hundred years of oppression and pent-up rage I've decided went into her elbow.

"Well," she hisses back, without missing a beat, "it was your kind."

Never mind that barely seventy years before our encounter at the newsstand, "my kind" were shivering in peasant hovels in a czarist Baltic province. Never mind that, given my mood that morning, the same rude jostling could have occurred with a Jewish woman or anyone else this side of Hulk Hogan crossing my path. The fact remains: I understood intuitively what the black woman was thinking; she knew that I knew; and as we acknowledged it, the earth seemed to open at our feet to reveal the depths of the wound.

But what, precisely, was the wound? Though I felt I couldn't take the woman's charge personally, it reminded me that even we whose forebears arrived long after slavery are indeed beneficiaries of that complex legacy. But by now, we white city dwellers have paid something for it, too, and in some quarters that has stirred resentments. Perhaps because I was new to the city in 1978, I felt no such resentment that morning at the newsstand. Had the woman been able to see me for what I am, I still tell myself, she would have known that not all beneficiaries of past black suffering are haters, that not all of us have it in for blacks.

In the 1930s and 1940s in Trenton, New Jersey, an hour by train from Manhattan, David Dinkins was growing up on a racially mixed block and attending a largely white high school. In Jamaica, Queens, Mario Cuomo was playing in street and sandlot ball games with black and other kids whose parents shopped at his father's neighborhood grocery store. Ed Koch shared a desk with a black youngster in a crowded, racially mixed junior high school in Newark. The former New York City schools chancellor Frank Macchiarola's family rented from a black landlord in Brooklyn.

For three summers in the 1950s, Les Campbell, the future black militant who would become Jitu Weusi, attended Camp Kinderland, a leftist Jewish summer camp, picking up friendships, pinochle, and an impressive repertoire of Yiddish idioms from veterans of the Abraham Lincoln Brigade who were friends of his father. In the early 1960s, Al Vann, a founder with Campbell of the African-American Teachers Association that was active in the Ocean Hill–Brownsville school wars and now chairman of the state legislature's Black and Puerto Rican Caucus, earned a master's degree in education at the Orthodox Jewish Yeshiva University. Representative Major Owens, of Brooklyn, having come North from Atlanta to be branch librarian in Brooklyn's Brownsville section, married one of his white graduate schoolteachers and became politically active with her in and around the American Labor party. Stokely Carmichael, a native of Trinidad, attended secondary school at the Bronx High School of Science. Jane Tillman Irving, a black New York City radio and television reporter, spent fifth through ninth grades in a voluntarily integrated class in Harlem with the children of liberal whites from nearby Washington Heights, including Joshua Muravchik, now a fellow of the American Enterprise Institute. The writer Pete Hamill and his younger brothers, growing up in an Irish community in Brooklyn, ran, read, and argued with black friends about civil rights and politics.

In the 1980s, Dominick Blum, the young court officer whose car struck Michael Griffith in Howard Beach and who was immediately branded a racist accomplice of Griffith's assailants by Maddox and Mason, turned out to be an amateur actor who'd played in Lorraine Hansberry's *Raisin in the Sun;* just before entering the parkway and colliding with Michael Griffith that fateful December evening in 1986, he dropped a black friend off at home after they'd watched a play at Brooklyn College. Jon Lester, then sixteen and one of the actual Howard Beach assailants, had dated a black girl at John Adams High School who insisted on speaking fondly of him after the assaults; he worked as a busboy at the Lindenwood Diner, where he was friendly with such regular black patrons as U.S. Representative Ed Towns and the black attorney Charles Simpson, who teasingly called him Elvis because of his hairstyle. A month before the Howard Beach assaults, Simpson represented Lester without cost and befriended his parents when the boy was charged with illegal possession of a gun he'd bought after some of his waitress friends had been robbed, by blacks, on their way home from work.

These are not the lineaments of a place we can call Up South, the more so because the important thing about these vignettes is that they are not "important" at all. That is, while many of those cited have become prominent or infamous, they certainly were not so at the time of these interracial encounters; nor are most of those who shared their experiences prominent today. There are no explicit politics in most of these citations of ordinary New Yorkers' experience of racial rapport, yet the information they give us is more structural than personal: they tell us that, even before the civil rights movement, portions of New York were "integrated" in ways the old South would never have countenanced, though not necessarily integrated on terms we would judge acceptable today.

From the 1930s on, countless white New Yorkers did back integration out of political commitment or conscience. At least one-quarter of the nation's one thousand white volunteers in the 1964 Mississippi Freedom Summer voter-registration campaign were New Yorkers. The United Federation of Teachers president Sandra Feldman, a key aide to the former president Albert Shanker during the bitter Ocean Hill–Brownsville battles over community control of the public schools in the late 1960s, had been a "freedom rider" on Route 40 and an early member of the Congress of Racial Equality; she is married to Arthur Barnes, a black who heads the New York Urban Coalition. Shanker marched in Selma and swung the UFT behind the civil rights movement. Koch was chased across the square of the Mississippi town where as a young lawyer he was helping blacks register to vote. Koch's first deputy mayor, Stanley Brezenoff, an early member of Brooklyn CORE, worked with some of today's militant black leaders against discrimination in housing and construction jobs. "Did you know that I used to help the blacks back during the Depression?" an elderly Catholic woman tells Jonathan Rieder in *Canarsie: The Jews and Italians of Brooklyn against Liberalism.* "I used to try to get their rents lowered. They were being exploited by the landlords, this was on President and Nevins streets in South Brooklyn, so I went to the Office of Price Administration to protest because I felt so bad about how they were treated."

The reader will believe that the rest of this book could be filled with citations like these, all dating from before the passage of the 1964 Civil Rights Act and the development of antipoverty programs and strong affirmative action. Out of such experiences came an unusual civic culture: of all the baseball teams in the country, it was bound to be the Dodgers who broke the color bar with Jackie Robinson, whose incarnation of grace under pressure carried delirious underdogs of all colors to triumph in the 1955 World Series. As *New York Newsday*'s Bob Liff puts it, "We're not the Mississippi of the early 1960s, because we New Yorkers will never 'know our places.' "

The simple truth is that, amid and despite the long train of brutality and hypocrisy recorded in the preceding chapter, hundreds of thousands of white New Yorkers harnessed their deepest insecurities and aspirations to build great educational, judicial, health care, and business networks that made the city a magnet for blacks and Hispanics in the postwar years. Since before LaGuardia's time, some broad-minded political and labor activists in the Irish, Jewish, and Italian communities, together with portions of New York's established middle class and the more indulgent members of its leading families (the Astors, Rockefellers, and Burdens), had been creating an unusual culture of institutions—public, collective, and universal—which tried to link the poor city dweller's personal upward mobility to a broader cosmopolitan purpose.

The resulting network of public transit, schools, hospitals, libraries, parks, and museums (New York still has 30 percent of the nation's mass transit riders, 60 percent of its municipal hospitals, and the only city university system) was meant to provide its beneficiaries with more than a leg up the ladder of personal advancement. It offered a social interaction different from the sort found elsewhere: a city of walkers and subway newspaper and paperback book readers instead of drivers; of brassy, better-educated workers; of intellectual development possible without the sums of money usually needed to cross the threshold of higher education.

What that social interaction provided, in a way a thousand scholarships to elite private schools could not, was an integration of proletarian strength with professional excellence and high cultural achievement. It was an enormous wellspring of American vitality whose sophistication inhered in its intimacy not with the city's glitter but with its glue. Skills of cultural transmission were honed by countless ordinary New Yorkers who shuttled across lines of class and ethnicity to run the institutions and movements that nourished the great rising Jewish, Irish, and Italian communities of the outer boroughs.

Most of these city builders did not think of its civic culture as racially exclusive. To be sure, some of its more well-known gestures toward inclusion were tokenistic. The International Ladies' Garment Workers Union's "Penn South" housing, in the West Twenties, built on a nonspeculative basis for the benefit of its members, proudly "bumped" its predominantly Jewish waiting list to give an apartment to Bayard Rustin; yet A. Philip Randolph had accused the ILG of racial discrimination. On the other hand, the late Ewart Guinier, chairman of Harvard's Department of Afro-American Studies in the 1970s, found such a cold reception as that college's only black freshman in 1929 that he moved to New York to complete his education at City College, Columbia, and New York University, joining the American Labor party and running for Manhattan borough president in 1949. Only in 1969 was Cambridge ready to receive him as respectfully as New York had done forty years before.

Yet we would be wrong to miss the profound racial ambivalence of even liberal white New Yorkers in the prewar years or to read too much into the instances of almost casual integration mentioned above. Macchiarola may have touched on that ambivalence when he said in an unsuccessful campaign for city comptroller in 1989, "We were so poor, our landlord was black." The press reported that as a gaffe, as if it were prescriptive, not merely descriptive, of the fact that in Macchiarola's youth most blacks were poorer than all but the least-fortunate whites. Mario Cuomo, even in recalling amicable boyhood relations with blacks, told me, "It was the prevalent white view that [blacks] were less intelligent, less entitled; it was something you took for granted." Cuomo added that German neighbors felt that way about his own group: "You're the new Italians," some German women said to his mother. "Just remember to keep your trash cans covered." She recalled the insult years later and chuckled at having outlived them.

Macchiarola and Cuomo are saying that such situations were normal in those years, not that they were right. In truth, we don't know what most of the whites mentioned above actually felt; the reminiscences of public figures take us only so far. But the neoconservative writer Norman Podhoretz undoubtedly spoke for many in a controversial 1963 essay, "My Negro Problem—and Ours," where he candidly recalled his boyhood fear and envy of loose, aggressive Negro youths growing up with him in Brownsville. The way those youths lived cost them later on, Podhoretz acknowledges, while he and other children of strict immigrant households reaped the middle-class rewards of their intricate restraints. What troubles Podhoretz is that these consequences were hidden in those all-important, formative childhood years; it seemed to him and to the black youths them-selves that they were being rewarded, or at least compensated, in boys' terms, for whatever deprivations prompted their license: spe-cifically, the black youths took great pleasure in exercising a seem-ingly inalienable right to whip Podhoretz's hide.

Podhoretz knows he shouldn't have had to endure that, no matter what his tormentors themselves had suffered at others' hands. And he isn't sure what can be done to help those among them who are not doing well now. Can there really be any programmatic, governmen-tal substitute for the wholesome childhood discipline they were not given then? Having fought his own way out of an impoverished Brownsville childhood, Podhoretz feels entitled to his success. Not all Jews from that community "made it" out of the neighborhood simply by being white; in the 1930s and 1940s, more than a few of them were lost to the warfare of gangs like the fictional Amboy Dukes, based on a real Jewish gang, as well as to organized crime and even drugs. If some of the black youths who attended the same schools Podhoretz did and who beat him up after class have not found success, what does he owe them?

And since Koch's, Cuomo's, Macchiarola's, Shanker's, and count-less other prominent and powerful New Yorkers' stories of interra-cial encounters have much in common with Podhoretz's, what does their generation of poor immigrants' kids owe the great-grandchil-dren of slaves? In the early 1960s, Podhoretz "discovered" and pub-lished James Baldwin in the pages of his *Commentary* magazine, bringing him to the attention of the world; Koch and Shanker went South in the 1960s; Cuomo appointed the special prosecutor in How-ard Beach and supports a strong anti-bias-crime bill; Macchiarola ran the public schools in the late 1970s and early 1980s, when they were 70 percent minority, and he did not do so solely for his own self-improvement. Isn't this more than anyone had reason to expect of these men? If they permit themselves to wonder about this when black leaders attack them for not doing enough, does that make them the "slavemasters" they've become in some of the rhetoric? Can such verbal assaults fail to remind them of old physical ones?

But these are rhetorical questions, posed in order to clear the way for a more fundamental query: If New York was not really Up South, and postwar white liberalism not quite a sham, then how was the city's liberalism flawed? Why did it fail? Why was it still possible in 1977 for a smartly dressed black woman at a newsstand in Forest Hills to hiss at me, "Well, it was your kind"?

The answer lies in an examination of New York liberalism's two great initiatives in the postwar years, which many of the people mentioned above helped to advance: first, a frontal assault on discrimination, an attempt to change Americans' attitudes toward race; and, second, ambitious public-sector programs, culminating in those of Lyndon Johnson's Great Society, intended to bring those who had won abstract rights and opportunities "up to the starting line" so that they might participate fully in society's rigors and rewards. In the late 1960s, radical blacks and whites came to suspect liberals' motivations on both fronts. The liberals' antidiscrimination efforts were cast as self-serving, particularly for upwardly mobile Jews anxious to secure their own opportunities in the larger society. The antipoverty and affirmative action initiatives were attacked for trying to finesse rather than confront the underlying, intractable racism in economic life.

Was Desegregation Good for the Jews?

The 1943 Harlem riot was one of many across the country during the war that galvanized Americans to what Carey McWilliams called the "crisis patriotism" of "civic unity" organizations working to promote racial harmony. Roger Starr, the young Yale graduate on his way to a career in housing and journalism, was one of many middle-class whites who joined the NAACP and hosted interracial gatherings in the early 1940s on the somewhat tautological assumption that segregation persisted because "Negro and white people did not meet each other very often." The gatherings were "dull as dishwater," he later recalled, "embarrassing to all present, and did nothing to solve the problem of segregation in the United States Army."

Yet such efforts were important because they came not from the left but from the broader white middle class. The emergence of integration on the liberal agenda bolstered LaGuardia's antidiscrimination measures and profoundly influenced a generation of rising New York business and civic leaders. So did the Supreme Court, which, confronted with compelling briefs by the NAACP, had since 1937 been establishing legal precedents that led to the landmark *Brown* v. *Board of Education* decision in 1954, declaring racially "separate but equal" facilities inherently unequal and therefore unconstitutional. By 1955, New York was the national center of northern, urban black life, and also of white left-liberal culture and politics—a wellspring of struggles for racial integration.

Enormous undertows gripped the city between 1950 and 1960, as 900,000 whites left and 800,000 blacks and Puerto Ricans arrived. Relatively few of the departing whites were fleeing crime and decay, which were not that far advanced in the 1950s; they were moving up, responding to the lure of greener pastures and the myth and market of suburbia, subsidized by government highways and cheap mortgage loans and artfully promoted by realtors. It may well be that the suburbanization of the 1950s thus "creamed off" some upwardly mobile liberals, leaving behind the elderly and the defenders of ethnic redoubts—those whites least hospitable to blacks, especially as their softening neighborhood housing markets made accelerated racial conversion attractive to speculators in ways described in chapters 4 and 5. But then, precisely because much of the city was relatively unscathed by the problems of the incoming poor in the 1950s and 1960s, many committed, liberal city dwellers remained and rose to meet the challenges the newcomers presented.

"Civic unity" efforts, which after the war fell under the rubric of "intergroup relations," seemed all the more urgent as the newcomers chafed within the great network of schools, hospitals, and other public facilities. These had become ethnic bulwarks as Irish, Italians, and Jews consolidated their employment gains in those institutions along group lines. Jews had moved into the Board of Education and social-welfare agencies under LaGuardia, wresting them gradually from the often politically appointed Irish by strengthening civil service regulations and expanding them under the liberal auspices of the New Deal; it may also be said that the Irish, who sent their children to parochial schools and got the best of the political machine's benefits, were less possessive of these agencies than of the police department.

By the 1960s, then, except for cops on the beat (and even among them, there were several thousand Jews), Jews had displaced the

Irish as the city's policers and tutors of the unwashed; they would be to the blacks and Puerto Ricans what the Irish had been to them and the WASPs to the Irish.

It cannot be surprising, then, that, to a southern black plunged suddenly into myriad encounters with Jews who decided whether he could get credit, welfare, an apartment, a job, a passing grade in school, or an acquittal in court, everyone in authority seemed Jewish. Nor was that perception, and the resentment that accompanied it, properly to be conflated with the genocidal anti-Semitism of Europeans who had power over Jews and hated them without even having to know them. "In most cases," notes Andrew Cooper of the *City Sun,* "the encounters were not unfriendly. But there's bound to be a reaction when you feel that people are manipulating your life and have power over what you can achieve."

Cooper is more than kind. New York in the 1950s could be a racially tawdry, petty, often brutal place. The hierarchy of humiliations blacks endured ran the gamut from subtle and not-so-subtle condescension by some teachers to outright exploitation by lawyers, merchants, and landlords. Other white-ethnic groups were often even tougher, considering the Jews "soft" and "easy marks"; blacks and liberal Jews had to embarrass George Meany into trying to get his old plumbers' union local in New York to take on Negro members (he failed). As late as 1960, proportionately five times as many Negro college graduates held low-paid service and laboring jobs as did white graduates; Negro women continued to work overwhelmingly in domestic and low-level clerical positions; construction unions were still assigning the occasional Negro journeyman to apprentices' jobs, demeaning him in the eyes of fellow workers in the hope that he would become discouraged and quit. Politicians vied for the liberal vote by promising to cancel city construction contracts with exclusionary unions, as they were required to do by law. Throughout the 1950s and 1960s, none was ever canceled. The unions were just too politically powerful, the politicians' edifice complexes too great.

But if Jewish providers of social services and education became, by comparison, "easy marks" for principled rebels and hustlers alike, that was also partly because they needed blacks in a special way. Some of the Jewish liberalism of the period had about it a tiptoe quality that enraged black activists because it strove not only for elementary social justice but also for something subtler—acceptance, admission of Jews to the club, by those above them in the social order. Upper-middle-class blacks today should find painfully familiar the catch-22 of anti-Semitism that drove Jewish calculations in the immediate post-Hitler years, when disdain for Jews was disguised in the winks and nods of "gentlemen's agreements": protests against such discrimination would only confirm WASP snobs in their belief that Jews were loudmouthed and grasping.

For Jews, this bind was all the more fateful precisely because no clearly visible barrier like skin color blocked the way; in some elite clubs and boards of directors, at least, a certification of "good behavior" could overcome discrimination based on "good breeding"—having the proper bloodline. If a Jew would speak out, then, better to do so on behalf of others less fortunate; there was some precedent for that in WASP tradition, going back to the abolitionists. The more upwardly mobile Jews, still barred in the 1950s from most prestigious resorts, residential developments, and bank and corporate boards, thus had their own reasons for pushing blacks forward as the bearers of a liberal civil rights agenda. Not only was it true that, as Nathan Glazer has noted, the same fair-housing law that allowed a Negro access to a modest apartment in Crown Heights admitted the Jew to a posh condominium on the Upper East Side; advocating for racial justice was also a way of presenting oneself to "society" as already well-enough established to have become magnanimous toward others. Or so some of New York's postwar Jewish liberals half-consciously assumed.

But even with these parochial side agendas fully acknowledged, and even with so many national forces apparently aligned in their favor, there is no belittling the struggles and sacrifices Jews and some other middle-class whites made to wrest the resources necessary to promote social justice from powers greater than themselves. Jews might just as well have sought to curry favor with elites by subtly denigrating blacks; by and large, to their everlasting credit, they did not. Throughout the 1940s and 1950s, they aggressively popularized the theory, developed by the writer Horace Kallen, that distinct ethnic and racial identities can be accommodated within a framework of liberal national patriotism—the theory of American pluralism.

Jewish organizations played an important role in Mayor Robert

Wagner's creation of the Commission on Intergroup Relations (COIR) in 1955 with a $500,000 budget and a mandate to avert or mediate interethnic and interracial disputes. When Martin Luther King, Jr., was stabbed in a Harlem bookstore owned by a white man while visiting New York on September 21, 1958, the police commissioner reached COIR's chair, Alfred Marrow, who in turn reached black leaders with the information that the assailant was a demented black woman; as crowds already forming in the streets were told this truth by people they trusted, violence was avoided.

Irving Levine, a native of Brownsville and an intergroup relations expert for the American Jewish Committee, recalls his profession as a proud and growing one in those years, with hundreds of members working to change attitudes through education and to pass new legislation against discrimination. The best-seller and movie *Gentlemen's Agreement,* which captured the subtle cruelty of genteel anti-Semitism, was conceived under AJC auspices, as was much of Theodor Adorno's research on the authoritarian personality. "Some social psychologists, including people out of the army's Office of Special Services, had idealized visions of how to change attitudes by education and counterpropaganda," Levine recalls. In the afterglow of victory over fascism and in the shadow of revelations about the Holocaust, these efforts, undertaken in concert with the National Urban League and other black and some Christian religious organizations, met with considerable success.

Countless seminars and workshops reached thousands of teachers, who in turn touched thousands more New York City schoolchildren with exemplary and often ingenious lessons in intergroup tolerance. The writer Barbara Grizzuti Harrison recalls that a teacher changed her life when she was a teenager in Bensonhurst by announcing that only students with blue eyes would have to do homework. Their cries of "That's not fair!" made the teacher's point for him, and as he drew from it the obvious conclusions about racism, Grizzuti Harrison felt scales drop from her eyes. It was the first time anyone in her narrowly tribal neighborhood had made her see that some people are animated by a commitment to fairness, not by blood loyalty.

Levine, who as a youngster had led in integrating the Brownsville Boys' Club, learned with other intergroup relations experts how to conduct "ethnotherapy" sessions that tapped and released participants' "extraordinary ambivalence about their identity. Ethnicity is as explosive as sex, death, and money because you have to factor in this ambivalence. Ten different explosions can be waiting to happen in a room. You have to know how to get at this. We know it's a racist society; the question is what you can do to create pride in kids despite that." Levine recalls a plethora of such efforts and brotherhood programs during the 1950s, initiatives later mocked by radicals but potent at the time in shaping the consensus for change.

Bensonhurst was also the childhood home of Eugene Genovese, the Marxist professor of black history, and of the civil rights lawyer Jack Greenberg, for many years the executive director and prime mover the NAACP Legal Defense Fund and now the dean of Columbia College. With his mentor Thurgood Marshall and other NAACP lawyers, Greenberg worked with the American Jewish Congress to draft many of the nation's civil rights laws. Levine traveled to many states with Arnold Aronson, Roy Wilkins, Bayard Rustin, and others to build the political coalitions necessary to enact them. In 1956, Levine was detailed by the American Jewish Congress to the staff of the City Commission on Human Rights to help enforce antidiscrimination laws, campaigning against banks and other institutions that still barred Jews from their boards and against restaurants and educational institutions that still barred or strictly limited the admission of blacks. It was a marriage of pragmatism and idealism whose fragility few Jews appreciated at the time.

Housing and Social Justice

Aside from a few celebrated cases like that of the exclusion of the black American UN delegate Ralph Bunche's son by the West Side Tennis Club in Forest Hills, most whites remained unaware of antidiscrimination efforts until 1958, when the city passed the nation's first fair-housing law and the human rights commission and activists in CORE set out to enforce it by sending out white "checkers." Marrow, of the Commission on Intergroup Relations, candidly acknowledged that the law did not win enthusiastic support from New Yorkers, black or white; too many felt deep stakes in neighborhood turf, as will be described in chapters 4 and 5.

By the late 1950s, it had dawned on at least some civic elites that the best way to eliminate discrimination in housing was to improve and expand the housing supply for all city residents. Roger Starr, the new executive director of the Citizens Housing and Planning Council (CHPC), became an advocate of this point of view on behalf of a remarkable generation of developer-statesmen caught up in the integrationist spirit of the times. Men like the realtor James Felt, New York City Housing Authority (NYCHA) director Ira Robbins, and developer Richard Ravitch had been shaken by the Depression and World War II but buoyed by the possibilities of the New Deal and the unexpected resiliency of the postwar boom. Led by Starr, they and their cohorts at CHPC, which Robbins had directed before Starr, staked their careers with an almost religious passion on the notion that curmudgeonly builders could coordinate their investments with the enlightened policies of a provident national government to produce an integrated, "slumless" city. They intended to improve on the example set by Robert Moses, the extraordinary housing czar, parks commissioner, and builder of public works, whose dazzling accomplishments had been shadowed by his dictatorial, often capricious direction of almost all city planning since the 1930s.

Surveying housing conditions on Manhattan's West Side, journalists, political reformers such as Hortense Gabel, and the members of CHPC brought to light the economics of ghettoization and crusaded for improvements under Wagner. At their behest, he committed vast sums of federal dollars to NYCHA's construction of what would remain into the 1980s a model public housing network sheltering half a million people. They also promoted massive urban renewal and "slum clearance" schemes, defending them not only against critics like Jane Jacobs, who considered them rapacious boondoggles that destroyed the fabric of neighborhood life, but also against suburban real-estate interests, which considered them creeping socialism. Socialism it wasn't, but Jacobs was right, too: the urban renewal projects which the developer-statesmen promoted "gave a veneer of social concern to classically political builders who made vast fortunes on public housing and Mitchell-Lama [middle-income] projects," the late urban analyst Paul Du Brul told me in 1983.

The developer-statesmen's determination to do well by doing good anticipated John F. Kennedy's spirited appeals to both hardheaded calculation and moral crusade. In 1959, Starr characterized the battle for low-income housing as

complex and costly total warfare, but in the war against slums, the price of victory may still be less than the price of defeat. It has taken New Yorkers many painful and arduous years to acquire some understanding, however partial, of the nature of the enemy—the city's internal forces of self-destruction. But over the same years, we have also amassed an arsenal of sophisticated skills wide-ranging enough to give us some valid hope of victory. We need only the courage to accept the cost, the maturity to face the difficulty, the determination to see the fight through. We have the weapons. Have we the will?

Before answering such a call, one might have been forgiven for wondering just what this enemy—these "internal forces of self-destruction"—was, and why Starr expected the Tishmans and Zeckendorfs of the city to arise and fight it. Perhaps the overblown rhetoric betrayed a subliminal awareness that, under the deluge of migration from the South and Puerto Rico, capitalist pragmatism and middle-class stability were breaking apart. Perhaps the "enemy's" lair really lay close to home, in the hardheaded calculations of slum realtors and developers, calculations that could be upset only by galloping socialism or a full-employment economy.

As they hoped that economic growth would raise the incomes and opportunities available to the broad mass of blacks and Puerto Ricans, Starr and others sought to "socialize" them into citizenship and employability by conceiving of the social service agencies and public housing projects as "normative" institutions—that is, as teachers and enforcers of the complex rules of civility so critical to the maintenance of urban life. Just as poor Jews and Italians had been introduced to the rigors and rewards of city living by the Irish schoolteacher, ward heeler, neighborhood cop, and other local symbols of authority, so now the (often) Jewish teacher, social worker, and housing-project manager would impart and enforce civic virtue.

In the housing projects, that meant tenant screening and the designation of special projects and programs for a group of troubled families a CHPC study called "The Small, Hard Core." In the 1950s, the housing authority developed a list of "Potential Personal Problems," grounds for denying residency in public housing to families with, for example, histories of behavioral instability or with members in prison for violent felonies. In some projects, prostitution had become a problem: investigators found that women needing money would open their doors to men going to work, saying, "C'mon in, honey, you don't need to leave just yet." Skeptical of such accounts, I asked Starr whether most of the women suspected of prostitution were black and Hispanic. He threw back his head and laughed. "Not at all! The projects in the early 1950s were 60 percent white. Welfare tenants, who, incidentally, included some whites, were around 18 percent of the population. Race wasn't the issue. We were completely committed to integration." For the early social reformers of the postwar years, that didn't preclude making people take responsibility for themselves and their children.

But civil rights lawyers, newly empowered in the early 1960s by government grants, recognized that the policy, even if not aimed specifically at blacks and Puerto Ricans, was likely to bar more minority households than others. "The problem we faced," Starr recalls, "was that of public ownership." Whether one was talking about a park, a public hospital, or a housing project, he noted, one was talking increasingly about "equal protection" and entitlement. "Courts saw housing as a natural right. They didn't see that people don't naturally grow up subscribing to a behavioral code or that, with the passage of time, most of those trying to uphold such codes and suffering from the misbehavior of people who didn't were themselves minority tenants." Indeed, by the 1970s, black and Hispanic tenants would be clamoring for the kinds of screening the civil liberties lawyers had challenged, often successfully, on the grounds that it was racially discriminatory. Starr believes that the abandonment of screening did hasten a white exodus from public housing to middle-income developments.

So did the sometimes absurdly bureaucratic lengths to which NYCHA went to promote "integration" under pressure from the activists. In 1959, the housing authority, which managed approximately 100,000 apartments in public projects, announced that it would give whites priority in mostly Negro buildings; move some Negroes and Puerto Ricans from overwhelmingly minority projects to new ones, where they would be mixed with whites; hold half of the prospective vacancies in predominantly white projects for Negroes and dark-skinned Puerto Ricans; and, in some overwhelmingly Negro projects and neighborhoods, hold vacancies for light-skinned Puerto Ricans. Thus substituting an abstract conception of integration by skin color for actual need, NYCHA wound up discriminating against dark-skinned applicants, generally the neediest of all and making up the majority of new applicants.

The plan was not entirely naive. NYCHA managers understood that if public housing became identified with Negroes in the public mind, their integration efforts would collapse entirely and, of course, NYCHA itself might suffer in its efforts to obtain increased federal funding. Yet the policy was unrealistic because whites were moving up the income scale and moving out of the city. By 1950, New York City was home to 750,000 blacks and 250,000 Puerto Ricans, many of them in young, poor families on the housing authority's growing waiting list.

And, the fact remained that while most of those families were law-abiding and seeking nothing more than decent housing and good schools, a small but growing minority of them were beset by social problems that alarmed their neighbors. It was a simple fact of life that crime rose wherever there were large concentrations of poor blacks and Hispanics, just as it had with concentrations of poor whites in earlier generations. The only way to save decent, low-income minority families from the stigma associated with large concentrations of the poor was to apply nonracial—that is, behavioral—screening criteria, and this was precisely what activist lawyers resisted, even as they pushed for wholesale integration.

Years later, a young lawyer mediating a dispute over the siting of a public housing project in middle-class Forest Hills tried to assess the validity of white residents' fears of project-generated crime by touring a number of projects and their surrounding neighborhoods. In his 1972 diary of his deliberations, Mario Cuomo noted,

Wherever there were large numbers of welfare people the attendant social problems were obvious and difficult to deal with. . . . I gather that the H.A. itself is painfully aware of this but is limited in what it can do about the problem because of the legal restrictions against screening.

... The opponents to the [Forest Hills] project are well aware of the legal limitations on the power to screen tenants and it increases their apprehension. They know, for example, that the H.A. is not even able to get Police Department records as to arrests or drug addiction. This is another illustration of the necessity to balance competing considerations. No doubt there is a danger in circulating arrest records; it presents a threat to civil rights. But then there is undeniable validity in making intelligent choices of tenants— for the safety of the project as well as the community. Surely, with some thought, a way could be found to serve both ends here.

But no way could be found, in part because project managers who did the screening were white, which some activists took as prima facie evidence that racism guided their decisions. It was a pattern that would be repeated again and again: because teachers, police officers, and social workers were predominantly white, they were charged with racism in conflicts that were often simply part of the age-old New York struggle among classes and competing white-ethnic groups. Crying "Racism!" put such conflicts into a new, more ominous light, bringing into play court rulings and government regulators. That short-circuited the informal, often extralegal bargaining and jockeying for place through which competing groups had always staked their claims in the city's institutions—the kind of bargaining that J. Raymond Jones would have argued was already bearing fruit through his style of politics.

By the 1980s, when blacks constituted much higher proportions— in some cities, majorities—of teachers, cops, and social workers, it was clear that rules and disciplinary actions once characterized as racist were nothing of the sort. That had been clear all along, of course, to those who believed with Starr that success in urban living is built not just by the assertion of rights but also by a difficult learning process that involves training, sacrifice, and conformity to norms whose validity knows no color. But that was a truth decidedly uncongenial to the spirit of the 1960s.

Education and the Abandonment of Integration

School integration highlighted even more dramatically the problems of mixing people across class as well as racial lines. In 1959, goaded by the pronouncements of Dr. Kenneth Clark, who simplistically attributed the age-old inequities in New York's slums and slum schools to racial segregation alone, the Board of Education bused Bedford-Stuyvesant children into underutilized schools in the conservative, predominantly German and Italian neighborhoods of Ridgewood and Glendale, in Queens, with minimal preparation of the participants in the experiment. As Queens field consultants to the City Commission on Human Rights, Irving Levine and colleagues tried in vain to smooth these first major public school integration efforts. Affluent white Manhattan parents proved no more accommodating: when the board tried to bus children from East Harlem to the Upper East Side in 1960, parents removed 50 percent of the white children to private schools.

Sweeping goals and timetables for integration had been demanded by the Reverend Milton Galamison, since 1955 the senior minister of Brooklyn's Siloam Baptist Church, to the plaudits of Daughtry and young black teachers like Vann and Campbell. Galamison's followers, armed with the moral force of the Supreme Court's 1954 *Brown* ruling, in which the court had relied heavily on Kenneth Clark's research, staged substantial school boycotts that pushed the Board of Education closer and closer toward massive, involuntary busing. Not only would that integration strategy have been a logistical nightmare; not only did it violate the actual wishes of most parents, black and white alike, who strongly preferred to keep their children in their neighborhoods; busing for integration was rapidly becoming a simple, demographic impossibility as the student population became increasingly black and Hispanic in composition.

But most important, Clark's premises and the thinking of the militant integrationists were deeply flawed. Frank Arricale, a longtime liberal political activist and today a community school superintendent in the northeast Bronx, cites two fundamental truths the activists ignored:

First, integrating different social classes hurts integrating by race, because people will tolerate racial differences only at their own class level. What they didn't understand is that integrating by class was always anathema in the city, even before nonwhites were involved. On the other hand, blacks living peacefully in [the affluent Bronx neighborhood of] Riverdale, for example, are higher up the scale than many of the whites.

Second, the greatest myth of all was that public schools in the past had taken kids from point zero—the least literate, least educated—to middle-class success, that schooling could bring economic opportunity to the poorest of the poor. That was just BS. The schools never, ever did that. You already had to be well up the scale in literacy and in middle-class aspirations and habits to make the most of the public schools.

In the white-ethnic slums of the past, for example, the school dropout rate had always been high; employment alone had trained and redeemed the vast majority of poor people who bettered their conditions. Busing the poorest of the city's children en masse into working- and middle-class neighborhoods now, simply because they were black, was no solution to poor education and certainly no cure for discrimination in housing and unemployment; it would only speed the departure of working- and middle-class whites from the system and, indeed, the city. Those most intent upon using the law to alter the urban ecology never seemed to grasp their strategy's central limitation: nothing in the Constitution could ever prevent aggrieved whites from picking up and leaving. "We began to realize only very slowly that you simply couldn't work one-sidedly for blacks without addressing white people who felt alienated by the bureaucracy and the courts," Irving Levine recalls.

Witnessing the ferocity of white resistance to integration by social class as well as by race—and the minimal response of black parents to voluntary busing programs that would have taken their children away from home—some black leaders, too, began to question Galamison's demands. The black *Pittsburgh Courier*'s New York edition criticized him in an editorial in 1960: "Instead of campaigning to have . . . more highly qualified teachers assigned to schools in Negro districts, the [New York desegregation] campaign leaders harassed the Board of Education into a plan to transfer Negro pupils to distant 'white' schools so that classes could be 'integrated.' "

COIR's Marrow, too, noted the shift in mood:

A community consists of a voluntary grouping of people who are alike in ancestry, ways of life and common ideals. A ghetto is also a community, but its members live together [partly] because they are compelled to do so by some external power. Many people who live there like it as a community and want only its ghetto stamp removed. They themselves do not want to move out. They would like to see their housing and schools improved, though they feel that those who want to move elsewhere should be free to do so.

On all sides, then, desegregation efforts were reconsidered. Levine reflects,

We knew that segregation was a disaster for blacks, and we wanted to smash it, but we did not know how to define integration. We had gotten swept up in moral rhetoric. Social engineering had become an unstoppable tide, but the [white ethnic] opposition was powerful and crafty. They built technical cases and spawned leaders like Jerry Birbach in Forest Hills or Louise Day Hicks in Boston, and even some national backlash movements. These were not evil people. The fact was that our movement had built up a head of steam based on detailed but shortsighted court orders. On the ground, it just didn't work.

That was a lesson which the federal judge Arthur Garrity refused to learn as late as 1975, when he accelerated the segregation of Boston's schools by forcibly integrating them through a busing scheme so draconian it drove white parents to transfer their children to local parochial and ad hoc private schools in order to keep them in their neighborhoods and away from the strangers flooding into their local public schools. Zealots like Garrity, an assimilated Irish "aristocrat" living in an affluent suburb, misread the changing black mood as well: certainly by the 1970s, many blacks supported desegregation— the removal of the stigma and barriers that had been set up against them—without actually embracing integration as their preferred way of life, particularly if integration meant "acting white" in pursuit of a generic American identity that did not exist.

But, even as they drew back from bureaucratic school integration, black radicals insisted on casting the failure of that initiative as a moral betrayal by whites rather than as a reflection, at least in part, of their own excesses. The parliamentary maneuvers against the Mis-

sissippi Freedom Democratic party in Atlantic City, like the weaving
and dodging of the Board of Education in response to their demands
for integration, had curdled their already strained faith in northern
whites' commitment to full racial equality. When Stokely Carmichael expelled whites from the Student Nonviolent Coordinating
Committee in the name of "black power" in the mid-1960s, his actions and rhetoric resonated among northern blacks disillusioned by
continuing white resistance to integration. The militants were also
enraged by their community's continuing dependency on white social service bureaucrats, organizers, and advocates—and, in a larger
sense, on having to face outward to white society in order to redefine
blackness itself. "Integration, black power, community control—
these were all attempts to deal with an unyielding system," Herbert
Daughtry explained to me years later. "If integration had worked,
okay. The most vociferous exponents of black power had been
through integration already, and it had failed them."

Now the only answer for black radicals was to build their communities from within, to establish some form of independence from
whites, who, they had come to believe, would never accept them
anyway. If white civil society wouldn't open itself socially or
economically to blacks, then at least its government owed them sus-
tenance, in the form of reparations: parochial schools within the
public system, supported by the taxpayers, and an end to all "mis-
sionary" social work—the "decolonization" of the ghetto. Liberals
protested that such a stark bargain was destructive of the traditional
mechanisms of urban upward mobility and of the American promise
itself. They wanted to make those mechanisms work for blacks. "All
ethnic succession involves sharp polarization, power struggles, accommodations and trade-offs that lead to coalitions, and, finally,
joint ventures to make money through polite graft," Levine observes.
If blacks could consolidate their electoral strength and develop their
own business and communal networks, they would win their place in
the sun while making institutions like the Board of Education more
responsive.

Yet black militants in New York after 1966 defiantly rejected
every concession short of full public funding for untrammeled "community control"; they became known as people who wouldn't take
yes for an answer. "Uhuru sasa!" they cried—"Freedom now!"—

little realizing that in a complex urban environment there can be no freedom without intimate engagement across racial lines. To them, the liberal Jews staffing the institutions had proven to be the most insidious racists of all. Never mind that Jews had led most of the antidiscrimination efforts and the attempts to integrate public institutions, while so many non-Jewish, white-ethnic unions and institutions remained closed to blacks. If the walls the Irish and Italians had put up around themselves were largely unbroken, that only made Jewish liberals the most accessible apologists and beneficiaries of an oppressive system, the closest of strangers, the easiest targets. By 1966, the politics of spite, laced with anti-Semitism, had triumphed: because you will never admit us, its practitioners seemed to be saying, we will break you by pulling out of your system.

3

The Politics of Polarization

The Elevation of Race

Liberal integrationists of the 1940s and 1950s had taken for granted a social order cohesive and self-confident enough to admit blacks on its own essentially white middle-class terms. After 1965, those terms came under determined assault not only from black militants and antiwar protesters but also from counterculture enthusiasts, all intent upon disrupting the conventions of a "sick" society. Their hostility to the assimilationist spirit of the civic unity, intergroup relations, and early civil rights movements presented opportunities to a renascent white left, which saw special revolutionary potential in black militants' rejection of the liberal consensus. As such movements brought new recruits to the struggle against "the system," it seemed to many on the left that capitalism's two most durable struts, racism and anticommunism, might at last be exposed and then shattered.

Such calculations figured in the creation of the National Welfare Rights Organization (NWRO) in 1965 by the radical white professors Frances Fox Piven and Richard Cloward, based in New York

City, and by the veteran black civil rights activist George Wiley. Accepting as a fact of life the left's isolation from the white working class, supposedly a bastion of racism and—after the McCarthyism of the 1950s—of mindless, cold-war nationalism, the NWRO's theoreticians prescribed a strategy of explicit racial polarization through minority demands for more welfare, demands certain to alienate white taxpayers. Piven and Cloward hoped thereby to shake up a national Democratic establishment that had come to need the growing black communities of the North as much as it did working-class whites.

The NWRO's tactic was to use rule-book technicalities to flood the welfare system with demands it was legally bound to meet, forcing it to collapse under the strain. Meanwhile, taxpayers who turned on the evening news to find welfare mothers screaming for increased toy or furniture allowances would be enraged. That would panic liberal national Democrats into replacing welfare with a guaranteed minimum income for all, thereby removing the stigma of selective welfare dependency and quieting the protests that threatened the traditional Democratic urban coalition.

The NWRO ideologues made two signal errors. First, perhaps swayed by countercultural visions of a noble poor free of bourgeois restraints, they misunderstood the importance of the obligation to work, not only in the traditional American value system but also in many liberal New Yorkers' lingering socialist vision of a collectivity to which everyone contributes according to ability in order to receive according to need. In both the traditional American and the left views, the purpose of welfare is to help those who cannot work to reach a standard of living and education that will enable them to join in productive labor. The NWRO activists nominally endorsed that goal, but in the late 1960s, when unemployment in New York City was running at 5 percent for blacks and even lower for whites—in other words, when there were plenty of jobs—they managed to triple the welfare caseload to almost a million recipients, promoting minorities' dependency upon predominantly white workers who paid taxes. If the activists' point was that society, not individuals who are chronically out of work, must be held responsible for unemployment, they picked a bad time and a bad way to prove it to anyone except the ideologically converted.

The caseload soared in part because in the mid-1960s the welfare-grant level, combined with supplementary assistance and other programs for the poor, had risen sharply against the minimum wage and because Lindsay and his welfare commissioner, Mitchell Ginsberg, were only too happy to accommodate the NWRO's demands. It was far easier for them to buy off minority protest with welfare and antipoverty monies, which most urban whites didn't want anyway, than to assail white unions and landlords for exclusionary practices in workplaces, neighborhoods, and schools. Indeed, in those days expanding the welfare rolls meant more jobs for predominantly white caseworkers. The NWRO's activities were, in effect, what the veteran activist and school administrator Frank Arricale calls "a subsidized revolution."

Piven and Cloward claimed they were helping those already on the rolls to break the cycle of dependency by channeling their anger into protest and empowerment. They even likened their movement to organized labor because, they claimed, it would show poor mothers that they could win real economic benefits through collective action. The demonstrations and legal challenges did politicize a thin layer of activist welfare mothers who exhibited organizing talent and leadership, but for most recipients the "subsidized revolution" merely enlarged bureaucratic munificence without their ever having to participate in political struggle. Most people master the skills of political or labor organizing only by working—that is, by getting out of the house, taking the subway, collaborating with others on a job. Conversely, the discovery that one can extract additional benefits from a system with minimal effort hardly induces one to work for its overthrow. The NWRO had few skilled organizers in part because it had relatively little real need for them and even less in the way of serious political training to offer them.

The NWRO leaders' second signal error was to make race the pivot of their strategy of polarization, which they dubbed "the politics of turmoil." Despite their analogy to organized labor, they characterized municipal and other unions as racist and therefore part of the problem of minority unemployment. Valid as a generalization, this assertion overlooked both the lessons of the "Don't Buy Where You Can't Work" campaign in Harlem in the 1930s, which demonstrated the necessity for unity among black and white workers, and the fact that public unions were certain to change racially, anyway, as urban minorities grew in numbers and electoral strength. Unfortunately, Piven and Cloward condemned electoral politics, a position they reversed in the 1980s, after discovering that the Democratic liberals they hoped to shake up would not be in office unless those who wanted something from them helped elect them. For the time being, the radicals saw electoral politics as co-opting and corrupting, while the poor's "power to disrupt" was pure. "They believed that out of chaos will come a new organization," says Arricale. "Out of chaos can come more chaos; they didn't know that!"

Despite their disdain for electoral politics, Piven and Cloward, like many radicals of the time, also indulged a wildly romantic view of the black community as a potential political power base. Sensing quite correctly that experiments in social engineering such as busing were doomed to fail, they, like many black radicals, resorted to a conception of black power whose base was geographical and, potentially, economic: ghettos were colonies to be liberated for self-determination. This surprisingly durable misunderstanding of the nature of power in America was later incorporated into interpretations of the Voting Rights Act that favor the creation of ethnic and racial bantustans as guarantors of minority "representation." Yet, because the activists of the late 1960s did little to promote electoral participation, they lost to entrenched politicians the control of local antipoverty boards that had been designed explicitly to help the poor make end runs around white-controlled political machines in the quest for self-sufficiency.

The mythos of the noble poor also undermined Roger Starr's notion that there are such things as public values and norms, transcending class and race, which urban society must impart to and, if need be, impose upon its newest residents. If instead black ghettos were colonies, then cops were an occupying army, and caseworkers, teachers, and other social-welfare professionals were missionaries or imperialists—a thesis rendered plausible to many activists, as we have seen, by the fact that in the 1960s these service providers were overwhelmingly white, while their clients were black and Hispanic. Instead of socializing the children of poor sharecroppers into employability and citizenship, service providers were told to withdraw and to hand over resources and institutions, without strings, to the poor themselves. "Rather than the intellectualization of the proletariat," recalls Arricale, "they preached the proletarianization of the intellect: only drug addicts could help drug addicts, only the poor could understand the poor."

Not surprisingly, as radical lawyers worked, with the acquiescence of the decade's newly libertarian liberals, to get teachers, social workers, and project managers off their clients' backs, they often became confused about who the noble poor really were and what most of them really wanted. The conservative social critic Charles Murray is right to complain, "We forgot the extent to which our solutions involved not transfers from the rich to the poor but transfers from some poor people to other poor people, mandated by us. When we said that impoverished inner city students couldn't be kicked out of class if they didn't perform, we exacted an incredible price on another set of poor students who were sitting in class ready to work. . . ."

Similarly, when "we" said that broken, devastated families couldn't be barred from any public housing project because of crime and delinquency, we exacted an intolerable price on another set of poor families trying to live decent lives. And when we said that poor defendants in criminal courts are so victimized by racism that they merit our special solicitude, we undermined the morale of the equally poor victims of their depredations. As a veteran Brooklyn prosecutor who prefers not to be named advised me, the real racism in the criminal justice system is toward black victims of crime, not defendants, thanks in part to zealotry of legal aid lawyers more intent upon protecting the latter than the former; even black defendants' crimes against black victims simply aren't taken as seriously as those against whites.

The radical extension of welfare and various other supports had one compelling justification: New York had been inundated by destitute, vulnerable people who did badly need protection. But the welfare-rights movement promoted a rhetoric of nonnegotiable demands based on racial grievances that carried with them no corresponding social obligations. The black poor and their putative spokesmen were suddenly beyond reproach when they did not conform to essential social norms. To many whites, the flamboyant, nose-thumbing career of Adam Clayton Powell, Jr., came to symbolize this attitude, particularly as he disintegrated personally in the mid-1960s: the joke went around among whites that NAACP stood for "Never Antagonize Adam Clayton Powell." Starr says, "I remember when a prominent New York woman complained in the 1950s that it was outrageous to stigmatize a woman with an illegitimate child in assessing her suitability for public housing. But we weren't discussing marriages that couldn't take place because the bride was a Capulet and the groom a Montague. Where were the men?"

Middle-class feminists and radicals condemned such reasoning because they were properly enraged at sexist abuses that had paraded for generations under cover of the sanctity of marriage; beginning in the 1960s, they worked heroically to establish alternative support networks, from battered-women's shelters to increased day care. But nothing in those efforts negated the fact that, for most people, it is still necessary and desirable to establish two-parent families and communities that grow from them. For them, the question is how to do it more justly, not how to create substitutes; when transient political communities ebb or, indeed, organize themselves out of existence by winning bureaucratic provisions of care, families remain the only communal alternatives to government abuse, nurturing as they do friendships and loyalties that are not subject to facile politicization. Even those radicals who railed most vehemently against the traditional family and neighborhood in the 1960s and 1970s drew almost surreptitiously on the strengths these admittedly flawed institutions had given them in their own childhoods. Yet, alienated from their own middle-class upbringings, they could not bring themselves to acknowledge that many of the "noble poor" are, of necessity, socially conservative. As the sociologist Christopher Jencks explains,

In poor communities as in rich ones, clergymen, teachers, mothers, and other moral leaders must continually struggle both to limit and to redefine self-interest. Censoriousness and blame are their principal weapons in this struggle: blame for teenage boys who steal from their neighbors, blame for drunken men who beat up their wives, blame for young women who have babies they cannot offer a "decent home," blame for young men who say a four-dollar-an-hour job is not worth the bother, blame for everyone who acts as if society owes them more than they owe society.

The unwritten moral contract between the poor and the rest of society is fragile at best. . . . But the solution cannot be to tear up the moral contract, or to deny that the poor are responsible for their behavior. . . . The only viable solution is to ask more of both the poor and the larger society.

Yet now, on the evening news, in the courts, in the pronouncements of community organizers, and in the examples set by celebrities, libertarians of every stripe—civil, sensual, other—were telling the poor that blamè was itself taboo and mocking the traditional authority figures of neighborhood life. Under such conditions, Jencks warns, society can "hardly expect the respectable poor to carry on the struggle against illegitimacy and desertion with their old fervor. They still deplore such behavior, but they cannot make it morally taboo. Once the two-parent norm loses its moral sanctity, the selfish considerations that always pulled poor parents apart often become overwhelming."

Today, the notion that social-welfare institutions ought to shore up poor families by recoupling obligation to entitlement comes increasingly from the ultimate authorities on the subject: the beleaguered poor themselves. In 1989, the *New York Newsday* reporter Nina Bernstein spoke with the Harlem neighbors of several young black women who'd just been arrested for roaming upper Broadway, sticking white female passersby with hatpins.

As two women interjected agreement, the tenant leader called for a more activist welfare system, the likes of which hasn't been seen in New York since the early 1970s, when clerks took over provision of public assistance. The women want an old-fashioned social worker who could threaten to cut the welfare grant of the 14-year-old's mother, who routinely lets her daughter stay home from school. They want a caseworker on the beat, who would demand that the grandmother's adult daughters go to work and would notice child neglect before it reached crisis dimensions. Instead, they said, welfare is still paying the rent on the seven-room apartment of one former hotel resident whose five pre-school children were taken from her a year ago and who now sublets rooms to crack addicts.

"Government policy has ended up creating a lost generation of children," a neighborhood leader told Bernstein. New ways have to be found, within civil society itself, to reweave familial networks and moral obligations. The state may find ways to support such efforts, but only if it can be acquitted of the charge of cultural imperialism.

Parochial Public Schools

The story of the bitter "school wars" of 1967–69 in New York City has been told so often that one hesitates to wade into its complexities yet again. The dispute turned on a minority community school board's bitter struggle to wrest from the Board of Education and the United Federation of Teachers complete control of the schools in a district which it was trying to run under an experimental program authorized by the central board and supported by the Ford Foundation in the Brooklyn neighborhood of Ocean Hill–Brownsville. Admirably balanced accounts appear in Jonathan Kaufman's *Broken Alliance* and Diane Ravitch's *The Great School Wars*. But a few important points, relevant to our survey of radical folly, do seem worth reemphasizing.

First, in theory, the district's overwhelmingly black and Hispanic parents deserved the right to exercise at least as much control over their schools as did parents in communities, rich and poor, outside the city. In New York in the mid-1960s, however, schools were run by the central Board of Education and the UFT. Black activists charged that the experimental program did not give them enough latitude. Their attempt to transfer nineteen teachers out of the Ocean Hill–Brownsville district without the due process hearings guaranteed in the UFT contract precipitated the citywide union strikes that ultimately led to the crushing defeat of "community control."

Contrary to popular opinion, however, when the Ocean Hill–Brownsville board defied the teachers' strikes by keeping its schools open with the help of "scab" volunteers, it welcomed and hired many whites. Given the available pool of applicants, it could hardly have done otherwise. Still, to all but the most angry black militants, the skin color of individual teachers was less important than the locus of power and the kind of teaching that flowed from it—and the governing board was certainly determined to break the power of the UFT over education in its district. Nor could anyone doubt that black students were doing so poorly in the stagnant ghetto schools of the period that almost anything the experimental governing board might come up with in pursuit of "community control" stood a fair chance of being better, provided it was allowed to take root and grow.

Second, while the skin color of teachers was less important to most of the district's activists than the question of who had authority, cultural affinities were indeed of some legitimate importance. Those whites who had opposed busing as a threat to the sanctity of "the neighborhood school" could scarcely deny that the vast majority of teachers of the city's black and Hispanic students were not from "the neighborhood," either geographically or, more important, by background. No one could deny that a cultural chasm yawned between the UFT's predominantly Jewish members and the poor children of recent arrivals from the South. The governing board prized black "role models" in the classroom, but the young white strikebreakers who joined blacks in replacing UFT members at the height of the crisis shared the local activists' assumptions about black empowerment; in the countercultural spirit of the times, they displayed a genuine if youthfully adventurous interest in ghetto children. (That their adventures in inner-city teaching also qualified many of them for draft deferments at a time when blacks were fighting and dying in disproportionate numbers was overlooked.)

On the other hand, Norman Podhoretz recalls no parental control over his own schools in Brownsville in the 1920s, and he has described a cultural chasm between him and his gentile teachers that was nearly as wide as that between Jewish teachers and black youngsters in the 1960s. It was the new attitudes toward race, not any dramatic deterioration in the schools themselves, that made the old arrangements intolerable. There were other searing ironies: like Podhoretz, many of the older UFT members did know the streets of the city's black neighborhoods with the intimacy of children who had grown up on them when they had held poor Jewish ghettos. If Brownsville had a Herzl Street, it wasn't because a Menachem Begin had persuaded Flatbush Jews to seize new land; if there were Jewish merchants on nearby Pitkin Avenue, it wasn't because they'd come there to exploit blacks as often as it was because the neighborhood had changed around them since the time when their customers had been their own relatives and friends. Even in 1968, some of the teachers who went out on strike in Ocean Hill–Brownsville still had parents or grandparents living in the community or in neighboring East New York.

Recall, too, that Brownsville had one of the city's first integrated public housing projects in the 1930s because the left-leaning Jewish community there had agitated for it. From the UFT president Albert Shanker on down, a majority of the union's Jewish teachers had come from precisely that liberal political tradition; ideologically if not always temperamentally, they had staunchly supported the civil rights movement and the antidiscrimination and antipoverty initiatives of the 1950s and 1960s.

That is what made the school wars so tragic. Whatever the legitimacy of their demands for black empowerment, militants such as Robert "Sonny" Carson and Leslie Campbell deliberately airbrushed the recent Jewish intimacy with blacks out of history. Moreover, however blighting the school bureaucracy, however narrowly defensive the trade unionism of the teachers, a chronicle of the governing board's negotiations with the central board and the union makes painfully clear its misunderstanding of and contempt for democratic procedure and due process for teachers; these precious legacies the activists characterized time and again as nothing more than the entanglements of a sick society.

Sonny Carson's politics, then as now, was that of intimidation, of blacks as well as whites; even the governing board's mild-mannered superintendent, Rhody McCoy, was enamored of the more strident antiwhite teachings of Malcolm X, at whose feet he and Carson had often sat in Malcolm's home on Long Island. "There exists," said McCoy, "a predetermined script, established by racist, capitalist America, which makes the education of black, poor white and Third World children in this country impossible. A violent revolution is necessary to have America's public institutions serve all of its people." According to participants' accounts cited by Ravitch, McCoy was not above orchestrating menacing appearances by "the community" in the form of Carson and his retinue at critical junctures in the confrontations. That the governing board ran off the rails under the influence of these men was more than a strategic blunder that cost it its power; it pointed past sophisticated black empowerment, to separatist nihilism and impotence.

The radical follies of the welfare-rights and community-control movements did nothing to mitigate continuing racism in employment, and they were powerless against the dramatic economic dislocations of the 1970s and 1980s. Given these developments, one can say with hindsight that, even had the real progress made by the civil rights movement in New York not been squandered by the militants, there simply wouldn't have been time, before the economic and fiscal decline of the 1970s, for the city to absorb its black and Puerto Rican newcomers on anything like the terms it had offered white immigrants.

But if radical excess did not by itself account for that failure, neither did white racism. Whether or not the broad mass of ordinary people who struggled up from the Lower East Side and Brownsville and toward modest security as caseworkers, shopkeepers, teachers, librarians, or union functionaries ever really loved blacks, they were willing up to a point to be held accountable to the ethic of fair play. But they were utterly overwhelmed by blacks' needs and frightened by demands that they cede to blacks their own hard-won places in the municipal bureaucracies and in neighborhood turf. At countless anguished meetings they convinced one another that the national liberal elites of the 1960s, represented by the Ford Foundation's McGeorge Bundy and by Lindsay, were only too happy to take black and Puerto Rican gains out of Jewish hides at relatively small cost to themselves. The "proof" was that the elite liberals sat silent in the face of chilling anti-Semitic rhetoric.

The fact that middle-level power brokers like the teachers' union president Albert Shanker magnified such rhetoric during the Ocean Hill–Brownsville school wars, inflaming Jewish fears until in some quarters they assumed genocidal proportions, didn't mean that all Jewish fears were hallucinations. If the anti-Jewish rhetoric of Campbell, Carson, and McCoy was not really the anti-Semitism of Nazis, neither was Jewish fear and resentment of blacks really the racism of the old South. What distinguished it from the blood hatred of the Klan was its almost purely reactive nature, its fear of very specific, wrenching minority encroachments on neighborhood turf and workplace prerogatives that truly affronted many Jews' notions of merit and due process. The perceptions of injustice fueling whites' indignation may not always have been accurate, but neither were the values they felt had been affronted always invalid.

The same, of course, can be said for angry blacks, but in the countercultural 1960s, liberal elites practiced a vicious double standard. Even as every expression of black rage paralyzed them or sent them into convulsions of explanation, they cavalierly abandoned white teachers, welfare workers, and other city functionaries to degradation and intimidation, in part because they considered them to be rigid, hostile, and materialistic, as measured by standards they have yet to apply to black occupants of those same bureaucracies today. As the city's economy lost entry-level jobs and the population of poor minority households grew, outer-borough Jews and white ethnics felt with anguish and rage the immediate impact of rising minority dependency, pathology, crime, and desecration in their communities.

It is no exaggeration to say that elite liberals couldn't have cared less. In their view, the burghers' very rage discredited their grievances. When Mayor Lindsay came to Forest Hills to open a campaign storefront in 1969, a woman threw a tomato at him but hit Al Ungar, head of the Lindsay association in Queens. On his way to Lindsay's Manhattan headquarters after the incident, Ungar remarked that he needed a change of clothes. "No," replied Deputy Mayor Richard Aurelio, "I want the people at headquarters to see you like this. You tell them what happened." At the headquarters, a couple of Manhattan liberal professionals whom Ungar dubbed "urban balloons" said they were glad he'd been out there, not themselves. "I remember thinking of Marie Antoinette and Louis XVI and wondering, 'What am I, the Swiss Guard?' " Ungar recalls. No one wanted to understand the Queens residents' rage.

Claude Brown touches a deep truth in *Manchild in the Promised Land* when he writes of his Jewish employers, "They were all little people, and I was demanding that they suddenly become big, tremendous, and understand this gigantic problem that the nation was trying to solve." If it is even remotely true that a sizable number of white New Yorkers, Jews as well as non-Jews, entered the postwar period with no special resentment against blacks, that they tried at least in the beginning to uphold an ethic of interracial fair play, then it is worth asking, finally, whether white-left and black activists and their liberal apologists should have been a little shrewder and refrained from baiting and reviling these vulnerable whites. The confluence of radical spite, absurd legal extrapolations, and liberal disdain for white ethnics that led to forced busing, the bloating of welfare rolls, and the man-mauing of white teachers broke the spine of New York's civic culture. Worse, it offered nothing in its place; though it spoke of black inclusion, in truth it held out no substantive vision of the city as a treasure to be shouldered and shared by all of its residents. The politics of too many white-left and black activists became, in the end, a politics of pure resentment, not of constructive confrontation and hope.

The World Caves In on Brooklyn

In the 1970s, those New Yorkers who had cheered the expansion of the welfare rolls and the struggle for community control learned at least part of the lesson Piven and Cloward had wanted them to learn: there cannot be Socialism in One City. Ultimately, the city's remarkable culture of progressive institutions could be sustained only by a national commitment to a full-employment economy whose investments were directed to meeting basic human needs in health, education, housing, and transportation—something neither the classical free market nor the new corporate consolidation provided. In retrospect, one can say that the builders of New York's civic culture in the 1940s and 1950s had taken advantage of a unique set of historical circumstances: industrial concentration amid growing American economic power; an unusual gathering of European socialist immigrants; the Empire State's special link to Washington through its former governor FDR and the New Deal. In the 1970s, the increasing liquidity of capital and mobility of corporations afforded much less room for municipal public-sector development. Other regions of the country without New York's peculiar burdens and visions could make themselves far more attractive to investors.

The flight of capital was abetted by federal welfare reimbursement formulas favoring other regions; by highway and housing policies favoring suburbanization; by skewed direct federal expenditures— military facilities, for example, which have the strongest multiplier effect in a local economy and which went where the conservative southern chairmen of congressional committees chose to put them. In New York, the downward spiral of capital outflow, consequent unemployment, shrinkage of the tax base, curtailment of public services, dependency of the unemployed on those curtailed services, and deepening social pathology gradually became disincentives to investment. As the public sector fell behind in meeting basic needs, liberal government became despised politically by hard-pressed taxpayers in the voting booth and became foreclosed economically by corporate disinvestment.

The 1960s had really ended in 1973 with the oil embargo and Richard Nixon's moratorium on federal housing funds. With the city hemorrhaging manufacturing jobs and the oil crisis widening the gap between tenants' incomes and what it cost the landlords to keep up their buildings, real-estate speculation took ugly new turns, playing upon whites' racial fears to accelerate disinvestment and even arson-for-profit in order to cash in on anticipated decay—a process to be described in the next two chapters.

By the time New York's fiscal crisis came to a head, in 1975, the city's unique civic culture had been routed, as all who could afford to, black as well as white, tried to replace deteriorating parks, mass transit, and schools with private consumption of expensive alternatives: walkers and subway riders became automobile drivers; a new generation of middle-class New Yorkers was lost to the social bond of public schooling. Among lower-income people who couldn't step up their private consumption, there followed a retreat to ethnic enclaves that gave dubious succor and further divided the city into warring camps. The civic culture hadn't exactly dissolved ethnic and racial tensions, of course, but one could argue that it had been moving in that direction. Now, its dreams became trapped in middle-class memory, dissipating into sentimental nostalgia at best, inspiring no new constructive action.

In Brooklyn's burgeoning black community, conditions worsened dramatically. Unemployment and housing abandonment in the mid-1970s reached rates that seemed to feed upon themselves, unleashing anarchy and despair, social disintegration accompanying the physical. Bushwick and parts of Bedford-Stuyvesant were devastated by arson and looting during a massive power blackout in the summer of 1977. In some poor neighborhoods, crime became almost a way of life, a subculture of violence with complex bonds of utility and affection within families and the larger, "law-abiding" community. Struggling merchants might "fence" stolen goods, for example, thus providing quick cover and additional incentive for burglaries and robberies; the drug economy became more vigorous, reshaping criminal life-styles and tormenting the loyalties of families and friends. A walk down even a reasonably busy street in a poor, minority neighborhood at high noon could become an unnerving journey into a landscape eerie and grim.

The city had to integrate Brooklyn's burgeoning, poor, young population into its public life; no one seemed to know how. Black voter registration remained pitifully low through the end of the decade, and the white bosses of the Kings County Democratic machine used "safe" black elected officials to contain electoral challenges from below—not by mobilizing voters, as J. Raymond Jones's elaborate clubhouse network had done in its Harlem heyday, but, increasingly, by isolating and demobilizing potentially aggrieved voters and bringing only loyalists to the polls.

In 1971, in the wake of the Ocean Hill–Brownsville debacle, Al Vann, then thirty-four, was running an Upward Bound talent-search program at Long Island University's downtown Brooklyn campus. A tall, somewhat austere figure, Vann had stayed rooted in Bedford-Stuyvesant among friends who'd played basketball together in high school, known angry solidarity in the school wars, and steadied one another in defeat. As they looked around at the rising tide of welfare dependency and single-parent families, unemployment, housing abandonment, addiction, crime, and infant mortality, they saw that the needs were too desperate for demonstrations alone. Besides, they had finally discovered that much of the black community was fundamentally conservative, that most of their neighbors were in no position to sneer at middle-class aspirations or to invoke injustice as an apology for crime. Many of those fortunate enough to have acquired education and training, often through the antipoverty networks of the 1960s, were scrambling quietly out of the ghetto with no intention of looking back.

Vann and his friends chose to remain. One of them, Franklin Thomas, was running the Bedford-Stuyvesant Restoration Corporation, a huge community development organization founded at the instigation of Robert Kennedy, and would continue to live in Brooklyn after becoming president of the Ford Foundation at the end of the decade. Others, like Les Campbell, who had changed his name to Jitu Weusi, had founded their own schools (Weusi's is described briefly in chapter 8), or, like Zeke Clements, were principals in the public system. Still others, like Malcolm Dunn, owner of an office-cleaning firm, made a go of it in business. Vann was restless. What was happening to the community hurt him deeply, but he wasn't sure what to do.

"When friends first encouraged me to think about public office, I didn't have much faith in it," Vann told me in 1981, speaking softly, with a characteristic reserve that seems awkward but sometimes approaches a shy grace. "We had a combination of professional and grass-roots people who wanted to do something. No political club ever wooed me." Vann challenged the local machine assemblyman, Calvin Williams, on the "Vannguard" independent line in 1972 and did fairly well. As he was sitting in the Vannguard storefront one day after the election, in walked a young stranger named Roger Green, a shorter, more animated young man who was dabbling in social work. Green, too, was restless; his father, a carpenter, had taken him to demonstrations to see King and Malcolm in the early 1960s, and he was pondering the lessons of his favorite book, *Protest at Selma,* when he first met Vann.

"It was a natural relationship right from the start," Green recalls.

Those early days were manic, alternating between anger and hope. We'd stay up all night working on issues. We had the principle of turning every setback into a broader offensive. If the state or city wanted to close a youth center or health clinic, we'd research and push for a broad youth or health program to meet the needs we'd documented. Rather than give up on an issue, we'd hang with it. We built networks and developed a reputation.

Vann was elected to the New York Assembly in 1974, just as Major Owens was winning a state senate seat in nearby Brownsville. Owens, a librarian by training, had been drawn into community organizing and had been tapped by Lindsay in the late 1960s to run the city's antipoverty Community Development Agency. Now he had returned to Brownsville and East New York to try to purge his community of the scourge of Assemblyman Sam Wright, an adroit politician in the Harlem mold who had opposed the militants in the school wars but had since turned the local school board and its resources to his own, corrupt ends. After winning his senate seat, Owens founded the Central Brooklyn Mobilization to free other offices from the grip of Wright, who was eventually convicted of extortion and sent off to jail.

Vann's and Owens's victories were muted by the arrival of the fiscal crisis, which brought cutbacks in essential city services and in job-training, day-care, and supplemental-assistance programs. City Hall was hostile to them under Mayor Abraham Beame, a product of the hated white Brooklyn machine. Such hostility continued under Koch, too, after a brief honeymoon: "It hurts a great deal when commissioners' doors get closed in your face," Owens told me in 1981. "It hurts to have your people put under the gun when programs are selected to be cut. Sometimes we're made to look a bit ridiculous when we arouse the community on the real issues and then can't get services delivered." In poor neighborhoods, the cost of bucking established power was great, because needs were desperate and politicians were the only leverage their constituents had, as Wright and his protégé, a state senator named Vander Beatty, never ceased to remind the insurgents. But Vann and Owens tried valiantly to behave in public office as representatives not of political clubs but of grass-roots movements.

In November 1975, Owens led his Central Brooklyn Mobilization and other groups in a citywide traffic stoppage when Beame threatened to cut all antipoverty programs by 33 percent instead of the 8 percent other agencies were facing. Activists charged that Beame was taking revenge on community antipoverty corporations for their unofficial backing of Herman Badillo against him in the 1973 mayoral race. In Bedford-Stuyvesant, Vann worked on the problem with Jitu Weusi and the Reverend Herbert Daughtry, who had founded the Black United Front, an organization including Daughtry's pentecostal House of the Lord Church, Black Veterans for Social Justice, Brooklyn CORE, the Sisterhood of Black Single Mothers, and Weusi's school, the East. They helped Vann and Owens bring busloads of people to Albany, stiffening the resistance of the Black and Puerto Rican Legislative Caucus, which held the state's budget hostage until Beame relented and set the antipoverty cuts at 8 percent.

Owens doesn't feel he has to apologize for the atmosphere of scandal which enveloped the antipoverty programs in the mid-1970s:

It was Carol Bellamy and I who studied the programs in a senate report and first coined the term "cesspools of corruption" to describe some of them. When Ed Koch used those words as a candidate in 1977, we welcomed the prospect of reform. I was one of the last to turn against him as mayor. But removing all power from the communities was wrong. There have always been responsible groups fighting local corruption, and these should have been empowered, not dismissed. Every ethnic group has used public institutional bases to solidify its power. The Italians had the sanitation department, the Irish had the police, the Jews the Board of Education. The community corporations were our foot in the door.

Assemblyman Frank Boyland, of Brownsville, a former Hospital Workers' Union organizer who was part of Owens's Central Brooklyn Mobilization, characterized their machine opponents as "hungry midgets." "They sell out for so little," he explained. "I don't entirely blame them because they haven't had much. But it's their duty as elected officials to look out for those less fortunate." Yet it was unclear how Boyland, Vann, Green, and Owens could substantially improve on the machine's sorry record, a dilemma that became all the more galling in the 1980s, as evidence mounted that public austerity was fueling private affluence in other portions of the city.

Ed Koch's Boom

As the void left by the public sector's decay became filled by divisive and predatory activities, a very different sort of change was occurring in another tier of the city's economy. OPEC and the negative national balance of trade brought huge foreign investment to New York and, with it, a boom in tourism and entertainment. Certain established and new industries—finance, insurance, real estate, advertising, corporate services—experienced a boom in the 1980s, sustaining a new middle class that could step up its private consumption, with some preferential tax help from all levels of government.

Amid general decay, the rise of this group seemed a godsend.

But measured against the need for full employment and a tax base that can meet basic human wants, the new industries and their workers were parasitical and nonproductive. As they manipulated words and symbols to consolidate the nation's investment decisions by a few thousand big corporations, they did provide some blue-collar jobs, but on the whole the skill barriers to entry were high, and, according to separate studies by Walter Stafford and Thomas Bailey, racial discrimination continued to foreclose opportunities even to blacks with the requisite education.

As the city's new economy became increasingly abstracted from the rewards and constraints of union and neighborhood roots, the social and political basis for LaGuardia's vision of a just, integrated city dissolved. Unlike the earlier middle class, which had risen from the tenements while building the culture of progressive institutions, the new tier seemed remarkably self-contained. Most of its tax dollars went right back into services and amenities for the new class, which required protection and hothouse nurture because it was skittish and highly mobile. Certainly many of its members were mortgage poor and harried by the high costs of making the city "livable" through private transit, schools, and recreation; no one accused $75,000-a-year professionals of accumulating great wealth. Yet they were much better off than most New Yorkers, and their style of consumption, lubricated by deductible expense accounts and tax exemptions that robbed the public sector of vitality, left little room for generosity to public institutions.

It was a self-absorbed, hedonistic style, corrosive of familial or neighborhood obligation; we know all about it because its practitioners couldn't stop writing and talking about themselves. In catering to it, the city shed the proletarian imagery of production for the lithe imagery of consumption: the old docks and diners became playgrounds and cafés. In the absence of any larger social purpose, frank decadence was purveyed—a big business in New York.

In 1978, Edward Koch greeted the new class in his jogging shoes, Fantasy Island's genial director. A product of Greenwich Village's white reform Democratic movement of the 1950s and 1960s, he understood his constituency's transmutation into an elite under the auspices of the boom. But Koch's genius was to anticipate the rise of a new dispensation, one he correctly sensed would hold more sway in the years immediately ahead than either new-class decadence or the liberal idealism of the 1960s: he would restore a measure of moral legitimacy to the broad, outer-borough white middle class which limousine liberals and radicals had so grandly disdained.

Unlike Philadelphia's Frank Rizzo and Boston's Louise Day Hicks, however, Koch hadn't come roaring out of the bowels of Bunkerville. His complex personal odyssey from liberal Village councilman and congressman to mayor of Canarsie and Forest Hills was the secret of his success at translating white ethnics' grievances and new fiscal constraints into a New York idiom that cowed even liberals and their clients. Even as late as 1977, Koch's most well-known campaign pitch wasn't the death penalty, as many later believed, but good—as opposed to profligate—government. His slogan was "After eight years of charisma [Lindsay] and four years of the clubhouse [Beame], why not try competence?"

Koch had come blinking into the sunlight of postwar Greenwich Village with others in flight from everything stunting in their outer-borough immigrant family pasts. Eagerly he and his new friends, like Dan Wolf, owner of the *Village Voice,* merged their own struggles to break free of old conventions with the period's larger struggles for civil liberties and, later, civil rights. The Village was the ideal crucible; rents could be covered by part-time work, the remaining hours given over to the pursuit of some art or political possibility. Modest prosperity came to them almost despite themselves. And as the proud liberalism of their time in the sun opened paths to professional advancement, they marched to Montgomery and summered on Fire Island.

And yet the promise and vision of those years was blighted for Koch by the winds blowing out of Ocean Hill–Brownsville. They reopened the wounds of a Bronx boy and hard-pressed adolescent Newark hat-check clerk, and he found himself returning, out of both expediency and conviction, to the other struggling Jews he'd left behind and who'd moved up a bit themselves. In 1972, Koch tried to float a mayoral candidacy by marching with the most vociferous opponents of the scatter-site housing in Forest Hills. Shaken like other New Yorkers of his generation by minority crime and the community-control, welfare-rights, and poverty-program battles, he denounced elitism in social engineering, nowhere more evident than in the original Forest Hills plan itself.

After Cuomo's compromise plan for Forest Hills was adopted, Koch's mayoral bid fizzled. But while the Cuomo plan would succeed, other redistributive measures, such as busing in Canarsie, continued to spark lower-middle-class rebellion. In 1977, Koch was back, appealing to outer-borough taxpayers more beleaguered and frightened than before. To his Village home base, he was still the earnest, sensible liberal, but even that constituency had begun to change: as Manhattan rents rose, the career lockstep descended; would-be artists and social reformers found themselves working full-time, manipulating words and symbols to consolidate corporate power. The reformers began dabbling in real estate, and their social agenda narrowed to those liberties protecting their own peculiar lifestyles and pathways to success.

Koch won overwhelmingly among both Manhattan liberals and outer-borough white ethnics in 1977. By 1981, he had lost most of the former but increased his popularity among the latter because he believed vehemently in the justice of their grievances. Yet he tried to leave them, too, by running for governor against Cuomo in 1982 because he didn't really like the lower-middle-class whites he'd played to so well. He had become trapped representing them to themselves, bodying forth their most intimate hurts with a penchant for self-parody some of them shared; he had become an ethnic comedian, bored with his material but unable to transcend it. "Remember," he warned them in his shrill, pedantic singsong, "you can always vote me out. I'll get a better job, but you'll never get a better mayor." A lot of them loved it. They knew what they'd become—and failed to become. He gave them the theater of their bitterness.

An aide recalls him fielding questions at a community meeting of politically conservative Jews who opposed even his modest affirmative action policies, his support for gay rights, and, sotto voce, his stinginess with patronage. A man got up to complain about new hiring standards designed to increase female and Hispanic representation in police ranks. "Mr. Koch, why do you lower the height requirements just to include these people? We need policemen who are big and tall and command respect. . . ." The speaker was barely finished before the mayor raised his eyebrows in mock astonishment and amusement and quipped, "Have you ever seen a five-foot-four Puerto Rican with a gun?" The audience roared as aides winced; happily for the latter, the big media weren't present, sparing liberal New Yorkers the spectacle of a mayor using racism to defend affirmative action.

Of such shabby paradoxes was Koch's mayoralty made. By showing frightened outer-borough ethnics that he shared with them a tissue of visceral understandings, Koch won their acceptance of an administrative record that, stripped of his rhetoric, was actually quite liberal by comparison with most others in the city's history. That may not be saying much; one can quibble about minority-hiring statistics, the depth of his support for gay rights, and the abuses of power by his subordinates; but the fact remains. Typically, he refused to grant official holiday status to Martin Luther King's birthday for city workers, except as a $23 million trade-off against municipal-union give-backs at the bargaining table; yet he hired back many of the minority workers laid off by the 1975 fiscal crisis.

But the cost of Koch's rhetoric to the civic discourse was tremendous. His critics rightly charged that his wisecracks only temporarily defused whites' racial fears by stroking them, ultimately reinforcing them, and so draining the political nervous system of resiliency. Koch was accused, with some justice, of sowing the wind that reaped the whirlwind of ghoulish applause for Bernhard Goetz. "Ed Koch *is* Bernie Goetz," said the political consultant Lou Gordon, a key strategist for Koch's 1981 Democratic primary opponent, Frank Barbaro, who carried every minority assembly district in the city. Koch danced in and out of Goetz's cheerleading line in a shameless series of flip-flops that aped the public's reactions to the contradictory disclosures.

But Koch countered that the city's white-ethnic and middle-class nerves were so far gone by the time he took office in 1978 that only his vaudeville, which dramatized their grievances, held the city together. And while history won't absolve him of the storm that ensued, he remained triumphant in its midst. For the truth was that, until his mouth got the better of him, Koch's convictions appealed to a broader spectrum of voters than his critics admitted. Minorities were as vocal as whites in the early returns for Goetz, for example.

And, as Koch delighted in reminding the Pivens, Clowards, and Bella Abzugs of the city, most minority New Yorkers accepted the paradigm of individual responsibility for upward mobility that he sincerely if abstractly held out to all New Yorkers, regardless of race. They knew that Koch had gone South in 1964 to fight for that paradigm, and when the social agenda shifted from civil rights to economic redistribution several years later, he was far from alone in digging in his heels. If you accepted the parameters and constraints of capitalist urban development, you were led inexorably to his conclusions. The dirty little secret on the left was that, until some of Koch's almost breathtaking personal misapprehensions about people of color became clear, not a few minority New Yorkers were with him.

By the end of his first term, in 1981, many of Koch's erstwhile Harlem and reform allies, including Paterson, Badillo, Kovner, and Fife, had turned against him—and he against them, with an affectation of magisterial disdain—over such issues as his austerity budgets; his hostility to municipal unions; his generous grants of city tax abatements and zoning variances to the wealthiest and most rapacious developers; and his hypocrisy in condemning both principled black insurgents and corrupt black "poverty pimps" while so indulging white political thieves that the city was rocked by scandals during his last term. The reformers were not wrong in feeling betrayed. Koch allowed luxury conversions of lofts and tenements to administer the coup de grace to blue-collar jobs and lower-income communities in Manhattan. He refused to use scarce housing subsidies to help keep lifelong residents in neighborhoods the new upscale market could convert; yet he also refused to recoup the millions of dollars in tax abatements and exemptions he gave to accelerate the conversions, tax dollars that might have prevented homelessness.

As City Council President Carol Bellamy's liaison to Manhattan community organizations in 1980, I attended many meetings of the Single Room Occupancy Hotel Task Force, composed of housing activists and elected officials who petitioned, begged, and harangued the Koch administration to impose a moratorium on the rapid conversions of SRO hotels into upscale residences. Hellish though SRO's could be, they provided shelter and mailing addresses for

thousands of marginally functional people dependent on state benefits. As more than 70,000 such dwelling units were lost to upscale
conversions during the 1980s, their low-income residents were forced
into the streets. It is impossible for me to pass them now without
thinking of Koch.

So have deepened the social divisions that commissions had been
warning about for a decade: enclaves of affluence amid realms of
despair, an isolation of social classes completed by segregated transit
(cabs, express buses) and schools, which permitted middle-income
people to ignore or even justify the suffering, the grinding down of
those who seemed, in their destitution, to have become members of a
different species. It was a bitter end to the city's unique culture of
progressive institutions.

Rambling across Brooklyn in the early 1980s, one could survey the
ruins of the postwar liberal promise. In Brownsville, that erstwhile
seat of Jewish radicalism, housing projects stood like armed camps
amid blocks of abandoned apartment buildings and rubbled lots
where prostitutes and drug dealers plied their trades and wild dogs
prowled near homeless men warming themselves by fires burning in
old barrels. In Bushwick, a massive, ornate cathedral stood abandoned, sealed against the devastation, dead as a tomb. At the edge of
Williamsburg, the former Rheingold Brewery lay ravaged, gaping;
one cold winter day, I picked my way over broken glass and utensils
strewn about the workers' lunchroom and walked past old time
clocks, my heels echoing down empty corridors to the president's
wood-paneled office, where pigeons nested on inset bookshelves
under an open sky.

Koch would carry out substantial rebuilding in Bushwick, the fulfillment of a campaign promise made just after the blackout looting
and arson of 1977. In his last term, he undertook a massive rehabilitation and construction program to provide thousands of low- and
moderate-income housing units in Brooklyn, northern Manhattan,
and the Bronx. But by then the perverse, if inexorable, logic of fiscal
austerity for the poor and lavish subsidy of the rich which Koch
championed had compounded the social divisions promoted by his
enemies through the politics of turmoil in the 1960s. Koch's own
charged rhetoric, mirroring theirs, had deepened those divisions. It
was a weary, dispirited city that finally turned him aside for David

Dinkins in 1989, in a political climate we will describe in the last two chapters of this book. To understand it fully, we first need to look more closely at the battles over neighborhood turf, legal rights, and racial claims which gripped the city in the 1970s and 1980s.

4

White Ethnics on the Block

All against All

A bloodied, hard-muscled Italian teenager tore down the block on Court Street in Brooklyn and spun round to face his assailants from the safety of the open, sidewalk counter of a pizzeria where I'd hopped off my bike for a slice in the warm Brooklyn dusk. The black youths faded into a deepening pool of shadows halfway down the block as the white teenager's pizza parlor friends stepped wordlessly into the street, brandishing bats, ready to "protect" him. The veins in his neck throbbed as, finding his breath, he cried out to the blacks in a register so deep from his gut it seemed to tap a hurt more startling than his anger.

"You *mutha* . . . *fuckin'* . . . *nigguhs,*" he moaned in a leaden, rhythmic dirge. "You're *all shit! Eh-* very *one-*a' yous! They otta *ship* yous *all* back!" He doubled over, gasping for air, hands on his knees, then straightened up, not satisfied. "I don' care, I tell ya da trut'. I wish *eh-* very *one-*a' yous was *dead.* You ruin *eh-* very *fuckin'* thing!" he cried in a despair so deep it riveted everyone on the street. "I spit on you *muthas!* I wish you was *nev-* veh *ee-* ven *born!*"

It was over. Another deposit to the hate bank that would burst soon enough in Gravesend, Howard Beach, Bensonhurst. I peddled off down quiet, tree-lined blocks, heading east through a little industrial ghost town along the banks of the Gowanus Canal and up toward my apartment in Park Slope, past tenement stoops and fire escapes jammed with black and Hispanic people whiling away the stifling after-dinner hour. Brick- and brownstone-fronted streets became canyons of russet, violet, ocher, their cornices and high windows glinting cobalt and gold in the last of the light.

"Julio! Hoo-lee-YO!" Velvety cries of young Puerto Rican kids echoed off the canyon walls, mingling with the melody chime of an ice cream truck a block away. Go-carts clattered along slate sidewalks, and in that gentle cacophony the block became an aviary, part cage, part jungle gym reaching to the vaulting opal sky. City kids call with their hearts, throw their whole bodies into it, as if they might scale those tenement walls on the backs of their own high, thick voices.

On my Carroll Street block at the western edge of "the Slope," elderly Italian-American men and women sat on lawn chairs in little paved front yards behind low, iron railings, chatting, watching the street. Trash cans and fire escapes wore a greasy sheen in twilight. A dank, oily breeze blew up out of the Gowanus. In back of these little brownstone walk-ups, I knew, others were sitting on terraces and decks, surveying the collection of gardens, painted pavements, and vine-laden fences that was the large, interior courtyard of the block. In one of the yards, ninety-year-old Tony Bottighlieri, a Con Edison worker retired since 1950, would be inspecting his fig trees, poking in the dirt around his shrubbery. Four kids would be playing basketball in a yard catty-corner to his, blocking and taunting one another good-naturedly as girlfriends called from the fire escape. From farther down the row of yards would waft a scent of barbecue and a tinkling of ice cubes in glasses.

I knew, too, what the Italians on the lawn chairs were muttering about. A large, multifamily apartment building and two adjoining brick walk-ups across the street had acquired in recent years a predominantly minority, welfare tenancy. The absentee owner of the buildings welcomed them because their shelter allowances for a few years in the 1970s were permitted to exceed what he could get under the rent-control system. Not that rent control had troubled the land-lord before local banks stopped extending mortgage credit to the area after racial change began at the start of the 1970s. That prevented him from engaging in the practices that really made ownership of such buildings profitable—"flipping" them from one of his dummy corporations to another in paper sales that allowed him to raise their value, refinance their mortgages, rework the various tax deductions to his advantage.

Now, for the first time, he needed to squeeze the rent roll for all it might be worth; hence the welfare tenants, the first of whom sent the remaining white, rent-controlled residents packing, increasing his take. With "the colored" in the building, he could reduce mainte-nance and services. Once they had run the place down and inflation and rising property values had eroded the value of their shelter al-lowances against other options, he could push them out in turn and do a substantial (and subsidized) renovation for the local upscale co-op or rental market. Should the local market turn sour, leaving the landlord with a decaying property, he—or a buyer with a stom-ach stronger than his—could freeze out the tenants one winter and, paying a "torch" to burn the building, collect the fire insurance. Whole neighborhoods in Brooklyn had already gone up in smoke that way.

The Italians across the street owned their buildings and weren't going anywhere. "Grow where you were planted," they would say. They'd been there since the 1930s—these were the first homes they'd bought in America—and they were going to keep cultivating their gardens. Their own tenacity and signs of gentrification up the block promised to contain "the element" in just one corner. They would have scoffed at the idea that their neighbors across the street would soon be yuppies and that the welfare people would be transported off to homelessness or the projects. But they did have vague hopes that things would take a turn for the better. For now, they hunkered down in a grim fatalism.

The Italians knew—and these were, indeed, incontestable facts—that at eight each morning, when the men in their families had gone to work and their sidewalks and stoops were already hosed down and the wash was hanging out back, garbage covered the sidewalks in front of the "welfare" buildings, whose residents were sleeping off another night of noise and mayhem. The nightly screams and shatterings of glass, the inevitable police sirens and bubble gum lights ricocheting through the Italians' blinds and around their parlors, had brought the block to the edge of war. Puerto Rican and black boys urinated against the fronts of the block's two abandoned buildings in broad daylight and strode down the street bearing boom boxes at full blast.

Occasionally, the Italian men would cross the street and stop them, without actually resorting to violence; everyone knew they had the upper hand, because there had already been a showdown. Two teenage black boys in the big building across the street had been preying on people, burglarizing apartments on their side of the street. Even tenants in the boys' own building had asked the landlord to get rid of them and their families, little knowing that having them there fit his plans well enough for now. But then the boys crossed an invisible, hitherto uncrossable line, mugging an elderly Italian man. A few young Italians and an Irish kid from up the street administered rough justice, firebombing one of the offending households' apartment doors right off its hinges in the dead of night.

"Race War!" screamed the headline in the *New York Post.* Down the Slope came a hundred of its resident lefties—"another curse," the Italians called them—marching to "smash racism" and handing out leaflets to black and Hispanic tenants advising them of their rights as "national minorities." Liberals clucked their tongues and pondered stronger enforcement of fair-housing laws and prosecutions of "hate crimes." State Senator Vander Beatty, a black politician whose district included a corner of the block, showed up at a "peace meeting" with white community leaders at the local parish, and he skillfully played all sides. The Italians boycotted the meeting, feeling that they'd done what they'd had to do—and would do it again.

The "problem family" left, the block quieted down, and by 1981 the shifting real-estate tide had emptied the buildings for "gut" rehabilitations that would turn them into tidy cooperatives with window boxes and elaborate alarm systems. The yuppies did not stop there. Some of them made the Italian brownstone owners irresistible offers, offers accepted by those whose children couldn't afford the Slope's rising prices and property taxes and so had departed to Bensonhurst or Long Island or other states, places where no one would ever let "the element" in. They barely noticed, at first, that "the element" was no longer their problem. What it hadn't managed to do, the yuppies were accomplishing.

As parish schools and social clubs lost people and closed, there was even less reason to stay. "Sorry about this mess, I don't want to drive down your property values!" chirped a young hostess as she tripped over shards of Sheetrock and buckets of spackling compound, carrying refreshments to thirty members of the block association sitting somewhat stiffly in her exposed-brick living room—including some minority tenants who'd have been relieved at that moment to have property values to worry about. Learning that another young professional had been living on the block for ten years, the hostess trumpeted, "You're really one of the pioneers!"—in front of the Italians, who'd been raising kids here for fifty years. Those who did stay through this, well, they would visit the relatives out on the Island on a Sunday, and be treated to the subtlest suburban condescensions, and then they would come home to these buckling pavements and old brownstones where no wall was straight, where the old, thick hands that had tended them had grown thicker still. And they would feel ashamed.

Anna Bruno had raised her kids in a rented apartment on the block and would look out at the world from a pillow propped on the sill of her ground-floor window, cursing the Puerto Rican kids on their go-carts. Then a renovator bought Anna's building and told her she'd have to move. At the parish bingo, her Information Central, she asked her neighbors about apartments. She went to the priests. Nothing. The realtors she spoke to kept telling her there was nothing she could afford; the neighborhood was "hot," now that yuppies and aging liberals streamed out of the Upper West Side and the Village in search of cheaper housing. Anna wouldn't believe it. Not in the only neighborhood she'd ever known in America. "Maybe if I dress nice," she thought, and put on her rusty black dress to hobble back up the Slope to see the brokers on Seventh Avenue.

Finally, Anna had to move to Florida to live with her daughter. She was stoic about it until her last morning on the block, when the movers arrived; then the dam of her dignity burst, and she hobbled up and down the street, weeping on the necks of her friends. A few forlorn letters from Florida—"There's nothing to do here. I'm all alone"—and then, back in the old neighborhood for a visit at Christmas, she keeled over onto a friend's linoleum kitchen floor and died. Stories like Anna's abounded. Men who'd sworn they'd die in their homes with the little grape arbors out back expired of heart attacks the week the movers were to come.

Death came, too, in neighborhoods not "saved" by the yuppies—Bushwick, East New York, places with little wooden bungalows and aluminum-sided walk-ups which the men had built with their own hands and had finally lost to the riptides of real-estate disinvestment, arson, and crime. Long before the first abandoned buildings forced them to avert their eyes in a flicker of befuddlement and hurt, their neighborhoods had known the stigma, the scent of decay. Brooklyn, the beautiful Brooklyn they had built and loved, would have to be left behind. Interviewing some of these exiles in the borough's still-white Canarsie section in the 1970s, the sociologist Jonathan Rieder learned how sometimes, driving home, they would detour through the old neighborhood on a gust of nostalgia and find their former blocks devastated, a part of themselves now devastated, too. What they saw struck them as "an insult to their memories and their ancestors," according to one such exile whom Rieder does not name and who recalled, "I couldn't believe it. The houses were all marked up, the streets were filthy, and there was garbage and graffiti everywhere. There was no respect for property. It was very sad. I started to cry."

Another sociologist coined a phrase for this feeling: "grieving for a lost home." Even those who were only teenagers when they'd moved out could feel it. Even the kid screaming his guts out in front of the pizza parlor on Court Street.

A Lesson In Moral Geography

But what about the minority poor? They grieve, if not for lost neighborhoods, then for not having neighborhoods to lose, for the silent storm of their endless migration, for heatless winter nights haunted by the specter of homelessness. Carroll Street's minority welfare tenants had escaped from neighborhoods far more troubled than Park Slope; those I spoke with mentioned Red Hook, Bushwick, and the Lower East Side. After their five-year interlude on

Carroll Street, some ended up in the most run-down and dangerous section of Coney Island. But to try to rate suffering by race in a discussion of the politics of race is to walk into a trap. The minority disadvantaged will win a moral ranking every time, but because we inhabit not a philosophy seminar, social-policy think tank, or mass movement for racial justice but a city drenched, even founded, in injustice, drawing such distinctions in political discourse builds no citywide consensus about what justice ought to be. On the contrary, it gives people fresh reasons to become afraid and to divide.

It is a bitter lesson, one which New Yorkers have had ample opportunity to learn since the Lindsay years, when white ethnics were first given to understand that they had become secure, even privileged; that their protests about encroachments on that security and privilege were not to be taken too seriously; that the resistance they put up against neighborhood racial change was the moral equivalent of the work of the Klan. The truth is that many New Yorkers, white and black, feel a little like exiles, and not always by virtue of their race; recall that it was white yuppies, not blacks or Hispanics, who displaced some Carroll Street Italians and made those who remained feel like strangers on their "own" turf. Only in granting the integrity of one another's experiences of uprooting can New Yorkers discover what they share. Before the white ethnics who have also been driven to the margins of the city can participate in that sharing, they, as well as people of color, must feel politically included; only then can both groups find common ground.

That is not to say that social initiatives to ensure racial justice can wait upon white conversions of the heart; only that, as Mario Cuomo discovered in mediating the Forest Hills dispute back in 1972, there is an inevitable, often terrible political price to be paid for not crafting those initiatives more carefully than court orders and urban renewal schemes generally allow. "We can ignore these facts [about white-ethnic neighborhood insularity] and continue to blow the trumpet for moral reaffirmations," said Saul Alinsky, a well-known activist for economic and racial justice, during a similar dispute in Chicago, "but unless we can develop a program which recognizes the legitimate self-interest of white communities, we have no right to condemn them morally because they refuse to commit hara-kiri."

There was some common ground between the Italians and welfare tenants on Carroll Street, though it went unnoticed, untilled. Whether or not either group wanted the other, neither could survive without defeating a common enemy that uprooted them—the real-estate speculation that eventually brought the yuppies. What if the decent Italians had joined with the decent minority working poor and welfare tenants, who, we recall, also wanted to drive the criminals and delinquents out of the neighborhood; what if, united by that victory, they had fought the speculators together? They might have lost anyway. But not necessarily, not if the common fight had extended beyond one block and one neighborhood. Certainly neither group looked very much like a winner in the aftermath of the three-way war among speculators, white ethnics, and the minority poor.

The Italians on Carroll Street did lose something precious, irreplaceable—even those among them who made a profit losing it. The old adage that money isn't everything takes us halfway into their story, a story shared by people of color as well. It is an accounting of the role neighborhoods play as refuges from the clamor and anonymity of the great urban market and as places of preparation to meet its challenges—launching pads for the urban young. And it is an accounting of the way those neighborhoods are bought and sold in the great urban market itself. So let us begin with a portrait of the kind of neighborhood life the best of the Italians thought they were defending, a portrait idealized, abstracted beyond color, in order to establish a conceptual framework for the more close-grained history that follows in chapter 5.

Neighborhoods that "work" manage to filter the hard knocks and sheer dissonance of the city. They keep alive some appropriate balance of relaxed play and obligation within which social commitments can flower and be shared. To children, especially, a good neighborhood life offers a wealth of spontaneous but manageable challenges and contacts beyond the front stoop or apartment door. When it works, neighborhood life introduces youths to the satisfactions of roles which the urban market rewards only indirectly, if at all: nurturer, defender, uplifter, communicant, teammate, lover, friend.

Adults may find such satisfactions in other, nonspatial networks, but, to an extent surely underestimated by the more cosmopolitan among us, New Yorkers of all ages find them at least partly in neighborhoods, at the local parish hall or synagogue and in the nearby tavern, diner, community center, or park. Where would Anna Bruno have been without bingo, or Tony Bottighlieri without the senior center to which he brought the fruits of his garden? In our idyll, it is neighborhood adults, after all, who become role models for the young: the priest, the local political leader, the basketball coach, the teacher, even the corner grocer and the cop on the beat. They hammer home simple norms: don't drop out of school unless you've got a steady job; don't parent offspring until you can support them; treat other people and their property with respect. For most people, neighborhoods that work keep alive such timeless affirmations and virtues, whose exercise nourishes personal dignity as well as social vibrancy and trust.

Neighborhood life that works well generates codes, understandings, expectations, and ironies that commingle with those of other communities to set the tone of what Kalman Siegel calls the "impersonal affection" of the life of the larger city. Neighborhoods are crucibles of the civic culture. New York City's capital and its cultural and human resources come from all over the world, but its capacity to keep drawing and synthesizing them into the achievements of a civilization depends in part on the moral geography of its neighborhoods.

Now we can complicate this ideal portrait. Some New Yorkers seem not to want neighborhoods at all—not only young transients using apartments as dormitories on their way to the stars, but also mature trendsetters and jet-setters who make their "homes" in the city's ungrounded, nonspatial networks of aspiration and achievement. Their sources of support and information are friends, associates, or colleagues living somewhere else in the city or even the world. New York is preeminently a city of collectivities that transcend geographical bounds—of business enterprises with national and international markets; of the headquarters of media, professional, and cultural associations, religious denominations, nonprofit institutions, unions, political movements and parties, and polities larger than the city itself, including even the United Nations. New York is home to hundreds of thousands of people who really "live" in these networks more than they live in their neighborhoods.

Many other New Yorkers seem not to have neighborhoods, even

though they want them desperately. They are not just the homeless but also those warehoused in projects at the margins and in the interior ghettos of the city. Or they are shunted along by the speculators from one place to another—"dumped" far less often into a Park Slope than into areas where neighborhood life has all but disintegrated and none of its vital functions are fulfilled. They are confined by racism and its economic legacy to ghettos whose genuinely communal characteristics are swamped by the deprivation and stigma that attend their demarcation by outside forces.

Between the non-neighborhoods of the mobile and the non-neighborhoods of the trapped are a dozen other varieties of community. There are tightly knit ethnic "urban villages," including the one the Italians of Carroll Street were trying to maintain, but also the new "villages" of Orthodox Jewish Hasidim, Chinese, Koreans, Indians, South Americans, Caribbean blacks, and other recent immigrants to the city. There are specially planned communities as diverse as Lewis Mumford's lovely Sunnyside Gardens, in Queens; the huge Starrett City development, in Brooklyn, an experiment in racially integrated living that has succeeded; and the various union cooperatives, like the ILGWU's Penn South and the Amalgamated's projects in Manhattan and the Bronx.

There are gracious, upper middle-class enclaves of freestanding, one-family homes, as in Forest Hills, Queens, and in Ditmas Park, Brooklyn. There are "old money" preserves: Sutton Place, Gramercy Park, Park Avenue, Brooklyn Heights. There are the seemingly endless tracts of modest row homes and garden apartments all over the city; not even most New Yorkers know that there are 250,000 owner-occupied, one- and two-family homes in the city's five boroughs. Many of these neighborhoods, even the more "suburban" among them, recapitulate the patterns of ethnic concentration characteristic of the immigrant "villages." Then there are the myriad bohemias in the West Village, the East Village, SoHo, the Williamsburg waterfront, and on the fringes of racially mixed neighborhoods like Park Slope.

One could refine this taxonomy endlessly yet miss the real story, which is not just about diversity but also about fluidity: most of these neighborhood types are constantly threatened or in transition under the impact of an endless churning, voluntary and forced. More than anywhere else in the United States, different kinds of neighborhood life in New York are forever changing their physical locations, conquering and reconquering turf with dizzying, often destructive speed.

The white-ethnic urban village of sturdy row homes becomes a black ghetto of subdivided rooming houses and boarded-up shells, only to metamorphose a decade later into a genteel preserve of middle-class white and black renovators. Yesterday's fashionable white middle-class community of grand apartment buildings with marble lobbies becomes today's Hispanic working-class neighborhood, only to be "invaded" tomorrow by new ethnic urban villagers—Hasidim, Koreans, Russian Jews.

There is another dimension to the fluidity of neighborhood life in New York: a half-dozen types of neighborhood life often jockey for place on a single block. Recall that on my section of Caroll Street there were not only blue-collar Italian families of fifty years' residency and black and Hispanic working-poor and single-parent families on welfare; there were also young professionals like the block association hostess; young transients like me; dedicated radicals like those who came marching down the street. The block was thus a sheltered, ethnic, urban village; a minority refuge from ghetto danger and decay; a charming collection of brownstones with unique Dutch façades, convenient to Wall Street; a way station for writers and artists; and a locus of revolutionary organizing—all at once.

There is a third dimension to the fluidity: as all these types of neighborhood keep moving around the city and bumping into one another, they evolve within themselves in response to new options and constraints. Who would have dreamed thirty years ago that young, middle-class families would aspire not to buy new, suburban homes but to wrestle with the buckling plaster of old brownstones? Or that Hispanic housing activists would fight to defend the "integrity" of tenement neighborhoods that were built for exploitation in the first place?

And there is a fourth dimension: many New Yorkers as individuals are in spiritual as well as spatial transition from one mode of neighborhood life to another, carrying within themselves past incarnations of communal struggle and belonging that they miss or are glad to be rid of—or both. Central to the New York idea for many people is the experience of breaking with "the old neighborhood," of cutting the ties, of striking out on one's own to try a new way of life.

An older middle-class couple of "empty-nesters," moving into an apartment in the fashionable, high-rise Battery Park City development in lower Manhattan, may have raised their children in a Long Island suburb after fleeing a Bronx neighborhood where they grew up in the 1930s. A black letter carrier raising his family quietly, protectively in a modest row home on Linden Boulevard in the East Flatbush section of Brooklyn may have grown up in a crime-ridden public housing project in Harlem, where his sister, who has married a lawyer, is renovating a nearby brownstone that used to be a rooming house, some of whose former tenants now live in the project she and her brother grew up in.

In *Saturday Night Fever,* Tony Manero leaves Bay Ridge for a new life in Manhattan. Jackie Gleason makes the long, circuitous trek from a dismal tenement flat in Bushwick to a penthouse in Miami, but, through "The Honeymooners," he gives Brooklyn to the world. LeRoi Jones moves down to the Village and changes the shape of the counterculture. When continuous movement doesn't bring personal disaster, it makes the New York character tough, tart, cosmopolitan. Many New Yorkers really have seen it all; scratch them and they'll make you see it, too. They bear worlds within worlds.

Neighborhoods for Sale

What causes all this churning, sometimes more brutal than benign? Most obvious is the city's ever-changing demography, people of wildly divergent lineage pouring in and out, seeking opportunity and freedom. They are responding, in turn, to ever-changing configurations of capital, technology, and culture—of the nonspatial networks I've mentioned. But a more intimate yet often invisible cause of neighborhood churning is a real-estate industry that is to New York City what big oil has been to Houston, a remarkable agglomeration of bankers, investors, developers, builders, owners, managers, and brokers who speculate frenetically on the sites of the great enterprises and headquarters and on the neighborhoods where their owners, managers, workers, clients, and customers might live.

These key players in the real-estate game have a culture and subcultures all their own; they sluice the currents of neighborhood investment and disinvestment that are so swift and unsparing. As they try to profit from various communities' emergence, stabilization, upgrading, or decline, they stamp the perceptions and preferences of New Yorkers, whose standing in the real-estate market is determined by income and tastes derivative of their relationships to the larger, nonspatial networks of the city.

Depending on who they are, what they aspire to, and what they have to spend, New Yorkers are told by developers and brokers and real-estate watchers in whatever publications they choose to read that a given neighborhood is congenial or even "hot" or that it is "going down"; or they pick this wisdom up from friends and associates who've already made the rounds. As the real-estate industry tries to profit from these projections by investing or disinvesting in them, it accelerates them, in effect creating self-fulfilling prophecies of neighborhood improvement or decay.

Yet ordinary people are far from passive recipients of the latest conventional wisdom. In their neighborhoods, they organize to make the city use its powers of taxation and zoning and its regulation of building codes, banking, and a dozen other realms to constrain whatever real-estate operations they feel are threats. But what they would accomplish through government with their votes, the real-estate industry tries to subvert with cash, and it initiates ambitious projects of its own, often in collaboration with government, giving the justification of public purpose to profitable private ventures. Since too many politicians are as receptive to income enhancements (and, to be fair, to promises of economic development) as to the promptings of public service, the public arena becomes a battleground.

The two "sides" are far from monolithic; there are really a dozen conflicting armies and allegiances. As on Carroll Street, conflicts may pit neighbors against one another according to their different standings in the real-estate marketplace, and speculators and politicians alike can manipulate those conflicts, which often run along and reinforce racial and class lines. Similarly, small absentee landlords may find themselves at odds with big ones or with brokers and banks. The quality of communication and of civic and political leadership becomes critical in determining how the battles play out.

But in all this confusion, there is an opportunity: even as each neighborhood takes its shape from some particular confluence of the economic, demographic, and cultural currents that are always transforming the city, it does so in complex ways that are somewhat negotiable in the public arena. That brings up the question of whether New Yorkers' growing sophistication about the dynamics of neighborhood change will make them more opportunistic and divided or more visionary and humane. After the devastation of the 1970s, has a collective "learning curve" emerged among all the actors in neighborhood change, a consensus that if everyone gives up a little edge, the more brutal and destructive cycles can be moderated?

There is evidence to support each view, and it usually hinges on how both the real-estate industry and New Yorkers in their neighborhoods come to grips with the most important variable, aside from economic conditions themselves, that shapes and channels these battles: race. It is not, of course, an independent variable. Race is what we have made of it, through public policy and economic decisions, including the economics of real estate itself.

To people like the Italians of Carroll Street, the beginning of the end of a viable neighborhood life is the appearance of people of color as neighbors. They associate it, again on the basis of incontestable experience, with three things: a rise in crime and other forms of social disintegration; a rise in speculative activity by outside real-estate operators that threatens their property, either by "destroying" market values or eventually, as in Park Slope, by escalating them and the attendant taxes beyond what they or their children can afford; and, finally, a rise in social engineering by interventionist government and liberal activists, which offends them morally and wounds them politically and economically.

Many white ethnics insist that it is not "color" per se they hate. Blacks who come in and out of the neighborhood to work in clearly prescribed roles during daylight hours are almost never hassled; white ethnics who leave the neighborhood for work often form on-the-job friendships and share a visceral camaraderie with black coworkers—if having black coworkers is already a given. Some can even point to individual families of color who've lived for a long time in a corner of the neighborhood without incident.

"When a typical WASP liberal says, 'Some of my best friends are . . . ,' it's an introduction to a bigot; when an Italian-American says it, it's a step forward in intergroup relations," quips Frank Arricale. "There's good and bad in all races," white ethnics will say. And they mean it. But they also mean that there is more bad among blacks than among whites, if by "bad" we mean violent crime and other threats to the fabric of neighborhood life.

Because white ethnics are right enough about this to feel terribly wronged by it, two obvious questions do not much concern them: What are the causes of black social disintegration? What about the decent, hardworking blacks who, within the bounds of their own legitimate race pride and cultural self-esteem, want only to uphold the same basic neighborhood norms the whites do? The Italians on Carroll Street have neither the time nor the security to ponder these questions, and I wonder if that should surprise us. What offends us is that so few show even an inclination to ponder them. Granting, if only for the sake of argument, that white ethnics are unfairly besieged in their neighborhoods, aren't they also complicit in the racial discrimination by construction and other unions and countless businesses, small and large, that has put blacks under such strain, producing the pathologies and crime that fulfill every prophecy of black doom? And aren't some of these whites, too, engaged in crime— organized, perhaps, white-collar, perhaps, but still predatory, racist, and violent in its impact upon blacks?

The answer to these questions is a qualified yes. In white-ethnic neighborhoods, "racism has usually existed in uneasy tension with a deeply held morality—almost as if whites whose life expectations have been thwarted project the moral aspect of their failure onto strangers through racism," wrote Gasper Signorelli in an essay for *New York Newsday* after the murder of Yusuf Hawkins in Benson-hurst. Signorelli, a native of Brooklyn's Bushwick section and a former colleague of mine on the *North Brooklyn Mercury,* the paper I edited during the late 1970s, explained that even whites who engage in violent crime or are simply delinquent in their social responsibilities sometimes keep up a façade of probity in their neighborhoods in order to demonstrate to themselves that they aren't like blacks.

These whites celebrate their neighborhoods, sometimes with justification, as solid communities upholding "family values." But, Signorelli wrote, because they are under siege by crime and economic decay and their own youngsters' options are limited, [some apologists think that] their local codes somehow aren't expected to enjoin moral responsibility for the murder of blacks. In post-mortem surveys of places like Bensonhurst, one always hears of the accused as good, decent kids who've never been in trouble. What's scary about these assessments is not their duplicity but the extent to which they're true. I've known many such "good kids" who, mysteriously, almost schizophrenically, veer off into disgusting stupidity in matters of race.

Exculpation [of these kids and their communities] is both stupid and wrong. As a lifelong resident of Bushwick, which has suffered in pain, dislocation and destruction what Bensonhurst only fears, I can still say with certainty that the killing of innocent strangers has never been sanctioned by my "tribe." People in such neighborhoods do know that living in a city means sticking to certain fundamental values: that killing is wrong, that racism is wrong, that the city belongs to all of us and we should be able to visit any part of it in safety.

Some whites in these neighborhoods who want to believe in these values—yet have been caught or accused of betraying them—resort to counter-protest to scream away the terrible judgment that is also, at bottom, their own. Acting out the world's caricatures of them as racists has become a way of exorcising those caricatures through parody. It also expresses contempt for a larger society that, they, believe, is more hypocritically racist and elitist than they.

Signorelli captures well the profound moral ambivalence of whites who, like those on Carroll Street, find themselves fighting it out with blacks under pressures of scarcity and inequity that are more powerful than either group. Signorelli clearly knows better than to succumb to the politics of resentment, and he insists that he is not alone. In this he resembles Gerard Papa, a lawyer and youth worker from Bensonhurst who organized an interracial basketball team, the Flames, that faced down threats and occasional assaults by some local whites and won the Brooklyn-Queens championship in 1974. "The next year we laid down roots a little better. Some of the former troublemakers started to help us," Papa told *Newsday*'s Alexis Jetter. "Some even joined the team."

In 1986, however, Papa and a black friend, Arnold Rampersant, were set upon by plainclothes cops who claim to have mistaken them for another interracial pair who had just snatched a purse. The cops shot at and beat Papa and Rampersant within an inch of their deaths, and four years later the two were given large awards by a jury for their experience of police brutality. Some members of the Flames believed, without evidence, that the cops were a racist posse bent on punishing them for their success in integrating the neighborhood's social life. But even a "legitimate" case of mistaken identity may have reflected how unusual it was for a white man and a black man to be driving together through the local streets. And yet the Flames persevered. Asked how Yusuf Hawkins's murder affected the team in 1989, Papa responded, "It didn't. We had one of the best years we've ever had in terms of race relations. You can't jump all over people because they have prejudice. When you force people into a situation where they have to be the most tolerant, non-racist people in the world, or bigots, they might choose to be bigots."

To understand that comment, we need to take a closer look at white ethnics' contention that what they hate isn't color per se but the emergence of color in association with crime, speculation, and social engineering. We need to understand how, in the 1970s, these three currents commingled to become a perverse torrent, each drawing strength from and reinforcing the others. So let us look more closely at white ethnics' rage at those currents, particularly at liberal interventionism. The liberals thought to relieve black urban distress by smashing—with busing, scatter-site housing, and other public-policy initiatives—the barriers white-ethnic neighborhoods had erected to wall out that distress. Was breaking down those walls with these particular battering rams really the best way to expand opportunity for all? Or was it something quite different—a way to blame white ethnics for black deprivations really caused by economic and social arrangements that benefited primarily the liberals themselves?

5

The Specter
of Neighborhood Decay

Black Crime, White Prejudice

Here is a classic account of white perceptions of the effects of racial change upon a community. A special grand jury investigates rising crime in a Brooklyn neighborhood, producing front-page headlines for over a month. After hearing more than a hundred predominantly white witnesses, the grand jury finds a state of "extreme lawlessness." As Harold X. Connolly, a writer, summarizes the findings,

School children had been robbed and mistreated; churches had curtailed or eliminated their evening services. . . ." Gangs of hoodlums" armed with knives and other weapons had assaulted, robbed, . . . and murdered innocent, law-abiding people. A part of the section was rife with prostitution. . . . Hundreds of "formerly very fine one-family homes" had been converted to multiple family usage. . . .

. . . To remedy the situation, the grand jury offered the forthright solution of saturating the area with police, and, if need be, state troopers and national guardsmen . . . [and] demanded vigorous and dutiful performances from city and state regulatory and administrative agencies. The department of welfare should root out fraudulent recipients of relief; the tenement house, fire, and health departments should rigorously enforce building and sanitary codes; the Alcoholic Beverage Control Board should police rowdy bars more diligently. . . . Additional suggestions included expanded recreation facilities, special cultural activities, the formation of "centers . . . for spiritual and moral training." . . .

. . . Not surprisingly blacks perceived the [report] as blatantly racial in character, denouncing its "strong . . . bias" and "witchhunting" flavor. Owing to . . . residential segregation . . . , the labeling of that section as unsafe and crime-ridden tended to paint all [blacks] as such. In addition, they argued, the report failed to "take into consideration the underlying social and economic causes giving rise to such conditions as they describe." . . .

. . . While there still seemed a possibility of preserving the racial integrity of the area, whites had schemed, protested, and lobbied. Once the transformation became inevitable, whites withdrew and fled. Only six members attended the [final meeting of a neighborhood block association] to disburse the remaining treasury among the Red Cross, the Hopewell Society, [and two clergymen], neither of whom was noted for his compassion for blacks.

The neighborhood was Bedford-Stuyvesant, the year 1943. The grand jury's report, printed in full in the *Brooklyn Eagle,* and the black community's response in letters to the editor and in the *Amsterdam News,* was the opening round in a great war that came close to destroying the mightiest city on earth. An echo of white alarms in Harlem between 1912 and 1920, it was the prototype of all the white perceptions and prophecies of neighborhood change that have shaped neighborhood life and real-estate investment in New York City outside Manhattan ever since.

Everything about the report and the debate it sparked is disheateningly familiar today. In response to black leaders' protests, the grand jury "vehemently denied that the problem presented to it was in any sense racial, insisting instead on its purely law-enforcement character," notes Connolly, who unearthed the report in the mid-1970s. As black leaders rightly retorted, the grand jury's disingenuous handling of the subject that was really on Brooklyn's collective mind made it possible to dodge any discussion of racial segregation or discrimination in employment, the "underlying causes" of decay.

Yet the grand jury did not confine its recommendations to increased law enforcement. It proposed various government and civic initiatives to improve the conditions and character of the black community—initiatives which Connolly shows were outmoded in law or custom even in 1943. Note, too, that while the report did not present crime statistics in a manner that permits comparison with present rates, other records and recollections make clear that nothing remotely approaching today's conditions obtained. The point is not that today's high threshold for outrage at crime is the standard we should apply but that something besides fear of crime may have been at work.

For example, the block association Connolly mentions had been scheming desperately with others to keep blacks out of the neighborhood since the early 1920s, when many of the newly arrived blacks were homeowners. The association even opposed the construction of a neighborhood playground, fearing "the race riot which a playground will invite"; race riots in those days were almost universally perpetrated by white mobs against blacks, not vice versa. Thus the "Minute Book" of the Gates Avenue Association is one of several documentary threads reaching back into the decades before the grand jury's report to establish that resistance to blacks antedated worries about crime.

Coming as it did a few months after the 1943 Harlem riot, the grand jury's report on conditions which it acknowledged had "existed for some years past" must be understood as part of a new stage in the development in white perceptions about blacks and neighborhood change. In 1943, Harlem had been a ghetto for thirty years, its population approaching 400,000 during the war. In Bedford-Stuyvesant, by contrast, blacks were just becoming a majority at the time the grand jury conducted its probe; the neighborhood's black population was in the process of nearly doubling, from 65,166 in 1940 to 137,436 in 1950. Moreover, the 1950 census would record the first decline, of 50,000, in Brooklyn's white population since the eighteenth century. For the borough's whites in 1943, then, the writing was on the wall or, more precisely, on the front page of the *Brooklyn Eagle.*

Connolly presents maps showing the concentration of Brooklyn's black population in 1950 and 1970. On each map, the densest concentration, of 80 percent black or more, in Bedford-Stuyvesant, is shown in stark black ink, with penumbras of lesser density radiating out in lightening shades of gray. By 1970, the black center has tripled in size and the gray areas have expanded to cover the northern third of the borough. The spreading slowed and stopped in the 1980s, when Brooklyn's black population approached 800,000 yet had begun to drop in proportion to that of the nonblack population. But no one could have foreseen this at midcentury, and, to most whites, the expanding black center on the map of Brooklyn might as well have been burning a hole in the page. Wherever it spread, the vivid imagery of the grand jury's report followed.

So was joined the battle that would consume much of Brooklyn and much of the city. The prophecy implicit in the grand jury's disingenuous handling of a "law enforcement" problem became self-fulfilling: discrimination in housing and employment segregated and impoverished blacks; their growing numbers, augmented by new arrivals from the South through the late 1950s, only expanded the misery and the number of violent crimes they committed; and that only reinforced whites in their determination to keep cordoning off the disaster. Indeed, following the grand jury's report, residential segregation intensified dramatically. In 1940, only 7.5 percent of Brooklyn's blacks resided in census tracts that were over 80 percent black. In 1950, 35 percent did, in overcrowded, ghetto conditions. As workplace discrimination persisted and, later in the decade, factory jobs began leaving New York, black employment barely held its own.

Whether or not the report had exaggerated the extent of crime in 1943, it scarcely needs to be recorded here that reality soon outdistanced everyone's wildest nightmares. Blacks were and would remain the primary victims, a point which black leaders were often as reluctant as whites to acknowledge. Equally tragic, as more forthright black leaders, from W. E. B. DuBois to Roy Wilkins, did acknowledge, fear of black crime eclipsed for most white observers the vast majority of young blacks who, to this day, have never stopped keeping faith with the larger society and want to share in its development.

Among white victims, who concern us here because of the role their experiences played in the reinforcement of neighborhood segregation, no accounts are more poignant—or more enraging—than those of the idealists, the whites who stood against flight and reached out to their new neighbors. The sociologist Gilda Zwerman, who grew up in Brownsville during the late 1950s and early 1960s, vividly recalled for me her experience of being taken as a very young child to a wading pool and coming out of the water to discover that her mother had given her clothes away to a poor, black family. "You fight for what you believe in. You don't run, and you don't give in," is the way she summarized her leftist parents' determination to stay and to send her in 1963 to the new Junior High School 275, a noble attempt by the Wagner administration to provide a high-quality, integrated school, zoned to include whites who'd already moved to neighboring East Flatbush.

A year later, Zwerman became one of the very last white youngsters to leave the neighborhood, as her parents realized that "we just couldn't go on stepping over the bodies." There had been no shortage of bodies in the Jewish Brownsville of Murder, Incorporated, as Irving Levine of the American Jewish Committee recalls. "But it was franchised crime, it was organized." And because it was controlled, you could fairly easily keep out of its way. More Jewish Brownsville boys were lost to organized crime and drugs in the 1940s than is generally realized; but, as Gerald Sorin movingly describes in *The Nurturing Neighborhood,* hundreds of the poor youths of that ghetto also developed remarkable mutual-aid networks, centered in the Brownsville Boys' Club, that won the hearts and opened the wallets of the civic-minded all over town, including club alumni, who still attend yearly "Brownsville Boys' " reunions by the hundreds in upstate resorts.

In Jonathan Rieder's *Canarsie,* we learn that the wives of some of those white war veterans mentioned earlier, who wouldn't go along with Jim Crow while in the South, were mugged several times by young blacks in Brownsville and East New York. Those who stayed on defiantly in racially "tipped" housing projects were assaulted by black girls in basement laundromats. They tell Rieder how feelings of betrayal and bitterness grew uneasily but ineradicably in their hearts, winning inner dialogues with statements like "It's a physical reality. You have to protect your body and your children."

Escape to modest homeownership in Canarsie brought fears that any property devaluation would foreclose retirement plans or medical care. We watch even those with no visceral objection to a black family moving in next door join neighbors in excluding blacks, in order to forestall a stampede that could destroy future security. We watch them distinguish, with pride and muted shame, between the welfare that let their immigrant families get back on their feet after a father's death and the welfare that seems to penalize working and sustain dependency on monthly payments nearly as large as what Canarsians take home after paying taxes to help support the dependents. Such dependency offends not only their self-interest but, in some cases, their fading socialist vision of a collectivity to which all contribute what they can.

Yes, some Canarsians have heard of structural unemployment and seen workplace discrimination; but they have also seen the long lines outside ghetto liquor stores on welfare check–cashing days and the vandalizing of the very buildings they had managed to keep clean when they were just as poor. We watch them rail at elites' concessions to such behavior; by the time school integration comes to Canarsie in 1973 through mandates from on high, the buses bringing black youngsters from the very streets and projects Canarsians abandoned in a hail of black crime, we comprehend the spectacle of middle-aged Jewish men beating white picketers (some of them undoubtedly Jewish, too) from Youth against War and Fascism who've come to Canarsie to "smash racism" during the school boycott. All across Brooklyn and the Bronx, especially, blacks' social disintegration under the pressures of unemployment coincided with their numerical and geographical expansion—milked and channeled into softening white real-estate markets, to be sure, by racist bankers and brokers who turned quick dollars by orchestrating self-fulfilling prophecies of neighborhood decay.

The vast majority of white victims were not idealists or political activists who'd put themselves in harm's way. On December 4, 1982, the *New York Times* reported "a three-hour spree of robbery, violence and death threats" early the previous morning in a middle-class, white-ethnic Queens neighborhood.

[T]hree gunmen kicked in the doors of eight homes . . . , staged three street holdups and escaped in a pair of stolen cars early yesterday after eluding police in two wild auto chases. Police said the robbers terrified householders with a shotgun and a handgun. They struck some victims and threatened to shoot others, including couples, families with small children and elderly people living alone, the police said.

It was the ultimate white urban nightmare: the intruders were black, and the horror occurred about a year after black gunmen had held up a diner just outside the community, forcing all the white customers to lie on the ground while they shouted threats. In between these two events, there had been so many robberies by young black men of whites coming home late on Saturday nights that the police at the local precinct had developed a system: as soon as a report came in, they would get a description of the suspect's car and stake out the highway that connected the community to a low-income, black neighborhood about a mile away. Predictably, the cops caught most of the suspects.

For some months, homeowners had contributed to hiring a private patrol, and the robberies had subsided. But by the fall of 1982, payments had lapsed and the private policing had been suspended. In their spree that December night, the gunmen rampaged through the community along a wild, zigzag route. At 3:40 A.M., they entered the home of the family of John Byrnes, where his mother, daughter, brother, and grandchild were sleeping, waking them up and menacing them. After several more terrifying break-ins, they arrived at the home of Mrs. Anna Scherma, sixty-nine, who told me that she had moved originally from Bushwick and then from South Ozone Park to the community in search of peace. The gunmen hit her husband, Philip, over the head and took his pants and $1,600 the Schermas had planned to use for a trip to Italy for their twenty-fifth wedding anniversary. They also struck the home of Cecilia Becker, an elderly woman who suffered a heart attack and was taken to the hospital. She moved out of the neighborhood soon afterward.

The community the gunmen ravaged that December night in 1982 was Howard Beach. The route they followed was close to that followed on another December night four years later by a pack of local white youths chasing three black men, one of whom, Michael Griffith, would be killed by a passing car. The home of the Byrnes family, where the gunmen struck first in 1982, is next door to that of the Kern family, where Scott Kern, one of the four 1986 Howard Beach assailants convicted of first-degree manslaughter, was twelve years old and asleep; he learned of the rampage the next day.

Cecilia Becker's house, at 86-20 Shore Parkway, is the same one from which Theresa Fisher witnessed the beating of Cedric Sandiford in December 1986. The 1986 Howard Beach assailants had been watching a female stripper at a party; the 1982 Howard Beach assailant convicted in the robbery spree, Larry Jeffries, then twenty-two, of East New York, had grown up in Brownsville and was a male stripper in a Brooklyn disco.

"When we had the press here every day in 1986," Anna Scherma recalls, "I went up to a reporter from Channel 7 and tried to tell him what had happened here in 1982. I asked him, 'Tell me, why weren't there any marches when this happened to us? Where was everybody then?' He wasn't interested. Nobody remembered. But I'll never forget."

That is not to say that 1982 excuses 1986, or that the line we have to draw against violent crime can separate black from white—where would that leave the vast majority of blacks who want to draw the same line, too? Nor is it to suggest that a neighborhood's legitimate refusal to see violent crime "in context," as a product of systemic oppression, excuses its angry victims from supporting social investments in prenatal care, early education, and jobs. Quite the contrary: it is only when "neighborhood values" like those invoked in chapter 4 are defended against criminal incursion that there is either the breathing room or the positive experience necessary to nurture a commitment to social justice. The reverse trek of Jewish Canarsians from lunch-pail liberalism to voting for Republicans after 1970 makes that very clear.

Gasper Signorelli, who has watched Brooklyn's Bushwick section succumb to the ravages of accelerated racial transition, evokes well the interplay of neighborhood codes and commitments to racial and social justice which activist lawyers and social engineers need to take into account:

I stopped a mugging. A woman was coming home from work, I was on the stoop. I saw a kid going toward her, then he saw me. I looked at him. He looked at me. He didn't do anything. But I knew. I knew. Everytime someone has assaulted someone in this area, I could see it coming. It's not skin color, it's a certain look about a person, they give off a certain vibration. You have to be a fool not to be on the defensive. . . .

People in the neighborhood say of certain minority kids who come through, "We know what they're about, either they're leaving the scene of something or making plans to do something." Like Goetz and those kids who were going to Times Square with those screwdrivers to open up pinball machines. A lot of people believe they deserved it just for that. You see, it's just that crime is so rampant.

In my neighborhood, if you look at a kid and have a sense that he's involved in illegal activities, if you have any street sense at all, you have a 90 percent chance of being right. It's not racism; it's that you're not stupid! [He laughs.] It's like if anyone gets mugged in the street, it's almost as if his friends say to him, "What the hell's wrong with you? Can't you see what's going on around you? Can't you distinguish people one from the other?"

A lot of blacks take great pride in their street knowledge, right? But if a white person evinces the same savvy, he's a racist, you know. Meanwhile the black kids I know are seeing the same thing he is. That's one of the reasons they're into combat so much, as a protective device, because they know, they're afraid themselves, there's a lot of validity to the fear.

It's not so simple. A friend of mine had one black kid on his softball team, and one day a guy from another team yelled a racial epithet at him. The whole team went and beat the shit out of him. On the other hand, a couple days later a black guy was chasing a white woman down the street and they ran and beat the shit out of *him!*

I'm all for social programs that keep people out of poverty and out of crime. Once they cross the line [and commit crimes,] okay, then that's it. That's how I cleared my head up on this. I would say to whites, I realize there are problems, I realize people have fears, but you can't have these insane attitudes toward minorities and political policies based on fear, vengeance, spite, insanity; you have to separate these things out. I don't see political leadership that makes these distinctions. They're kowtowers to fear, they say we should keep "them" on the reservation.

Signorelli's concluding comments cast an important light on his opening ones. His ability to uphold justice and fair play for minorities is inseparable from his ability to make the subtle, sinuous, sometimes extralegal judgments that preserve his family's safety. If you discredit this second set of judgments by calling Signorelli a racist or a vigilante, denying him the integrity of his experience as a filter for what he sees on the street, you also dry up the wellsprings from which come his first set of judgments on behalf of social justice. In Signorelli's case, at least, both kinds of judgment, woven into the fabric of his neighborhood life, do promote justice. Understanding how his perceptions differ from those of the 1943 grand jury and the youthful bigots in Howard Beach and Bensonhurst is the beginning of wisdom.

Sitting one evening on his front stoop in Bushwick, just a few blocks from the arson-ravaged, abandoned housing and drug-infested tenement life that constantly menace his own, quiet block, Signorelli and I talked about the disorientation New Yorkers feel when visiting low-crime areas outside the city; they become objects of ridicule for locking their cars at high noon on streets where no one so much as rolls up a car window even when parking overnight.

"Actually, it doesn't take me very long to let down my guard when I'm outside the city," I volunteered. "I guess it's 'cause I grew up in a crime-free neighborhood in western Massachusetts."

"Yeah," Signorelli mused. "I grew up in a neighborhood like that myself."

"Oh, really? Where?"

"Right here."

Social Engineers and Other Operators

By the late 1950s, the burgeoning black population of Brooklyn could not be confined to Bedford-Stuyvesant. White working-class resistance, sometimes manifested in ugly violence against those who tried to cross the color lines, delayed and deflected the inevitable expansion just enough to help ensure that the economics and pathology of segregation would replicate themselves. Not only did blacks lack adequate income because of job discrimination; residential segregation—the "dual market" in real estate—enabled landlords to continue subdividing apartments and forcing the new residents to pay higher rents per square foot than whites in similar buildings did.

Jewish neighborhoods like Crown Heights and Brownsville were often the first to turn, perhaps for three reasons which Nathan Glazer suggested in 1964. First, some Jews, like Zwerman's family, were more liberal on racial questions than other whites, and even the many who were not were far less inclined to use violence to settle disputes. Second, unlike white ethnics, especially Italians, who were passionate about homeownership, Jews in those days were overwhelmingly apartment dwellers, and most blacks were too poor to bid on homes. Finally, most Jews were more mobile than other whites, more likely to be moving, anyway—the older adults to more "modern" apartments in places like Flatbush, their children to homes in the suburbs or suburb-like sections of the city. Real-estate brokers and landlords, many of them Jewish, understood that Jewish neighborhood markets would be the first to "soften." And as they did soften, the single-family brownstones that dominated the side streets between the multifamily apartment buildings on corners and avenues could be purchased, too, and profitably subdivided into rooming houses, re-creating the ghetto conditions which blacks were trying to escape.

That said, the very intransigence of Italian and Irish resistance to blacks often meant that, once a white-ethnic neighborhood was finally "breached" after pitched battles, it would "turn" even more quickly than the Jewish neighborhoods, becoming all-black with blinding speed. There would be few of the valiant efforts to "stay on" which a number of left-wing Jews made on principle in places like Brownsville. The color line would be redrawn in another place and the black population contained once again in properties which absentee white owners with no commitment to the neighborhood would run down in order to maximize their returns. That my former block on Carroll Street didn't "turn" this way was probably a reflection of its diversity, which sustained at least some intimations that property values would rise.

If indefensible prejudice had sown the wind in 1943, by 1963 it was beginning to reap a whirlwind of crime and destruction that had yet to approach its peak force. For that to happen, two more storm systems would have to be added. One was the social engineering of "integration" by black activists and liberal whites, described in chapters 2 and 3. The other was a disastrous new turn in the economics of real estate itself.

In the softening white urban neighborhood markets left behind by the first suburban exodus of the 1950s, ghettoization speeded up as realtors began carefully to steer blacks and Hispanics into new areas of confinement and dual-market exploitation. Blacks who were making it into the middle class thanks to the achievements of the civil rights movement did manage to escape the dual market in some neighborhoods and in new, middle-class enclaves of their own; but, as the sociologist William Julius Wilson has demonstrated, that depleted the institutional and communal life of those left behind.

When some of the new low-income ghettos began popping up not in Brownsville or the South Bronx but on the Upper West Side and other Manhattan neighborhoods outside Harlem in the late 1950s, the city fathers took alarm. They turned for answers to the city's developer-statesmen and their peripatetic spokesman, Roger Starr, who proposed urban renewal to develop each parcel of land for its "highest and best use." On the Upper West Side north of Moses's brand-new Lincoln Center, that meant sparking the revival of white, middle-class urban living competitive with suburbia. But the West Side Urban Renewal Plan's proponents also saw it as a genuine effort to promote integration—not, this time, by intruding minorities into white areas, but the reverse. The watchword of the planners was "marketability" of the area east of Amsterdam Avenue between Eighty-seventh and Ninety-seventh streets to liberal, white families renovating the brownstone rooming houses into owner-occupied homes. Unlike beleaguered white ethnics in the outer boroughs, these homeowners were willing to live among minorities—but only if they could be guaranteed a ceiling on the number of subsidized, low-income units in the area.

The novelty of introducing into a predominantly minority area thousands of middle-class whites whose incomes and attitudes gave them more flexibility than white ethnics could summon reopened the debate that had been all but closed with the Brooklyn grand-jury report of 1943: need a sizable concentration of low-income minority people always and everywhere portend decay? The new debate became the prototype for discussions a few years later in "gentrifying" areas of the city like Park Slope and other brownstone neighborhoods ringing downtown Brooklyn. But while the West Side plan differed enough from the dual market to reopen the debate, it still accepted, as fully as would the block association hostess on Carroll Street, the primacy of white perceptions about race as the determinants of investment and public policy.

In a private market where most blacks had yet to make their way, there was simply no alternative, the plan's proponents argued. At least, under urban renewal, public subsidies and incentives could be carefully crafted to facilitate a modicum of integration to give thousands of people of color some respite from the spiral of ghettoization. Whites needed dominance, they argued, because bitter experience had taught them, and, indeed, all New Yorkers, that whenever the poor reach a certain critical mass in an area, crime and pathology begin to feed on themselves, "tipping" it from integrated to all-minority as whites (and middle-class blacks) flee.

Low-income-housing activists responded that these perceptions were racist, stigmatizing decent, hardworking, and welfare-dependent people on account of crimes most of them did not commit. And white perceptions were doing this, as usual, because the poor were nonwhite. As the housing activist Bill Price put it,

The real nature of the "tipping point" is that it institutionalizes white fears and defines a percentage level to white tolerance. In this sense, we are building racism into our community by administrative decree. As in many forms of racism, this process identifies the oppressed as the oppressor and thereby creates a rationalization through which whites can maintain power without feeling guilty about it. The causes of "tipping" are not black. The causes are white anxieties, white attitudes. But the cure is to control blacks.

Were those anxieties and attitudes unfounded? The question was never resolved, for, as the West Side plan went through many permutations, the middle-class private market did take hold. Thousands of units of low-income housing were built, but thousands more low-income people were displaced, sometimes through the thuggery of speculators anxious to renovate buildings for upscale occupants. Urban renewal's critics called it "Negro removal" because, in Manhattan at least, it displaced tens of thousands of people of color—and sent them packing for precisely those softening, white, outer-borough neighborhoods already under siege.

But the West Side plan also gave impetus to another set of social-engineering schemes in those outer-borough neighborhoods, this time promoted by the liberal opponents of urban renewal. They would use federal legislation, court orders, and funds, along with the city's powers of condemnation and zoning for land and school districting, to prove that white-ethnic resistance to integration could be broken in the North as it had been through the legal and political triumphs of the civil rights movement in the South. The availability of massive federal subsidies was critical to these new initiatives. Without subsidy, the conviction that integration was justified by any means necessary begged too many questions. After all, ghettoization reflected not just white neighborhoods' segregationist impulses but also the economic imperatives of a real-estate industry confronted with black poverty. If blacks had nothing but welfare shelter allowances—and many of them not even that, their sources of income unclear, erratic—how could a landlord make a profit off them except by cramming them into little spaces in buildings he let run down?

How would merely allowing blacks into white neighborhoods change that desperate situation? Even if one could leave aside problems of crime and culture clash, how could residential integration work economically for landlords, unless they were willing to keep on subdividing homes and apartments in the neighborhoods into which blacks were being integrated? What would that mean for the rest of those neighborhoods, even if all the whites in them were color-blind? The answer was that white tolerance would make no difference, because real-estate markets are creatures of class as well as race. Of course, "poor" meant "black": there were relatively few poor whites in New York during the expansionary 1960s. Still, from the real-estate industry's profit-maximizing point of view, the race problem was at bottom a convenient shorthand for a class problem. The industry's discrimination against the rising but still-small black middle class was a concession to that shorthand's overall utility as a guide to maintaining profits.

Ironically, were poverty not as important a problem for blacks as segregation itself, there ought by the early 1960s to have been more housing units vacant and available to blacks than ever before, for the city's population was dropping, freeing up units. But who could run those newly available units at a profit if the tenants had no money? The continuing overcrowding of blacks seemed the only answer, and that meant that, beginning in the mid-1960s in Brownsville and parts of the South Bronx, desperately overcrowded buildings in the process of being milked stood next to empty buildings that had outlived their usefulness and that no one in the private market wanted to run. Community-based efforts to rehabilitate and operate such buildings on a nonprofit basis with government subsidies were years away. For the time being, instead of relieving the pressure on white neighborhoods by serving as a resource for new black arrivals from the Upper West Side and the South, the abandoned buildings became cancer cells—firetraps and refuges for hoodlums and thieves—that endangered whole blocks. They were the beginnings of the holes being burned into the black center of Connolly's maps, accelerating rather than slowing the desperate flight of black tenants toward the ghetto's white margins.

As places like Brownsville and Bushwick began to resemble war zones under the pressures of abandonment, their former white residents became ever more determined to defend their new homes across the color line in places like Canarsie, which lies literally across the tracks from Brownsville, and the Ridgewood-Glendale area— Archie Bunker's territory—just across the border from Bushwick in Queens. In Chicago, Alinsky proposed that all-white communities agree to accept blacks up to but not exceeding 5 percent of each neighborhood's population. Like the "tipping point" debate in Manhattan, that proposal was a crude concession to white racism, Alinsky acknowledged; but, given whites' bitter experiences with the dynamics of neighborhood change, there was no other way, and it was better than nothing. As time passed, such a quota system might prove to traumatized whites that blacks could be decent neighbors, that there was an alternative to the spiral of ghettoization. Not surprisingly, considering the acrimony surrounding debates over the far higher "tipping point" in Manhattan, low-income-housing advocates opposed Alinsky's idea as staunchly as did white ethnics.

The liberal answer to problems black poverty posed for neighborhood integration was more public funding and initiatives: the wholesale busing of minority children into underutilized white-neighborhood schools; higher welfare shelter allowances and the payment of special cash incentives to landlords in white neighborhoods to accept minority welfare households, ideally without subdividing apartments; and the "scattering" of new, mostly low-income, minority housing projects into white neighborhoods to enable poor blacks to live decently outside the imperatives of the private dual market.

Within the ghettos themselves, large tracts of deteriorating and abandoned private housing had already been replaced by projects. But there never was enough funding, and government interventions of this sort did nothing to remove the stigma and pathologies used to justify segregation.

And yet in the mid-1960s, at a time when white ethnics who'd fled disaster had every reason to associate the appearance of even solid, economically qualified black tenants or home buyers in their midst with a repetition of the cycle—to them, the statement "There goes the neighborhood" was no joke—activists and sympathetic bureaucrats decided to plunk down new, predominantly black public housing projects in the middle of white neighborhoods, including the one that hung on in a portion of Bushwick itself. Advocates of scatter-site housing were riding a moral and legislative tide. As vice-chairman of the Kerner Commission on Civil Disorders, Lindsay was instrumental in including in its 1968 report the famous warning that America was rapidly becoming two societies, one black and one white, separate and unequal. Segregation was unconscionable and, for blacks, lethal; the only way to break the self-fulfilling prophecies that kept it so was to leapfrog blacks over the color line and, in effect, make defensive white ethnics see that their world didn't have to collapse simply because blacks lived among them, even if in high-rise projects towering over their little homes.

That is just what was decreed in 1966 in new federal mandates ordering cities, on pain of losing public funds, to disperse blacks out of ghettos by building new public projects in white neighborhoods. In the center of Bushwick, still a solid ethnic German and Italian community of frame homes and yellow-brick, three-story walk-ups with granite cornices and varnished doors, the City of New York demolished two whole blocks of such housing in 1968 to make way for a scatter-site project of several fourteen-story towers. White homeowners promptly fled the blocks surrounding the demolition. Holdouts were given a rough shove by speculators, who jammed the remaining brick and frame structures with welfare tenants—whose shelter allowances had increased considerably by that time—and milked the buildings for all they were worth. Some of the speculators posed as civil rights champions for renting to minorities, receiving finders' fees and certificates of appreciation from a Human Resources Administration desperate to find homes for its clients. But as more white homeowners fled, more of the area became a dumping ground for tenants being displaced from Manhattan into the hands of the speculators.

"[The white flight] wasn't racism," Father James Kelly of St. Brigid's Church insisted to me in 1978. "It was a class problem. Our white families wouldn't have fled just because there were Hispanics and blacks around. After all, one of the most stable sections of Bushwick today is the eastern end, where blacks bought homes in the early sixties. It was because these were welfare tenants, whose landlords let the buildings run down." What no one could have foreseen was the brutal, calculating way the speculators would milk the buildings into abandonment and then torch them for the insurance, relocating the worst tenants to new blocks to begin the cycle again. There was more money to be made that way than in simply collecting rents; unlike Park Slope, whose distinctive brownstones and convenience to Manhattan made it attractive to middle-class renovators, Bushwick, with its nondescript little walk-ups, would never attract upscale conversion.

The speculators had discovered something important about racial change: because it had become a convenient shorthand for poverty and antisocial pathology, it could be used as an accelerant of a neighborhood turnover that was more profitable than neighborhood stability. When the Federal Housing Administration (FHA) finally introduced to inner-city neighborhoods like Bushwick and East Flatbush the same mortgage guarantees it had offered in suburbia, the speculators knew what to do: they deliberately sold their buildings to poor, naive minority buyers, bribing the FHA inspectors to certify their creditworthiness. The sooner default came, the better; the speculator would collect his mortgage insurance from the government, which would foreclose on and board up the property. That would induce the remaining white homeowners to sell for a song to speculators whose songs were very scary indeed—warnings of impending decay and total loss if the owner did not sell now. Then the prices would be jacked up for more federally insured sales to unqualified newcomers. There were investigations and convictions, but the real sentences were meted out to the neighborhoods. By the mid-1970s, Bushwick was burning, a prison of traumatized welfare recipients reeling in rage and despair. And because of fiscal constraints, the city left the two-block site at the center of the storm vacant for eight full years.

Bushwick lies eight miles southwest of Forest Hills, a Queens neighborhood of predominantly Jewish homeowners and middle-class tenants where another scatter-site project was proposed in 1966 and formally announced in 1971—a trio of twenty-four-story towers intended to house 840 low-income, mostly black families. The home-owners went wild. "This," declared Lindsay, "is a fundamental test as to whether those who argue for integrated communities have the courage of their convictions." Lindsay and other proponents of the plan like the public housing authority chairman Simeon Golar failed to see that such "convictions" had already been tested severely in other neighborhoods.

Indeed, although Ed Koch, then a liberal Manhattan congress-man, took up the Forest Hills homeowners' cause, few of the city's liberals charged him with racism; four years later, he even had the support of most minority leaders when he defeated Cuomo, the For-est Hills mediator, in a runoff for the Democratic nomination for mayor. Cuomo, too, had found himself learning to separate the rac-ism of some Forest Hills homeowners from their legitimate com-plaints. "From the beginning," he wrote in his *Forest Hills Diary,* "[the project] has been a series of mistakes and miscalculations. The very idea of scatter-site was, to start with, virtually untested—almost purley a social experiment—and the attempt to move on it massively in several different locations appears now, in retrospect, to have been a great error, no matter how noble the intentions." The Forest Hills project did work successfully because it was scaled down, trans-formed into a cooperative, and opened to an unusually high propor-tion of elderly tenants; it became the exception that proved the rule.

When David Dinkins defeated Koch in 1989 to become the city's first black mayor, he did not do so with votes from Forest Hills. Because blacks made up less than a third of the electorate, Dinkins had to win by reaching out to other minorities and liberal whites, especially Jews—he got nearly 40 percent of the Jewish vote. But the once liberal Forest Hills went for Dinkins's opponent, the former U.S. district attorney Rudolph Giuliani, by better than three to one. The Glendale-Ridgewood area, just over the color line from Bush-wick, went for Giuliani better than four to one.

Lessons—and a Ray of Hope

The irony, as we have seen, is that by the late 1960s black activists and some white radicals were having second thoughts about racial integration, which some of them had come to see as a threat to the consolidation of black power. A few claimed that white resistance to integration had disillusioned them, leaving them to concentrate on black self-development. But what, in the end, was that white resistance all about? Much of the black middle class was also opposed to integration that mixed welfare recipients with people of moderate incomes, whatever their race. As Cuomo told me in 1989,

[People said] it was blacks against Jewish people in Forest Hills, [but] a lot more of it was poor, welfare against middle class. When [low-income housing was proposed for] Baisley Park, where the black middle class was controlling the entire community, they were more ferocious about resisting the black poor than Forest Hills was. It was happening at the same time, yet the story never got written. They stood in the street, and you wouldn't have believed it, the curse words. . . . So what does that say?

What it says is that, for all their struggles against racism, liberals and activists only compounded the mistake of the Brooklyn grand jury that had investigated conditions in Bedford-Stuyvesant nearly thirty years before. The grand jury was disingenuous about the implications of its probe; unspoken fears about race drove its work. By the mid-1960s, many white liberals and black activists prided themselves on exposing such hypocrisy, bringing unacknowledged racism to the surface. Yet, no less than the white Brooklyn burghers of the early 1940s, the liberals and activists of the late 1960s were using race to dodge their moral and political responsibility to confront something even more profound: a system of economic injustice that would impoverish some of its people and drive them to pathology and crime even if everyone in that system were white.

To be sure, race had long been the coding system whereby some Americans could be marked for social damnation without posing fundamental questions about society's economic and moral soundness. For that reason, mobilizing blacks to cast off the stigma and to demand equal treatment was sure to send shock waves through the whole society, exposing its inequities and lies. But as long as those shock waves were interpreted solely in racial terms, only part of the problem could be addressed. The emergence of a black middle class—and the beginnings of the emergence of a white "underclass," not only in midwestern, industrial ghost towns but also in Bensonhurst, where decent people feel helpless before the increasingly criminal rage of white, jobless youth—would cast doubt on the Kerner report's use of race as the lens through which to examine our society's disorders. And it would cast grave doubt on the race-based social experiments that flowed from that examination.

Whatever it may have been in the South, and however deeply ingrained it may have become in the North, society's obsession with race deflected its attention from the real problem, which is poverty, and the real need, which is jobs. To "expose" racism without addressing that problem and that need is to invite responses from one's opponents that only deepen racism itself. That the underlying injustices in our society have to be resolved systemically, not simply by social experiments in integration and various forms of redress to people of color, becomes clear from a close look at some of the enraged Bensonhurst whites who ridiculed black protesters marching through their community after the slaying of Yusuf Hawkins in August 1989. At the march, a southern WASP journalist told the black writer Playthell Benjamin, "Most of these [Bensonhurst whites] look like mulattoes. You know, we never thought of Italians as real white people back home." And, Benjamin adds,

most of the people of Bensonhurst, who are largely southern Italians, weren't thought of as real white people back home in Italy, either. . . . A common joke in the North was that Africa begins in Florence or Rome. . . . There are signs all over the North, saying, "Southerners Go Home." And, in an ultimate irony, Dr. [Silvia] Federici [of Hofstra University] observes, "The two main reasons most often given by Northerners for discriminating against Southerners are: they are criminals, and they take away jobs." Then she points out, "These are the very people who migrate to Bensonhurst."

That color is relative has not been lost on everyone. Back in Park Slope, the Fifth Avenue Committee did score some successes by uniting Italian merchants and homeowners with low-income minority tenants to push for low-rise, attractive subsidized housing and other protections against a rising market that would help both groups. All across the city, similar community-based housing organizations sprang up in the 1970s, rehabilitating and running abandoned housing for low-income people of all races in an effort to forestall both decay and overheated, overpriced conversions. In Flatbush, Brooklyn District Attorney Charles Hynes, who prosecuted the 1986 Howard Beach assailants, told me that homeowners in his area had refused to panic when blacks moved onto the block and that both integration and property values had held up very well. In Starrett City, a huge development on the outskirts of Brooklyn that is home to such "refugees" from Brownsville as Gilda Zwerman's parents, integration has been successful (see chapter 6). The "learning curves" among actors in neighborhood change have grown, with a little nudge from new laws that make it harder for banks to withhold credit from qualified applicants in "marginal" areas and easier to stop arson-for-profit and block-busting speculators.

Most dramatic and heartening has been the rebuilding of a portion of Brownsville itself, as well as a part of East New York, by East Brooklyn Congregations (EBC), one of four neighborhood-based, doggedly interracial, and brilliantly successful "power organizations" in New York City that draw from organizing techniques pioneered by Alinsky. In 1979, a small group of East Brooklyn ministers who had been trying for years to save their devastated neighborhoods retained the Alinsky-inspired Industrial Areas Foundation to help them train clerical and lay leaders. In hundreds of individual meetings with congregants and house meetings and training sessions, EBC rewove the "relational fabric" of neighborhood life for tens of thousands of politically moderate, churchgoing local residents. They studied the structure of local power, meeting with officials and developing winnable goals: new street signs, cleanups of local food stores under polite but dauntingly credible threats of boycott, crackdowns with the district attorney on local smoke shops.

Few of these gains were won without confrontation. Busy commissioners and city officials gave EBC priority only when they began to realize that the group had been tracking their political interests and professional performance. EBC representatives stunned the local political establishment in 1980 by handing Brooklyn Borough President Howard Golden their resignations from politically wired local community boards and demanding instead a meeting with his shadow boss, the Democratic county leader Meade Esposito, to talk about the city services they weren't getting.

Without once using slogans like "black power," EBC registered 10,000 new voters, 70 percent of them black, and doubled the turnout in its area during the 1984 elections, turning politicians' heads all over town. "Who are these people?" they began to ask. The group's growing clout also caught the attention of its congregations' national parent church bodies, which together contributed almost $9 million to begin construction on the "Nehemiah" homes, named for the biblical prophet who persuaded his despondent neighbors to rebuild Jerusalem's battered walls. The visionary developer and civic curmudgeon I. D. Robbins designed the single-family row homes and promised to bring them in at prices that many public housing residents could afford. The city donated thirteen nearly abandoned blocks and a $10,000 federal "community development" subsidy to write down the cost of each house. The state provided low-interest mortgages.

But the initiative and ownership remained EBC's, and that meant that it had to stand up to local elites—bankers, public officials, and others who suddenly began to look predatory and capricious as they tried to profit from EBC's discipline and probity. All of them wanted a piece of the action—business for friends, bribes for inspectors. They got nothing. EBC used its clout to go over their heads, Brooklyn's Bishop Francis Mugavero calling Mayor Koch when necessary to expedite bureaucratic reviews. The houses did come in at prices which nurses, paralegals, transit workers, and young teachers could afford; and a third of the buyers did come from nearby public housing, bearing small nest eggs they'd dreamed of investing in local homes.

And so, on a freshly fenced ball field in Brownsville in October 1982, gaily colored banners marked off a milling throng of eight thousand blacks, Hispanics, and a small number of whites by congre-

gations: Lutheran Church of the Risen Christ, Our Lady of Consola-
tion, RC, St. Paul's Community Baptist Church, and on. "Contrary
to common opinion," cried the Reverend Johnny Ray Youngblood
of St. Paul's, EBC's cochair, "we are not a 'grass-roots' organization.
Grass roots grow in *smooth* soil! Grass roots are *shallow* roots!" His
incantatory power caught his listeners, summoning their strength
and spontaneous amens. "Our roots are *deep* roots!" Youngblood
continued. "Our roots have fought for existence in the shattered glass
of East New York and the blasted brick of Brownsville!" ("Aw-
right!" "Praise God!") "And so we say to you, Mayor Koch, we love
New York!" And we say to you, Council President Bellamy"—the
crowd on its feet now, thundering with him—"WE LOVE NEW
YORK!" shifting the emphasis gradually to "we," as in "Listen to
us: *We* love New York!"

The mostly white officialdom was stunned. Bishop Mugavero
blinked back tears. Here, in 1968, watching people pick their way to
the elevated IRT past rows of abandoned buildings and over rubble-
strewn lots prowled by wild dogs, a visiting Mayor Kevin White of
Boston had made the *Times*'s "Quote of the Day" by sputtering that
he had just seen "the beginning of the end of our civilization." In
1975, with virtually nothing left standing but public housing, the
then city housing commissioner Roger Starr had proposed "planned
shrinkage" of the area—the calculated withdrawal of services and
resettlement of population.

Now, at the rally, Mayor Koch led the crowd in a dramatic count-
down, and a bulldozer roared, opening the earth for the new homes.
Huddled at the edge of the crowd were a couple hundred dazed-
looking, middle-aged whites who might have stepped out of Archie
Bunker's neighborhood—and who, in fact, had come by bus from
"his" area of Queens. They were members of EBC's sister IAF
group, the Queens Citizens Organization. Their president, Pat Oettinger, took the mike and cried, "Our trip to Brooklyn today has
reinforced our belief that there is no boundary between us. We are all
one neighborhood, one great city. Your struggles are our struggles!
Your heartaches are our heartaches! Your victories are our victories!" The crowd roared back its welcome. The Queens visitors loosened up, smiled, waved. The elected officials, accustomed to shut-
tling two-faced back and forth across the color line, were visibly

impressed. "Two years ago," Oettinger later confided, "you couldn't have gotten my neighbors here in a tank."

The EBC effort is but a straw in the wind. What the Queens visitors experienced would have to happen to many thousands more like them to change the civic culture of New York, and a viable new politics would somehow have to address their grievances as well. The odds are daunting; a tank, indeed! If one measure of civility is the degree to which force and fraud are kept at bay in the calculations of daily life, then New York is a place less civilized today than in the 1950s and early 1960s, though not, perhaps, before that. And the virtual collapse of a centrist Jewish and white-ethnic political culture in places such as Forest Hills reflects its former adherents' belief that the rules have been changed against them by policymakers who sometimes act as if a dark skin alone ought to command economic and political preferment.

The city's beleaguered white ethnics know that, in the larger scheme of things, it isn't really minorities they're losing out to; there are the eternal rich and a new managerial elite that, in an exquisite irony, includes radicals who tormented them in the 1960s and then cleaned themselves up in the 1980s to claim their class prerogatives. Every day, luxury buses sweep through Brooklyn and Queens, picking up blue-haired ladies and paunchy men in leisure suits apparently determined to lose millions to the likes of Donald Trump in Atlantic City—white ethnics gripped by the boredom and hopelessness they ascribe to blacks.

Still, stark connections between neighborhood racial change, rising crime, and lower property values are seared into their hearts; their inability to escape has demoralized them. Ever since the race-based social experiments of the 1960s and 1970s assaulted their claims to moral legitimacy, their political idiom has degenerated from one that expressed its grievances in tart humor, irony, and flashing insight into one of sullen, evasive rationalizations for attacks on blacks. From Ralph Kramden, the garrulous but decent "big mouth," and Archie Bunker, a quiver of barbed retorts against shrinking horizons, we have come down to a word spoken anonymously in the street: "Fuggedaboutit."

The new silence is so eerie, so ominous, that I was almost relieved to hear it broken by that Italian-American youth on the street in front of the pizza parlor. He was wrong about blacks, but then, he was only playing the activists' own game of using race as the lens through which to view all social change. Five years later, I was far more gratified to hear the city's tense, racial silence broken at EBC's ground-breaking rally in Brownsville. I wish the kid from Court Street had been there. From out of the black hole in the center of Connolly's burning map, he would have heard the thundering of Johnny Ray Youngblood—and of a white woman, Pat Oettinger. Her rousing speech was a priceless contribution to reversing white ethnics' racial perceptions by changing the sad realities on which they rest.

6

Rights and Reciprocity

From Color Blindness to Color Consciousness

One of the most appealing aspects of East Brooklyn Congregations' projects in Brownsville and East New York is that
they have been accomplished not through racially charged
lawsuits or court mandates but through a politics that employs organizing, education, and, when necessary, confrontation to advance the
interests of an *interracial* community. Nationwide, groups trained by
the Industrial Areas Foundation generally avoid litigation. They prefer to win concrete gains rather than abstract rights by wielding their
power in face-to-face negotiations with public officials and corporate
leaders. That power comes not primarily from asserting moral claims
or legal rights, important though these are as frameworks for all
political action, but from the groups' own performance—their ability
to turn out voters and stage effective, intelligently targeted appeals,
rallies, and boycotts across race lines.

That, of course, was the basis of the early civil rights movement's
power as well. But black militants and their white radical and liberal
apologists squandered their political capital in the late 1960s and
1970s by organizing poorly, selecting the wrong targets, and, ulti-

mately, fleeing to the courts when they began losing at the polls and in the economy as voters and investors turned away. Defenders of the radical politics of that time might argue that the activists had no choice: the voters would never have come around through persuasion alone. The truth is that the activists needlessly isolated themselves and alienated potential allies by framing the issues racially and legally rather than in political terms calculated to enlighten and draw the broadest possible range of supporters. As their demands for immediate school and neighborhood integration engendered fierce resistance, they were drawn into courtroom battles over the law's ability to shape American society in defiance of the popular will.

The Constitution enumerates individual—not group—rights which no electoral majority may violate. If judicial rulings constrict or expand rights beyond what most voters can accept, they can elect officials who pick new judges. So any group wanting to defend or expand rights must assemble a voting majority through political persuasion and only then rely on the force of law to "persuade" the rest. The civil rights movement did this brilliantly in the 1960s; later, with judicial momentum on its side, it could forget about voting majorities and simply go to court and have extrapolations of earlier rulings imposed on communities. In 1980, the political bill came due, in ways we must try to understand.

We can begin by remarking how wildly fighters for social justice have zigzagged across the constitutional battleground since 1965. After the landmark Civil Rights Act of 1964 and the Voting Rights Act of 1965 were passed, judges and government administrators rapidly elaborated their provisions in response to suits brought by activists lawyers. The transformation of American political culture they effected was nothing short of astonishing. In twenty-five years, government moved from ensuring that people were not formally categorized on the basis of race to ensuring that they are so categorized today, whether they want to be or not. (As we will see, not everyone does.) Liberals and black civil rights activists thus shifted from demanding equality of individual opportunity, which entails color-blind respect for a person's merits and rights beneath the skin, to demanding equality of condition, which submerges individual dignity beneath a color-based emphasis on the putative "rights" of historically deprived racial or ethnic groups.

That shift increasingly constrains individuals to think of themselves primarily as members of persecuted groups as defined by color. Such thinking represents a fateful, typically American dodging of the reality of social class divisions, which are arguably more fundamental than racial divisions in perpetuating social injustice. In legal terms, there is a good reason for the dodge: the law can address injustices based solely on race, but, because it protects private property and the freedom of capital to invest or disinvest as its owners see fit, the law cannot as easily address injustices rooted in economic class distinctions.

Not surprisingly, then, our national conventional wisdom on the subject of class has always downplayed its importance. There may be dramatic, even intolerable disparities of income and opportunity in our society, the conventional wisdom says, but there is also a saving grace: the sheer dynamism and fluidity of our market economy, democratic polity, and open culture ensure that no specific individual or group need be trapped at the bottom of the social scale. Low birth and bad luck are formidable obstacles, but they are also less decisive in America than anywhere else. Any family may go "from shirtsleeves to shirtsleeves" in a few generations as fortunes are won, lost, and won again. Thus, in the traditional American capitalist view, individual capacity and our protean economy reinforce each other, creating a kind of permanent revolution; each generation of Americans, from the lowliest immigrants to scions of wealth, must be sent out onto its playing fields and trained for its rigors. No matter which players win or lose, society as a whole reaps the rewards of their strivings.

There has been a great deal of merit to this argument. Capitalism's ability to free society from the constraints of stultifying traditions and castes was a great human triumph, a source not only of its own dynamism and innovation but also, through its promotion of the law as a way to protect contractual relations, of considerable individual freedom. Marx was more forthright in acknowledging this than many of his followers were. But he also held that the human liberation offered by the bourgeois social contract had its limits, and he noted that even America's unusually fluid and dynamic form of capitalism had a permanent exception—blacks, who were denied basic political and economic rights by the framers of the Constitution. Even after slavery, in the left's view, capitalism was impelled by its very nature to exploit labor, driving down wages by maintaining "a reserve army of the unemployed"; the classical liberal capitalist society thus had to marginalize and, in effect, dehumanize a portion of its people. Racism, by excluding black people from the social compact, gave the rest of America a continuing rationale for that dehumanization.

The historical necessity of racism thus kept most of the society, through its media, popular culture, electoral politics, and formal government, from addressing straightforwardly the deepening of social class divisions. That is why the left, eager to discredit the American fantasy of a society without permanent classes and to sow a different sort of revolution whose goal is classlessness itself, championed racial equality. Weaving the black thread right into the center of the social fabric by organizing for economic justice is really a way to unravel the fabric itself, exposing its contradictions and lies: with blacks visible and insistent, Americans won't be able to delude themselves any longer about the exploitation at the heart of the system.

In the 1960s, as we have seen, liberals welcomed the left's challenge, confident that the wealthiest and most powerful nation on earth could offer opportunity to everyone. All that was needed was some collective action to curb monopolies and to lift the bottom of the social scale in order to give people the basics of opportunity. Indeed, the New Deal and the wartime and cold-war economies outflanked the radical left for more than forty years. So abundant was the economy of the late 1950s and 1960s that liberals believed that legal guarantees of civil rights would by themselves unleash economic freedom for blacks and, through their progress as producers and consumers, greater prosperity for all.

But a catch in the liberal dispensation has caught up with it: the wealthiest and most powerful nation on earth has become an increasingly interdependent part of a larger world capitalism that has no stake in America's resolution of its own inequities. If the Communists earlier failed to win Americans to their vision of inevitable confrontation and complete social reconstruction, liberals seem now to have failed in their promise of energetic legal accommodation based on an ever-expanding, ever more balanced economy. Expanding, the economy might still be; balanced and controlled by Americans, it is not. Unskilled, low-skilled, and blue-collar workers and the unemployed—categories encompassing a majority of the nation's blacks—are the losers.

For them, the default of the liberal promise is all the more galling for the fanfare with which it was affirmed by the War on Poverty, the Great Society, and the New York liberal tradition. At the 1963 March on Washington, Martin Luther King characterized constitutional guarantees of liberty and the pursuit of happiness as a kind of "promissory note" which blacks had finally come to cash. "We refuse to believe that the bank of justice is bankrupt," he added, putting liberals on the line not only politically but, as his metaphor suggested, economically. Nearly thirty years later, with the emergence of the very term "underclass," the old left's insistence on the intractability of social class divisions seems to have reasserted itself in American life with a kind of spectral vengeance, mocking liberal integrationists' faith in the equal-opportunity myth.

Traditional liberals cling to the faith that the economy can be variably taxed, regulated, and subsidized in order to forestall destitution in some quarters and buy social peace in others. So doing, they hand easy targets not only to the Marxist left but also to conservatives like George Gilder, Charles Murray, and Lawrence Mead. Like most liberals, the conservatives accept the basic economic structure as given; but as liberals' tinkering with that structure fails, conservatives charge them with coddling the poor into chronic dependency and distorting capitalism through irresponsible impositions that also undermine the culture of individual merit and initiative. In other words, liberals and blacks are to blame for unemployment and its ravages—not capitalists and their apologists. Stung, some liberals have edged rightward, blaming the left and even the underclass itself for the intractable new poverty. They have largely acquiesced in the conservative drive for a restoration of the classical myth of individual opportunity, calling for the social rehabilitation of those who, despite liberal efforts to expand opportunity, have declined to suit up and come out on the field.

But it isn't only or even primarily poor people who weasel out of the risks and rigors of the opportunity game; working, middle-class, and rich people do it too, through such elaborate protections as union featherbedding, political "seldom show" jobs, regressive taxation, and exotic but enormous tax deductions on everything from vacation homes to deliberately unproductive investments. These only harden class lines and deepen the poor's isolation, even amid legal progress against overt racial discrimination. No wonder the early civil rights movement's faith in legally mandated racial integration as a way out of poverty has been rejected by so many of its black legatees. No wonder, on the other side, that a minor branch of neoconservative scholarship has dedicated itself to exploring not the new economic underpinnings of class division that render legal progress against racism almost moot but the extent to which King was a tool of Communist advisers intent upon sowing such division.

In fact, King did have Communist advisers, and his evolution was consistent with the left's hope that if blacks could be mobilized to demand civil rights and, through them, more jobs and public services, they would help delegitimize the system by putting it under unbearable strain. Thus, while the language of the latter-day civil rights movement has remained that of legal rights, its agenda has been deeper, potentially more revolutionary: it aims to redistribute benefits according to race as well as according to individual effort and achievement, in order to drive home its point that racial discrimination masks economic injustice. Yet it is impossible to uphold both individual merit and racial-group claims at once; defending the latter constrains not only black but also white individuals to define themselves, at least provisionally, as members of aggrieved groups. One's surname or skin color becomes by itself a means to advancement, and that undermines the classical liberal American ideal in which individuals are held significantly responsible for their fates and rewarded according to their performance. That ideal has never been realized, of course; the question is whether we should be striving to realize it. Explicitly or otherwise, the latter-day civil rights movement says we should not.

A compelling example of the problem arose in 1985, when the New York Police Department promoted to sergeant 180 black and Hispanic officers who had failed the examination for that rank, in order to settle a suit brought by minority officers charging that the exam had been biased against people of color. A far higher proportion of black and Hispanic officers had failed the sergeant's test than had whites. That didn't prove that the test was discriminatory; it

might simply have meant that proportionately fewer minority officers were prepared to handle the exam, which emphasized levels of
reading and writing skills that minorities notoriously lack by virtue
of poor early schooling. But, under the law, the minority plaintiffs
didn't actually have to prove racial discrimination; they had to prove
only that skills the test demanded were irrelevant to job performance—presumably evoking memories of the exotic "civics" exams
administered by southern elections officials to prevent blacks from
qualifying to vote.

That analogy is outrageous, of course; the city badly wanted more
minority officers and brass to police its increasingly minority population. But, according to a mayoral panel and consultant who studied
it, the test was indeed poorly correlated with the skills actually demanded by the job; and the city, believing that it would lose the
minority officers' case on that ground, agreed in a settlement to promote blacks and Hispanics, under a one time racial quota, in the
proportions in which they'd taken the test, not the much lower proportions in which they'd passed. But this meant that while whites
who'd failed the test were not promoted, many blacks and Hispanics
who'd failed it were. Not surprisingly, white officers whose scores
had been equal to or better than those of the new minority sergeants,
yet who had not been promoted, brought their own suit, to no avail;
the courts held that they had filed too late.

At that point, six officers who were classified in police records as
white, and some of whom were in fact light complexioned, stepped
forward to announce that they were really minorities. They invoked
the rule that if one of an officer's parents is black or Hispanic, the
officer may be classified as such, too. Thus, officers who upon entering the department had identified themselves as white suddenly
claimed, by virtue of their own or their mothers' surnames or either
parent's race, to be members of groups entitled to redress. They were
duly promoted—a blunt demonstration that individual merit and
performance, as measured by the department's admittedly flawed
examination, had become irrelevant to advancement in at least one
highly visible sector of American society. It was a long way from
Martin Luther King's hope that his children would someday be
judged by "the content of their character, not the color of their skin."
Liberal legalism had made that impossible.

Litigation versus Politics

The dubious racial remedies applied in the case of the police sergeants' exam show that if America's capitalist "permanent revolution" is flawed, so is the overreliance of black and leftist activists on the law as an agent of social change. Ultimately, as blacks and leftists ought to know, laws are not handed down by Olympians; within limits set by the Constitution as it is interpreted by judges, laws are written in response to the power which organized groups bring to bear on public officials through elections. Elections, in turn, influence not just legislation but, as the historian Fred Siegel has demonstrated, the appointment of the judges who interpret the Constitution, to which all legislation is answerable.

As Siegel summarizes their dilemma, liberals and the left, confronted with the seemingly implacable racism of defensive majorities, made those majorities even angrier when they substituted litigation like that which produced the police quota for the politics of the early civil rights movement. From risking their lives to register blacks to vote during Mississippi Summer to ringing doorbells for Eugene McCarthy's antiwar presidential candidacy in 1968, from organizing community groups in the slums of Newark to fielding suburban political crusades led by the peripatetic activist Allard Lowenstein, hundreds of thousands of young Americans had thrown themselves into the politics of persuasion and made the system bend.

But it did not bend far or fast enough, so, "instead of attempting to reconcile popular concerns with procedural fairness," Siegel writes, "liberals fled to the courts to impose their vision of justice. More and more dependent on the courts, liberals forgot how to talk to most Americans, forgot how to build public support through persuasion." That spawned an electoral backlash, leading to the Reagan counter-revolution and, through it, a more conservative judiciary, which has begun to reverse the liberals' legal gains. Not surprisingly, the Reagan Justice Department entered a friend-of-the-court brief in support of the white police officers who had not been promoted. Though they did not prevail, their sense of grievance was a harbinger of things to come.

In a dozen other realms and fields, radical lawyers and liberal administrators had throughout the 1970s used the equal-protection clause of the Fourteenth Amendment to conjoin rights with race. Reasoning backward from obvious inequalities in the conditions of blacks and whites to "find" discrimination whether or not it had actually occurred, they prescribed racially targeted legal remedies. So doing, they soon discovered the limits of the law's ability to untangle the pathologies of white racism in a capitalist economy. By substituting court-imposed formulas for communication and bargaining, they eroded community standards, like those discussed by Bushwick's Gasper Signorelli, cited in chapters 4 and 5, that were sometimes provincial but also sometimes profoundly supportive of human dignity. Legal activists mistook communally supported restraints, such as expulsions of disruptive students and screenings of applicants to housing projects, for racist repression, simply because those mechanisms disproportionately affected blacks. By substituting racial-group entitlements for opportunities and sanctions dependent upon individual behavior and communal consensus, they sundered the bond between rights and responsibilities, with tragic consequences for those most in need of the security and, through it, the freedom that communal restraints provide. Siegel explains,

In the name of equal opportunity, court-ordered liberalism replaced merit testing for teachers with pass/fail tests and quotas, so that academic mobility for minority students was undermined by professional mobility for minority teachers. In the name of integration, court-ordered busing resegregated the big-city school systems. In the name of fairness, judicial liberalism demanded due process in order to reprimand rowdy pupils, producing a disorder manifestly unfair to the vast majority of their classmates.

The result is a diffuse demoralization as both blacks and whites who can afford to do so desert public institutions en masse. Black parents who do not want their children confined with troublemakers in public schools make every effort to pay parochial school tuitions. Good teachers seek appointments in good private schools or in public systems in suburbs, sometimes even at a cut in pay. Stable households escape public housing whenever they can, causing the projects to decline.

The tenant screening discussed in chapter 2 is worth examining more closely in this light. Without question, screening out households with histories of crime, delinquency, and antisocial habits denies housing to needy, predominantly black families unless they're given alternative housing with support services. But that same screening is a significant boon to needy, predominantly black families who remain in the projects. It also provides a powerful incentive for all potential applicants to conform to basic social norms. And, one might argue, it expresses the faith that people can indeed "conform," whatever their economic condition. Such early postwar low-income-housing advocates as Roger Starr and Ira Robbins saw in the creative public housing manager a socializing agent for urban newcomers; the manager's efforts could complement those of the teacher, local cop, and ward heeler.

But in the late 1960s these agents of social control, most of them white, came under assault by people who could not understand that the respect for rights which they were demanding takes shape only in a delicate social ecology. Eventually, courts upheld some nonracial screening criteria, but too late to save many public housing projects. Opponents of screening forgot that not all social institutions with strict regulations are enforcers of racial caste distinctions, that not all discipline is repression, that project managers are not southern sheriffs. As Siegel puts it,

Liberals have always rightly worried about the threat of state and corporate power to individual autonomy, but they should worry as well about how unfettered appetite can undermine the self-discipline necessary for that autonomy. . . . Liberals at one and the same time have insisted that neither they nor anyone else had a right to tell the black poor how to live and that it was the financial and social responsibility of the government to see to it that people were lifted out of poverty. It's been an unworkable combination.

For "government" read "taxpayers," and another dimension of the problem becomes clear. If we would ask the voters and taxpayers to support the expansion of civil rights and foot the bill for improving opportunities for the poor, then we have to present them with collective results beyond the expansion of minorities' civil rights. We have to show them another return on the investment: a spirit of social reciprocity, obligation, and productivity on the part of those who have been helped. If we do not, people will vote against social-justice initiatives.

Above all, it is important to be consistent. We cannot ask people to condemn the occasional injustice perpetrated by an overzealous project manager, teacher, or cop and at the same time ask them to overlook the occasional abuse perpetrated by an affirmative action program that drives out a competent person in favor of someone ill prepared for the job. We cannot mute our concern for due process, as the New York Civil Liberties Union did during the Ocean Hill–Brownsville battles, when a black school board abruptly expels white teachers, and then call for the suspension of a white school board that has resisted the "due process" of a court-ordered busing plan, as the NYCLU did in Canarsie in 1973. When black leaders convened a "blacks only" meeting at a public high school in Brooklyn after the Howard Beach tragedy, the NYCLU condemned this obvious violation of civil rights only after some hesitation and confusion, and then only because it had been challenged to do so. In such cases, politically moderate whites rightly suspect civil libertarians and civil rights activists of working primarily to advance black interests as part of a larger, radical political strategy based on race.

Nowhere has this been clearer than in the realm of crime and law enforcement. Middle-class communities besieged by crime have become mistrustful of the courts, which they see as hamstrung by due process considerations that release criminals to strike again, and of the police, who sometimes excuse their inaction against predators by citing the civil libertarians' abolition of loitering laws and their tightening of the search and seizure provisions of the Fourth Amendment. Whatever the real reasons for court and police inaction—understaffing and bureaucratic self-protection also come to mind—such communities are turning to private justice through private patrols, paid and voluntary, and residents like Signorelli are forced to refine their sense of danger and their responses to it.

To such people, the civil libertarian Gara LaMarche, a former executive director of the Texas CLU, has an answer. In a 1988 *New York Newsday* essay, he wrote,

Obviously, it's a lot easier to blame the ACLU for police inaction when that's convenient than it is to build the community relations that are vital to effective law enforcement. Clearly-defined laws which proscribe criminal conduct, not bad attitudes or low status—these are not some recent efforts at misguided social engineering. They originate in the Constitution. In the tension between liberty and order, individual freedom and state power, the Bill of Rights declares a clear preference. When schools fail to educate, when jobs aren't there anyway, when the most prosperous and admired person in the community is the pusher or the pimp, the exclusionary rule and loitering laws are the least of the obstacles we face in the battle against crime.

To civil libertarians, loitering laws and the admission of evidence that has not been seized in technical compliance with the law open a slippery slope toward state oppression. "Should we restore the anti-loitering laws and give cops the power to round up people who've committed no crime? Reading [a Brooklyn resident's] account of his middle-class neighbors' loose application of the term 'underclass,' it's not hard to guess who would be the targets of enhanced political activity in this area." But this is too easy: to clinch his argument, LaMarche stereotypes neighborhood residents like Signorelli in much the same way he accuses them of stereotyping transients or familiar vagrants and derelicts on their blocks, and that simply is not fair.

LaMarche misses the fact that there is another slippery slope, one that leads from the toleration of destructive or threatening behavior in residential communities to the collapse of those communities. Regrettably, the battle against crime has to be fought in the streets as well as at meetings of the police precinct's community council or in the political arena, where LaMarche would rightly have us call for jobs and justice. When informal local restraints break down, people are more likely to wind up killing than tolerating or supporting one another. There is an essential cultural and emotional connection, discussed in chapter 5, between neighborhood residents' hard-won street savvy and suspicions of certain strangers, on the one hand, and their ability to trust and act on their more generous impulses, on the other.

A liberal legalism that devalues those street instincts forces people to live a lie—to pretend, for example, that they don't really know whether the woman wearing a tight, short skirt and standing at one in the morning near a streetlight on a corner where there has been much prostitution is a prostitute, or that the young men prowling a street that has been hit with a number of burglaries and muggings recently are not to be confronted and driven away if they cannot account for themselves. If you can tell yourself that Signorelli and others who would confront such strangers are racists, your task is made easier. It certainly is made easier by the actions of youths, less sophisticated than Signorelli, who engage in irresponsible vigilantism against strangers, and by the actions of cops like those who mercilessly beat Gerard Papa and Arnold Rampersant.

But such exceptions cannot always determine the rules. Especially maddening to those who would restore a balance between rights and responsibilities is the inconsistency between civil libertarians' responses to abuses by predators and their responses to abuses by community residents fighting crime. Was a violent criminal released on a technicality to prey again on innocent people? That's the price we pay for upholding civil liberties, liberals might say. The courts aren't perfect; you will get some mistakes. Why, then, if a community patrol member or cop oversteps his bounds to frighten away a loiterer, won't liberal legalitarians accept the same response?

The answer, I think, is that left-leaning civil libertarians want to raise our sights, as LaMarche does in the passage cited above, beyond the immediate danger to the larger sources of misery that produced it. They are right to emphasize that even the most draconian law enforcement will never bring safety to a society that does not provide its poor, and especially its minority members, with decent education and jobs. But they are wrong to think that residents of beleaguered communities don't know this and, like Signorelli, endorse social programs to lift people out of poverty and crime. Civil libertarians don't seem to understand that knowing all about capitalist exploitation and racism and working to change them don't make any difference to neighborhoods besieged by violent criminals.

A final example of the folly of litigation driven by racial agendas has been the activists' charge, since the 1960s, that New York's electoral system is permeated with racism. With their approval, three of the city's five boroughs have been subjected to such detailed scrutiny by the Justice Department under provisions of the Voting Rights Act that Washington has to approve the change of a polling place's location, let alone the redrawing of an election district line, as racially neutral in terms of its likely impact on election outcomes. They persuaded the courts to abolish at-large City Council seats on the grounds that minorities could not hope to win them. They charged that the city's runoff primary system made the election of a minority candidate virtually impossible (a second primary must be held among the top-two vote getters in any contest for citywide office, should neither receive 40 percent of the vote in the first round). They won abolition of the city's central governing body, the Board of Estimate, rather than the weighting of its members' votes to conform to the principle of one person, one vote.

Yet, in 1989, with the supposedly racist runoff primary and Board of Estimate still in place, Dinkins won the mayoralty; a woman, Elizabeth Holtzman, won the comptroller's office; and three of the five borough presidencies were won by two women (one of them replacing Dinkins in the Manhattan borough presidency) and a Hispanic man. No one inquired whether these and other minority electoral successes, which can be expected to grow as the city becomes less white, should trigger the removal of Manhattan, Brooklyn, and the Bronx from the purview of the Justice Department under the Voting Rights Act.

The failure to draw distinctions between systems that are clearly racist in intent and those that do not prevent minorities from registering, voting, and winning office has also led to the ludicrous "empowerment" of an enlarged City Council under the same new City Charter that virtually dethrones the presidents of the city's five boroughs. The theory is that more—and hence smaller—council districts, drawn "correctly" by a commission whose membership reflects the city's racial mix, will reinforce racially homogeneous communities, thereby all but ensuring the election of more minority members. The reality is that such council members, who will no longer have to forge consensus among diverse constituencies in order to get elected, will be even more parochial and hence more manipulable by the council speaker and the mayor than the lackluster crop that preceded them. That is a prescription for tyranny in matters of substance and for increased racial polarization in matters of principle. The old system badly needed rejuvenation, but structural reorganization that reinforces turf-based racial distinctions was not the way to do it.

The use of the law to advance racial-group rights rather than to guarantee color-blind opportunity will always backfire in American political culture, not only because it generates racist backlash but, more fatefully, because as in the abolition of tenant screening by nonracial criteria, it dissolves the consensual norms without which there can be no opportunity and no inclusion. Institutions that have been procedurally "cleansed" according to strict due process criteria become sterile; Siegel cites the old aphorism "If you purify the pond, the water lilies die." That is the heart of the American Dilemma: how to revitalize a consensual politics that doesn't have to rely on racially motivated legal cleansings of our institutions as its primary levers of social change.

A Gilded Cage

In the autumn of 1987, as the Howard Beach case was coming to trial, a state civil servant showed Assemblyman Dov Hikind an affirmative action "training manual," already distributed to ninety employees of the State Insurance Fund, that contained the following statement: "All White individuals in our society are racist. Even if a White is totally free of all conscious racial prejudice, he remains a racist, for he receives benefits distributed by a White racist society through its institutions."

Hikind represents a young, politically conservative, religiously Orthodox Jewish constituency that has grown dramatically over the past fifteen years in the Borough Park section of Brooklyn. The only thing remarkable about the vehement protest he lodged was the minimal response it received. The legislature's Black and Puerto Rican Caucus issued a statement saying that the manual had been designed merely "to promote discussion" and accused Hikind of "inflaming" racial tensions. The newspapers carried obligatory reports of the exchanges. The manual was duly withdrawn. But from the broad political plain that separated the perfervid Hikind and his defensive black colleagues there issued little more than a few angry letters to legislators and newspapers.

There is, of course, a theoretical analysis behind the manual's statement, which is really a kind of shorthand explanation of the concept of institutionalized racism. As the Queens College sociologist Stephen Steinberg elaborates it, "if the cumulative disadvantages that ensue from past racism leave many blacks without the education and skills to compete for the better jobs, we are left with patterns of racial exclusion and inequality even if employers are not personally motivated by racial prejudice." Whites, it follows, remain the beneficiaries of inequities that are the bitter fruits of slavery and the degradation of blacks under Jim Crow. Those inequities persist not simply through whites' conscious discrimination—of which there is plenty—but, more subtly and tenaciously, in the blighting legacy of low skills, low income, psychological damage, and pathology into which so many blacks are born. To the extent, then, that whites wave the flag on the Fourth of July or otherwise celebrate institutions allegedly built on these historic deprivations, they are racists.

But what are the remedies? How are whites to get out from under such opprobrium? Presumably, a program of affirmative action, which the manual was meant to introduce, offers one answer. It reflects the notion, unique to America, that because there is such a thing as institutional racism, it is appropriate for government, under the equal-protection clause of the Fourteenth Amendment, to mandate the reconfiguration of institutional hiring and admissions procedures with the intent of increasing minority representation in the ranks of employees or students. Not only does that set a far higher standard of social justice than any applied by organizations that document abuses of human rights in other countries around the globe; it grates on the sensibilities of many Americans who do hold themselves and their society to a high standard when it comes to providing opportunity free of racism, "institutional" or otherwise. Certainly, if the manual's finding of universal white racism was intended to administer a moral shock that in turn would generate a thoroughgoing reform of American institutions, it has proved a rather poorer goad than the court rulings and laws under which Jim Crow was dismantled in the South.

That is because, unintentionally, the manual poses a far more troubling question: if the society remains incorrigibly racist after all the efforts of the past twenty-five years, institutional and informal, collective and personal, to open up opportunities for blacks, is there really anything more to be done, except, perhaps, for blacks to dream of turning the tables and kicking whites out of jobs in order to take them for themselves? Hikind thought the manual was headed in precisely that direction.

But then, why did the manual's statement occasion so little protest—or, for that matter, so little determined support from blacks? Quite possibly it was ignored because it was widely, if only implicitly, understood not as a black call to arms but as a waving of the white flag of black despair. It was a reflection of what Shelby Steele calls the "race fatigue" of a black affirmative action elite: the unending, tiring, and ultimately tiresome effort to expand the definition of racism as a way to explain so many blacks' dispiriting failure to advance—or, as we have seen in the case of voting rights, to keep on expanding it even when blacks have indeed advanced.

Proponents of the state manual's analysis have adapted this explanation, if not their political style, from nationalist militants who believe that blacks must retain an adversarial stance toward a society that does not wish to absorb them. The manual has been but one of a number of efforts to extend, by legal and bureaucratic fiat, special provisions that guarantee upward mobility or, failing that, a unique, protected status to blacks in the economy and the polity. (Attempts to reconfigure the public school curriculum along the lines of the manual's assumptions are discussed in chapter 8.) And yet, while affirmative action has indeed helped some qualified blacks enter fields which antidiscrimination laws had not opened, there is less and less evidence today that such special protections will bring many gains, even in the affirmative action elite's own job development terms. They don't seem likely to outweigh by very much the capacity of whatever political muscle blacks can develop, as other groups did before them, to compel ethnic succession in public and private institutions. In case of New York City's police department, for example, the election of a black mayor, and his appointment of a black police commissioner, makes it unlikely that examinations for promotion will be racially biased or that litigation and quotas will be necessary to increase minority representation on the force.

Nor can affirmative action provisions outstrip by very much the actual credentialing of blacks for the positions they seek, even under relaxed certification standards. With fewer blacks graduating from college now than ten years ago, even the drive to alter college admissions standards in their favor has not produced significantly more black applicants for positions as teachers, academics, lawyers, and doctors. For all the talk about white public school faculties that don't reflect their minority student populations, school systems are hardly besieged by black applicants. With or without affirmative action, the teaching staff of the New York City public schools is expected to turn over by up to 50 percent over the next ten years, yet there is simply a dearth of blacks with the requisite minimum qualifications applying to replace departing whites. Surely such a system, so desperately short of teachers and under such pressure to field a faculty resembling its students that it imports hundreds of teachers from Puerto Rico and South America each year, would leap at the opportunity to hire qualified blacks.

The bewilderment experienced by white administrators who desperately want but cannot find qualified blacks was evident in the city corporation counsel Allen Schwartz's response "more in sorrow than in anger," to a charge in a *Village Voice* article that his office had shut out black lawyers. Schwartz detailed an aggressive outreach program that had included pleas, by mail and phone, to minority elected officials to forward to him the résumés of young black lawyers. An embarrassing silence had been the only response. Schwartz recounted that almost all the minority candidates he did try to recruit through other means had turned him down; they were intent on working for the much higher salaries offered by private firms.

Something similar was highlighted in 1989, when the Reverend Ben Chavis of the National Council of Churches wrote to seventeen well-known environmentalist organizations charging them with "racism" because they employed so few blacks. Only in the most apologetic manner, filled with acknowledgments that their minority-hiring record is "miserable," did the heads of those organizations suggest that one of the reasons might be that few blacks seek careers in environmental science or in poorly paid activism that isn't oriented toward civil rights. Even if racism somehow accounted for the paucity of black applicants, was it the environmentalists' racism, as Chavis charged? Wasn't it rather true that many of the civic idealists in these organizations who apologized to Chavis would, like the city's corporation counsel, have fallen all over themselves to hire any qualified black person who'd walked through their doors?

Experiences like these lead many white bureaucrats and professionals to two sad conclusions. First, if the attitudes behind the activists' pronouncements are representative, too many blacks who are positioned to take advantage of special tutoring, scholarship, and other assistance programs have failed to do so; some have stopped following Martin Luther King's admonition to "burn the midnight oil" in order to compete with their white counterparts, demanding instead a formulaic inclusion on the grounds that stipulated qualifications are not only irrelevant to job performance but intentionally racist as well. Second, blacks who make such bureaucratic demands have stopped making King's emotional and spiritual demands that whites "give a damn," that they reach out to minorities as individuals, to welcome them into the shared work of the society, as more than a few whites did try to do in the 1960s. The black affirmative action elite has given up all this in exchange for a bureaucratically sanctioned slice of the pie. It has given up, in short, on interracial trust, on any sense of a common endeavor. The claim "All White individuals in our society are racist" says, in effect, that since whites once drew a rigid color line against blacks, some blacks will now use what little moral advantage they have gained from persecution to draw a color line right back against whites.

That posture and whites' defensive and by now often cynical reactions to it foreclose honest discussion of the reasons why so much effort to end discrimination and segregation in the 1960s produced so little. By positing racism as the only explanation, Chavis and the manual paradoxically let whites off the hook; morally safe behind the color line which blacks, too, have now drawn, those whites who are inclined to be cynical, or who are offended by charges that they are racist, can enjoy a reprieve from self-examination as long as they fork over a few more jobs. The new color line assures them that no one expects a genuine moral commitment to social justice. When Carolyn Pitts, a black affirmative action officer at the State Insurance Fund who had prepared and distributed the manual, was fired a month after the controversy because she had falsified her résumé to claim that she had graduated from Brooklyn College—in fact, she had not attended college at all—some whites I spoke with in state government rolled their eyes, winked at me, and yawned. "What did you expect?" one asked. Justifiably or not, he had no expectation of personal accountability, honesty in public communication, or interracial trust from those blacks he regarded as "affirmative action cases."

And so the noncontroversy over the manual raises familiar questions: At this point in our history, is there anything to be gained by such frontal assaults on racism? Or is it time for blacks to do more with what they have—to take advantage of such open doors, scholarships, stipends, and affirmative action programs as are already in place to become teachers, lawyers, and engineers? Why does the affirmative action elite keep demanding more guarantees? Shelby Steele suggests it is because blacks are afraid to walk through those doors:

Integration shock is essentially the shock of being suddenly accountable on strictly personal terms. It occurs in situations that disallow race as an excuse for personal shortcomings and it therefore exposes vulnerabilities that were previously hidden. . . . When one lacks the courage to face oneself fully, a fear of hidden vulnerabilities triggers a fright-flight response to integration shock. Instead of admitting that racism has declined, we argue all the harder that it is still alive and more insidious than ever. We [blacks] hold race up to shield us from what we do not want to see in ourselves. . . .

To be sure, whites who take a perverse moral comfort from debacles like Pitts's are also using race as a hedge against personal responsibility; they, too, would rather point a finger of blame—"Blacks are ruining everything, dragging standards down"—than confront their own laziness or ignorance. Steele's insight is that such white hypocrisy no more excuses blacks' evasions of personal responsibility than blacks' failings, whatever their origins, excuse whites.

A Hard Case

That vigilance against discrimination is preferable to formulaic affirmative action is best illustrated by a case in which the benevolent management of Starrett City, a huge Brooklyn housing development, attempted a policy of affirmative action for white applicants in order to promote an integrated, rather than an all-minority, community.

Rising on former marshland on Jamaica Bay at the edge of Brooklyn, just a few hundred yards but also a world away from the ravaged neighborhood of East New York, Starrett City's gleaming towers and neatly landscaped grounds are home to a community of 15,000, with its own public school and shopping center. The country's largest federally subsidized housing development, Starrett was built in 1973 as part of New York City's answer to the suburban exodus— part of an effort to hold the middle-income tax base. This "new town" was also a response to racial change in the neighborhoods many of its residents had left behind. "A monument to fear" was how some critics described Starrett, with its original quota of 30 percent for minorities. Local politicians feared losing white votes they needed to stay in office, and the Starrett Corporation (then teetering at the edge of bankruptcy) feared a threat to profitability.

None of these fears were spurious, least of all those of Starrett whites bludgeoned out of Brownsville and East New York by black crime and the many effects of disinvestment accompanying blacks' arrival. Yet now qualified minority applicants who'd had nothing to do with crime—except that they'd often suffered it themselves and, just like whites, were trying to flee it—were enduring discriminatory treatment on the part of Starrett management. White families obtained apartments in two months, whereas blacks, on average, languished for twenty.

Starrett management's assumptions were clear, and Jefferson Morley, writing in the *New Republic,* articulated them well: "If the minority population . . . grew much larger than 30 percent, Starrett would almost certainly 'tip'—whites would begin to move out. . . . Starrett was sure to attract black tenants. But if it wanted a stable, middle-income project, it had to attract—and keep—a large number of whites." Racial tipping, in short, inevitably brings instability and decay. Integration isn't just an admirable idea but, as Morley put it, "a practical necessity" to protect black residents as well as whites— even if that meant relying on stigmatizing quotas that allowed whites to "buck" Starrett's waiting list, which had many more qualified blacks than whites.

Must racial tipping always bring decay, as it did in Brownsville and East New York? A different scenario is to be found in the city's experience. Whites might move out as more blacks arrived, but they might well be leaving a Starrett City as exemplary as the middle- and solidly working-class black developments of Esplanade Gardens, Lenox Terrace, Riverton, River Bend, Atlantic Plaza Towers, and others whose success is apparently unknown to most commentators. Starrett, too, might remain a model community were it to accept, on a racially blind first-come, first-serve basis, the many fine applicants it could cull from the 9,000 minority families on its waiting list of 14,000. Starrett could screen them by nonracial criteria which courts had by then upheld and which black residents have been the first to demand and use successfully in many developments where they predominate.

If site-specific integration isn't always a precondition for black social stability, then the demise of integration at Starrett, if it indeed occurred, has to be weighed against the gain for blacks of thousands of decent apartments in a housing market that has limited their options even more severely than those of whites. There are compelling arguments for integration, but blacks' putative need to live in integrated communities in order to be protected from themselves simply isn't among them. Housing opportunity, not integration, was certainly the primary goal of five black plaintiffs who in the early 1980s brought a class action suit on behalf of the 9,000 minority applicants on Starrett's waiting list. They argued that preserving integration at Starrett City through a race quota could not be society's primary goal if achieving it meant limiting the housing options of disadvantaged yet deserving blacks.

Nonetheless, in 1984, Starrett management won the day by insisting on the negative consequences of tipping. Under a settlement hammered out in a federal district court, Starrett's race-based occupancy controls would be preserved, with a ceiling of 40 percent minority tenants. It was an accommodation built, ironically, on affirmative action principles—this time benefiting whites, in the service of integration. As Morley noted, if one believed in affirmative action as a legal strategy to promote integration, one had to defend Starrett's ceiling on blacks. "I am a social engineer," Starrett's manager, Robert Rosenberg, declared proudly.

For a Reagan Justice Department opposed to affirmative action, here was an opportunity not to be missed—a chance to establish legal precedents against affirmative action by siding with the black plaintiffs and the NAACP in opposing the Starrett settlement. The department sued to overturn the agreement, arguing that only a color-blind admissions process meets the essential test of due process. It won on appeal, and Starrett has since had to admit applicants on a racially neutral, first-come, first-served basis.

The NAACP, embarrassed at being joined by the Justice Department, tried to save the principle of affirmative action by distinguishing "inclusionary quotas," designed to bring in those historically kept out, from Starrett's ceiling on the number of blacks, which was clearly "stigmatizing and exclusionary," designed to keep a majority of blacks out in order to cater to whites' fears of racial change. In rebuttal, Morley contended that blacks excluded from Starrett are no more unfairly treated than Brian Weber or Allan Bakke, two white men who had brought suit challenging affirmative action programs which had in effect denied them, respectively, employment and admission to medical school. Morley added, "Occupancy controls at Starrett City can be viewed as 'inclusionary'—for whites and, notably, for blacks who would otherwise not get to live in an integrated community."

That last point recalls the old "Jewish quota" of 12 percent at a number of Ivy League colleges in the 1930s. Its purpose, of course, was not to remedy a dearth of Jewish representation but to restrain what, on demographics and merit alone, might otherwise have been a surfeit. Did that mean that Ivy League admissions officers feared Jews? Heavens, no! Some of them would have insisted. The point was to open to a reasonable number of Jewish students the felicities of gentlemanly life. As private educational institutions, these schools had every right to control their population mix in the interests of diversity, of course. The housing market, particularly a publicly subsidized portion of it, is something else again. Even if housing developments may screen tenants on the basis of behavior, they have no right to do so on the basis of race, as Roger Starr and other public housing advocates always acknowledged.

Consider what color-blind admissions at Starrett means. Whites on the waiting list lose only the preferential treatment they enjoyed, not equal treatment; no whites on the waiting list are denied on the basis of color. Surely, no stigma results for whites under such circumstances. Meanwhile, blacks gain equal, not preferential, treatment. That is why there is something mystifying about the argument that blacks excluded from Starrett under its old quota system were no more unfairly treated than Bakke or Weber. These men's frustrations were real, precisely because they were acknowledged to be as well qualified as blacks hired or admitted preferentially instead of them. No one had argued that these two would bring deterioration with them, and therefore no stigma attached to their exclusion. Rather, they were being asked to share the burden of scarcities that blacks had hitherto borne disproportionately. Even that might be too much to ask: that blacks and whites must fight over scarce jobs, training programs, and housing is an indictment of society's leaders and investment priorities, not an argument for affirmative action. But at least the traditional affirmative action programs did not reinforce negative assumptions about those they excluded. Starrett's occupancy controls did.

That the Justice Department was right is evidenced by the subsequent history of Starrett City. It has remained integrated, and whites have continued to apply for apartments. As we have seen, developments and neighborhoods that have tipped racially have decayed in part because managements and landlords have reduced their investments in security and repairs, ultimately turning their buildings over to exploiters as blacks arrived in numbers. Such policies increased white hostility toward the newcomers and hastened white flight. Not so in Starrett City. Working closely with the tenants in place at the time of the new ruling, management rallied to keep up the development. Even if Starrett does tip racially, the success of other middle-class black developments in the city highlights the critical issue that defenders of the quotas ignored and that the Justice Department may have raised only opportunistically: the unconscionable imposition of a stigma upon blacks by excluding them.

If blacks are ever to be truly integrated into society so that whites no longer need fear them, their access to decent housing and jobs must be considered more important than integration as such at any one site, particularly integration achieved through discriminatory practices. Broad-based equal opportunity—not quotas—is a necessary, even if not sufficient, condition for the dissolution of white fears. One needn't revert to hoary defenses of "separate but equal" facilities to argue that color-blind but otherwise cannily managed opportunity such as that maintained now at Starrett is the only route to stability and decency, for blacks as well as whites. The relatively unimpeded advances of other ethnic groups, from Jews to Koreans, in neighborhoods they "take over" from older, white residents is ample testimony to that fact.

Racial tipping can be culturally disruptive, but its linkage to "inevitable" deterioration is illusory and unacceptable as a premise for public policy. Starr, even though he has become a neoconservative in the years since he first championed public housing, told me that he could not have supported Starrett's "benign" quotas against blacks, because he could never bring himself to, in effect, post a notice telling black applicants that they need not apply or that they must wait a year and a half longer than white applicants to secure an apartment. This time, the NAACP and black housing activists who opposed Starrett's controls were right, even if they were joined by a hypocritical Reagan Justice Department intent on removing every vestige of affirmative action from the law books. The law must be used vigorously to attack discrimination, but it is not a vehicle for turning skin color into a badge of entitlement.

7

Black Militants' New End Game

A Matter of Trust

It was only a straw in the wind of racial discord blowing through the city that winter of 1987, following the previous December's outrage at Howard Beach—a shift so subtle in the tone of a friendship that even an observant third party might not have noticed it. Yet what happened unsettled me, and, as other straws blew by in a gathering storm, I pondered it in a deepening disquiet.

Dan (I have changed his name) was a black teacher, forty-nine years old in 1987, thoughtful, tweedy, comfortably established with his wife and children in an integrated middle-class Brooklyn neighborhood. A sometime journalist, he moved easily across the broad spectrum of black politics and activism in New York, and through white reform Democratic circles as well. He struck me as one of those civil rights movement veterans, black and white, who've kept talking to one another past old wounds. Dan had been a source of good counsel to me ever since I'd met him in the late 1970s while running the *North Brooklyn Mercury.* His wry sanity about the vagaries of black community politics was all the more welcome because he was as unsparing in his witty criticisms of demagogues and hustlers there as he was in skewering white officials, whose hypocrisy he delighted in baring. Even when Dan sent some of his barbs my way, I knew that he meant to test and temper me against the rigors of struggles he, too, had known, and that he held everyone, black and white, to a single standard. Or so it had seemed, until I called him one day to talk about Howard Beach.

I thought Dan would help me understand what had gone wrong with black protests and legal maneuverings over the brutal assaults. Political activists have often used exemplary criminal cases to heighten their followers' awareness of social justice. Unlike civil litigants discussed in the previous chapter, activist defense attorneys want not only to squeeze concrete gains from the legal system but to expose its hypocrisy. But I was sure Dan would agree that the Howard Beach victims' attorneys, Alton Maddox, Jr., and C. Vernon Mason, were pursuing such an agenda in an unusually dangerous way. The lawyers might well be right to withhold their clients' cooperation from the authorities in order to compel them to replace the Queens district attorney with a special prosecutor. But surely they were wrong to try to justify their noncooperation by branding Dominick Blum, the motorist whose car had struck Michael Griffith, as a racist accomplice in the assaults, whom the cops were protecting because Blum was a court officer and his own father was a cop.

When I called Dan, it had already been widely reported that Blum was an amateur actor, a decent young guy of twenty-four who, on his way home that night after watching a play at Brooklyn College, had just dropped off a black fellow actor. After colliding with what he claimed to have thought was a tire or an animal, he had left the scene of the accident. But then, after consulting with his father, he had returned—how many would have?—and had offered tearfully to waive immunity and testify to establish his innocence of the charges Maddox and Mason were heaping upon him. Blum was no hero, but that was just the point; in his very ordinariness, he seemed to me to exemplify the sort of fair-minded, working-class, white New Yorkers whom any movement for racial justice would have to embrace, not enrage.

Yet, as evidence of Blum's innocence had begun to mount, Maddox and Mason had kept shifting their story. Maybe he hadn't started out as an accomplice, but, driving by, he had witnessed the chase and joined in it by car; if not that, then Blum had simply seen a black man running across a highway and, figuring he could get away with it, decided to hit him. That the authorities wouldn't arrest him was reason to withhold all cooperation. In saying this, ironically, as the special prosecutor Charles Hynes would point out, the lawyers were making a tactical blunder, for if Blum were in any sense guilty of murdering Griffith, then, legally, those who'd chased him would not be. In the court of public opinion, meanwhile, by using Blum so cynically as a focus for gratuitous smears, Maddox and Mason were contemptuously writing off essentially fair-minded New Yorkers who identified with Blum.

What really bothered me was that so many black ministers and civil rights movement veterans had gone along with these obvious offenses against the most elementary principles of morality and good political organizing. I called Dan to ask him why. His response astonished me. As I listed my concerns over the phone, he began a series of long, low chuckles that kept punctuating my comments and, in the end, my silence. Dan's heavy, humorless laughter told me that while he couldn't deny the dishonesty of the black attorneys and their supporters, he was enjoying their strategy because it was winning. "This isn't about fairiness and intellectual integrity," he said, finally; "it's about power—and, sure, maybe it's the same, morally bankrupt power whites have held over us through institutions like the Queens courts for years. When was the last time the 'fair-minded-ness' of white folks in Queens ever got us justice?"

Maddox and Mason had been "naughty," he continued, but they had "gotten the system over a barrel." Governor Cuomo and the state legislature had refused to create a special prosecutor for race-related cases even after the 1983 death of the graffiti writer Michael Stewart in police custody went unpunished. Now they'd had to respond, thanks to the lawyers' withholding cooperation, which threatened to torpedo any prosecution and so embarrass the state in the klieg lights of the national media. The lawyers' victory, compromised and polarizing though it might be, overrode its flaws.

But did it? Only, I countered, if you're narrowly focused on the legal victory without caring about the political coalition building that must, in the long run, sustain such victories. Ronald Reagan's landslides ought to have taught us that administrative and even legal gains can be undermined at the polls if there's no broad consensus to sustain them. As Cuomo himself had warned black nationalists, a disgruntled electorate might well choose a very different governor who, using the same "easy" special-prosecutor precedent, could start superseding better local district attorneys whom blacks had helped to elect. Ironically, there had been no organized white opposition to a special prosecutor. Now the lawyers' dishonest Blum strategy had turned acquiescence into resentment, alienating for the future the very people whose forbearance and fair play had been, in its own way, critical.

What I learned that moment on the phone was that Dan no longer much cared. Something had snapped in him at Howard Beach. Tribal truth counted for more than interracial consensus. The latter can be won only by keeping to certain standards of personal account-ability and public honesty and trust, and, for the time being, at least, Dan found it more satisfying to hurt than to hope. While newspaper polls and my own soundings showed that many blacks doubted the truth of Maddox's Blum scenario, Dan was by no means alone. The city's two black weeklies went full-tilt in support of the lawyers; the chief reporter covering Howard Beach for the *Amsterdam News,* Peter Noel, doubled as a kind of press secretary for Maddox, re-buffing all requests for interviews from the "white" press by lecturing us white writers on our sins.

Few black organizations or leaders openly challenged the lawyers' strategy. That didn't necessarily mean they agreed that blacks must write everyone else off and go it alone. In fact, a few prominent blacks had some reason to believe that even at its worst, the truth behind the outrage at Howard Beach was more complicated than either Hynes or the black militants had made it seem. I have cited the black attorney Charles Simpson, who, with Congressman Ed Towns, the City Council member Priscilla Wooten, and other black politi-cians, had been friendly with Jon Lester, a busboy at the diner they frequented, before he was charged in the case and eventually con-victed of second-degree manslaughter. Simpson recalls,

Jon would always give us special treatment, for a busboy. He'd get a wait-ress for us if we needed something or take our order himself if she was too busy. He'd sit and talk with us all the time. We enjoyed him, we kidded him about looking like Elvis on account of his hair. When I represented him in November 1986 on the gun-possession charge, I could tell the DA and the judge, in all honesty, that this was a hardworking kid with no criminal record who was doing adequately in school. He bought the gun, a .22, on the street after a couple of the waitresses had been robbed going home. The cops caught him half-drunk with a friend, shooting at a wrecked car in a vacant lot, because he'd had the gun for six months without using it and wanted to try it. The judge adjourned the case until January 5 and said that if Jon kept his nose clean until then, he'd get probation. Jon was shaking in his shoes. I came home with him afterward and had a nice lunch with his parents. When he wound up on the cover of the *Daily News* a few weeks later, we were shocked. "It's Elvis!" we said. We couldn't believe it.

To the surprise of Maddox, Daughtry, and others involved in the protests, Simpson showed up in court on January 5 to ask that Lester be allowed out on bail. To this day, he maintains that Lester, portrayed in the press as an aspiring "capo" and the ringleader of the assailants, was a socially precocious but otherwise typical teenage boy who let "the group mind" get the best of him that fateful night as he tried to impress his friends. He thinks it was a teenage turf battle that got out of hand.

It troubles me that no one involved in the case ever tried to find out what kind of kid Lester really was. Hynes and the protesters—and I consider Alton and Herb [Daughtry] to be my friends—were willing to sacrifice the truth about Jon Lester to make a statement of principle and lock him away. Of course Jon should have been punished. But ten years [in jail] is only going to turn him into everything Hynes and the press said he was. He'll be a racist for certain. I like Jon. I don't like what happened to him.

Simpson's position is at the opposite end of the continuum of black opinion from that of the militants. One may doubt the accuracy of his perceptions, yet acknowledge that his insistence on the complexity of the human truth—an insistence the ACLU would have us make on behalf of black criminal defendants—sets an extremely high standard of responsibility. Recall that in response to the ACLU, residents of crime-ridden neighborhoods defend their right and responsibility to make subtle choices: they would not threaten every stranger, but neither would they hold every backyard prowler innocent until proven guilty. Simpson, too, insists on his right to choose, even defending Lester after he was found guilty; and he has just as often condemned people, white and black, who were found innocent. In Howard Beach, practitioners of the politics of paroxysm peferred to convict not only Lester but also Blum and to indict all whites as accomplices. Thus mirroring victimized whites' often indiscriminate rage at young blacks, they ratcheted up the cycle of racial recriminations—at special cost, I believe, to blacks like my friend Dan and to all of liberal society. For, as we will now see, casting everything in terms of white racism ironically leaves blacks the victims not only of whites but also of one another, just as whites' casting everything in terms of the black threat subtly alienates whites from one another by grounding their alliances in fear.

Racism, Liberalism, and Personal Dignity

Racism of any kind is intolerable in liberal social thought because every victim of racism is presumed to have a personal dignity that runs deeper than color—deeper, even, than any culture bounded by color. Precisely because dignity is personal, it is violated whenever color or ethnicity is used by others to frame one's options and opportunities. But liberals believe that ultimately it is not within the oppressor's power to grant dignity or take it away. Even in oppression, individuals can make choices, and dignity that runs deeper than color carries with it a personal responsibility that transcends color. When a victim of racism responds intelligently, dignity has reaffirmed itself in the very act of choosing—in freedom.

These truths about moral responsibility in adversity animated the civil rights movement in its confrontations with a rigid, monolithic racism. They also explain why nothing is more anguishing in the Jewish memory of Nazi concentration camps than the fact that some Jews were forced by their captors, at gunpoint, to drive their fellows to death in order to save their own skins. Under that kind of duress, these individuals' last embers of dignity died before their victims did; short of martyrdom, they had been stripped of their ability to affirm life.

Twenty-five years after the monolithic racism of the South was dismantled, some blacks still liken their oppression in American cities to that of the Jews in the Nazi camps. That perverse analogy has even driven some of them to rationalize black-on-black murder: when blacks kill other blacks in the "concentration camps" of Brownsville and East New York, it is certainly horrible, but racism makes them do it. The cumulative, dehumanizing pressure of unemployment, bad schooling, inadequate health care, police brutality, and the drug conspiracy is the equivalent of holding a gun to the head of everyone who kills another in order to survive.

If that were true, then in Brooklyn, as in Bergen-Belsen, the battle against racism would be over. This issue was very well focused at a conference on drugs that was held in Manhattan late in 1989, where a white friend of mine found himself in an otherwise all-black workshop of half a dozen middle-class educators and social workers. The small discussion group quickly developed a horrific, if by now familiar, picture of drug wars in low-income African-American and Hispanic neighborhoods. More shocking than that picture, though, was the group's interpretation of it, for everyone present embraced the view that the drug wars are the unfolding of a white, genocidal conspiracy against blacks.

Everyone, that is, but my friend. A historian, he knew that conspiracy theories had raced around the black community for years, at least since heroin's rise in the 1950s, and that they had drawn a measure of credibility from incontrovertible evidence that J. Edgar Hoover conspired against Martin Luther King, Jr., and that other law enforcement agents plotted against the Black Panthers. Still, my friend was surprised to see the conspiracy idea enunciated with such certainty by professionals who'd seen so many barriers fall in their own lives—people who, if truth be told, were doing reasonably well in this supposedly genocidal society. So my friend cleared his throat. The idea is preposterous, he ventured, a paranoid delusion utterly self-destructive to anyone who indulges it.

A smartly dressed, middle-aged bureaucrat from the Board of Education, a woman with a sense of history, told him to open his eyes. "It's no different from the slow but steady deterioration of Jewish people in the ghettos under the Nazis before the 'final solution.' At the rate things are going, there won't even have to be a 'final solution' for us, 'cause there won't be anybody left."

That was ridiculous, my friend retorted. And what kind of white conspiracy would let drug enforcement agents and police officers, white as well as black, die trying to protect not the ghetto's perimeter but African-American witnesses to drug crimes and the African-American residents of apartment buildings where officers went to make undercover buys?

"Why haven't you gotten the message of 'Miami Vice' and 'Crime Story'?" snapped a younger man in a three-piece suit, the director of a black community-based social service agency. "Sure, for the sake of appearances, low-level law enforcement is hung out to dry—make that 'to die'—by superiors in Washington who're in cahoots with the international cartels. There's just too much money to be made." This conspiracy, the man added, is as lucrative as it is genocidal.

At that, my friend threw up his hands. "Okay, you're right! Whites got together in secret and decided to funnel this stuff in. And their racist, genocidal plan is moving like clockwork. Now what?"

A silence ensued. My friend continued. In a society where whites outnumber blacks nine to one and armed uprising is impossible, there is only one answer to the drug question, he said, and those of us who reject conservative ideology can't help that it was Nancy Reagan who first put that answer into three simple words. The only conceivable answer is that the black community will have to stop drug dealing and drug using on its own.

Now it was the group's turn to explode. The "community" in drug-ravaged areas is already too fragmented, too terrorized, too addicted, too desperate to pull itself together and "stop" anything, they said. The conspiracy has done too much damage already.

My friend was implacable. "Your alternative?" he pressed them. "Go quietly, like the Jews?"

"No," growled one man through clenched teeth. "We'll go like the Muslims, and we may take a few Jews with us."

Never mind that in citing the Muslims the speaker had undermined his own argument that blacks could do nothing, or that he'd whisked Jews from victimhood to villainy in the twinkling of an eye. Quite without intending to, by positing the white world's unrelenting hositility, these black professionals had stumbled upon some hard questions about the meaning of personal and communal responsibility. My friend was saying that unless blacks' options are truly as constricted as those of concentration camp inmates, they can rail at the heavens and develop elaborate diagrams of conspiracies, but they dare not scant community organizing that builds upon and reinforces personal accountability.

But accountability to what? The larger society may not be a concentration camp, but is it something to keep faith with? Should one, rather, confine one's accountability to other blacks? Do appeals to racial solidarity in the teeth of oppression invigorate or retard the development of personal dignity and accountability? I believe Dan was wavering in his responses to these questions, and, in truth, the answers from history are mixed. As the historian Christopher Lasch has noted, "American history seems to show that a group cannot achieve 'integration'—that is, equality—without first developing institutions which express and create a sense of its own distinctiveness." He reminds us of the black sociologist E. Franklin Frazier's observation that the black man's "primary struggle" in America "has been to acquire a culture—customs, values and forms of expression which, transmitted from generation to generation, provide a people with a sense of its own integrity and collective identity." Only within such a culture can individual dignity be nourished and cohere. That is certainly the claim of a large community of Muslims in Brooklyn, who redeem drug addicts and violent criminals by indoctrinating them in accountability through faith.

Can an embattled minority acquire a culture through politics, especially a politics that defines itself primarily as a struggle against the white racist devil? Those who think so defend not a culture in the classic sense but an ideology and, to my mind, a delusional system, a separate reality. Such a system has its points of congruence with the consensual reality of the larger society, and often enough it unearths important correspondences the larger society has missed. But its most salient characteristic is that it explains too much too easily, and when otherwise intelligent people buy into it, they can go on elaborating it forever, almost effortlessly, in response to every challenge.

Liberal individualism makes radically different demands. It holds that periodically, at each important moment of decision, the responsible person stands alone. Even when he or she is a member of a tightly knit, disciplined community, individual initiative and periodic independence are critical to the rejuvenation and maintenance of the community itself. That is the mystery of human dignity at this pass in the history of liberal societies, perhaps nowhere more so than in America, where countless whites as well as blacks are generations removed from any recoverable religious or ethnic community. Life in polyglot, liberal America daily reminds most of us that our dignity is not wholly reducible to our group memberships, whatever they are. Certainly, to recapitulate even a racist society's apparent obsession with one's blackness is not necessarily to enhance one's dignity, much less one's resources; it can become an escape from a genuine self-confrontation that is always postponed in the name of building group solidarity against racism. I think Dan recognized these pitfalls most of the time and cherished his own, sardonic brand of independence.

So did blacks who won important victories toward the end of the 1980s: that of a predominantly black but interracial hospital workers' union in forging a strong settlement in New York; that of the predominantly black but interracial builders of the Nehemiah homes in Brooklyn; and that of David Dinkins's predominantly black but interracial coalition in his election as mayor. These victories showed what folly it is to write off in advance, as the Howard Beach attorneys had done, that stratum of whites who are willing to live by the rules of fair play. They showed that there are ways to trust from strength. Maddox, Mason, and other black militants had missed this lesson. They had fled to ever more baroque elaborations of white genocidal conspiracy, producing the styles of protest that so alienated New Yorkers of all colors during the same period at the end of the decade. Their attempts to reopen festering wounds and, through the media and the courts, to attribute every injury to white oppression overlooked the importance of honesty to any community that is organizing to build real power.

Murder and Honesty

It seems to me that Reverend [Timothy] Mitchell [of Queens's Ebenezer Baptist Church] and his colleagues should in fact be fighting for more law and order, since his people are the most affected. . . . Every low-income black is now paying the price for "street violence," no matter how unfair the attribution. . . . Five years ago it might have made sense for the blacks to

take the position that an emphasis on law and order was somehow the signal of bigotry and a willingness to permit the oppression of the blacks. We're way past that now. . . .

—MARIO CUOMO,
Forest Hills Diary, entry of October 7, 1972

Not until the end of the 1980s did Mitchell and other black ministers and militants who'd led twenty-five years of protests against
racism in New York begin to acknowledge in public that Cuomo was
right. In a grim irony, it was only in the aftermath of the murder of
Yusuf Hawkins—as pure a martyr to white racism as could be imagined—that a wave of murders of young blacks by other young blacks
forced militants to say publicly what Ed Koch and his black police
commissioner, Benjamin Ward, had been saying for more than a
year: nothing further can be gained by blaming racism as such for the
mayhem engulfing poor neighborhoods.

To say this is not to propose that racism has ceased to exist. It
would be dangerous to pretend that it has. No case in point is more
wrenching than that of Hawkins, who died at sixteen on a Bensonhurst street, holding a Snickers bar in one hand, his young eyes wide
with uncomprehending fright. It isn't enough simply to say that
Yusuf was blameless on that particular night, having come to the
neighborhood simply to look at a used car, or even that he had
always been a good boy, with no police record and a dream of attending Transit Tech High School that fall. More than that, Yusuf Hawkins was a racial innocent. Watching a videotape of *Mississippi Burning* at a neighbor's house just before leaving to meet his death, he
said, according to friends, that he couldn't believe people could be so
cruel to one another for no reason other than the color of skin. Growing up in black East New York, he hadn't yet begun to comprehend
the weight of white hatred pressing in upon his community and everyone in it. A white person who visits poor black communities finds
such innocence in the faces and speech of more black teenagers than
one would ever have imagined possible. And the unwelcome thought
crosses one's mind that some of these hopeful children would be
terrified if they knew what awaits them.

An August 27, 1989, *Daily News* photo of the Reverend Al Sharpton and a claque of black teenagers marching in Bensonhurst to

protest Hawkins's death shows that they are not really "marching."
They are stumbling along, huddled together, heads bowed under the
storm of hatred breaking over them, eyes wide, hanging on to one
another and to Sharpton, scared out of their wits. They, too, are
innocents—or were until that day, which they will always remember.
And because Sharpton is with them, his head bowed also, his face
showing that he knows what they're feeling, he is in the hearts of
black people all over New York.

Yet something is wrong with this picture. Sharpton did not invite
or coordinate with Bensonhurst community leaders who wanted to
join the march. Without the time for organizing which these leaders
should have been given in order to rein in the punks who stood
waving watermelons; without an effort by black leaders more reputa-
ble than Sharpton to recruit whites citywide and swell the march,
Sharpton was assured that the punks would carry the day. At several
points, he even baited them by blowing kisses. Instead of mounting
an unforgettable tableau of the city, Sharpton provoked a symbolic
reenactment of Hawkins's murder, in a way calculated to make it
easier, not harder, for Bensonhurst residents to embrace denial. That
denial surfaced in the trial, where little people who'd told cops they'd
seen the killing suddenly developed amnesia.

In a sense, Sharpton's strategy was brilliant. If it eclipsed one
reality, it certainly exposed another. But because the city is in fact
better than the reality the demonstration exposed, those moments in
Bensonhurst may well have accounted for David Dinkins's stunning
defeat of Koch in the Democratic mayoral primary two weeks later.
While Sharpton would take credit for that, it was far from clear that
victory was what he'd intended, for Dinkins was more threat than
boon to any politics that finds it more satisfying to hurt than to hope.

In a little-reported denunciation of Sharpton's organizing tactics
in another Bensonhurst march early in 1988, Sarah Lee McWhite, a
black resident and tenant activist at Marlboro Houses, a predominantly black enclave at the edge of the neighborhood, criticized
Sharpton for conducting an ill-planned, media-oriented march following a brutal assault on two black youths. "If you're gonna mess
with two of us, you're gonna have to mess with all of us!" Sharpton
had cried. The march sparked a predictably ugly counterdemonstra-
tion, alarming black residents. "He never contacted anyone here or

spoke to white leaders in the community," McWhite said, adding that she and her neighbors, not Sharpton, would be left "to pick up the pieces."

To many angry blacks, Sharpton's practice of the politics of resentment was irresistible. But it was part of the reason that, at some point in the late 1970s, the politics of race in New York had begun to turn more and more on death—on recitals of the names of blacks murdered by whites: Randy Evans, Arthur Miller, Willie Turks, Samuel Spencer, Michael Stewart, Eleanor Bumpurs, Nicholas Bartlett, Jonah Perry, Michael Griffith, Yusuf Hawkins. Among blacks, it seemed, the politics of victimization had triumphed: along with murderous white racism, militants cited drugs, AIDS, and doomed boarder babies, parables of hopelessness and despair spiraling easily into projections of white genocidal conspiracy. Sharpton claimed that he and other protesters had forced the murders and plagues upon the conscience of the city. They were not wrong. But where would that lead? What real power did it build? And how, without power, could the violence and plagues be stopped?

These questions took on new urgency as another deadly roll call forced itself upon the activists' and the city's attention, this time without Sharpton's help. It was reported well enough in the mainstream press, yet this roll call was not read aloud at protests in the streets or in solemn memorials within the black community itself. It just swelled and swelled until it could not be ignored, until it eclipsed all that had gone before.

Two weeks after Hawkins's death, thirteen-year old Sean Vaughan, a young black participant in the "I Have a Dream" program, which guarantees college tuition for ghetto kids who stay in school through high school graduation, was gunned down in a parking lot near his home in the Soundview section of the Bronx. He was not the intended recipient of the bullet that killed him. The man later charged with the killing, Ronald Reid, eighteen, had allegedly fired at others at the the behest of a woman who'd asked him to defend her "honor."

A few days later, on September 11, opening day at Brooklyn's Prospect Heights High School, the student Duane Lewis, eighteen, was gunned down in front of the school by one of three assailants as scores of students watched. On Friday, October 27, Gemel Kalek

Mitchell, a nineteen-year-old student at Julia Richman High School in Manhattan, was shot and killed by another student on a subway train in the culmination of an argument they had begun in the school cafeteria. That night, a fifteen-year-old sophomore at Stuyvesant High School was shot in the head in a discotheque in Jackson Heights, Queens.

Early on Sunday morning, October 29, Donald White, a seventeen-year old honor student at Murry Bergtraum High School for Business Careers, in lower Manhattan, a young man celebrated as role model by all his neighbors, was shot in the head and chest by a crack addict trying to rob him as he went to do his mother's wash at a laundromat near their home in Jamaica, Queens. The man charged with the murder was another seventeen-year-old, Michael Allen, whom neighbors described as a drug dealer and thug.

On Monday, October 30, Edward Caban, a Julia Richman High School student, was shot and killed in East Harlem in what was ambiguously described as a drug-related shooting. On Friday, November 17, Melvin Smith, twenty-four, a popular ministry student, was shot and rendered brain-dead by thieves who got five dollars and his wristwatch as he was heading home from a Bedford-Stuyvesant grocery store. A graduate of Baruch College attending Church of Christ Seminary in Manhattan, Smith held Bible study classes twice a week in his home.

On Thanksgiving Day, fourteen-year-old Preston Simmons, known as Little Man, was killed, allegedly by a twenty-four-year-old who pumped thirteen shots into him in the courtyard of their Castle Hill housing project in the Bronx because Simmons had been selling drugs independently instead of through the murder suspect. On December 2, Arnulfo Williams, Jr., nineteen, was shot and killed while trying to shield his younger brother from bullies at a bus stop in South Jamaica.

In four days beginning on December 21, there were four unrelated killings of innocent bystanders. Two of the victims were young black women in Queens, one of them twenty-five years old and nine months pregnant; she died at the hospital several hours after giving birth to a six-pound, seven-ounce boy. Another victim was an eleven-year-old boy whose family had moved out of East New York to escape violence; he was back in the neighborhood visiting a relative and getting a haircut when a bullet flew through a window and killed him.

They were all young blacks, the hope of their people, killed allegedly by other young blacks who had become the scourge of their people. During this period there were many other murders of blacks besides those I have mentioned. In the four months after Hawkins's death, more blacks were killed by other blacks than had been killed by whites in the preceding two years. In a departure from past patterns, many of the assailants and victims did not know one another. As the toll rose, most black militants, ministers, and civil rights lawyers and their white activist apologists were as silent as the graves into which the bodies were being lowered. There were no marches. There were no speeches.

Finally, the silence could no longer be borne. Some black rap groups had already begun to sing out against black-on-black violence when Sharpton delivered the eulogy for fourteen-year-old Preston Simmons in a tiny chapel inside a Bronx funeral home. According to *New York Newsday*'s William Douglas and Doug Haberman, Sharpton

blamed Preston's death on the black community and black leaders, who he says have allowed drugs to invade and take over their neighborhoods.

"I think it is now the responsibility of the community and activists to be responsible for the drug killers of our race as well as the race killers. We've lost two young men this year [*sic*], Preston at 14, Yusuf Hawkins at 16. One was our fault because we should have policed our community and taken a more active stand against drugs." Sharpton said he and Preston's family plan to organize an antidrug patrol in the Castle Hill community next week.

"This was a tragedy equal to what happened to my son in Bensonhurst," Moses Stewart [the father of Yusuf Hawkins] said. "This time, we are at fault."

Coming from men known for denouncing racism as the alpha and omega of black suffering, this new, more introspective line was surprising. So was a column in January by Sheryl McCarthy, a black columnist for *New York Newsday*. McCarthy cited the indictment of a sixteen-year-old black youth in the rape and torture of a twelve-year-old girl—and rejected the "familiar litany" of social problems often recited to explain if not to justify such vicious crimes:

I take issue with [the] portrait of black men as helpless victims of society who have no control over the direction of their lives. In my career, which has included interviews with jail inmates, junkies, alcoholics, and troubled juveniles, all have told me the same thing: that the turning point for them was the decision to end the self-destructive behavior. Until then, all entreaties to shape up and all offers of assistance were useless. . . . [The rape] was an act of choice, and for this horrific choice there are no excuses.

McCarthy's sentiments were echoed in a comment by Ned O'Gorman, headmaster of a Harlem storefront alternative school, when thirteen-year-old Robert Cole, a former student, was killed by a police officer in February as he brandished a gun (which turned out to be broken and unloaded) after attempting a robbery in a corner grocery. O'Gorman, who has written movingly about how ghetto life crushes children's spirits, refused to blame everything on poverty and the pressures of the streets: "To take from [Robert] his free will, to say he was a wild child thrown into chaos by his environment, is to make him a nonhuman. The pressures on him to make the trek into darkness were real. But along the way, he exercised free will."

In a transcribed conversation with a white Bensonhurst priest two weeks after Yusuf Hawkins's murder, Daughtry had edged toward a similar expression of concern—and then pulled back. Confused, I asked him a few months later why activists didn't march to protest black-on-black murders; or surround the homes of the suspects and invite their families to join them in prayer; or show up at court and demand that the suspects be held without bail, as they had in Bensonhurst and Howard Beach; or raise all the larger questions about personal and communal responsibility that lay behind the continuing slaughter. Daughtry didn't really answer my question. He told me of a vigil he and other blacks had kept for the white Central Park jogger assaulted and raped by black boys who lived north of the park. He told me of his success in getting Donald Trump, who had placed a heinous newspaper ad demanding revenge in that case, to pay the medical expenses of a black woman who'd been raped by other blacks in Brooklyn that very same day and had received scant public attention.

But these correct, even noble actions by Daughtry were still guided by the race lens. What about blacks killed by blacks when there is no analogous white victim such as the Central Park jogger to highlight their deaths, by association? True, the public double standard is partly the media's fault. Perhaps it reflects many whites' obtuse thinking that, since blacks are disproportionately the perpetrators of violent crime, they can damn well perpetrate it against one another; that, if "they" don't care about themselves, why should "we"? But does even such ignoble and destructive reasoning prove that the mayhem on ghetto streets is a manifestation of white racism, perhaps the consequence of a white genocidal conspiracy? Is that what one tells the detectives assigned to investigate the murders? Is it what one tells the victims' grieving relatives?

The halting movement by Sharpton and Daughtry toward acknowledging black individual and communal responsibility, even amid racist adversity, has more potential to improve matters than they may recognize. It frees us from the game of racial finger pointing which whites, too, have played, using black crime to "explain" and excuse their racism and thereby encouraging some blacks to counter that racism does explain and excuse black crime. By declining to blame whites at Simmons's funeral, Sharpton and Stewart implicitly affirmed that racism is intolerable precisely because most blacks are worthy people who hold one another responsible for their actions. That deprives censorious whites of the moral advantage of condescension. The vicious spiral is broken.

As that happens, blacks also have an opportunity to rethink some of the legal and political strategies of Maddox and Mason. During the Howard Beach trials, for example, when Maddox was denouncing the criminal justice system for routinely acquitting whites who murder blacks, he managed, deftly and cynically, to win acquittal for Andre Nichols, a nineteen-year-old black man who confessed to killing a white priest who, Nichols claimed, had solicited him for sex. According to Nichols, the priest, Frederick Strainese, had invited him into his car in a known pickup area. The priest was unarmed; Nichols had a gun. He claimed he'd used it because the priest had used excessive force trying to detain him. Trading heavily in the worst sort of reverse racism and homophobia, replete with imagery of the white sexual exploitation of black youth, Maddox persuaded the jury to acquit Nichols. The integrated jury, members of Strianese's parish, and, apparently, the assistant district attorney were all para-

paralyzed by Maddox's lurid characterizations. Strianese, he told them, had enjoyed "good food, good wine . . . and now he wanted some good flesh."

Hynes, the prosecutor in the Howard Beach case, stopped by the courtroom to pick up Maddox and caught a few minutes of the Nichols trial. "Maddox was totally prepared. The assistant DA on the other side seemed disinterested; he sat on his ass, lobbed objections from his seat. That jury was angry about something. They didn't like the case, what the priest was allegedly doing, out trying to pick up kids. They even acquitted Nichols of gun possession." Maybe they were angry, but *murder?* Did the priest deserve that? It took Maddox's most diabolical talents to seal the judgment. Less than a month later, Nichols was arrested for armed robbery and held without bail.

In another celebrated case that winter, Maddox defended one of two blacks charged with slashing the white model Marla Hanson, demanding an acquittal on the grounds that her own, hysterical racism had caused her to misidentify her assailants: "Seeing two black men, she went absolutely nuts. . . . She thought she was going to be raped" because "she had racial hangups," he told the jury as Hanson sat shocked, weeping, in the courtroom. Maddox tried to convince the jury that she had attacked the men and precipitated the violence—that they, like Nichols, were the victims. Though he didn't win this one, the message was clear: murder and attempted murder were morally variable according to race.

It can be argued that, in both these cases, Maddox was doing what any good courtroom attorney would. But he had more on his mind than making the system work through a vigorous defense of his clients. "[Black juveniles] are the majority of people being arrested and tried and imprisoned. Ain't nobody givin' up nothing in New York. If you want to survive here, you have to take your turf!" he told Jill Nelson of the *Washington Post.* Because Maddox conceives of his cases as racial battles, he sends his community the message that personal accountability is dissolved in collective grievance and entitlement. The system acquitted the murderers of Michael Stewart, the young graffiti writer who "died in police custody"? We'll acquit the murderer of the Reverend Strianese. The system smeared Jonah Perry, the Harlem honor student accused of mugging a cop? We'll smear Marla Hanson. Tit for tat. When we get control of the system, we'll turn the tables.

Shelby Steele characterizes the tactical use of racial grievance as "victimization metamorphosed into power via innocence." In every case, Maddox does not simply try to acquit the defendant; he tries to recapture the innocence that was his when he suffered a brutal beating at the hands of police in his hometown of Newnan, Georgia, in 1967. While Maddox was convicted of the usual trumped-up charges of disorderly conduct and resisting an arrest, innocence like his moved a nation; such innocence "gave blacks their first real power in American life," says Steele, who comments,

But this formula . . . binds the victim to his victimization by linking his power to his status as a victim. And this, I'm convinced, is the tragedy of black power in America today. It is primarily a victim's power. . . .

So we have a hidden investment in victimization and poverty. One sees evidence of this in the near happiness with which certain black leaders recount the horror of Howard Beach and other recent (and I think over-celebrated) instances of racial tension.

As one is saddened by these tragic events, one is also repelled at the way some black leaders—agitated to near hysteria by the scent of victim power inherent in them—leap forward to exploit them as evidence of black innocence and white guilt.

There is, after all, a way other than Maddox's to reduce racism in the criminal justice system. It is to apply a community's electoral muscle, to elect judges and district attorneys who feel a political debt as well as a moral obligation to blacks—Hynes, for example, who was elected Brooklyn DA in 1989 with a strong black vote. And there are ways other than Sharpton's to organize public protests; there can be demonstrations that embarrass whites into decency by embracing them in the process of confronting them. But doing that would mean rising above victimhood to display a disarming magnanimity. Maddox isn't up to that. His intimations of such dignity are blocked by his pain. Every trial he casts in black and white becomes a reenactment of his own attempt to vindicate what he suffered. But one can never escape pain this way, vicariously, and certainly not in a courtroom; for while Maddox was black and innocent in Newnan in 1967, and the police officers who beat him were white and racist, not every black defendant is innocent, and not every white plaintiff is racist. Because, emotionally, Maddox cannot admit this, he cannot lead a movement for racial justice, only one for racial revenge.

The support Maddox enjoyed among militant nationalists even as these trials unfolded suggests that his kind of pain is widely shared. Often enough, it will "fit" the facts of a case. "[Responsible black leaders] couldn't attack Sharpton and Maddox during a situation like Howard Beach or Bensonhurst, because they were the only ones giving open expression to a rage we all felt," Jerry Hudson, a black organizer at the Hospital Workers' Union, Local 1199, told me. "To delegitimize them at moments like those would have left many of us feeling that we had delegitimized our own anger and, therefore, ourselves." But that places an intolerable burden on the rest of us. Because so few from their own community had restrained Maddox and Mason, it fell to Mario Cuomo to save them from themselves in Howard Beach by ignoring the lies they'd told to justify their noncooperation and demand a special prosecutor. In the Brawley case, no special prosecutor could have saved them from their lies, which gave every appearance of having become their delusions.

Psychodrama and Public Truth

Not long before my friend Dan's virtual endorsement of the lies in Howard Beach, the fragility of respect for truth was underscored when Sonny Carson threatened blacks who might be tempted to speak out against the vilification of Blum. At a crowded news conference, he said, "There are tires all over this city," a reference to the South African practice of "necklacing" suspected informants—putting tires around their necks and setting them aflame. My castigations of Maddox and Mason in a Park Slope weekly newspaper and *In These Times,* a socialist weekly, brought angry letters from white radicals who called me a racist and contemptuous rebuffs from black activists I'd known for years. Manhattan liberals, too, were oblivious to the moral problem, with a few exceptions like Richard Emery of the New York Civil Liberties Union, who told the *National Law Journal,* "Maddox's methods are sabotage and the pursuit of racial division; I will never work with him again."

I tried presenting my arguments to a racially mixed audience of activists at a conference that spring of 1987, quoting an observation by Christopher Lasch:

It would have been impossible for [Martin Luther] King to mount any moral attack on segregation if he had taken the position that black people, by virtue of their special history, had developed a special set of moral principles that whites could not appreciate. . . .

King did not, of course, expect an appeal to moral principles to settle the issue. . . . The genius of the civil rights movement lay in its insistence that a resort to coercion was by no means inconsistent with an appeal to moral principles that both sides in the conflict could be made to acknowledge.

. . . It was not the rejection of violence as such but the rejection of resentment . . . that enabled the civil rights movement to speak from a position of overwhelming moral authority.

My listeners' responses were troubling. A black activist suggested that I reexamine my motivations for criticizing Maddox and Mason, which were probably rooted in a profound but unacknowledged sense of my white guilt. A union organizer suggested that I was propounding a notion of citizenship and of the civic culture "too idealistic, too ethereal" (she might as well have said "bourgeois") for hard-pressed, justifiably angry minorities to accept. An activist lawyer reminded me that controversial, confrontational legal tactics had often been used to heighten social tensions as a way of shifting a movement's frame of reference beyond the law to larger questions of justice. Nobody evinced the slightest concern over what had happened to Blum or, more broadly, over what the treatment of him and its reception among whites of his background might portend for the "movement building" they all claimed was so important.

By the time of the activists' next conference the following year, there was a new "Dominick Blum," surrounded by more strategic lies: Maddox and Mason had accused the Dutchess County assistant district attorney Steven Pagones of raping and sodomizing Tawana Brawley and had likened the State Attorney General Robert Abrams to Adolf Hitler. Mason declared that Abrams had masturbated over photographs of Brawley, repeating the accusation on the air and for print reporters. Assemblyman Roger Green, of Brooklyn, a young activist whose father was a veteran of the civil rights movement, publicly criticized the lawyers for the "cavalier use of words like 'racism' and 'fascism.' To equate at this point in time the Attorney General of the State of New York with a fascist dictator and . . . the system with fascism does a major disservice to all those who fought and died against that most heinous form of injustice."

Sharpton immediately charged Green with buckling to pressure from the governor's office: "He's obviously doing the bidding of his sponsors. . . . [It] shows where Roger's heart lies as an apologist for the system." The next day, State Senator Velmanette Montgomery, who represented the same area of Brooklyn as Green, announced her intention to oppose Green's reelection as chairman of the legislature's Black and Puerto Rican Caucus, saying she thought it inappropriate for Green to have attacked "a citizen leader such as Al Sharpton" and that it was "time for a change" in the caucus leadership. A few days later, she abandoned her candidacy because she did not want to "continue to project a sense of disunity," and Green was reelected. But the flare-up had been revealing, and distressing.

In my contribution to papers circulated in advance of the activists' second conference, I wrote a short essay citing developments in the Brawley case and challenging the readers to embrace my assertions of a year before. But when the day of the conference arrived, I could not bring myself to attend. As for Dan, I still call him, and we trade stories and references; but it is not the same as before.

Accountability, Honesty, and Trust

"Efforts to stop the polarization in the city can't be geared totally toward race anymore," says Roger Green, who is pushing the schools to teach adolescents how to resolve conflicts without resorting to violence. "It's a point I have to argue, but folks do realize it. Sometimes we're captive to our own rhetoric, as opposed to looking at what's really happening and analyzing it. For example, after Howard Beach, I saw in the demonstrations something entirely new to me: that those white kids are a lost generation, too, that there is a poverty of spirit that doesn't just come down to race."

Green's view is endorsed by the hundreds of thousands of working-class blacks and Hispanics who participated in the strike by the hospital workers' union, helped build the Nehemiah homes, and turned out to vote for David Dinkins, who was anathema to the militants, as we will see in chapter 11. The practitioners of racial paroxysm have nothing comparable to these victories to show for their efforts. They claim that their demonstrations and demands have aroused blacks and shoved whites in directions that made the moderates' victories possible. In reality, their brand of racial politics has established a stereotype of public protest which the church groups and unions have had to work hard to break in their own rallies, and it surely cost David Dinkins white support that would have widened his two-point margin of victory.

The militants express jealousy and misunderstanding of those who have gained real ground. Of the Reverend Johnny Ray Youngblood, cochairman of East Brooklyn Congregations, which built the first round of Nehemiah homes, the Reverend Calvin Butts of Harlem told an out-of-town reporter,

As a clergyman, he's a premier example of the strong, new black clergy today. But in terms of whether he's had a profound impact on the major issues this city faces today, I say he has no public presence. On the issue of police brutality, when you look at the number of people who took radical stands, Johnny Ray Youngblood is not there. When you think of the lack of proper health care for the poor, Johnny Ray Youngblood is not there. And at a time when we need new leaders in this city to improve the climate of racial tension, he has not spoken out.

Jesse Jackson answered Butts, though not by name, in a speech at Youngblood's St. Paul's Community Baptist Church in East New York. Noting that some people had criticized Youngblood, Jackson said, referring to the Nehemiah homes, that what Youngblood had accomplished was so real and had afforded so much hope that "people sleep in it at night."

Daughtry, too, is confused about Nehemiah. In a conversation with me, he kept circling around his suspicion that Industrial Areas Foundation groups like Youngblood's East Brooklyn Congregations are somehow dependent on whites:

I'm ambivalent about IAF. You don't want to berate an effort that provides goods and services and has a Christian element. But the question is how much they have to compromise with the powers that be and give up the prophetic posture. They're subservient to [the IAF leader] Ed Chambers, the bishop [the white Roman Catholic Brooklyn bishop Francis Mugavero], a white leadership. . . .

Responding to Butts's and Daughtry's criticisms in a conversation with me late in 1989, Youngblood said it was true that for some years he'd avoided what was commonly thought of as social action because he'd become disillusioned by protests of the sort Butts and Daughtry conducted—"a numb repetition of the strategies of the sixties." Finally, he agreed to attend an IAF ten-day training session.

It was one of the most effective, informative, and challenging ten days I've ever spent. I learned four things: That power is not a term or a reality to be afraid of. That imagination and creativity have a place in the power arena, that system and structure too often cancel out imagination. That people who hold sway in the precincts of power are human. That all people have a stake in American society; blacks will not do it alone, whites will not do it alone. Being with the IAF people, the motliest crew you could imagine, I realized that I do have a piece of the rock as an American citizen, with the right to see the democratic ethic realized to its fullest potential in my lifetime.

What Butts and Daughtry can't quite let go of, I think, is an unconscious need for powerlessness; so long as whites have the real power, these black leaders can remain righteous victims. Daughtry is better than this. I believe he knows he's between a rock and a hard place as nationalist militancy spirals off in directions no Christian—and, for that matter, no Marxist—can defend. Though he will not admit it, a reliable source assures me that as the Brawley psychodrama approached its nadir, he summoned Maddox and Mason to his church and told them they simply couldn't go on making their wild, gutter attacks on Cuomo and Abrams. Regarding the Brawley fiasco, Daughtry told me,

History teaches us that the most vocal leaders are often charlatans. When I first heard of Tawana's rape, I dropped everything and went to Newburgh. Deep inside I felt something was amiss. I never got to see Tawana. I said so at a Brawley rally, on the eve of Martin Luther King's birthday, a couple of days before *New York Newsday* broke the story of Sharpton as an FBI informer. I kept telling people, just think for yourselves, don't let people paint you into a black/white corner. If all whites are always wrong, then you have no check on your own leadership. Don't you see, I told them, the greatest thing Bob Abrams could do for himself is solve the case, with all the world press on him. Yet they skillfully made it a black/white battle: everything my enemy says is wrong.

Daughtry was not alone among black activist leaders in regretting the direction Maddox, Mason, and Sharpton had taken. When someone at a Harlem meeting of activists made reference to Maddox's ferocity, Mason's dishonesty, and Sharpton's FBI connections, the Reverend Lawrence Lucas said, "Oh, you mean Fire, Liar, and Wire?" "That brought down the house," recalls one who attended. "Jitu Weusi almost fell out of his chair laughing." It became a gallows humor, though, as the group considered its impossible situation. Most of its members would not break ranks; they felt increasingly trapped as the case wore on.

Dinkins triumphed over the inevitable white hostility to his candidacy because he doggedly refused to make things "black/white" and to blame everything on racism. He denounced Minister Louis Farrakhan. He condemned the Brawley advisers. He called the assailants of the Central Park jogger "urban terrorists," and when a black listener objected, he responded, "I called them that, Bill, because that's precisely what they were." Finally, he told a group of black high school students during his campaign,

I know that we, the adults, have not done all we should, and all we must, to make this city all it can be. And I pledge to you that I will do my part as your next mayor. But I want a pledge, in turn, from you. A pledge that you will never use those obstacles and barriers as an excuse. I know that life is not always fair, that it's hard to get ahead, but your obligation is to work hard, respect the law, be disciplined and strong—and take responsibility for your actions.

For saying these sorts of things, Dinkins has been denounced for defending "the system," and in chapter 11 we examine the ways in which that may be so. But sometimes militants like Sonny Carson have made his stance easier by staking out too despairing and vindictive an alternative. In Bedford-Stuyvesant and Flatbush, for example, Carson led raucous black demonstrations against Korean grocers during Dinkins's first few months in office, accusing them of having "an attitude" toward black customers and even of assaulting some they suspected of shoplifting. In a manner reminiscent of Sufi-Abdul Hamed, "Harlem's Hitler" of the 1930s, Carson and associates demanded that the offending stores be transferred to black ownership, charging that Koreans were out to "destroy" the community's culture and economy. The truth, of course, is that they provide twenty-four-hour-a-day convenience and some security on dark streets where none existed for years.

Rebuffing mediation efforts, Carson declared, "The fundamental issue is who is going to control our economics. That's why we continue the boycott." An associate, Coltrane Chimurenga, told a hundred people gathered at Bedford-Stuyvesant's El Hajj Malik Elementary School, which Carson commandeered for a boycott meeting, "We are going to take back our community by any means necessary." Yet one "means" never mentioned is the recruitment and training of a few hundred young blacks prepared to work fifteen hours a day at low wages and in close family units, as the Koreans do, in order to pay their debts to immigrant lending societies. Surely capital could be found to invest in such a work force.

One of the characters in Spike Lee's *Do the Right Thing* notes that a local store had been vacant for years until a Korean turned it into a thriving grocery; no one from the community had taken advantage of it even when it could've been had for a song. But somehow, for Carson, the time to "put up or shut up" never comes. Hearing of Carson's demand that all Korean merchants leave the black community, I imagined them closing their thirty-odd stores in Bedford-Stuyvesant and referring their customers to him. For that matter, who is stopping Carson and his followers from opening up their own, competing chain of cooperatives, farmers' markets, or stores and urging local residents to "buy black"? Since nothing remotely like that has ever emerged from his organizing, his sad parody of "black activism" rallies only adolescents, real and perpetual; that, in turn, merely strengthens Dinkins's legitimacy in the rest of the city.

A mural at Bedford-Stuyvesant's Slave Theater, where Sharpton holds forth at weekly rallies, depicts a young, barefoot black man crying, "I don't know who I am! Lost my name. My tribal language. My homeland. African wealth. I have nothing!" Another mural depicts a muscular, blond white man in chains, his captor a much smaller black field hand. "Sam," the white man cries, "you chained me up when I was asleep, you S.O.B.! Cut me loose or I'll charge you with white man's slavery." The field hand replies, "Shut up, Pete, you chained me up when I was asleep, too. Now it's my turn. I gotcha, boy."

To which the definitive response comes from the writer Leon Wieseltier:

The memory of oppression is a pillar and a strut of the identity of every people oppressed. It is no ordinary marker of difference. It is unusually stiffening. It instructs the individual and the group about what to expect of the world, imparts an isolating sense of apartness. . . . Don't be fooled, it teaches, there is only repetition. For that reason, the collective memory of an oppressed people is not only a treasure but a trap.

. . . In the memory of oppression, oppression outlives itself. The scar does the work of the wound. That is the real tragedy: that injustice retains the power to distort long after it has ceased to be real. It is a posthumous victory for the oppressors, when pain becomes a tradition. And yet the atrocities of the past must never be forgotten. This is the unfairly difficult dilemma of the newly emancipated and the newly enfranchised: an honorable life is not possible if they remember too little and a normal life is not possible if they remember too much.

8

Militants, "Professional Blacks," and the Culture of Schools

Black Nationalism in an Armory

Late one hot July afternoon in 1982, I drove to a cavernous armory in Bedford-Stuyvesant, where I'd been told I could typeset and lay out a newsletter. The area around the armory was a mix of attractive brownstones, abandoned apartment buildings, and neighborhood corner stores, not unlike the block a few streets away that would become the set for Spike Lee's movie *Do the Right Thing*. Men lounged on the street, drinking beer and talking; kids opened hydrants, seeking relief from the heat. But unlike Lee's buoyant community, this one was bleak. The storefronts were seedy. A gaunt woman in hot pants and a halter top pawed through a garbage bag amid broken glass. Two rough-looking teenagers eyed me from the window of an empty building. I worried about parking my car.

But as I stepped inside the armory I crossed a threshold in space and time. From the formal, correct young man in Muslim garb at the door to the bright murals adorning the massive, carved-wood staircase leading up to high-ceilinged rooms where dance and martial-arts classes were in progress, everything about the place radiated a fantastically disciplined energy. I climbed the stairs to music and the rhythmic thumping of feet and located the print shop, where Brother Segun, the pleasant director of this enchanting place, handed me the tools necessary for the layout and arranged my schedule with the typesetters.

I had stumbled upon the East, a cultural center founded in 1969 by Jitu Weusi, formerly Les Campbell of Ocean Hill–Brownsville infamy. Weusi, who a year earlier had read an anti-Semitic poem by one of his Ocean Hill students on Julius Lester's program on WBAI and been accused of inciting his public school students to assault whites, was a social pariah when he began cleaning out the old loft building that first housed the East. He was no longer associated with the center by the time I arrived there in 1982, and I didn't meet him until 1989, when he was being ejected from David Dinkins's mayoral campaign after the *New York Post* and Rudolph Giuliani had dredged up his past indiscretions. I would find him to be a gentle giant, albeit a Marxist-Leninist–Black Nationalist whose politics could be difficult to follow, a lovable man who'd been badly misunderstood because he'd been badly confused.

Without question, the East was something Weusi had done right, a remarkable achievement that built and saved young lives. I spent several nights there that summer, working nearly till dawn, and the memory of its sleepless energy haunts me, the more so because it has since been closed and the armory is now a shelter for the homeless.

In its prime in the mid-1970s, the East included an independent, fully accredited, 470-student African-American school called Uhuru Sasa ("Freedom Now" in Swahili) and food and clothing co-ops, a bookstore, and summer programs for black youths. An evening "School of Knowledge" taught low-income mothers and some fathers everything from dressmaking and first aid to African dance and martial arts. There were lectures and plays about African culture. "When you walked in, you walked into a paradise," Weusi claims, reinforcing my own and others' first impressions. "It was a totally positive atmosphere, no drugs, no drinking; you could feel comfortable, safe and relaxed. White people who'd come in, like the telephone man or an electrician, would be awed. 'This place blows my mind,' they'd say."

Weusi's method was to take all comers, however shell-shocked, give them some kind of responsibility to make them feel needed, and then dote on their accomplishments, no matter how small. "Sometimes he trusted people too much," recalls Atchudta Barkar, an organizer for the Hospital Workers' Union, Local 1199, who came to the East in 1973 after stopping in at its "Freedom Bookstore" one day and reading a flier about the school.

I had been a street kid, a Dewar's White Label girl, drinking on the corner. I got pregnant in junior high school and lost my husband to Agent Orange. When I saw the flier, my son Ali was in first grade in public school and I didn't like the atmosphere.

I saw some of the recitals and drills the kids did at Uhuru Sasa, and I wanted the best for Ali. He went there through eighth grade; it wasn't so much the academics that got to him, it was the role models. It was just a very decent environment in which people were tender and concerned, in which parents came with their kids to lectures and special programs; we'd go with teachers and students to demonstrations, like the ones in downtown Brooklyn that Herb Daughtry led after the shooting of Randy Evans [by a police officer, in 1978]. Those of us who were parents became part of what we called the East Family.

Black workers and college students would come to the East from all over the Northeast to Saturday-night concerts by the likes of Max Roach and Betty Carter, but the heart of the place was Uhuru Sasa, whose students were dropouts from the public system, their parents paying $100 a month, when they could, to send them to Weusi. Uhuru Sasa took surplus food from a day-care center run by Velmanette Montgomery, a public school board member and now a state senator from the area, and Weusi cooked up thousands of "hellified meals," as he fondly recalls them—"thick, split-pea soups, sauteed brown rice and vegetables, a special, exotic punch." A 1960s-style communalism sustained the place—two doctors and a dentist who sent their children to the school would examine all the students for free; lawyers would donate their services.

By the early 1980s, the economy and the mood in the neighborhood had changed for the worse. Parents were defaulting on tuition payments; top artists began refusing to do the center's fund-raising concerts for little or no pay; there was a shooting at a concert late in 1983, and ultimately the school and center closed, victims of the founder's departure and the changing spirit of the times. "I guess the only weakness of the place was that it was so good it shielded people from reality," Weusi muses.

In fact, Uhuru Sasa was part of a larger "shield" of half a dozen independent schools founded by some of Brooklyn's most aggressive and independent black parents, who took their children out of the public school system in the wake of Ocean Hill–Brownsville. These schools' strengths—their nearly convalescent insularity and obsessive preoccupation with cultural self-discovery—were also their weaknesses. "I taught at Uhuru Sasa for a year, and it instilled a tremendous discipline and pride in people," says Michael Johnson, now director of the Science Skills Center, an independent, nonprofit institution that uses public school space in Bedford-Stuyvesant to supplement youngsters' education with early-morning and after-hours programs in biology, chemistry, and physics. "I left because I wanted a certain level of expertise in science which I knew the kids were capable of but which I doubted the school was ready to support."

As we will see, it's doubtful that even the African history taught at the East would have passed muster with serious scholars. Yet perhaps, in that setting, it didn't much matter. The center helped young blacks reach back beyond the amnesia of the slave ship for a sense of heritage and cultural direction; for the first time, through the lectures, dramas, and films, students and their parents experienced, as if in a delayed reaction, the traumas of abduction, enslavement, and cultural dismemberment, much as Jews born after the Holocaust first encountered its horrors through Adolf Eichmann's trial in Jerusalem. Like those young Jews—like me, attending the Hebrew-speaking Ramah summer camps as an adolescent in the 1960s—young blacks discovered inner nerve ends extending back to a collective historical journey which had deposited them in America, and of which they were now themselves the repositories by grace of cultural memory.

But, unlike Jews, blacks leaving the East for the bleak ghetto streets saw something of the trauma of the past continuing in their own lives. That discovery was part of a force that spurred the formation of a Black Panther chapter and several Muslim sects in Brooklyn. As that militancy got nowhere or was suppressed, it turned at times to an impotent fury which only deepened some whites' conviction that it must be destroyed.

Perhaps African-American cultural nationalists needed more time and resources to develop institutions like the East into stable bases of community life that could also prepare more of their participants to join the larger society—much as, say, the Orthodox Jewish Yeshiva of Flatbush, whose graduates go on to elite colleges and professional careers, does only a few miles away. It is a tragedy that the black community did not have the strength to sustain such institutions. In retrospect, it's astonishing that whites who make so much of the importance of cultural moorings can reject the anger of blacks awakening to their own history of cultural devastation and of their heroic efforts to surmount it.

But it's also astonishing, I think, that Weusi and others ever believed that the rich but informal communalism they nurtured at the East could have been re-created in the public schools of Ocean Hill–Brownsville. What black advocates of community control of the public schools had been demanding, in effect, was that taxpayers subsidize parochial schools for them through the Board of Education.

Blacks do have a unique claim on our public institutions, which, in conjunction with private interests, enforced their degradation here in America. As Deborah Meier, principal of the public, innovative, integrated Central Park East schools in Manhattan, explains, "The issue of parental trust in a child's school is a real one in all communities, but nowhere more so than among blacks. Every parent feels an enormous vulnerability in sending a child to school: Do the teachers like my kid? Will they blame his failures on me? For obvious and not-so-obvious reasons, black parents have a larger-than-normal doubt and self-doubt about those things." To reduce those doubts to a tolerable level, such parents may indeed have to found their own community schools or make special demands upon the public system.

Moreover, blacks do have some claim on the content of the education which whites, too, receive—or, more often, don't receive—about black contributions to American history. As the black historian Harold Cruse put it in 1969, ironically, just when Weusi and others were leaving the public schools to try to educate themselves,

In the midst of this racial crisis, this deep conflict in cultural values, whites of all ages and classes sing the black people's music and dance to the black people's bodily rhythms, and there is no cultural history written and taught in the educational systems that explains why this is so, and is so American. History books . . . cannot truthfully reveal how the black people's presence, hovering in the background of white men's thinking and plans, shaped white men's political and economic decisions, influenced white men's military strategies, delayed or advanced westward expansion, arrested or encouraged industries, created wealth by being wealth that laid the basis for banking systems, and influenced the national character. We are witnessing at this moment visible efforts to correct our accumulated intellectual deformations in these historical and cultural concerns, and it must be recorded that these efforts came about in response to demands of black cultural nationalism, in varying degrees of insistence.

There are several good reasons, then, for a school system to honor ethnic and cultural affinities, reasons that aren't just stalking-horses for bellyaching about racism or school jobs. But the notion that a school system—from a chancellor defined as cultural "role model" (even though most children never see him) right on down to the precise percentages of minority children depicted in textbook illustrations—must be formulaically reflective of its student body is suspect as serious pedagogy.

Beyond a point which we would be wise not to fix too hurriedly, that notion can just as easily be little more than a rationalization for extra patronage lines and fat consultancies. The schools now deliver far too much patronage in response to electoral muscle, but even that is arguably better than efforts to dress up as pedagogy the ancient grievances and careerism of the next group in line. Indeed, the same systemic abuses, such as the protectionism and featherbedding that were cast as racist, now serve increasingly to protect incompetent black as well as white teachers and principals. In some districts, white superintendents don't dare move against obviously derelict black principals.

That is not what the militants intend, and they are quick to spot blacks who they think are "tools of the system." Still, here I find myself shifting from admiring Weusi's efforts at the East to defending the schools' far more pressing and urgent mission—to equip all children, black and white, with survival skills for the twenty-first century.

Cultural Nationalism versus Universal Culture

In 1985, East Brooklyn Congregations undertook a major effort to link graduates from several troubled East Brooklyn high schools to employment and college opportunities in the city and, in so doing, to improve the high schools themselves. EBC recruited ten major commercial banks, the New York City Housing Authority, and private colleges and universities from the area, including Pace, Adelphi, St. John's, the Pratt Institute, and Long Island University (which has an innovative campus in downtown Brooklyn). Despite a succession of three chancellors and three high school division heads in three years, Nehemiah II, as the program was called, had by 1989 placed 600 graduates and made 150 of its parents, ministers, and lay leaders more knowledgeable about schools. In more that 2,000 one-on-one meetings with students, the EBC people found overwhelmingly good, normal kids whose main problem was that they were poorly educated and knew it.

The schools themselves, however, did not change. As EBC's co-chair, the Reverend Johnny Ray Youngblood, put it,

[T]he New York City Board of Education is not a school system. It is a jobs program, a massive, consolidated hiring hall, set up partly to replace the union halls and clubhouses of the past. The system's real product is employment. Its business is bureaucracy. Its customers are paid personnel. Its god is quantity—more programs, more payrolls, more and bigger buildings, more equipment.

[Its growth depends on] the multiplication of needs and the discovering of lacks in students. Everyone in the system—administrators, teachers, consultants, custodians, local community groups, community school boards, politicians—knows this sad, unspoken secret: the poorer the performance of the students, the larger the payroll. . . . Failure is funded, success ignored. There are no countervailing incentives for improved performance by teachers, administrators, or students. . . . At the administrative and programmatic levels, the system is a swamp of patronage, cronyism, and incompetence. . . .

To the resolution of these problems, the black cultural nationalism which several alumni of the East and of the streets have attempted to bring into the schools has contributed worse than nothing. This small but highly visible group seems torn between attacking the school system rhetorically and trying to play it for all it's worth through bureaucratic infighting, patronage, and even corruption. Some of the activists hold graduate degrees yet have little real education; they form a sort of lumpen intelligentsia of embittered militants and educational martinets. Their proposals for curricular reform would make Harold Cruse cringe; filtered through the system, they would amount to a ludicrous bureaucratization of fantasies about peoplehood, ennobling no one.

Beyond the militants and their immediate followers lies a penumbra of generally supportive black clergymen, journalists, and other professionals who work primarily within and for their community—I call them "professional blacks." At their most pedestrian, they mirror the shabbiest of the Jewish and white-ethnic patronage and featherbedding they pretend to oppose on principle. But their efforts to cast struggles over ethnic and racial succession as profound, pedagogical imperatives pose new dangers. Leapfrogging over the fact that they represent far fewer African-Americans than they claim, they have effectively cowed the many who disagree with them. And they enjoy at times a bizarrely inflated influence on white radicals and liberals who have their own, complicated reasons for going along, not only in the major news organizations but also in public agencies, legislatures, courts, and private churches and foundations.

But let us know them by their works. In December 1989, *New York Newsday*'s Nina Bernstein offered an exhaustive portrait of two dramatically different Bedford-Stuyvesant public schools just three blocks apart and not far from the armory that had housed the East. "At P.S. 21, the Crispus Attucks School, children consistently learn to read and do math at least as well as other children in America," she reported. "At P.S. 262, the El Hajj Malik El Shabazz [Malcolm X] School, they fall far behind."

In every respect—physically, economically, and demographically—the two student bodies are the same. Yet, Bernstein found,

the difference in citywide test scores is stark. Last year only 27.4 percent of the children at P.S. 262 performed at or above grade level in reading. Only a quarter reached that level in math. At P.S. 21, the figures were almost reversed: more than two-thirds of the pupils tested at or above grade level in reading, and nearly three-quarters made the grade in math.

What accounts for it? P.S. 21, Bernstein found, "could be a textbook illustration" of the key factors the Harvard researcher Ronald Edmonds identified ten years ago in trying "to determine what distinguished unusually effective inner-city schools from so many others that failed to educate the children of the poor: strong administrative leadership, an orderly school climate, high expectations for student achievement regardless of family background, frequent monitoring of student performance and a staff consensus that pupil learning is the school's top priority." In contrast,

at P.S. 262, no one has been in control. Four years after the last tenured principal retired, leadership of the school . . . remains the subject of a bitter struggle that divides staff and parents. The battle has resulted in bomb threats, teacher flight, mass staff absences and the beating up of a principal, Lester McDowell, in his office last December [1988], allegedly by a community activist [Ali Lamont]. Appeals for help went largely unanswered at every level of the school system, despite several official inquiries that called for the chancellor's intervention. The investigations supported McDowell's contention that he was being forced out by Brooklyn activist Sonny Carson.

What is this struggle about? In essence, Carson and some teachers and parents who'd left the public school system after the Ocean Hill–Brownsville debacle and helped found Uhuru Sasa, had, after its demise, reentered the public school system; they wanted to establish PS 262 as a black cultural center where they could run meetings, rallies, and a Saturday youth group and control some of the funding and patronage. Carson led this group in persuading the community school board and the Board of Education to rename PS 262, which had been called the John H. McCooey School after a deceased

Brooklyn Democratic party leader, for Malcolm.

Ironically, Carson had once had similar proprietary feelings about the neighboring PS 21, whose principal throughout the 1960s and most of the 1970s was his fellow activist Adelaide Sanford, a committed nationalist who succeeded in transferring most white teachers out of the school and discouraging white applicants from entering. Sanford's assistant principal in the 1960s and Carson's longtime ally, Herman Ferguson, was denied a principalship in the Ocean Hill–Brownsville district in 1967 because he was under indictment for plotting to kill the civil rights leader Roy Wilkins (he was later acquitted).

The Brooklyn assemblyman Al Vann, who was president of the Afro-American Teachers Association and a close ally of Carson, Ferguson, and Sanford at that time, explained the militants' educational philosophy to a reporter from *Ebony* magazine during the 1968 school wars:

By no means are we saying that it's not important to read, write and manipulate numbers. But we're saying, it's also important that you begin to understand yourself, that you've had a glorious past and can have a glorious future, and therefore you can achieve. We want a program that will produce big black men, not little white men. The Man is not going to give us these values. They have to be earned by a new kind of black man that we don't have yet. . . .

Schools are big business. The average school probably has about $1 million money flow in a year's time. You control a lot of jobs if you control the school system. You control all the contracting and purchasing. . . . The black community has not really begun to speak to this economic aspect of community control because it's wrapped up in the very humane problem of "How can I educate my child? How can I educate him to become mobile in this society?" Black people see community control as that vehicle.

Since the time I first met him in 1981, Vann has often made a good deal of sense to me, and I find his views here at least arguable, not much different from those which leaders of other ethnic groups have held. But Carson takes them further. It has long been Carson's belief that the education of black children belongs literally in the hands of "big black men"—a belief Weusi thinks he carries to extremes: "In

1986 Sonny, who has a lot of influence on the local school board, put out a call for a black male principal at PS 262; the irony is that they gave the job to Lester McDowell, who some people felt was weak. He got it just because he wore some pants. Women often make the greater fighters." McDowell is black but lives in Brooklyn's integrated Park Slope neighborhood, not in Bedford-Stuyvesant.

Whether inadvertently or not, McDowell locked some of Carson's people out of the school when they scheduled meetings there. Carson began denouncing him as "a tool of the system . . . driven by those downtown whose mission is to make sure that all our children are miseducated." "The day that school became the El Hajj Malik El Shabazz School," he said, "it was destined that that school would have turmoil. The powers that be will never let anything happen there successfully." Actually, as Bernstein reports, the school had been targeted for special programs based loosely on Edmonds's research, but, largely because of Carson's interventions, its staff, parents, and administration became too divided to collaborate. After some of Carson's supporters were elected to the community school board in May 1989, tensions rose.

Carson enlisted the support of Basir Mchawi, another community activist whom Chancellor Richard Green had hired as a special aide. Some critics said this was a way of buying peace from militants who thought Green an Uncle Tom when he first arrived in New York from Minneapolis with the support of Mayor Koch, Board of Education President Robert Wagner, Jr., and the UFT. A Board of Education investigation would find that Carson and Mchawi lunched at Junior's Restaurant in downtown Brooklyn with McDowell and urged him to transfer out, promising to arrange a better assignment and threatening him if he refused.

McDowell declined. Not long afterward, Ali Lamont, another associate of Carson's, entered McDowell's office and beat him severely, according to an indictment of Lamont for assault. Weusi told me, "I resolved a long time ago not to get involved in these low-level battles—'We want so-and-so for principal, for superintendent.' It's a power play, not based on any principles I can defend."

Principled or not, the militants seem to have a mesmerizing effect not only on many blacks who are angry or afraid of being called system tools and Toms but also on guilt-ridden whites like Bernard Mecklowitz, the acting chancellor after Green's death. Mecklowitz did not act decisively to vindicate McDowell, who was transferred out.

Shoot-out at the Ethnic Corral

More problematic than what Weusi calls "these low-level battles, which are really based on personalities and power," is the subordination of formal curricular and credentialing standards to questions of race. Both the good and the bad in such initiatives got a big push forward late in 1986 when Adelaide Sanford, the former PS 21 principal, was nominated by Assemblyman Vann and, to the applause of Carson and many other community activists, elected by the legislature to the Board of Regents, the state's highest educational governing body. At a time when East Brooklyn Congregations was developing its scathing indictment of an overly politicized system, Sanford declared that black children were dropping out of the schools in disproportionate numbers because insensitive teachers and an archaic curriculum were telling them nothing about themselves and their cultural backgrounds, thereby fostering low self-esteem.

An excerpt from an edition of *Increasing High School Completion Rates,* a New York State Board of Regents booklet distributed to 15,000 educators throughout the state in the summer of 1987, showed the lengths to which Sanford, one of three regents appointed by the full board to study the relation between cultural learning styles and school completion rates, was willing to go to impose the prism of race upon educational policy. At her behest, the booklet included the following findings of a black researcher:

> Children's racial . . . backgrounds . . . influence the manner in which they learn. . . . For example, qualities noted in African-Americans include: . . .
>
> • tendency to approximate space, number and time instead of aiming for complete accuracy;

- focus on people and their activities rather than objects;

- possession of a keen sense of justice and quick perception of injustice; . . .

- general tendency not to be "word" dependent, but proficient in nonverbal as well as verbal communication.

This effort to institutionalize a recognition of special cultural learning styles is reminiscent of black-power advocates' claims in the 1960s that, as Julius Lester put it then, black culture's "emphasis is on the nonverbal, i.e., the nonconceptual. . . . It is experience that counts, not what is said. . . . The black man knows the inherent irrationality of life." Fortunately, the regents' booklet created a storm in the fall of 1987, though not only among blacks. Hispanic teachers protested an item stating that their children are known for their "acceptance of work in moderation"; Asians were furious to learn that their children are known for their "intolerance of ambiguities."

Most of the regents, too, were appalled by the assertions; one of them called for Sanford's resignation when a news account quoted her as saying that white and Native American high school dropouts were not on her agenda, because her top priority was the salvation of her people. Edmond Gordon, a black Yale psychology professor whom the regents asked for comment, endorsed the booklet's "good intention" but called its language "unfortunate" and warned of the dangers of racial stereotyping. "That's the risk we have to take, perhaps, in order to give these children a ray of hope," Sanford responded.

What no one seemed to notice was that Sanford and company had managed to re-create in the four items above not only a bureaucratic parody of black-power pronunciamentos from the 1960s but also traditional stereotypes about women which feminists showed had been reinforced by sexist schooling. There is an irony in the fact that many white girls, like many black children of both sexes, have indeed exhibited these qualities. For they are essentially avoidance strategies, protective anticipations of the sexist and racist rejections which societies worldwide have delivered to women and minorities in their midst.

One reason so many people emigrate from such societies to America, and specifically to New York, is to enable themselves and their youngsters to win self-esteem by proving that they're just as good as those who might undervalue them. They want to do so precisely by demonstrating the prowess and precision which elitists (or sexists or racists) always believe are their special preserve. For prowess and precision are demanded today not by "elite" or "white" culture but, as the Japanese and others are demonstrating, by a new, universal culture enveloping the globe. Many of the immigrants still think of New York City as a free, cosmopolitan place where that culture is respected.

Staking a claim on admission to the universal culture and making it stick is especially difficult for African-American kids, say the psychologists Signithia Fordham and John U. Ogbu, because the long history of whites' low expectations of blacks and hostility to their achievements has engendered a defensive group solidarity, enforced by peers at school, that penalizes successful black students for "acting white." Reading Fordham's and Ogbu's vignettes of lonely, bright black youngsters' desperate efforts to submerge their academic achievements—because they dread being shunned by black peers and doubt that whites will accept them even if they succeed—one can't help marveling that adults like Sanford are touting cultural learning styles that reinforce such destructive "solidarity."

No one can fault blacks for resenting and highlighting white racism in education and elsewhere; it was WASPs, after all, who used to tout their own cultural learning styles, including their putatively "keen sense of justice," and they employed plenty of "nonverbal" understandings to hurt blacks most cruelly. Nor were other white-ethnic groups far behind the WASPs in such treatment of blacks. Teachers should know this. They should try to nurture black pride and redress ancient grievances where they can. But bureaucratizing that redress through manuals hawking stereotypes only deepens the racist double standards it means to dispel. Thankfully, in this instance, the regents removed the offending passages, over Sanford's objections.

Of Chancellors and Role Models

Shortly after the booklet was withdrawn, its defenders found a new cause in the demand that the next public schools chancellor be an African-American. In the 1987 search that ultimately produced Richard Green, the Reverend Sharpton declared that the new chancellor must be black, no matter what, "because the last two were Hispanic." Indeed, in the 1983 selection process that had produced Anthony Alvarado, the first of the Hispanic chancellors, Weusi, the NAACP state coordinator Hazel Dukes, and Bill Lynch, now a deputy mayor and then an aide to Representative Major Owens, had been arrested at Board of Education headquarters for demonstrating in support of Thomas Minter, a black deputy chancellor who they felt should succeed the outgoing Frank Macchiarola. The demonstrators' lawyer was C. Vernon Mason. Now, in 1987, the candidate favored by Sharpton, Mason, and the New York Alliance of Black School Educators, of which Sanford had been president before joining the Board of Regents, was Sanford herself.

Whether supporting her or not, those who called for a black chancellor spoke only in passing of the sorts of qualification, besides a high level of race consciousness, which black candidates should bring to the job. Rare was the acknowledgment that a black chancellor, no less than a black astronaut or chairman of the Joint Chiefs of Staff, could be a role model for black students (and, for that matter, for all students) only if his or her color were incidental to a selection process that evaluated the candidate's talent and experience. In 1989, Sanford made this unconcern remarkably explicit on Gil Noble's black Sunday-morning television talk show, "Like It Is":

> There have certainly been many, many instances in which I have been asked to evaluate Dr. Richard Green and certainly I will never do that, because I see every male of African ancestry so tied to my destiny and my future and that of my people—it is as though you ask me, do I want to fight the person who is the victim or do I want to fight the oppressor?

At least Sanford was candid; others who demanded a black chancellor were disingenuous both about their lack of interest in transracial standards and about their political agendas. Without saying so in public, they looked not just for blackness but for cultural nationalism like Sanford's; blackness was really a necessary but not sufficient condition. There was deafening silence from the New York Alliance of Black School Educators, for example, when Bernard Gifford, a talented, black former deputy chancellor and dean of the Graduate School of Education at Berkeley, was mentioned in newspaper headlines as a leading contender. No wonder: Gifford told *New York Newsday* he worried that the selection process might "be contaminated by the race question." He added, "No one wants to be reduced to a racial statistic, including me. The position is far too important to be allocated on [that] basis. . . ."

The Board of Education search panel that interviewed more than a dozen candidates for the position in December 1987 found that Sanford "lacked the experience and ability of the [eight] finalists." That didn't stop fifty demonstrators from showing up at board headquarters to demand her appointment. When the selection of Green was announced soon afterward, C. Vernon Mason, who had backed Sanford, bared her supporters' politics by warning, "Koch will be calling the shots. We will have a figurehead in the name of Green." The chancellor-designate's response showed greater dignity. "I would suggest that [Mason] ought not to use the politics of the moment to diffuse the opportunity that we have. He should think very carefully about where he chooses to place his energy," Green told *New York Newsday*'s Barbara Whitaker from his home in Minneapolis.

Fortunately, Green was well qualified and an inspiration to the teachers and children he met. And it must be said that, with the activists, he understood that today's schools cannot simply offer staged introductions, through tests of all sorts, to the rigors of life beyond the family circle for youngsters presumed to come from warm, supportive homes. For better or worse, Green knew, the city's schools now must engage in the most basic efforts at socialization, teaching children about conflict resolution, harnessing youthful peer pressure to constructive ends through special programs, and, yes, helping youngsters respect their own and others' cultures. Unfortunately, as one education reporter told me, "Green's sense of racial politics was nil." He was astounded by the depth and narrowness of racial preserves in New York's public life, and he usually tried to keep the militants at arm's length. They were suspicious of him, and to allay that suspicion, he sometimes indulged them, as when he hired Basir Mchawi. When Green died of an asthma attack in May 1989, not a few black activists felt that the system had "killed" him, and they marshaled the rhetoric of redress to call for another African-American chancellor.

A comment by Weusi about the original 1983 campaign to make Deputy Chancellor Thomas Minter the system's first black chancellor reveals something important about the larger, racial political agenda behind such efforts. Weusi recalled having been interviewed for a high school principalship in 1981 by Chancellor Macchiarola and Minter and remembered that the latter had "been bad" to him:

Macchiarola was playing the nice guy. It was good cop, bad cop, and Minter was doing his job. See, Minter had been brought in and touted all over town as Macchiarola's successor, so he was doing what he was told. I knew they were just using him. [Yet] when the search for a new chancellor began in 1983, I called up Vann and Daughtry and said, "We've got to do Minter." I knew he wasn't gonna get the job, but it was part of our strategy to convince the black middle class that they have power only when they ally themselves with the masses and don't allow themselves to be used, as Minter did.

Well, by that time they'd disrespected Minter so badly that he was furious, and he knew he wasn't gonna get it, either. And during our campaign he was transformed. It's only when they have a Tom Minter experience that they realize how they've been used. It's like [former deputy mayor] Haskell Ward; Koch brought him up from Georgia and just used him up like an old rag. And Haskell told me, "They'll just throw you away when they're done."

Culture by Cookie Cutter

The nationalists' and professional blacks' maneuverings over cultural learning styles and black chancellors are but two expressions of their flight to racial double standards in the schools. Another is their relentless opposition to all standardized testing and curricula allegedly built around the dominant, "Eurocentric" corporate culture. Since Sanford and others had insisted on redefining and circumscribing standards in ways that could inhibit black children's proficiencies in science, mathematics, and Standard English, it wasn't surprising that they also tried to discredit, as inherently biased, all standardized testing that measures such proficiency.

That effort failed, too, and not just because the Board of Education bureaucracy cannot justify itself without test scores. The consensus among parents and the public is strong that, as the Queens College political scientist Andrew Hacker puts it,

the SAT reveals how far students have adapted to the kinds of thinking that are widely thought to be necessary for success in the United States. The test calls for an ability to impose formal systems on reality. Arithmetic, mathematics, and standard grammar are such systems; so are other modes of thinking central to academic work such as reasoning by analogy and quickly extracting the point from passages of exposition. Ours is a society built on science and technology and on highly organized activities concerned with abstractly formulated pieces of information (however useless some of that information may be). Those who wish to join these enterprises must have minds attuned to the ways that world works.

That the "world" Hacker describes is not a "Eurocentric" one is made clear by the ethnic and racial distribution of SAT scores. If the SAT is culturally biased, it is in favor of Asians, who score higher than whites.

The activists now beat a tactical retreat to politically safer efforts to revise the cultural content of the curriculum. We must try harder, they said, to recognize the contributions of all minority cultures to American society. That worthy end in their minds was freighted with responsibility to bolster what they called the "basic self-esteem" of minority students. The current curriculum's scanting of students' cultural histories in social studies and other classes wasn't just unfair; it was a form of genocide because it denied African-American children self-respect and a clear connection to their studies, and so figured in their dropping out of school.

That sweeping assertion became the premise of a draft report, "A Curriculum of Inclusion," submitted in 1989 to New York State Commissioner of Education Thomas Sobol by his Task Force on Minorities: Equity and Excellence. The body comprised primarily noneducators; its chair, Hazel Dukes, heads the state NAACP and is a paid official of the state's Off-Track Betting Corporation. The report's principal author, Harry Hamilton, a professor of atmospheric science at the State University of New York at Albany, was assisted by one consultant from each of the minority groups studied—African-Americans, Hispanics, Asians, and Native Americans.

Noting that nonwhites will make up 29 percent of the new entrants into the state's labor force by the year 2000, twice their current share, the report cited Latino and African-American school dropout rates that are over 50 percent higher than those of children of other cultures. Staying in school is critical, the report noted, because "the fastest growing jobs will be in professional, technical and sales fields requiring the highest education and skills. . . ."

Lest anyone think this an argument for teaching the things Hacker tells us are measured by the SAT, the report quickly explained that minority kids were turned off by the schools' Eurocentric curriculum, which was deficient at portraying the images and content of their own cultures' contributions to America and New York State. If that can be remedied, the report stated,

children from Native American, Puerto Rican/Latino, Asian American and African American cultures will have higher self-esteem and self-respect, while children from European cultures will have a less arrogant perspective of being part of the group that has "done it all."

European culture is likened to the master of a house ruling over a dinner table, himself firmly established at the head of the table and all other cultures being guests some distance down the table from the master, who has invited the others through his beneficence.

. . . Again using the dinner table analogy, the [task force's proposed] new model is likened to the fabled Round Table of King Arthur, with all cultures offering something to the collective good, each knowing and respecting others. . . .

The point is that we can boost kids' self-esteem by changing the cultural seating arrangement. But it is unclear that we can, and the report's dubious scholarship (and syntax) begged the question of whether we must pass from inclusion to distortion in rewriting history to accomplish this goal. It may not have been wholly by accident that the report invoked a European emblem, King Arthur's table, to make its point. For, as a *Newsday* editorial criticizing the report noted,

The American notion of respect for diversity that the task force holds up as a model comes, ironically, from a unique constitutional scheme rooted in the European Enlightenment. Students must learn that this scheme was flawed and has often been improved through the heroism of African-Americans and other minorities. But that this ethic exists at all reflects a history of noble collaborations in which whites, too, can take pride.

A curriculum should indeed teach students the humbling lesson that all great ideas and social experiments progress laboriously and are distilled, if at all, through struggles in which the oppressed, like the oppressors, sometimes fight heroically, but also sometimes blindly and destructively. All this seemed lost on the task force, which focused on removing what it called the "deep-seated pathologies of racial hatred" permeating the curriculum. As Assemblyman Arthur Eve of Buffalo explained, reiterating what has become something of a catechism among professional blacks, educators "literally destroy" black children because there's nothing in their schoolbooks to give them self-esteem, and "it is a form of genocide."

And how is such destruction to be stopped? Presumably through curricular evaluations like this one, by the task force consultant Leonard Jeffries, chairman of the Africana Studies Department at City College:

On the cover [of the Board of Regents' social studies syllabus] is a multicultural collection of families which is appropriate because the focus in the initial educational level is on social interaction and family relations. . . . Upon a more detailed analysis, particularly utilizing an Afrocentric perspective, it is clear that multicultural substance has been sacrificed. The white family is represented by three generations, the Asian family by two generations, and the African American family includes just a single parent. This example could be referred to as Eurocentric Multiculturalism.

What a "more detailed analysis, particularly utilizing an Afrocentric perspective," might have revealed to Jeffries is that a large body of black scholars believes that single-parent-family modes should be presented as legitimate and that, when they aren't, black children without resident fathers are unfairly scapegoated. More research might have informed him that a majority of the families of black students in the New York City public schools are single-parent families. In what sense, then, is their representation in the booklet an example of "Eurocentric Multiculturalism"?

The report apologized for not having time and resources to examine other cultures beyond the Native American, Black, Asian, and Latino:

It should be emphasized at this point that there is great cultural diversity within all of the cultural groups referred to in the report, and care must be taken to recognize and respect the variations. The task force firmly believes that the manner in which the European American culture has interacted with these four general cultural groupings is basically similar to the way it has interacted with all other cultures.

But the last sentence contradicts its predecessor. Is it professionally responsible to lump Italians with Norwegians, Slavs and Germans with Polish Jews, or, for that matter, within these groups, to equate Hasidic Jews with secular Jewish radicals, or Sicilians with Florentines? That history written by the "victors" may be untrustworthy and unfair is no excuse for the "losers" to engage in what amounts to fanciful, wishful thinking disguised as history. Yet the task force offered nothing but romanticized portraits of tribal chieftains, minority fighters for justice, and white racist oppressors.

Fairy tales from out of the mists of the past may be fine for the East or for the youngest students in any school. But on "Like It Is," the task force consultant Jeffries joined Professor John Henrik Clarke, a Hunter College historian who once lectured at the East, in a fabulistic tour de force of African history of the sort that presumably would find its way into all public school curricula if the task force's recommendations were followed through.

NOBLE: Professor Jeffries, many today wonder how so many great civilizations in Africa came to be overwhelmed by the slave trade.

JEFFRIES: . . . In the period before the trans-Atlantic slave trade, which the European nations were heavily involved in, . . . Europe was in chaos,

. . . land-poor, resource-poor, people-poor. The bubonic plague had wiped out a good part of the population in the 1300s. . . .

There was a golden age along the west coast of Africa, . . . in the high Andes of the Inca peoples and in the Central America of the Mayans, and the Aztecs later contributing to that development. So, we have to ask ourselves what happened. My approach is that there was a 50-year turning point in history, 1482 to 1536. . . . By accidents of history, the European was able to move from the wings of history on to the center stage and push everybody else off.

NOBLE: But how could a people from a continent in decline overwhelm a continent that was in full flower?

PROF. CLARKE: Well, you got to take into consideration who had the gun. . . . In Europe's isolation, they had lost the concept of longitude and latitude. The Africans, Arabs and the Burburs [*sic*] in Spain had preserved information on the maritime skill coming out of the great technical nation of that day, China. Once the European learned what to do with ships at sea, again, he realized that he had to get outside of Europe to find some food. He's looking to Asia for the great spices, looking for something to put on that awful European food so he could eat it.

One might suppose that viewers eventually got an answer to Noble's query about how the backward Europeans conquered flowering civilizations of the sun. It never came.

The task force report called for a new special assistant to the commissioner (of education) for cultural equity—quickly dubbed "the cultural equity czar." In one of its few specific suggestions for curricular change, the task force urged that children studying the conquest of the American West be told that Chinese laborers laid the track for the Central Pacific Railroad. To which Andrew Hacker responded, "They should also learn how Leland Stanford and Collis Huntington conceived of the project and supervised its completion." In other words, students may need more, not less, of what Jeffries thinks is Eurocentric history, since much of world history now turns on technological and social developments that transformed the globe and are no longer the monopoly of Europeans.

Sobol, according to a news release from his office, expressed "his appreciation to the Task Force and the consultants for their 'valuable contribution to the dialogue on this important issue" and "pledged to carefully review the recommendations and work diligently to implement a comprehensive program" of multicultural inclusion. Then he publicly distanced himself from the report, whose language he acknowledged had "offended" some readers, and recommended to the regents that a new panel of scholars be assembled to help revise the curriculum to promote inclusion. The regents adopted his plan unanimously, in effect starting all over.

No one said anything about *Newsday*'s editorial recommendation that "the state should review the complaisant way it assembled this task force and disseminated such divisive, misleading writ." One thing such a review might disclose is Sobol's own acknowledged anxiety to placate professional blacks, who were angered when the front-runner for his job, Bernard Gifford, the black former deputy chancellor of the city schools, withdrew his name from consideration and, with it, the activists' hopes for the first black state commissioner of education.

Toward a Universal Culture

The central confusion behind all the reports and agitation about learning styles, standardized testing, and curriculum was identified years ago by the black sociologist Orlando Patterson, who drew an important distinction between "European culture" and America's "dominant culture." There is, Patterson explained,

a universal culture which is partly a product of the . . . new socioeconomic order and, on the symbolic level, draws on the most convenient cultural patterns of the groups which make up the society. These symbolic borrowings are largely a matter of convenience and timing. . . . The Anglo-Saxons effectively conquered and settled the United States and, as a result, their language became the national language. It is silly for an Italian or Pole to moan over this.

. . . But there is another reason why it is trivial to complain about the fact that the generalized culture may have borrowed unduly from certain groups. Once an element of culture becomes generalized under the impact of a universal culture, it loses all specific symbolic value for the group which donated it. It is a foolish Anglo-Saxon who boasts about "his" language today. English is a child that no longer knows its mother, and cares even less to know her. It has been adapted in a thousand ways to meet the special feelings, moods and experiences of a thousand groups. . . .

What is true of language is also true of other areas of the universal culture. . . . Jazz is now the music of the universal culture of America. It is no longer a black-American music, although some blacks have desperately tried to hold some special claim to it. . . .

We are . . . told by the chauvinists that the melting pot was merely a smokescreen used by the WASPs to ensure the continued domination of their own culture. It is never possible, however, for peoples to meet for any sustained period of time without mutually influencing each other. More important is the way in which the chauvinists [fail] to see that ethnic WASP culture is no longer the culture of the group of Americans we now call WASPs.

Patterson is reminding us that WASPs listen to jazz, eat Chinese food, and are in other ways assimilating to a "dominant" American culture that is by now more universal than purely European in character. Patterson thinks the chauvinists insist on calling that dominant culture a WASP culture because, in so doing,

they kill, ideologically, two birds with one stone: WASP cultural domination and the universal culture. The latter, of course, is the real enemy. But the enemy cannot be named, for it is still too powerfully sanctioned. Furthermore, the rewards of the universal culture are still being enjoyed even while it is being attacked. Most chauvinist works are composed in suburban homes or elegant apartments.

Epistemologically and politically, there is no longer an official historical or cultural "line" in America; we are all of us hurtling into a brave new world, hoping we'll be strong enough to wrest new myths and truths from our shared experience on a shrinking planet. Doing so could indeed mean unearthing long-suppressed cultural traditions in our midst, an exciting prospect. But, like parochialists of every color, black-nationalist educational reformers fear and mistrust that excitement and the new world it will bring. Unlike those who reject modernity on principle and are willing to pay the price, the chauvinists desperately crave—no, demand—the benefits of the dominant culture they attack.

When I was a substitute teacher at Manhattan's elite Stuyvesant High School briefly in 1983, my biggest discipline problem was trying to stop Asian kids from studying the chemistry books they kept open in their laps during a class on labor history. Ironically, I was recounting how immigrant groups, including the Chinese, had been channeled into specific industries and exploited in the building of America. But if the self-esteem this material was supposed to impart to my Chinese-American students was important to them, they gave no evidence of it; they seemed to have acquired self-esteem at home.

Certainly, they needed to learn about the other cultures around them. And, yes, to repeat, African-American students have a special claim on public schools to teach them about themselves, for it was American institutions, public as well as private, that suppressed and tried to destroy the culture they'd brought with them onto the slave ships. The question is whether a public school class can ever give back what America has taken away or can impart the sense of group pride Weusi was able in some measure to impart at the East.

The purpose of public school is to enable children to locate themselves, not just as blacks, but as individuals, in the broader human experience and endeavor, a process that ultimately requires the courage to "act white," to forsake the crutch of role modeling based solely on group identification. Ralph Ellison knew that in order to be a great writer, he had to broaden the horizons of his community:

[I]n Macon County, Alabama [Ellison wrote], I read Marx, Freud, T.S. Eliot, Pound, Gertrude Stein and Hemingway. Books which seldom, if ever, mentioned Negroes were to release me from whatever "segregated" idea I might have had of my human possibilities. I was freed not . . . by the example of [the black novelist Richard] Wright but by composers, novelists and poets who spoke to me of more interesting and freer ways of life. [Their work gave] me a broader sense of life and possibility. . . . It requires real poverty of the imagination to think that this can come to a Negro only through the example of other Negroes. . . .

Neither Ellison nor the Chinese-American students in my class were interested in adopting "white" culture as much as they were interested in becoming part of the larger "universal" culture of constitutional democracy and technological development.

By no means do all Chinese-American students excel. In New York City, most of them are quite poor, living in crowded tenements with parents who work in restaurants and garment sweatshops. Yet a disproportionate number of them are on their way to becoming rocket scientists, computer designers, biomedical researchers, and, presumably, artists, writers, and political leaders. Certainly no one stands over them telling them that they have a "tendency to approximate space, number and time instead of aiming for complete accuracy" and to "focus on people and their activities rather than objects." Nor do they have "defenders" like Sonny Carson assuring them that the system is dedicated to their miseducation and that they must choose between being, as he puts it, "tools of the system" and "political prisoners." Free of such obfuscations, the Chinese-American students will not lay the metaphorical rails of the next railroad; they will help design and guide new technological and cultural systems.

Black students can join them if they follow the example of Michael Johnson, a black educator who has founded the Science Skills Center in central Brooklyn. With the support of the former superintendent Jerome Harris in Brooklyn's District 13, which provided some empty classrooms, Johnson began a few years ago to use antipoverty and private-foundation funding for a program to draw 150 "latch key" children into his labs each day after school and interest them in scientific discoveries and experiments. To counter absurd charges by a few jealous black educators that he was somehow "creaming DuBois' talented tenth" by working exclusively with only the brainiest children, Johnson asked for some of the district's toughest junior high school kids and recruited them into an "Early Bird" science program that meets every morning at seven-thirty. "Those kids get there before I do, and they're great. It shut the critics up real fast," he chuckles.

But we don't do "rap" in the classroom; we don't allow gold chains. We set a larger cultural standard. I believe in a curriculum of cultural inclusion, and we do a series on black and Latino scientists to show these kids that they can do anything other students can. But kids also know they have to be able to go out into the world and take an exam. I have a fifth grader who just passed the Regents' tenth-grade science test.

We have had to go outside and physically defend our kids from others who made fun of them for coming here. We try to create a cultural membrane—to borrow a term from biology—and create within it our own social activities. I tell the kids, "Look, I was on welfare for a while, my father wasn't around; kids used to say horrible things to me because I liked to read." They can't believe it.

But, growing up in Brooklyn, I had teachers, white and black, who didn't care where I came from, they just put it on me. It's very dangerous to have low expectations of kids; that's one of my pet peeves. I get into conflict with people because of it. But I know that students will rise to the level of your expectations. You have to be careful not to back into racist notions.

Johnson was a student teacher at PS 21, when Adelaide Sanford was its principal.

I love Ms. Sanford; she's an inspiration to me. And she loves this program—that's the educator in her. But I suppose that as a political figure she's under a lot of peer pressure of her own to take certain positions. She may have to maintain her credibility with certain people, and if she asks for educational excellence, some are gonna say, "You're leaving too many behind."

[Superintendent] Jerome Harris had to stand up to that. He'd come into schools and say, "I want you to teach these kids like you would teach students on [mostly white, middle-class] Staten Island. I don't care if they're on welfare. If they need something to eat, give it to them. But then you teach." Harris wasn't liked by some people for that.

Indeed, Harris, who applied for the city chancellorship on two occasions, was never supported by Sanford and the others demanding a black chancellor, even though some of his all-minority elementary schools showed the most dramatic increases in reading scores in the city. When I asked him about this in 1988, he told me he'd just been chosen to be superintendent of schools in Atlanta, a position he assumed later that year.

But Harris's legacy survived: on the same WLIB program where Maddox and Sharpton often hold forth, the host Gary Byrd held a Science Skills Center contest between two teams of Johnson's students late in 1989 as part of Ujima, a day devoted to "collective work and responsibility" during the season of Kwanza, an African holiday which black cultural nationalists increasingly celebrate instead of Christmas. The radio contest was exciting and impressive. When it was over, Byrd said, "The real winners are the community; look at the minds being turned out, the scientists of tomorrow! Don't let anyone tell you it isn't happening, because it is!"

I couldn't help hoping that these black and Latino youngsters will someday know the exhilaration of holding their own with white and Asian teammates. That won't happen on WLIB, but perhaps it will in high school and in at least some colleges. If so, they'll have become part of the universal culture that transcends race, and I envision them looking back fondly, proudly on their experiences at the Science Skills Center, including their studies of black and Latino scientists. They won't think of themselves primarily as black and Latino scientists, however, but as New Yorkers and Americans, free of crippling, special "cultural learning styles," free of the fear of acting white; free, too, of the clutches of Jeffries, Mchawi, and Sonny Carson. "The 'political' people in education really don't like science, I've found," Johnson says dryly.

The Forgotten Parent

Speaking in Chancellor Green's behalf at an April 1, 1989, community forum on education sponsored by the Coalition of 100 Black Women in Brooklyn, his nationalist aide Mchawi stated, according to one outraged black parent who took notes and protested to the chancellor, "I work for the Board of Mis-Education—and I mean that. Don't think that because there are two black men in the chancellor's office that the revolution has started. It hasn't. Nothing's changed. The only way change is going to come is if you do it."

Sadly, Mchawi's rhetoric stirred many in his audience to applause. But the dissenting parent, Norbert Pierre, has two children doing very well in a special program supported by his district's white superintendent, Harvey Garner, administered by a white woman, Joyce Rubin, and "taught by a corps of teachers committed to excellence." Pierre resented Mchawi's "sinister implication that whites have been knowingly in charge of alleged mis-education." "This is a slanderous insult to the many diligent, committed white teachers and administrators who every day make a difference in the lives of all our children," he wrote to Chancellor Green.

Confronted with nonsense like Mchawi's, Green, State Education Commissioner Sobol, and the former CUNY chancellor Joseph Murphy have sometimes acted as if they felt guilty about their responsibilities as gatekeepers to the universal culture of the future. Honorable men all, they know they preside over institutions badly distended by discriminatory racial fiefdoms, black as well as white, and by a pervasive cynicism and inertia which they have not managed to dispel. But guilt is no excuse for rushing, as they so often have, to conflate the noisiest of black agitators with the long-suffering majority of black students and parents like Norbert Pierre.

Even when their institutions don't exemplify the best, educational leaders have to stand for standards and for society's noblest visions of achievement. Even as they battle entrenched, mostly white interests that subvert good education, they have to be willing to be called racists or Toms in fighting to save minority children from the professional black chauvinists. When educational leaders compromise or temporize about this, they fail parents like Pierre, who had invested his own children so deeply in a color-blind concept of excellence that he felt compelled to protest to the chancellor the racially charged misrepresentations of Mchawi. He got only a form letter in reply.

The system's politician-administrators also leave dedicated teachers to fend for themselves. Like Pierre, Stanley Schwartz, a teacher on Staten Island, felt compelled to fire off an angry letter, this one to the *Daily News,* when a black activist priest from Manhattan laid the "damage" done to black children at the feet of Jewish teachers:

Father Lawrence Lucas must have known all about me when he condemned Jews "who are killing" black children in the classroom. Yesterday, I murdered two with an evil test. Last week, I poisoned six with Shakespeare. . . . Others have I strangled with poetry by Countee Cullen, Paul Laurence Dunbar and Langston Hughes. I never let up. From the moment a black student enters my room, I crack the whip: memorize this spelling, study that grammar, learn these definitions; prepare for the Regents [examinations]. . . . Nag, nag, nag. Push, push, push. Achieve, achieve, achieve. Some killer am I.

9

Folly on the Left

A Troubled Marriage

Ever since the left and the Negro community first met over battered tin coffee pots in the city's cold basements early during the Depression, their destinies have been woven together more tightly than many black leaders would like. Perhaps the time has come for white leftists, too, to reassess the relationship.

In the 1930s, as we have seen, the downtrodden Negro badly needed the ascendant and more powerful left; Communists and socialists were able to open new doors for blacks by successfully casting their plight as part of larger oppressions which all Americans must fight. As Mark Naison explains in his book *Communists in Harlem,* the left, "by defining Black America's struggle for cultural recognition as a source of creative energy for the entire nation, . . . helped give [whites] a sense that they had a personal stake in black empowerment and that cultural interchange between the races represented . . . the affirmation of a democratic impulse rather than a journey to the heart of darkness."

Less often noticed was that the Popular Front helped white leftists themselves to affirm their tenuous grasp on American life. Children of immigrants driven by their own profound insecurities and ideals, they used radical politics and their alliances with blacks to stake their own claim in an America where they, too, might feel at home. The historian Fred Siegel notes that McCarthyism in the 1950s was a long-delayed revolt by white ethnics, particularly Irish- and German-American isolationists, against Roosevelt's war, the alliance with Stalin, and, perhaps most important, the Popular Front's success at redefining Americanism in terms of tolerance, brotherhood, and integration. Former Vice-President Henry Wallace's leftist campaign for the presidency in 1948 had seemed to continue those efforts, enraging the right and stoking the fires of reaction. McCarthyism voided white leftists' fevered social progress by telling them they were "un-American," after all. Thereafter, some on the left seemed to need blacks in a new, more desperate, less condescending way as a cat's-paw of revolution.

Neither the left nor the black community has been quite able to let go of the other, then, but, oh, what a bruiser this marriage of class and color, of Marxism and black nationalism, has been, its noisy basement fights sending tremors through the edifice above! Usually those living upstairs have been able to reassure themselves that the disturbances were only squabbles among the domestics, not the dread thunder from below that might someday make them run for their lives. But there *has* been real thunder: recall the importance of the left to the "Don't Buy Where You Can't Work" campaign of the 1930s and, indeed, the civil rights and antiwar movements of the 1960s. Even today, the left remains a leaven of diminished but still discernible importance in New York City's politics and culture. Still mostly white, but including increasing numbers of blacks and Hispanics, the core of the left in the city consists of a few thousand people, most of whom live in four neighborhoods: Manhattan's Upper West Side, Greenwich Village, the Lower East Side, and Brooklyn's Park Slope, with sprinklings in neighborhoods at the fringes of these.

More than half are teachers, writers, or students who talk mostly to one another, pursuing a politics of self-definition through moral posturing and the taking of "positions" that are occasionally expressed in leaflets. But a couple thousand more are dedicated, full-time activists, lawyers, professional policy analysts and advocates, elected officials, and community and labor-union organizers. That is not without consequence, nor is there anything conspiratorial about most of it. Nor, finally, can one blame the left entirely for its relative impotence, since its critique of capitalism, while valuable, remains alien to American political culture and has yet to fare well as a basis for a decent politics elsewhere in the world.

Precisely as the left insists, capitalism has been gobbling up civil society—the family, the churches, the voluntary service organizations—and it has rendered many individuals marginal to the market, dehumanizing them. But these valuable diagnoses, elaborated well by such social critics as Barbara Ehrenreich, do not excuse more orthodox leftists' characteristically delusive prescriptions, especially their frequent resort to a mixture of elaborate deference and unspoken condescension to blacks, who are presumed to have revolutionary potential by virtue of their oppression and their marginality to capitalist enterprise. These romantic beliefs, conjoined in such efforts as the left-inspired welfare-rights movement described in chapter 3, have only widened old rifts in the troubled marriage that began in the 1930s.

Consider this classic example of the left's often disingenuous touting of blacks, in an editorial in the leftist weekly the *Nation:*

The extraordinary publicity that [the black veteran prizefighter's] twelve-day visit to the Soviet Union generated in the American and world press was to be expected. [He] is one of the best-known Americans of his time. . . .

. . . He was tactful and shrewd and set an example other famous American visitors might well follow. . . . He had come to the Soviet Union, he said, to meet the people of a great country, to learn how they live, and what they think. He had pleasant things to say about aspects of Soviet society. "They give a man free medical and hospital care, low rent and a job. . . . I didn't see no hustlers, no prostitutes. . . . I haven't saw one person hitchhiking, one person begging or in bad, bad poverty, and I never felt so free of being robbed." . . . [The Soviet Communist party chairman] he found to be "as cute as he can be . . . a quiet, meek gentleman." . . .

[B]ut totally credulous and uncritical [the prizefighter] was not. . . . The Russians, he grimaced, had a tendency to be very serious: "I didn't see nobody laughin' or jokin'. Everybody was serious." He didn't like the absence of ice and a coffee shop downstairs in his hotel, with those "big juicy cheeseburgers," and he said so. . . . His patriotism . . . was impeccable. "I love my country. I think it's the best in the world, I don't want to live in any country but America. . . ." The head of the DAR could hardly ask for a more emphatic affirmation. But how rare it is these days to hear an American visitor to the Soviet Union say anything favorable about Russian society and its people; how rare and how refreshing. . . . It took a prizefighter to sound a more civilized, a more tactful, a more pacific tone. Yet one may be sure [he] was not deceived or oversold; he is natively very shrewd.

Surely this is a specimen, or at least a good parody, of the Communist Popular Front line of the 1930s. All the elements are there: the authentic Negro hero; the peace-loving Soviet people; the hero's simple patriotism for an America that can be taught to love peace, too. The essay is permeated with a manipulative condescension, not only toward the prizefighter but also toward the reader: in a feint toward "balance," the author tells the reader that the boxer didn't like some things and "said so"—the absence of "jokin' " and "big juicy cheeseburgers." Since these are all the criticisms of Soviet life the essay reports, the reader is invited, implicitly, to join the writer in patronizing the big Negro, whose simple nature it is to miss such little pleasures of home. We can be counted on to supply the insight that such frivolities aren't really to be expected of the Soviets.

If much in the history of the white left's approach to Negroes is a noble record of struggles for economic justice and "integration" *avant la lettre,* much of what is ignoble in that same history is encapsulated in this embarrassing, even racist screed. It was written not in the 1930s, however, but in 1978 by Carey McWilliams, then the editor of the *Nation,* about Muhammad Ali's visit that summer to the USSR. The essay marks a sad descent from Williams's brilliantly nuanced book *Brothers Under the Skin,* published first in 1942, which exposed the cool bargains whereby the North allowed the South to crush the Negro after Reconstruction.

As much as any other document one could cite, "Muhammed Ali for Congress" (McWilliams urged him to run) shows us why black-power advocates who tried to declare their political and cultural independence of white society in the 1960s were fleeing not only redneck racism and white liberal piety but also the left's anticipatory flutterings over every real or imagined stirring in black conscious-

ness. If such a left held out the only hope of black-white reconcilia-
tion, no wonder some black activists concluded there was no hope at
all. There is a forty-five-year tradition of such leftist myopia about
blacks, stretching from the Popular Front to McWilliams's 1978
essay; and a mere decade separates his celebration of Ali from Andrew Kopkind's breathless encomiums, again in the *Nation,* to the
far more "shrewd" Jesse Jackson, the left's latest "ambassador for
peace," who has run not for Congress but for the presidency. Here is
Kopkind in 1989, even after Jackson's ornery independence has
begun to make some wonder whether he is faithful to the left:

> Jesse Jackson does not stop running. In the year since he sought the
> Democratic presidential nomination, he has barely missed a day on public
> view or a chance for extending his sway. . . . Every night he is on the TV
> news somewhere, and in the morning in the headlines, marching with the
> masses, exhorting schoolchildren, supporting strikers, eulogizing fallen
> comrades, considering his options, circumnavigating the globe, parleying
> with world leaders and cajoling politicians in the promotion of his many
> projects. . . .
>   It's fashionable for many white leftists, black intellectuals and lesser or-
> ganizers to trash Jackson as an egotist, a grandstander. . . . A local Rainbow
> leader said recently, . . "He's an opportunist in every sense of the word,
> good and bad. But there's no other leadership. None." For in the face of
> criticism, . . . [Jackson] has traversed lines of class and race to create a
> genuine populist force that can play serious politics in the national arena.
> And he has not given up the game.

To be sure, Muhammad Ali was no Jesse Jackson. If Ali was a
pleasant, passing daydream for the left—he never did run for Congress—Jackson is a real, live lover, flawed, sometimes faithless, but in
the end, apparently, irresistible. Why didn't the left choose him over
Ali in the late 1970s? Perhaps it was because Jackson was then leading rallies against abortion, which he called "murder," and warning
that "when prayers leave the schools, guns come in." He told the
Village Voice writer Paul Cowan that opposing abortion had saved
his own family. Cowan asked how. "Well, you know, my life is very
dynamic and, variety being the spice of life, alternatives keep occurring. But no outside woman could compete with my children for my
affection. So my wife has kept some babies, but she's kept more than

that. She's kept her husband and a house and some other things, too." So much for the meaning of adult fidelity—which seemed to trouble Cowan but not Kopkind. But because Jackson, always running, keeps reinventing himself, the feints toward balance in Kopkind's disco-paced agitprop have to be more adroit, more elaborate than McWilliams's. With the local Rainbow organizer, he frets about whether Jackson is really being faithful to the left. But Kopkind sticks with him because, as the organizer puts it, Jackson is the best we have. And because, as Joe Louis said of Ali, "He makes his people proud, and I love him for it."

And that much is true. In the national political arena, Jackson is the only one who can mobilize millions of blacks and raise fundamental questions about liberal politics and the larger American experiment. The questions are real; many Americans do want them raised; and it is entirely fitting, if by no means inevitable, that an African-American raise them. But why the silly fluttering on the left about his raising them? What does it tell us about the left's relationship to blacks?

The Costs of Condescension

A compelling answer to these questions—and, in this case, ultimately, a happy one—emerges from Leon Fink's and Brian Greenberg's *Upheaval in the Quiet Zone: A History of Hospital Workers' Union Local 1199*. Fink and Greenberg portray David White, a black nationalist and former Communist party activist who in 1983 played a disastrously pivotal role in supporting a black opportunist, and almost destroying the union, until leftists of broader vision prevailed. White learned fierce racial pride from his father, a railroad stevedore and member of a colored railway brotherhood who despised white craft unions for their racism. Father and son supported various Popular Front institutions through the 1930s. In 1948, after being fired from the Brooklyn Navy Yard for refusing to sign a loyalty oath, David White took a job as an attendant at Bellevue and wound up working closely with 1199's old Communist party leadership on organizing drives. Local 1199 was Martin Luther King's "favorite union," offering a tremendous material and moral uplift to underpaid, mostly female hospital workers of all races, the people who keep cities running, salvaging their dignity from emptying bedpans, laundering sheets, and mopping floors.

But, as Fink and Greenberg record, the union's white, old-left leadership, personified in its dynamic, curmudgeonly president Leon Davis, was in the midst of making a serious mistake. Committed nobly to their own eventual replacement by a leadership more representative of the predominantly black rank and file, Davis and other old-left pros had taken to dubbing 1199 "the soul union" and were grooming Doris Turner, a woman described to me by union activists as not above using her color as a club with which to claim bourgeois privileges, even if that meant destroying the union. "She represents the Negro Opportunity Society," Jitu Weusi told me contemptuously; according to Fink and Greenberg, Turner had little vision or understanding of the labor movement and was not disposed to learn. "How do you teach a world view?" Moe Foner, a top Davis aide, asked the authors plaintively. "To us it was like breathing."

The left has never really known what to do with black nationalism (indeed, with any nationalism), especially those affectations of it that so regularly deflect its potential power into little more than posturing. Many blacks, for their part, have resented the left's casting them as the opening wedge of revolution, a big stalking-horse for white radicals' dreams of a society beyond class and color. Yet if the Davis crowd's racial paternalism and unspoken condescension were bad, its dreams were not impossible. Turner's use of black nationalist rhetoric to discredit nonblack opponents was far worse. Fink and Greenberg write that, as 1199 was negotiating an auspicious merger with another hospital workers' union in 1983, Turner began nursing the paranoid conviction that the merger was a ploy to dilute black representation and deny her the union presidency after Davis stepped down, and she began to organize against him and the merger.

Enter David White. As an old leftist who understood Foner's "world view," he doubted Turner. As a black nationalist, he resented the Davis crowd's little condescensions even more. He bolted to Turner, bringing some leadership secrets, helping her outmaneuver the pros. When Turner became president, she all but destroyed the union, swaggering around with armed guards, using race as "a trump card that paralyzed us," one union official recalled. She distanced

1199 from the city's larger progressive coalition and negotiated a disastrous contract that nearly wrecked the union. Davis told Fink and Greenberg, "If we were victims, we were victims of our own strategy"—of equating blackness with entitlement in a tough business where leadership must be earned.

But, as in the "Don't Buy" campaign of the 1930s, there is a happy and instructive ending to this story. After Turner's faction was caught rigging an election, the union vice-president Dennis Rivera and a committed group of fellow veterans of the Puerto Rican Socialist party who constituted the union's Latino Caucus assumed overall leadership. Rivera and his group were able to negotiate astutely among the union's warring racial factions: "I knew the message of racial unification and dignity was a winning combination—the message the members wanted to hear," Rivera recalls. They integrated the best of the old leadership (Davis had retired, but Foner and others came back), rebuilt the organization, and led it to a stunning victory in the 1989 contract negotiations with municipal and voluntary hospitals. The union thus helped to redefine the parameters of the city's budget crunch at decade's end and to make Dinkins's mayoral victory an important if symbolic gain for the union's heavily black rank and file. Whenever parochial black nationalism threatens to destroy coalitions, 1199 can be expected to provide a powerful check on such delusions.

Would that the union and Rivera were more representative of the left as a whole. Because they are not, because the left has many David Whites who blunder into nationalist excess, we cannot leave the story with Local 1199. Too much of the left, white and black, is putty in the hands of the Sonny Carsons, the Alton Maddoxes, and the affirmative action elite—susceptible, that is, to notions of virtuous blackness that are as narrow as Doris Turner's. Some of the black revolutionaries themselves teeter back and forth between nationalist romance and old-left orthodoxy. Jitu Weusi, whose father was a Communist, cautioned that black nationalism becomes a trap if it is not tempered and broadened by Marxism-Leninism and Third Worldism, which call for a united front of all races against capitalism, here and abroad. Weusi and the Reverend Herbert Daughtry even traveled to East Germany and Libya during the 1970s to express their solidarity with the Communist left and to proclaim their local activism a part of the international struggle. They were wined and dined, and the thought occurs that blacks of talent and passion are drawn to the left not least for the very nonnationalist reason that here, at last, they find whites who treat them as people of importance.

Describing the January 21, 1987, marches and boycotts of businesses to protest the events in Howard Beach in an interview with a radical journal, Weusi recalled his pleasure at seeing so many "young people out in the streets with posters of Malcolm X and Mao Zedong." "It almost brought tears to our eyes," he said, "to see our young people identifying with the actions and the ideas of these revolutionaries after everybody else had told us that these people were forgotten. . . . If we can turn our youth towards politics and away from drugs, a mighty force will be unleashed in the streets of cities all across America." Daughtry, who calls himself a "rainbow nationalist," constantly repeats the phrase "radical national grass-roots activism," which he says stands for "human rights and self-determination for all nations" in a context of international socialism. "[Black] nationalism and Marxism can walk together more comfortably than nationalism and capitalism," Daughtry told me, adding that while "Marxism talks the talk of humane socialism, you need liberation theology; Marxism's violent repression can't be employed."

It is hard not to think of Daughtry and Weusi as deluded, even if noble. They career too easily into positions that couldn't be better calculated to preclude a "united front" with any but the most demented of white and other nonblack activists—supporting unreliable characters like Sonny Carson, for example, or falling for the Maddox-Mason line in Howard Beach (Weusi, too, was calling the motorist Blum an accomplice several months after the event). Again, these errors are magnified by the white left's romanticism about blacks, which too often conflates the noisiest, most aggressive black leadership with the entire black community. That leads not only to the disingenuous celebration of a Muhammad Ali, a Doris Turner, or any of the nationalists just mentioned, but also to an implicit contempt for defenders of more pedestrian virtues. Recall that in organizing the National Welfare Rights Organization in 1966, Piven and Cloward pursued strategies of explicit polarization calculated to enrage white working-class taxpayers.

As we have seen, too, Piven and Cloward were among the first white leftists to join black nationalists in challenging the wisdom of integration through busing and fair-housing policies. They did so not out of any solicitude for white ethnics hurt by overzealous social engineering but out of the belief that only by concentrating their power in compact areas could blacks become the vanguard of social change the professors wanted them to be. But the white left's dogged insistence on miscasting the black community as an assailant of bourgeois morality and politics is best illustrated by following closely how it handled the dilemmas posed by rising violent crime and the Howard Beach and Brawley cases. How did the white left meet the challenges of personal accountability, public honesty, and interracial trust?

Seeing Murder "in Context"

In the fall of 1989, Representative Major Owens, a veteran of left-inspired community organizing going back to his chairmanship of Brooklyn CORE in the mid-1960s, called upon Governor Cuomo to deploy the National Guard in portions of his district to control the raging drug wars. Citing increased levels of "despair, disease and substance abuse that create fertile ground for drug racketeers," Owens also called for more funding for essential social services and doubling the number of officers in two local precincts.

The sympathetic Mark Naison, who, in addition to writing and teaching, runs youth sports leagues in inner-city neighborhoods, explained Owens's predicament in an essay for *New York Newsday*. Following the black sociologist Harry Edwards, Naison described the reigning outlaw culture in drug-ravaged neighborhoods as

a "pediocracy," a world run by children without significant adult influence. In the eyes of some "homeboys," every institution run by adults—schools, churches, places of employment, community centers—is a trap. The only good things available to young people are what they can grab for themselves through their own physical strength. The future doesn't exist. Nor does the past: the elderly are frequent victims.

The drug dealers are as aggressive in cultivating their market as any advertising executive on Madison Avenue. There are no neutrals because of the ferocity of the competition. Community, family and neighborhood in the traditional sense are gone. What we have is a new form of capitalism gone wild in an environment without government or law, in which human bodies and souls are for sale and the market is regulated by the power of the gun.

Yet the call for troops by a black community leader and a sympathetic white writer "freaked out" Naison's colleagues on the left, he told me. They were accustomed to view the police and the armed forces as agents of racist oppression, and crime as an "adaptive" response to it. Calls for law and order were almost invariably racist, in their view, because such calls traded in stereotypes of black criminals and begged all the important questions about the social and economic roots and contexts of crime. They were correct to insist that crime is a social, not just a personal, problem, but they were wrong to insist that black crime is essentially an adaptation to economic exploitation. As the sociologist Elliott Currie notes, crime and social disintegration began to soar in the 1960s, when economic growth presented society with the "troubling paradox of a postwar prosperity increasingly haunted by delinquency and violence."

But if economic deprivation alone isn't the reason for crime—poor communities in traditional, precapitalist societies are often relatively stable and crime free—then economic growth, even with additional social spending, won't by itself "cure" crime. More fundamental changes in the nature of capitalist production and marketing would be required, and those changes, in turn, could be spurred only by movements of people who are capable of self-discipline and a sense of social responsibility—which the left has no more idea how to encourage than do capitalism's most enthusiastic celebrants.

By the late 1980s, it should have been clear that there is no substitute for drawing the line against violent crime and holding its perpetrators responsible for their actions. Yet, like black nationalist militants who'd been so busy denouncing racist killings that they'd barely addressed the blood rising around their own feet, the white left was so preoccupied with rebutting white racist stereotypes of violent black criminals that it barely noticed that such "bigotry" was, increasingly, empirically grounded. When cab drivers, black as well as white, wouldn't pick up blacks who struck them as suspicious (we leave aside those drivers who wouldn't pick up blacks at all), they were making quick judgments based on hard-won experience. Even white liberals' children, attending integrated schools, developed certain rules of thumb: the writer Charles Morris explained that not every black kid knocked his son off his bike and stole his lunch money—but only black kids did. It was something one had to know in choosing a route to school.

For some time, writers on the left fought a tenacious rearguard action against granting the integrity of these perceptions. Only grudgingly did watchdogs of racism like the Queens College sociologist Stephen Steinberg acknowledge that while skin color does in some circumstances serve as a warning flag for whites (he never suggests that, as in the case of cab drivers, it serves blacks, too), their concern is not with sweeping racial assumptions but with narrowly circumscribed behaviors.

[W]hites have learned to discriminate between those respectable blacks who are reasonably tolerated, and those other blacks who bear the stigma of the ghetto and are still the objects of racial stereotyping, fear and scorn. Nevertheless, the fact that middle-class blacks may encounter minimal racism does not mean that ghetto blacks are so fortunate.

But surely it does mean that white perceptions have changed since the 1950s, and one has to wonder if Steinberg realizes how much he has conceded: he nearly acknowledges that the standard here has shifted from race per se to behavior, over which even the poorest blacks have some control. That returns us to questions of personal accountability, questions to which people as diverse as the Muslims and the IAF church groups have begun to offer answers that stop short of overthrowing capitalism. Steinberg cannot deny that bad behavior, not race, is what drives the fears Morris's children experience while bicycling to school. He does not tell us, possibly because he honestly doesn't know, what he would do as the parent of such kids in a neighborhood like Morris's or as a cab driver.

Yet Steinberg cannot quite let go of the race lens. He even denies that the behavior is really as bad as we think, citing Douglas Glasgow's jargon-clogged analysis of crime, which shows to what lengths some people will go to hang on to the race lens:

Behaviors of young inner-city Blacks are . . . consciously propagated via special socialization rituals that help the young Blacks prepare for inequality at an early age. With maturity, these models of behavior are employed to neutralize the personally destructive effects of institutionalized racism. Thus, they form the basis of a "survival culture" that . . . is not a passive adaptation to encapsulation but a very active—at times devious, innovative and extremely resistive—response to rejection and destruction. It is useful and necessary to young Blacks in their present situation.

Like Carey McWilliams writing about Ali, Glasgow is telling us, in effect, that violent ghetto youths are actually "natively very shrewd." But his premise—that crime must be understood in the context of institutional racism—has been overtaken by events in a city where black youths are gunning one another down at the rate of several a week. What Glasgow calls "survival culture" does not promote survival, nor is it "adaptive" to anything. And if, as others might claim, this is genocide, then it is auto-genocide. Even if Glasgow and Steinberg could somehow show crime to be "adaptive" for the youths who commit it, they would be hard put to show that it is adaptive for blacks whom the criminals rape and bludgeon to death. The sociologists have fallen into the left's trap of conflating the criminal with the community and assuming that by "explaining" the former in terms of social forces, they are somehow defending the latter.

It is a bankrupt enterprise. There is simply no credit left in the claim that such crimes are "economic" and in that way distinguishable from the "hate" crimes of white racists. As often as not, these are hate crimes, too, responding less to brutality by the white police than to brutality in the black home. That, in turn, may reflect the internalization of white racist hatred, but the more such extenuated links one draws between gratuitously violent crime and its putative social causes, the farther one is from what most blacks themselves think about violent criminals. Recall Christopher Jencks's description, cited in chapter 3, of the importance of moral censure in the lives of the poor.

Old beliefs die hard. Here is the veteran radical attorney William

Kunstler explaining why he decided to defend a Chinese immigrant store owner who'd killed a black Haitian intruder:

It was the first time I had ever represented someone who killed a black person. Pang [the store owner] was Third World, the decedent was a hopeless psychotic with drug problems. He was twice the size of the defendant. It was clearly self-defense. And even then I had misgivings. It's been such a lifetime of representing black people abused by white people. I'm not sure, if Pang had been white, I would have taken it.

But this is racist. That is, Kunstler resorts to an oppressive racial stereotyping in this handling of real people and evidence. He certainly hasn't absorbed the fact that many Asians and other "Third World" people in the city are registering as Republicans because they resent what they believe is the Democrats' coddling of blacks. It is one thing to represent, as Kunstler did, Larry Davis, the young black man charged with shooting six police officers; Kunstler convinced the jury that Davis was firing in self-defense at cops who'd lured him into dealing the drugs they seized on their rounds and who'd then come to stop him from ratting on them. It is quite another thing to agonize about representing a shopkeeper such as Pang—and to conclude that one wouldn't have done so had Pang been white! Indeed, had Pang been white, and had the Haitian intruder killed him instead of vice versa, we can only conclude that Kunstler would have defended the Haitian without hesitation.

The story of Pang shows precisely how the left's perverse logic about violent crime breaks down. To interpret street violence strictly in terms of racist, capitalist exploitation is to turn people away. Naison reflects,

I don't even like to make an issue of race anymore, because I'm organizing kids' sports leagues all over the city and traveling with white kids into black neighborhoods and black kids into white neighborhoods, to play ball. These kids are vulnerable. We can't afford to subject them to polarization that might lend itself to raw feelings, especially when what they're doing is overcoming racism itself.

These are the same sentiments Gerard Papa expressed in discussing the success of his interracial basketball team, the Flames.

Another questionable use of the race lens came in a moving, digni-
fied, but deeply flawed editorial in the *Nation* shortly after Bernhard
Goetz shot four black youths who he claimed had been menacing
him in the subway. The editorial warned against blurring the essentially racist nature of Goetz's crime, as it said the mainstream media
had done in quoting a few blacks who defended Goetz, including the
mother of one of the youths he shot, who said her son deserved it.
The editorial cautioned that even whites outside the city with little
fear of crime and little contact with blacks were using the Goetz case
to indulge

a metaphorical rage, the function of a pervasive sense of powerlessness that
fixes primarily—though not exclusively—on race as a cause and revenge as
a cure.

. . . Goetz . . . seems perfect for his part in this modern morality play: the
story of a lonely yuppie terminator, neurotic, freelance and divorced in the
anomic city; but blond, brave and Germanic in battle against the invading
dark barbarians. . . . In the play, the blasts from his silver gun arouse a
powerless people, and the wounds of his victims redeem a fallen land.

The myth as well as the reality evoke frightening historical analogies.
Our nightmares are filled with images of tribal violence rationalized as
political necessity. We know what results when racial tension is exploited to
empower a populace whose pride and patriotism have been offended. . . .
Nothing good comes from acts of social vengeance. . . .

With most of this one can agree, but something is missing. For if
one really does agree, then one must criticize, as Assemblyman
Roger Green did and the white left did not, the tactics of Maddox,
Mason, and Sharpton. "Frightening historical analogies"? Consider
Sharpton's telling blacks to think of Robert Abrams as Adolf Hitler.
"Our nightmares are filled with images of tribal violence rationalized
as political necessity"? Consider Maddox's going to court to vindicate the young black killer of the Reverend Strianese and one of the
slashers of Marla Hanson, whose acquittals he sought as political
victories. Where were the editorials in the *Nation* protesting these
rationalizations for acts of social vengeance? Are these not instances
where "racial tension is exploited to empower a populace whose
pride and patriotism have been offended"?

The journal is stuck because—as it permitted me to say in a published letter in response to the Goetz editorial—it fails to comprehend Naison's insight: sometimes the only way to address racism, to break its spell, is to stop casting events as purely or primarily racist in character. Not because racism isn't real and destructive, but because we can't get at it by oversimplifying it this way. The truth is that the minority supporters of Goetz who appeared on the television were not aberrations. The early polls showed heavy minority support for Goetz, until his vindictive side was revealed in his shooting a second time at a youth who was already down. Goetz's initial shooting of the youths was understood by many blacks as something other than "blond, brave and Germanic."

The real myth being nourished in the Goetz case is even more perverse and central to American life than that of white redemption through black pain. It is the notion, common to all races and urged upon us daily in a hundred television programs, that it's better to blow away nineteen-year-old criminals than to struggle to educate and employ seventeen-year-olds experimenting with crime. Only when the left stops dismissing as racist the trepidation whites and blacks alike feel in the shadow of that challenge can it hope to break the spell of racism itself. In the meantime, it must hold people accountable for their actions—Goetz, certainly, but also the youths he shot, some of whom had rap sheets as long as their arms, filled with charges of rape and armed robbery.

The Left's View of Public Truth

As the Brawley fiasco unraveled in the spring of 1988, the *Nation* published a piece on the implications of the case by the Albany-based writer-activist Jeff Jones. He recounted two gruesome racial incidents in the Hudson Valley unrelated to the Brawley case, one of them an assault on some black men witnessed by Haywood Burns, the black dean at the City University Law School and president of the National Lawyers Guild. Jones then cited marches against racism in the area which the Brawley case had sparked, and concluded,

In the weeks ahead, the mainstream press is likely to focus on whether the Brawley family's account of what happened to Tawana is accurate. But more important is the exposure of racist violence, and the institutionalized racism of police and prison guards in Hudson Valley and around the country.

After the case had fallen apart completely, the *Nation* let the anthropologist Stanley Diamond try his hand. "In cultural perspective," he wrote,

it doesn't matter whether the crime occurred or not. . . . It was described with skill and controlled hysteria by the black actors as the epitome of degradation, a repellent model of what actually happens to too many black women. The perpetrators supposedly included more than one white law enforcement officer, also echoing a social fact and creating the occasion for indicting once again the system of white justice. . . . It may be asking too much of the white community to excuse the Brawley deceit; but they misunderstand it at their peril.

Kunstler was giving out the same line, in an interview with *New York Newsday:*

It makes no difference anymore whether the attack on Tawana really happened. . . . It doesn't disguise the fact that a lot of young black women are treated the way she said she was treated. [Maddox and Mason] now have an issue with which they can grab the headlines and launch a vigorous attack on the criminal justice system.

The *New Republic,* a political weekly far less predictable than the *Nation,* also published essays on the Brawley case. They were tightly reasoned, they stuck close to the facts, and one of them, by William Tucker, was the first I know of to suggest in print that the case might be a hoax. If the *New Republic*'s pieces might have been improved by acknowledging the troubling racism in the Hudson Valley and the deeper cultural antecedents of the case, nothing can excuse the *Nation*'s astounding indulgence of lies or the contempt for working-class white opinion in the Hudson Valley which its indulgence of lies entailed.

Why couldn't Diamond, a distinguished anthropologist, find in this case even a faint echo of the fable of the boy who cried wolf? As it leaps from the depths of the Brawley story, the fable reminds us that while there may be a wolf of racism in the valley, crying out that it's there at a moment when it's not will only convince people that it's not there at all. Diamond's condescension to whites who might not want "to excuse the Brawley deceit but [who] misunderstand it at their peril" is breathtaking. At his own peril, he misunderstands the relationship of factual truths to mythmaking in public discourse. By his logic, it wouldn't have mattered if the Scottsboro Boys had really committed the rapes with which they were charged in 1931.

A final example of this racially blinkered thinking comes from Jim Miskiewicz, a former colleague of mine on the *North Brooklyn Mercury* who was a third-year student at the CUNY Law School in 1987. The school boasts a diverse student body that encompasses veteran activists as well as political moderates, including housewives starting careers after raising families. The general cast of the student leadership is leftist, however, and, even as the Brawley case was falling apart in the winter of 1988, a committee of students voted to give the school's annual public-interest lawyer award to C. Vernon Mason. Although the committee was only to nominate honorees for Dean Burns's approval, one member telephoned Mason an invitation just hours after the vote.

At that time, Mason had already asserted that "everyone" in Brawley's hometown knew the names of her assailants. That prompted Miskiewicz, in a conversation with a member of the committee the day after the vote, to question the implications of honoring a man whose professional integrity so many had begun to doubt. The committee member—who'd often said he hoped to be the first CUNY Law School graduate held in contempt of court for a righteous cause—responded, "Hey, people don't like Mason? Tough, that's why we nominated him." Another member, who had quietly abstained from the vote, told Miskiewicz in a hushed stairwell conversation that he thought Mason was obstructing justice, but added, "I was afraid to say that. I didn't want to be called a racist." Miskiewicz sent an open letter to all students and faculty asking that the invitation be withdrawn. He listed Mason's unsubstantiated charges, including those against Dominick Blum in the Howard Beach case. "In the days following," Miskiewicz would recount in an essay for *New York Newsday,*

I got icy stares, a mumbled slur that I was a "privileged white boy" (by a woman who knew nothing of my upbringing in Brooklyn's Greenpoint neighborhood)—and private encouragement from both black and white students. . . . The next committee meeting drew most of the graduating class. Dozens spoke up. Most of those who opposed Mason were whites who, like me, had done enough community work to deserve a serious hearing from his defenders. Still, the eyes of many of the Mason critics filled with tears and they stammered like the accused at a trial.

When I'd finished repeating my own reasons for opposing Mason, a black woman student stood up and shouted furiously, "Why don't you just admit you don't want the man there because he's black!" As I tried to respond, she and I were drowned out by shouting from all sides.

What shocked me wasn't being labeled, in effect, a racist. More stunning was to see the pretense of reason jettisoned by so many in this group of future guardians of legal process and fairness. How much of the essential value of the law, its historical role in effecting social change, have Mason's supporters absorbed in three years of study at this unique, "public interest" law school?

Of the ninety graduates who voted on secret ballots, about 60 percent voted against honoring Mason, and he was disinvited. But Miskiewicz's questions remain. Why do so many on the left persist in believing they can drive home certain essential truths about racism only by violating public truth itself? Why is the left's tenacity in the pursuit of truth so selective? Perhaps, burned by McCarthyism in the 1950s, clubbed by hard hats and hounded by law enforcement agents during the Vietnam War, or simply despondent at the sheer weight of established injustice and the lies that support it, many on the left cannot bring themselves to trust people who aren't toeing a clear line. Lost in tracking the labyrinths of the others' "false consciousness," the left drowns in its own documentation of their delusions, convinced that only a media conspiracy keeps others from embracing its truths.

Or maybe the problem is that many on the left simply can't afford to admit to themselves that racism, however virulent, however pervasive, isn't the fulcrum for systemic change they want it to be. Perhaps the left can learn from Mark Naison and Gerard Papa and the young participants in their sporting leagues in Brooklyn and the Bronx: like travelers in the dark, who can discern an object only by looking slightly away, they have learned to look slightly askance at the constant invocations of racism in order to see it for what it is—and for what it is not. Then again, perhaps some people at the *Nation* are learning. After the assault on the Central Park jogger, the journal editorialized quite sensibly that an understanding of the incident "must begin with the wider problem of violence against women."

Even what remains of the Communist Party U.S.A. is finding some flaws in the race lens, too. Tony Monteiro, a member of the party's national committee, speaking in the summer of 1989, described racism as a pivot of capitalist oppression, but then he vehemently denied that the majority of white working people are racist and rejected black nationalists' and the romantic left's retreat to "plural but equal" strategies that tout cultural nationalism over integration.

Twenty years ago, in an analysis of the Ocean Hill–Brownsville school wars, Martin Mayer captured well some white apologists' betrayals of these essential truths:

As they say around the criminal courts, the lawyer always goes home. Like the criminal lawyer, the academician or the foundation officer has no continuing relation, no enforceable responsibility, to his clients. His job is secure however many mistakes he makes, and if his advice gets his clients into even worse trouble, he just never sees them again. . . . Excusing bigotry or terrorism or fraud in Negro life because of "three hundred years of oppression" is discrimination directly comparable to police failure to prosecute assaults or gambling or narcotics in the slums; whatever the revolutionary or empathic jargon in which such double standards are expressed, what is really being said is that you can't expect any better from these people.

It is useful to keep Mayer's comment in mind while reading these remarks by Kunstler in the *Newsday* interview cited above:

Q: Don't you think the credibility of the black civil rights leadership here could be severely damaged if the whole [Brawley] case is a sham?

KUNSTLER: Not in the black community, because it knows that there are many Tawana Brawleys out there. I don't think Maddox and Mason are further inflaming racial tensions in the city. But maybe there has to be some sort of cataclysm before anything constructive can happen. The more the white community is afraid of the black community the better off the black community will be.

Q: You are . . . representing Darrell Cabey, who was wounded by Bernhard Goetz and is now suing him. Will you call Goetz to the stand?

A: He'll have to testify or lose the case. Goetz is a victim of American racism. I would like to expose his fear of young black males, which generated this tragedy in the first place.

This was too much for David Greenman, a Woodmere, Long Island, resident who wrote, in a letter to the editor,

I was saddened to see a man I've always admired espousing a philosophy of reverse racism that is filled with holes and contradictions. . . . The thing that upset me most was Kunstler's reckless use of the word (and philosophy of) fear. First he states that "the more the white community is afraid of the black community, the better off the black community will be." Then he goes on to say that it was Goetz's fear of black people that "generated this tragedy in the first place." When Kunstler helps to promote this fear, doesn't that make him responsible for spreading the tragedy of racism?

Well? Doesn't it?

10

"Vote Your Hopes— and Your Fears"

The Electoral Politics of Race

If the city's desperate need to transcend the politics of race has been frustrated by white leftists and black militants, periodically it has found some hope of resolution in electoral politics, where millions of New Yorkers speak their minds on at least some of the day's pressing questions through the medium of the secret ballot. In a society whose economic inequities limit the exercise and sway of democracy, politicians are the most denigrated of activists: winning our trust by campaigning in the name of the whole, they often disillusion us by succumbing to the blandishments of the most wealthy and powerful—or the most parochial and selfish—of its parts. But in all their impurity, politicians have this saving grace: unlike visionaries or social scientists, they do actually have to develop a "feel" for the everyday needs and concerns of those ordinary people who must get around town and conduct their daily business across racial lines.

The larger their districts and the more they are subject to wholesome disciplines like runoff primaries, which force them to forge working, interracial majorities, the more politicians transcend the rantings of hucksters who work narrow constituencies for limited electoral gain. Time and again, most recently in such personages as former Governor Hugh Carey, former Assembly Speaker Stanley Fink, Representatives Charles Schumer and Charles Rangel, and, some would argue, Mayor Dinkins himself, New York has been blessed with political leaders who, even as they rise from parochial ethnic enclaves, keep pressing the flesh of their own and other constituencies, responding to shared needs. So doing, they understand how profound is the yearning for communication beneath the posturing and the genuine rage that characterize interracial disputes.

In Harlem, as we saw in chapter 1, J. Raymond Jones was the progenitor and champion of such a race-transcendent politics, dependent though he remained on political machines that arguably reinforced the capitalist system's residually racist inequities even as they strove to mitigate their effects. In contrast, the Brooklyn insurgents believed that most blacks would never advance until these contradictions were bared, and they broke the mold of the clubhouse compromises that reconciled people to the system. Yet, like Jones, they soon learned that important offices and systemic reforms can never be won by blacks alone, that it is necessary to make strategic alliances with whites who also oppose the machine.

In 1981, Al Vann, Major Owens, Frank Boyland, and Roger Green were able to mount an enormous vote-pulling effort to give Elizabeth Holtzman, a liberal Jewish former congresswoman from Flatbush, her margin of victory in a close race against the machine for Brooklyn district attorney. One of the biggest Holtzman victories came in Owens's and Boyland's area of Brownsville, the battered Fifty-fourth Assembly District. In a community 70 percent of whose people lived in public housing because almost everything else lay burned and abandoned, where over 30 percent of the families lived below the poverty line and 90 percent had incomes under $15,000, Holtzman received 2,334 votes to the machine candidate's 989.

But the real victory for the insurgents was that Holtzman carried black areas nominally controlled by patronage regulars answerable to the old West Indian elite. That introduced a portentous imbalance into the familiar patronage/apathy equation under which, in return for their plums, machine loyalists were supposed to keep the voters quiet and their own legislative votes safe for the directives of the white machine bosses. In 1981, they couldn't. Though blacks cast no more than 35,000 of the borough's 181,000 votes in the primary for district attorney, Holtzman's 9,000-vote margin of victory among them was roughly her margin boroughwide.

Three months after the 1981 election, Daniel Patrick Moynihan, the first U.S. senator to visit Brownsville in decades, spoke at a revitalization conference sponsored there by Owens—no small tribute from one looking for vote-pulling strength the following year. But not even Moynihan could have dreamed that Owens would be joining him in the Congress a year later or that half a dozen new assembly and state senate colleagues would join Owens and Vann in founding the Coalition for Community Empowerment, sweeping away most of Brooklyn's black West Indian elite and helping to carry Cuomo past Koch in the 1982 Democratic gubernatorial primary.

A Baptism in Brooklyn

One of the most important elections in that watershed year was a bitter contest between Owens and a black state senate colleague, Vander Beatty, to replace the retiring Shirley Chisholm in the House of Representatives. The campaign, which I followed closely for the *Village Voice,* drew some national attention, and its outcome had national implications. It showed that even as black insurgents built tentative alliances with white reformers, they had to fight strenuous rearguard actions against demagogues like Beatty who mask their subservience to machine politics in strident appeals to racial solidarity. Even when the more race-transcendent insurgents like Owens defeat such a politics of racial resentment, I learned, they often have to go on fighting its seductions within themselves.

Late in the summer of 1982, the *Voice* published a lengthy investigative article of mine documenting Beatty's impressive twelve-year record of election fraud and misuse of state funds. The piece began on the paper's cover under the dramatic headline "The Battle for Black Brooklyn" just three weeks before the Democratic primary, which Beatty was heavily favored to win—a victory that would guarantee him the November general election. The stormy reaction to my modest effort to break his stride bared the depravity and tenacity of machine politics at its worst.

Central Brooklyn's Twelfth Congressional District stretches eastward from its brownstone parlors in Fort Greene, near downtown Brooklyn, across the vast tracts of brownstones, rooming houses, and apartment buildings in Bedford-Stuyvesant and Crown Heights; south among once grand apartment buildings jammed with large, low-income families in Flatbush; and east again across the owner-occupied row houses lining the boulevards of East Flatbush. To walk these broken streets of stooped, still-southern gentility, new Caribbean vitality, and rampant drug warfare is to wonder whether political leadership can do anything to help the youngsters coming up on the asphalt.

Chisholm had decided by 1982 that nothing more could be done. Among Brooklyn's 700,000 blacks in 1982, indicators of social distress were rising both absolutely and in comparison with those for whites. Roughly half of the borough's 2.3 million residents were black or Hispanic; 31.5 percent of the black households and 42 percent of the Hispanic households lived below the poverty line, compared with just 10 percent for whites, most of whom were elderly. Seventy-five percent of all births in the borough were to minority mothers, 40 percent of whom were unmarried; 75 percent of the public school enrollment was black and Hispanic, with a minority dropout rate in excess of 50 percent.

Yet Chisholm's demands for societal redress, steeped in the imagery of white guilt and black moral advantage, were falling on deaf ears amid Reaganite exhortations to bootstrap responsibility. She found herself echoing the conservatives' admonitions, even though she knew them to be empty and impolitic for many of her constituents. Beneath the fiery rhetoric for which she had become known in the expansive, liberal 1960s, Chisholm had always maintained an unswerving if somewhat gloomy obeisance to the Kings County Democratic organization of Meade Esposito. She had seldom challenged Esposito's connivances with special interests exploiting her district and had never endorsed black reform candidates, even against white machine holdovers in racially changing neighborhoods.

In 1982, Brooklyn's blacks would surely have reelected, on a "Thanks for the Memories" ticket, the first black woman ever to run for president. But with white attention waning, Chisholm couldn't translate her dramatic political past into a future that would hold her interest. Congratulating herself for having served as the "mother of the community" through fourteen years of alternating hope and despair, she announced her retirement to the halls of Mount Holyoke College.

In his corner of Chisholm's district, which included most of Bedford-Stuyvesant and Crown Heights, Beatty had become a power who often left opponents feeling weak-kneed, breathless. He was a still-potent emblem of the passing political style that "Battlin' Shirley from ol' Bed-Stuy" and Adam Clayton Powell in Harlem had embellished over the years, a style that masked in colorful poses of militancy their shrewd accommodations to predators who were milking their African-American and immigrant black Caribbean constituents. At Esposito's behest, Chisholm endorsed Beatty to succeed her.

Beatty, I reported in the *Voice,* mixed equal parts fraud, intimidation, charisma, money, and a sprinkling of jobs to keep his area's community school and planning boards "safe" for the schemes of the white slumlords, developers, corrupt union locals, and prospectors for state and city contracts. To them, he was "someone you can deal with" behind closed doors. He steered them government contracts and low-interest loans while keeping inspectors away; they gave him kickbacks and other crumbs to dispense to his loyal, sometimes brutal retainers; and the retainers, in turn, sustained him in office by turning out his loyal vote amid a deepening electoral apathy. The white machine stood ready to take care of insurgencies through its control of the election apparatus, the courts, and the police. In short, Beatty was a satrap in the much larger municipal kingdom that routinely sells off its powers of taxation and public planning to the highest bidders, who invest or disinvest for short-term gain as poor, black districts like his slide slowly into hell.

Like Chisholm, Beatty was invincible because he offered his constituents terrific racial theater. Unlike Chisholm, he often sluiced his listeners' grievances into feelings about white society that bordered on hatred. No one was really very surprised when he opened his congressional campaign by telling the *New York Post* that Owens, his colleague representing the neighboring, impoverished Brownsville and East New York sections, "talks black but sleeps white." Even when, on his best behavior during a radio campaign debate, Beatty assured interracial audiences of his ability to "work with my friend Bishop Mugavero and with the Hasidim and so on," his subtext, well understood by black listeners, was, "Let me handle whitey; you know he hates us, but I'll cop us what we need to get by."

"He appeals to a lot of people in our community with larceny in their hearts," the former state senator Waldaba Stewart told me; since white society could not be redeemed, Beatty seemed to be saying, it might as well be ripped off. With his silver Mercedes, bulging billfolds, expensive suits, licensed revolver, and impressive connections, he certainly got that message across. Where Chisholm had merely accommodated all the special interests, Beatty actively melded them into a juggernaut carrying him into the 1982 race with ample funds and, through the county machine, control of the election apparatus.

My *Voice* exposé ended with a pitch for Owens, by 1982 a member in good standing in the city's loose coalition of black activists and white Democratic party reformers. I acknowledged that, to the dismay of some of his own supporters, Owens wasn't particularly adept at "copping" what they needed "to get by." He believed, rather, that as people learn to confront established power in staged, disciplined actions—pickets, boycotts, and the building of institutional alternatives to the clubhouses and social service bureaucracies—they not only wrest more resources from society's misspent wealth; they also wean themselves off the fears and dependencies which Beatty and his backers manipulated so well. A "closet" scholar and writer from his days as a librarian, Owens carried this message with him a bit like a musty preacher. He was a stocky, deceptively placid-looking man whose few words in private conversation seemed to come up out of a deep well; but in public he became a silver-tongued orator who could move crowds with words of love, and his honesty and intelligence were irresistible.

The problem in a ghetto situation, of course, was that opportunism like Beatty's easily scrambled such principled politics; under the circumstances, it got more services out of the establishment than did Owens's fitful organizing for systemic change. According to a member of its editorial board, the *New York Times* came within an inch of giving Beatty its endorsement; the board member Roger Starr was drafting it when a respected black journalist who doesn't want to be named convinced him that Owens was better. The resulting editorial betrayed its mixed origins, describing Owens as "windy" and given to talking "about what a wonderful world this would be if only he ran it," while praising Beatty as "a pragmatic and successful politician" who, however, didn't quite have congressional stature.

The irony is that Congress is generally more comfortable with a Beatty than with an Owens, and so is New York's political establishment. Nevertheless, I wrote in the *Voice,* Brooklyn's black community could scarcely afford a flamboyant but clubbable hack like Beatty at the dawn of the Reagan era, when, for once, principle might prove more important in a Democrat than scrambling for nonexistent crumbs. I concluded with an appeal to the city's political leaders:

Beatty has flourished because we have not met Owens halfway [and] because black leaders who should know better are avoiding confronting Beatty, or because they've let themselves be taken in by his manipulations of real grievances, or because, like [the Brooklyn organization's octogenarian dean, Wesley] Mac Holder, boastful now in old age, they've become terminally cynical: "I care only that I have a willing candidate; I don't care what he does between elections, and I've never lost an election, never." But perhaps Holder should consider whether Beatty is the legacy he wants to leave his people. And perhaps those who've kept quiet, like Percy Sutton, David Dinkins, Carl McCall, and Charlie Rangel, should think it over, too.

At a Gracie Mansion breakfast for state senators two and a half years ago, Ed Koch strode up to Owens and, towering over him, wagged a finger in his face. "I know you've been criticizing me, and if I were a different kind of guy, you wouldn't be getting any programs out there." Owens chuckles as he recalls the incident. "What he really meant was, shut up or you won't be getting any programs!"

Perhaps white society owes Owens an apology, on behalf of Ed Koch. Perhaps influential blacks do, too, for letting him go it alone so much of the time. Perhaps we all owe him an important debt. If so, it comes due this month.

The day the article appeared, my phone would not stop ringing. Pablo Guzman, a talk show host at the time on WLIB, invited me on his call-in show, and he opened the program, quite appropriately, with a question Beatty himself might have posed: since this was a contest between two black politicians in a largely black congressional district, why had I, a white writer for a "white" weekly newspaper, undertaken this exposé?

I threw the question back at Guzman. Why, indeed? Why hadn't the city's black print and radio journalists investigated Beatty's record? That would have been welcome. Blacks often criticize the so-called white press for ignoring their communities and dismissing all ghetto politics as gutter politics, I said. Here, for a change, was a serious, lengthy treatment that not only exposed a political hack but spotlighted a constructive alternative in Owens.

That prompted an angry call from a Beatty supporter, one Reverend Al Sharpton, who charged, "White radicals from the *Village Voice* are trying to pick the next black congressman by telling us how to vote." I'd already heard this from Sharpton a few weeks earlier at a campaign debate between Beatty and Owens, when Beatty stuck a finger in my face and a thug smashed the *Voice* photographer's flash attachment by hurling it to the ground. ("We're just trying to 'dialogue,' " Sharpton told a cop who crossed the courtyard to see what the noise was all about.)

Other callers supported my article, but I knew that Sharpton's charge had struck reliable chords when it was echoed in an editorial attack on me by Beatty's campaign manager in the weekly numbers sheet *Big Red:* "Every time a strong-willed, . . . not-for-sale Black leader arises, a white would-be 'nigger-breaker' is sent down from the 'big house' to break his will. . . . Now the neo-slavemasters have decreed that it is Sen. Beatty's turn." I even got some death threats on the telephone answering machine in my Park Slope apartment, which was just inside a remote corner of Beatty's senate district.

All in all, it was a crash course in an abiding black resentment which Beatty expressed better than anyone else: "First, whites shut us up and shut us out, push us into a corner; then, they come in after us, picking us over with their hypocritical morality, while we're struggling to survive." But at a fund-raiser for Owens at Stewart Mott's house, the former deputy mayor Haskell Ward told me the article had caused a stir among the black elite; while Adam Powell's successor, Representative Charles Rangel, was sticking with Beatty, Rangel's close friend City Clerk David Dinkins might come over to Owens, bringing other endorsements.

Then Beatty overreached. He had Chisholm send a telegram to every voter claiming, falsely, as it turned out, that Martin Luther King, Sr., had endorsed him. The claim was plausible because on a trip to Atlanta Chisholm had introduced Beatty to the civil rights establishment, which knew nothing of its more faithful but also more modest son Owens, a Memphis native and a graduate of Atlanta's Morehouse College. When the lie about King's endorsement was exposed, an outraged Representative John Conyers of Michigan, who'd founded the Congressional Black Caucus, flew into New York to campaign with Owens. Chisholm was embarrassed and Beatty discredited, and the public-sector unions and liberal groups supporting Owens worked hard and well to capitalize on it. Even with machine loyalists presiding at the polls, which mysteriously opened late in areas outside Beatty's senate district, Owens won with 54 percent of the vote, by a margin 2,900 votes, only half of them white.

Now Beatty showed what he was made of. A couple of weeks after the primary, he and thirty-five loyalists descended on the Board of Elections in downtown Brooklyn to "review" the voter registration cards. Sitting at tables in the stacks' long aisles, they forged thousands of signatures on the cards of people who hadn't voted, making it look as if they had come to the polls. Now that there were thousands more signatures than actual votes tallied, Beatty could claim that the election had gone amiss; while one cannot tell from a registration card which candidate the voter actually supported, Beatty could submit the forgeries in Kings County Supreme Court, which was run by the county machine, as evidence of massive fraud supposedly committed on election day itself—fraud that, given the outcome of the race, would seem to have been committed by its winner, Owens. The court did not actually have to decide who was guilty in order to find that the election had been improperly conducted and to call a new election.

I nearly caught the forgers in the act, thanks to a tip, and managed to expose the scam in a *Voice* article, which prompted a column by Sydney Schanberg in the *New York Times* as the courts took up Beatty's charge. It was a breathtaking gamble. Since a court-ordered rerun would have to preceded the November 2 general election, less than six weeks away, Owens would have little time to mobilize against whatever Beatty's war chest might buy. "Look at it this way," said a veteran Board of Elections watcher of Beatty. "The man is either going to jail or he's going to Congress."

As Owens partisans sat staring in disbelief, Acting Supreme Court Judge Eugene Berkowitz, a longtime political associate of the Queens Democratic boss Donald Manes who'd been imported to Brooklyn for the occasion to present a semblance of impartiality, granted Beatty a rerun on the grounds that the election had been "permeated with fraud" that "shocks the conscience of the court." Berkowitz so ruled despite overwhelming evidence submitted by Owens that the forgeries were entered in certain registration books in patterns that could have occurred only at the Board of Elections itself—and hence after the real voters had already spoken in the primary. A jubilant Beatty seemed certain to "win" his rerun. Owens said he felt as if he were in Mississippi; even the Harlem establishment was unnerved; David Dinkins showed up to stand with Owens at a rally to protest the decision.

Not until the day before the new election was to take place did the state court of appeals void the rerun, securing Owens's victory, after hearing a plea from the *Voice* attorney and now city corporation counsel Victor Kovner. Even when Beatty was convicted some months later of vote fraud and sentenced to prison, it was hard to believe he was finally gone, especially because, through it all, some of his connections in the civil rights establishment held firm: at a second trial for theft of state funds, Beatty was represented by none other than a surprisingly arrogant Ramsey Clark, Lyndon Johnson's former attorney general, who was persuaded to go back home to Greenwich Village only after Beatty decided to cop a plea halfway through the trial. Black Brooklynites had proven themselves sharper than Clark in seeing through and repudiating Beatty's patronage/apathy model of politics.

What are the lessons of this battle?

First, that a larger war continues. After all, it was a court in Albany, a place Brooklynites will tell you is just this side of the moon, that rescued Owens. Back on earth, all the local officials who'd graciously accommodated Beatty's romp through the Board of Elections and the courts remained in thrall to the machine, and they could be checked only by sustained mobilization of an informed constituency. Beatty's conviction didn't prevent the organization from promoting a less objectionable candidate against Owens two years later (he has survived all challenges).

That leads to a second lesson, one which J. Raymond Jones would find uncongenial: we should be done with the nostalgia fashionable in some quarters for the putative blessings of urban political machines. In shrinking economies, they accelerate a perverse logic of scarcity and submission, blighting democratic institutions and public planning while grinding ordinary citizens' expectations to a smallness unimaginable to more fortunate outsiders. If the machines stay in power, they orchestrate governance and politics, land use and economic development, to benefit antisocial interests; and one survives only by playing along.

Third, this perversion of politics too often feeds on racism. Through false messiahs like Beatty, it generates hatreds based on understandable resentments, beguiling blacks into a destructive isolation from interracial politics. Ethnic- and racial-group bargaining and jockeying for succession are inevitable in American life. But Beatty's brand of racial politics only deepened division and darkness. Haskell Ward's comment that the *Voice* exposé had shaken up the black elite unnerved me as much as it pleased me, because it showed how comfortable with Beatty those leaders had been.

But, fourth, Owens's victory was a profound tribute to the black electorate, which saw through Beatty's mystifications and managed to keep faith with the larger society, whether or not that society fully deserved it. The voters walked out on Beatty's racial theater and responded instead to a language that acknowledged both their hurts and their collective responsibility to reach beyond those hurts. It was only a first step, but in 1982 it was unprecedented at the congressional level in New York, and, given the odds, it was breathtaking.

As more cities inaugurate their first black mayors, an important shift is occurring in young blacks horizons; for the first time, some of them can imagine themselves entrusted with political power by a whole polity and responsible for the well-being of whites as well as blacks. That breaks down the political double standards which leaders like Beatty accepted and exploited within their own small fiefdoms. Their new horizons make his style and message seem smaller than before.

But here enters an unexpected, perhaps unwanted poignancy. Precisely because most blacks have long been excluded from white society's routine, subtle corruptions, many whites have almost expected them to come to public life as bearers of moral redemption. Blacks like Martin Luther King, Jr., have presented themselves on just such terms, brilliantly, and Jesse Jackson trades on liberal whites' yearnings for "inspiration" from the oppressed. Even Beatty carried something of that mythic charge, and it gave him a certain credibility with knee-jerk white liberals like Ramsey Clark, as well as with the black civil rights establishment.

To see black mayors settling down to the technocratic, often tawdry business of running municipalities is to watch the angels withdraw along with the demons. It means giving up something as well as gaining. For whites, it means letting go of a romance whose underside has always been condescension and guilt. For blacks, it means unlearning the "lessons" Beatty taught with a compelling if perverse logic: since white society cannot be redeemed, it might as well be ripped off; when in doubt, "run your mouth" about racism; it is safer and more satisfying to hurt than to hope. Just as whites will have to change the way they view and treat blacks, so blacks will have to surrender, along with their marginal status, whatever was perversely comforting in leaders like Vander Beatty.

Beatty's disingenuous balancing of predatory interests and voters' populist impulses isn't really very different from what happens in most American electoral politics. What else was Marion Barry's third term as mayor of Washington, D.C.? What else was George Bush's 1988 "Willie Horton" campaign but racial theater, an effort to deflect voters' fears of crime away from a discussion of the roots of the problem and into hatred of his more principled opponent? If the voters are willing to succumb to such blandishments, what are an honest politician's alternatives? Owens is but one of many elected insurgents who've had to wrestle with that question, who've learned that merely rising above racial resentment and egregious corruption doesn't by itself bring lasting and constructive change. Even David Dinkins's 1989 mayoral victory, and certainly his fiscally strapped first year in office, has only underscored the truth that while transcending racial division is a necessary condition of social and economic justice, it is not sufficient. The lessons of the Owens-Beatty race can help us examine how the struggle to transcend race in the face of economic undertows that make for racial division has haunted Dinkins's own career.

The Honorary Black Insurgent

Dinkins stood with Owens outside the Brooklyn Board of Elections in October 1982 because, he said, he was outraged at Beatty's racially charged rhetoric and flamboyant electoral fraud. Well he might be, for Dinkins's traditional Harlem politics of patronage and brokerage differed from Beatty's mainly in that the Harlemites had become too sophisticated to resort to racial theater or egregious graft. Dinkins seemed to feel that Beatty must be discredited because his extreme tactics had become an embarrassment to the system— not because, as Owens believed, there was an alternative to the system itself. One might have questioned where Dinkins's threshold for "embarrassment" really lay; several years earlier, he had chaired the defense committee for Owens's nemesis and Beatty's mentor, the povertician-assemblyman Sam Wright, convicted of extortion in the manipulation of community school board funds. Suffice it to say that Dinkins's Harlem cohort had scarcely more empathy for Owens and the other elected veterans of Brooklyn's grass-roots insurgencies than for Vander Beatty.

But then, with a quiet determination underestimated by many who knew him, Dinkins was looking beyond his own political roots. In a sense, he always had, supporting Robert Kennedy when Jones was still at war with him. In 1977, Dinkins tried unsuccessfully to appeal to white reformers and the broad mass of white voters in his bid for the Manhattan borough presidency when his mentor Percy Sutton left the office to run for mayor. Dinkins confronted a special challenge: Sutton was the last of a line of black borough presidents who hadn't actually had to face the voters before assuming the office and running for reelection as incumbents. Jones had always arranged for the Tammany-controlled Manhattan delegation in the City Council to appoint them first to serve out the remainder of terms which their predecessor borough presidents had "graciously" left incomplete— Hulan Jack resigning amid allegations of corruption, for example, or Constance Baker Motley leaving early to become a federal judge.

Now Dinkins, whom Beame had managed to make city clerk despite the income-tax debacle of 1973, was in line to succeed Sutton as borough president in just this way. But Sutton broke with tradition, deciding he couldn't resign his post for Dinkins's sake without opening himself to charges of black cronyism during his own mayoral campaign. (It was unlikely that the council's Manhattan delegation, which reformers had wrested from Tammany, would have named Dinkins anyway). Dinkins was forced to run on his own, relying on the borough's black base, which made up less than a third of the electorate, and on whatever white liberal support he could muster.

He lost badly because the reformers, delighted that the borough presidency was at last up for grabs without an incumbent, put forward Robert Wagner, Jr., and Ronnie Eldridge, who battled Dinkins and an unwelcome young upstart, the wealthy assemblyman Andrew Stein of the Upper East Side. Then, too, there was the problem of Dinkins's lingering association with the clubhouse system: to the reformers, it was bad enough that he'd supported Beame in 1973 and even worse that he hadn't paid his taxes. Neither Dinkins nor the reformers could consolidate enough strength to defeat Stein, whom a *Village Voice* headline characterized as "Too Rich to Steal, Too Dumb to Lie." Meanwhile, Koch beat Abzug and six other contenders to become the mayor.

As in 1973, Dinkins took his lumps, remaining loyal to Sutton, becoming an investor in Inner City Broadcasting, and doggedly mending his fences with white reformers throughout Koch's and Stein's first terms. He showed up at everyone's fund-raisers and marches for good causes, from Soviet Jewry to gay rights. He genuinely enjoyed getting around and lending a hand, and in 1981 most of the reformers backed him against Stein, in part because the potential candidates among them realized that no one could beat the monied incumbent, who had grown in office. Dinkins ran against Stein anyway, shrewdly taking the longer, more disciplined view, as his mentor Jones would have done. While the reform councilwoman Ruth Messinger of Manhattan's Upper West Side cut a deal with Stein— she decided she couldn't keep criticizing the increasingly apostate Koch and at the same time attack Stein if she wanted to service her constituents—all the other prominent, white reformers lavished support on the doomed Dinkins candidacy, strengthening his claim to their endorsements the next time around. To everyone's surprise, he got 47 percent of the vote against Stein in 1981.

By 1983, it was clear that Stein was restless in the borough presidency; he'd lost a 1982 congressional race against the East Side incumbent Republican Bill Green and was rumored to be considering a higher office. So Dinkins set his sights yet again on becoming Stein's successor in the 1985 election. Yet he also kept dropping in on Brooklyn. He went there in 1983, for example, as part of the broad coalition of activists, led mostly by the Brooklyn insurgents, demanding a black chancellor for the public schools. When Jesse Jackson came through town in 1984, firing up the city's African-Americans with his campaign to be president of the United States, Dinkins was quicker than much of the Harlem establishment to join the Brooklyn insurgents in supporting him. Jackson assiduously courted the other Harlemites, though, and put Percy Sutton on the board of the National Rainbow Coalition.

Jackson posed a problem for the ecumenically minded Dinkins that year because he was sending something of a double message. To white reformers, he presented the Rainbow as a coalition for jobs, peace, a clean environment, and better public services. Blacks wanted those things too, of course, but Jackson gave them something else—the message that blacks' own empowerment as a mobilized electoral bloc must somehow precede their joining with others effectively to address such issues. Jackson's coalition in 1984 was really a shell within which blacks were to develop themselves; they were the Rainbow's biggest and most central band. Actually, Jackson's black "nation time" rallies in 1984 were short on political content and substantive proposals for black development. They were really group exercises in the sort of therapeutic self-assertion which Brooklyn's beleaguered masses often welcomed. In a triumphal procession across black New York with a jubilant Al Vann, cochair of his campaign in the state, Jackson lit bonfires that warmed blacks but didn't do much to illuminate the political and economic landscape beyond.

Still, the rhetoric of the Rainbow was compelling, and strange bedfellows were made in Jackson's New York campaign as Sutton and Dinkins worked with Vann and Bill Lynch to get out the vote. Aside from some vague talk about using the new Rainbow network to elect a black mayor in 1985, it was unclear just what Jackson's supporters would be able to accomplish once he was no longer in town. Grass-roots activists complained of being let down, even snubbed by Jackson when they tried to reach him after his departure. Perhaps, for the time being, that didn't matter. Black voter registration rose to double what it had been in 1980, though part of that reflected efforts in 1981 and 1982 as black political leaders reacted to the ascendancy of Ronald Reagan and Ed Koch. In the 1984 primary, an impressive 60 percent of the black voters came to the polls, and 87 percent of them voted for Jackson. Mondale still carried the city, but Jackson's accomplishment there was unprecedented, a breakthrough in black politics that gave new hope to Brooklyn's insurgents.

In Jackson's wake, and sometimes with his direct endorsement, half a dozen local black candidates around the city that September and the following year mounted racially charged challenges to white legislative incumbents representing predominantly black districts— to Representative Joseph Addabbo in southeastern Queens, State Senator Martin Markowitz, Assemblywoman Rhoda Jacobs, Councilwoman Susan Alter in and around Brooklyn's Flatbush section, and Councilwoman Carolyn Maloney in a northern Manhattan district that included part of Harlem.

But here the limits of Jackson's issueless organizing reasserted themselves as black voters in these districts sent mixed messages about the politics of racial solidarity. They'd seemed to endorse it in voting for Jackson himself, but then, his opponents, Walter Mondale and Gary Hart, and, indeed, the presidency itself, were so distant, so symbolic, that Jackson might as well have been running a referendum on black pride. At the local level four months later, black voters turned out in far fewer numbers, and those who did opted to retain the popular white incumbents, even in the most overwhelmingly black districts, giving them half or more of the black vote. Andrew Cooper's militant weekly, the *City Sun,* shocked black politicians by refusing to support two of the black challengers; it actually endorsed one of the white incumbents, Assemblywoman Jacobs, who, with 66 percent of the total vote and half the black vote, did even better than she had against a black opponent two years before.

Why didn't the challengers' "Our Time Has Come!" appeals work? Why didn't black voters think that replacing white incum-

bents with black ones would promote racial or even, perhaps, economic justice? The answer, in most of these contests, at least, was
that blacks who'd moved to the racially darkening districts represented by the white incumbents wanted not racial solidarity but an
opportunity to join the larger society in communities as integrated as
possible. They seemed to reason that when white incumbents were
effective at delivering services and principled enough to stand against
white flight and disinvestment by affirming longtime neighborhood
ties while appealing to black newcomers across racial lines, black
prospects were better.

For Brooklyn insurgents like Owens and Vann, who'd supported
most of the challengers, these were bitter and puzzling defeats. The
election results affirmed the political wisdom of J. Raymond Jones,
which has since been developed theoretically by the black political
scientist Martin Kilson and summarized well by the historian Jim
Chapin: "It is an encouraging irony of our politics that solid minority
backing goes only to candidates who reach unambiguously across
racial and ethnic lines. . . . Minority candidates in heavily minority
districts who make calculated appeals to [racial] solidarity always
fail."

Dinkins as Racial Deal Maker

The workings of Chapin's law would be all the more evident in
heavily white electorates like Manhattan's in 1985, when Stein finally
left the borough presidency to run for the City Council presidency.
True, Dinkins would have to count on racial solidarity among Manhattan's black voters and, at the same time, on white reform leaders'
deferring to such an expression of black pride by not running candidates of their own. But Dinkins would also have to hope that at least
half of the broad mass of Manhattan's white voters, who made up
better than 60 percent of the electorate, would pay no more attention
to race than had the black voters who'd supported the white legislators' victories a year earlier in Brooklyn and Queens. In short, he had
to rally blacks without alienating whites.

The principle linking these seemingly contradictory appeals to
black solidarity and white ecumenism lay in the nature of the candi-

date and his politics, which conformed to Chapin's observation, re-phrased in *New York Newsday,* that "black candidates do best with black voters when they're doing well enough with whites to have a real chance of winning." Dinkins could command a solid black vote precisely because, in a majority-white electorate, he could not—and by temperament would not—make the explicitly racial appeals the failed black legislative challengers had made in Jackson's fiery wake. The same combination of scruple and constraint had moved black voters in those contested districts and would certainly do so in Manhattan as well: even Jackson was the beneficiary of that truth when his far more racially inclusive 1988 campaign won him a higher proportion of New York's black vote (97 percent) than he had received in 1984 (87 percent). And, significantly, Jackson drew more white voters, too, carrying New York City this time against Michael Dukakis and Al Gore.

The white legislative incumbents who beat black challengers in heavily black districts had promised blacks better race relations and services. Dinkins could promise Manhattan's whites better race rela-tions, too, and, with the kind of white establishment help Jones had taught him to secure, he could also promise better services and access to power. As far back as 1978, Governor Carey had recommended Dinkins's wife, Joyce, for a position in the state Division of Taxation and Finance; in 1984, her husband had been appointed to the board of the state Urban Development Corporation. There he disappointed reformers by voting in favor of the power brokers' massive Times Square renewal plan, which Councilwoman Messinger and other re-formers had been trying to stop. But Dinkins had paid his dues to the reformers in so many others ways over the years that he had staked his claim to the borough presidency. Only Assemblyman Jerrold Nadler of the Upper West Side, an incorruptible maverick, dared challenge Dinkins and the new, cozy reform/Rainbow consensus.

And so, in 1985, Dinkins finally became Manhattan borough pres-ident the old-fashioned way: he earned it, not just by inheriting the local black band of Jackson's Rainbow but by befriending the new, white reform establishment, which suppressed its lingering misgiv-ings and embraced him at last. Dinkins had also proven himself to the more conservative "permanent government" of realtors, develop-ers, and contractors who'd always been close to his mentors in Harlem. His vote for the Times Square plan marked but one of many occasions over the next few years when housing advocates felt Dinkins had gone over to the developers; he moved comfortably among them, playing tennis regularly with Koch's housing commissioner, Anthony Gliedman, who would become Donald Trump's executive vice-president.

In the 1985 race, Dinkins even endeared himself in two ways to the mayor, a villain by then to both white reformers and blacks. Dinkins very courageously denounced Minister Louis Farrakhan's anti-Semitic statements. And, less courageously, he collaborated in a deal among minority pols to scuttle the Rainbow mayoral candidacy of Herman Badillo and to advance instead Assemblyman Herman Denny Farrell, of Harlem, whose candidacy helped Koch by siphoning votes from his challenger Carol Bellamy, the reform City Council president. Yet Dinkins kept his black base and white liberal allies: Farrakhan did him the unwitting favor of threatening him with death, an excess that offended black voters. Dinkins's support of Farrell was largely a deal behind closed doors. He trounced Nadler and another white opponent, taking 90 percent of the black vote and over 50 percent of the white—65 percent of the whole. Four years later, Dinkins's assiduous cultivation of the same three power bases—blacks, white reformers, and the permanent government— would carry him past Ed Koch and Rudolph Giuliani to Gracie Mansion.

11

A Politics beyond Race?

Black Politics: Progressive or Parochial?

Dinkins's election to the Manhattan borough presidency in 1985 vindicated his mentor Jones's conviction that a racially integrated—indeed, a race-transcendent—politics is the only way to secure high public office in New York. But as electoral success brought with it increasing governmental responsibility, it posed a dilemma: must a viable transracial politics also be "establishment" politics, a collaboration of economic special interests and narrow ethnic and racial brokers that subverts enlightened governance and hence, in the long run, interracialism itself? As it turned out, Dinkins and his supporters were forced to expend so much energy trying to curb both white racism and militant black nationalism that they had neither strength nor time to address this big question. Still, it surfaces again and again in any examination of his rise to the mayoralty.

It is interesting to speculate, for example, about how Dinkins would have handled the Beame administration's 1975 showdown with Owens, Vann, and the other Brooklyn insurgents over cuts in the antipoverty program had he become Beame's deputy mayor as originally planned. It would have been a confrontation, in effect, between Harlem's and Brooklyn's divergent responses to the seductions and compromises of establishment politics. It would have revealed much about Dinkins's own beliefs on the subject and might well have cost him a political future in Brooklyn. Because he did not become part of Beame's fiscal-crisis administration, Dinkins would not deal extensively with the Brooklyn insurgents until 1983, and then it was to forge friendships in a popular black cause, the campaign to make the deputy schools chancellor Thomas Minter the first black to head the system.

The Minter campaign was a natural fight for Brooklyn's insurgents to lead: Vann and Weusi were former teachers and Ocean Hill–Brownsville veterans; Minter and the outgoing chancellor, Frank Macchiarola, both lived in the borough, and the Board of Education was headquartered in downtown Brooklyn's infamous 110 Livingston Street. There, police would arrest several demonstrating Minter supporters who tried to crash a board meeting, including Weusi, Hazel Dukes, and Bill Lynch, the veteran organizer who had managed Owens's victorious congressional campaign the year before and was comfortable among the Brooklyn insurgents. But Dinkins and other Harlemites were drawn to the fray because Koch had tried to appoint his former deputy mayor Robert Wagner, Jr., as chancellor, only to be overruled by the state education commissioner because Wagner did not hold the required doctorate in education. The irony, lost on no black person who read a newspaper, was that Koch, a champion of "standards" against affirmative action goals and timetables, had tried to bend standards in seeking a waiver for Wagner while passing over Minter, who held the requisite credentials.

It was in the Coalition for Tom Minter that Dinkins first became friendly with Lynch, eventually drawing him to Manhattan to manage his 1985 campaign for borough president, after which Lynch became Dinkins's chief of staff. "That was the first time the African-American community of New York City had ever come together in a broad-based coalition," Weusi declares. "It was the beginning of the struggle that ultimately led to Dinkins's victory in 1989." In the end, both Wagner and Minter lost out to Anthony Alvarado, the charismatic superintendent of East Harlem's School District 4, but the alliances formed during the campaign remained. Two powerful ministers, Calvin Butts of Harlem's Abyssinian Baptist Church and Timothy Mitchell of Queens's Ebenezer Baptist Church, met there for the first time. Like Dinkins and Lynch, they next worked together in the Coalition for a Just New York, a group of forty-two black leaders who agreed to unite their own and other constituencies behind a single challenger to Koch in 1985.

For the hitherto fragmented black community, the Coalition for a Just New York was yet another ambitious leap forward, proposing as it did to unite blacks and at the same time reach out to other minorities and white party reformers. All the rhetoric of progressive social change was there, encapsulated in the coalition's very name: this was a movement not solely for black empowerment but for social justice that transcended race. Under the slogan "Strive for '85," the coalition interviewed mayoral aspirants, including former Bronx Borough President Herman Badillo and City Council President Carol Bellamy. It tried to impose on all comers an exchange: it would endorse one of them for mayor, in return for the candidate's support of Vann's own intended candidacy for Brooklyn borough president against the machine incumbent, Howard Golden.

Bellamy was unwilling to cut that deal, to the sorrow of Major Owens, Roger Green, and others who'd worked constructively with her when she was a state senator from Brooklyn Heights in the 1970s. Badillo agreed to the Vann bargain and became the coalition's apparent choice. Before making it official, the group's members lobbied the city's anti-Koch elites, including Bellamy, to yield to Badillo just as they were yielding to Dinkins's bid for the Manhattan borough presidency.

Badillo's candidacy seemed to be gaining momentum when, at an extraordinary, eleventh-hour meeting late in February of 1985, Denny Farrell, the flamboyant Harlem assemblyman and Manhattan Democratic party chairman, little known outside his borough, asked the coalition to withdraw its endorsement of Badillo and support him instead, on the grounds that a black candidate was preferable. As the coalition was all-black, it had heard grumbling about its failure to come up with a black standard-bearer; some of its members also felt that Badillo had double-crossed them on past deals. Then, too, coalition outsiders like the *Village Voice*'s Jack Newfield, at the time quite active in Badillo's effort, were annoying coalition members by loudly and prematurely praising the group's sophistication in building a black-Hispanic alliance—another case of white radicals from the *Village Voice* trying to tell blacks how to vote.

The Vann-led coalition's last-minute deliberations with the dapper Farrell might have been another classic Harlem-Brooklyn confrontation, but for the irony that Farrell's call to the group to return to black solidarity was antithetical to the Harlem tradition. If anything, it was calculated to stike chords among some of the more nationalist Brooklyn insurgents. Almost incredibly, it worked, speaking volumes about the Brooklyn insurgents' insecurities and about the coalition's flawed composition: not only was this nerve center of the citywide progressive coalition all-black; thirty-seven of its forty-two members were male, while the city's black electorate was 60 percent female. Newfield and others on the left who'd taken the coalition seriously had never questioned why such a group should hold a moral veto over candidate selection for the whole anti-Koch coalition. It was a classic case of undue deference to blacks as the vanguard of social change.

Then again, as long as the Puerto Rican Badillo was the group's apparent choice, criticism of its racial exclusivity might well be muted; it must be said, too, that Owens, Green, and others were acknowledged advocates of programs to aid women and children. One member of the coalition told me that when a Harlem activist called Bellamy "that white bitch" during the closed-door deliberations, Owens leapt to his feet and shouted, "We won't have that kind of talk in this room! The real test of what we are is what we say when we're amongst ourselves!"

But the group's last-minute dumping of Badillo eclipsed all these strengths, unleashing a torrent of criticism to the effect that a club of insecure, macho black nationalists had destroyed the city's chance to rid itself of Koch. Butts and C. Vernon Mason stormed out of the coalition, and when Farrell formally announced his candidacy on the steps of City Hall the next day, Mason stood with a group of Hispanics shouting "Judas!" at him for blindsiding the enraged Badillo. Chairman Vann reacted defensively: "We understood there'd be a reaction [among Hispanics], but there could even be a reaction to the reaction if it continues." One could almost feel the veteran nationalist teetering backward into old ways, a personal and political tragedy. Now there would be no moral pressure to stop Bellamy from announcing, too.

Conspiracy theories flew all over town. Farrell had made a deal with Koch, it was said, to divide the mayor's opposition in exchange for the mayor's implicit support for his reelection as Manhattan Democratic leader. Dinkins was said to have promoted the deal in the hope that Koch wouldn't undercut his third try for the Manhattan borough presidency. While Dinkins admitted backing Farrell, no evidence emerged to support these claims. Still, the ensuing primary unfolded as if they were true: Farrell ran a shoestring campaign as "the black candidate," winning only 40 percent of the black vote to Koch's 38 percent. Overall, Koch won a landslide—68 percent of the primary vote against 13 percent for Farrell and 19 percent for Bellamy. In Brooklyn, meanwhile, Vann, running against Golden and two other white candidates without benefit of the strong, citywide ticket the coalition had promised, failed to reach out to the borough's whites, concentrating too much of his effort in the minority communities. He lost badly, nearly losing the black vote itself. Both Farrell's and Vann's dismal performances thus confirmed Chapin's dictum that black voters strongly support only those black candidates who are credibly reaching whites.

When the smoke had cleared at the close of 1985, Koch was still mayor, Andrew Stein was the new council president, and Howard Golden continued his reign in Brooklyn's Borough Hall. "We laid the Farrell thing at Dinkins's feet," Andrew Cooper recalls. "He resented it. He said so years later: 'How long are you gonna blame me for that?' " In a supreme irony, though, only David Dinkins, the one black leader to adhere steadfastly to transracial politics—at least in public—joined the city's governing elite as Manhattan borough president, the only minority member of the Board of Estimate, a spokesman, he said, for the city's downtrodden. Since his days in the assembly, Dinkins had, indeed, supported the best of the civil rights and labor movements; and now, standing by Dinkins's side as if to bolster his promise "to empower those who have been underserved" was his campaign manager and new chief of staff, that veteran organizer of the insurgent poor—Bill Lynch.

But, unlike so many other members of the Coalition for a Just New York, Dinkins had never felt he could be an effective fighter for justice without maintaining cordial relationships with established powers in the manner prescribed long ago by his mentor. Four years later, a week before the 1989 mayoral triumph, Jones, then eighty-nine and retired to his native Virgin Islands, told *New York Newsday*'s Kevin Flynn and Ellis Henican, "Dinkins understood the rules and played according to the rules. It's no surprise, is it, that the Harlem man—not one of those Brooklyn militants—is the one to do it." In a long list of "thank-yous" on the night of his mayoral victory in 1989, Dinkins did not even mention the names of three of his key supporters: Brooklyn's Owens, Vann, and Green.

Once again, then, Harlem would best Brooklyn, in two ways: first, by observing Chapin's dictum that "the choice between marshalling black unity and courting white support is a false one"; and second, by securing links to powerful patrons in the permanent government. The question facing the Brooklyn insurgents would be: could blacks ever hope to transcend the politics of race, as Dinkins was clearly doing, without at the same time embracing the politics of the establishment, as Dinkins was also clearly doing and as his mentor Jones had always prescribed? In 1985, the insurgents had succumbed to the politics of race, never even reaching the second part of the dilemma. Would they succeed in posing both parts of the challenge in 1989?

Lip Service That Counts

One might think that the debacle of the Coalition for a Just New York had settled the debate between the partisans of black racial solidarity and those of race-transcendent politics in favor of the latter, opening the door to broader questions about the relation between social justice and electoral politics itself. But throughout the 1989 mayoral campaign, debate raged among the city's black politicians and pundits over whether candidate Dinkins was sufficiently loyal to his black base. Typical was a discussion on October 29, a week before the election, on Gil Noble's talk show, "Like It Is":

EARL CALDWELL [*Daily News* columnist]: [Dinkins] said right up front, "I am not the black candidate," and he is not running on the Harold Washington model: this isn't the black community putting forward a candidate and saying "Our time has come" and showing that we have the muscle to take it. Rather, this to me is the best example of the Rainbow Coalition.

WILBERT TATUM [publisher, *Amsterdam News*]: David is the candidate of the Democratic Party. That means white, black, green, yellow, polka dot, and he is prosecuting his campaign as if that were the case.

NOBLE: But hang on, . . . Harold Washington was a Democrat.

TATUM: But as Earl said, he ran a different model [stating openly that his candidacy was contingent on the black community's organizing itself for victory]. That model cannot be run here. In this town, the largest voting bloc is the black bloc, 32 percent of the vote. [But] the next is the Jewish bloc, with 28 percent. The next [which Dinkins hopes to win] is the Hispanic, with 9 percent, and this comprises the coalition. . . . He has to appeal to a vast section of people, and I understand his campaign very well. He is campaigning to win, not to feel comfortable or obligated to any group . . . , because he will have to be mayor of all the people.

UTRICE LEID [managing editor, *City Sun*]: . . . The reality, nonetheless, is that his political base is overwhelmingly black. There has got to be some kind of return based on that investment, and that is the quintessential question.

Leid's "quintessential question" was posed vigorously to Dinkins by her own newspaper and by militants in Brooklyn. A particularly harsh *City Sun* editorial slamming Dinkins for neglecting the African-American community brought his campaign manager, Bill Lynch, to a lunch meeting in July at Brooklyn's Gage & Tollner's restaurant with Leid, her publisher, Andrew Cooper, and Jim Bell of the Coalition of Black Trade Unionists.

"Lynch said, 'We're doing the black constituency quietly, we're not ignoring it,' " Cooper reports.

"He recited the problems of putting together a real citywide campaign as opposed to promoting a national figure like Jackson in a symbolic race. He explained the difficulties in reaching the territories, groups, and constituencies which you don't have to reach in a presidential campaign. He told us that for Dinkins to build these bridges, he had to be consistent in what he

said from one group to the next. Which means you don't say very much! We
said, okay, but we want to meet David."

Lynch did not follow up, Cooper says. "Everything was dropped.
No phone calls, no nothing. After *Newsday* reprinted our editorial on
its op-ed page, we got a call from Percy [Sutton] inviting the black
press to a meeting with David, where he would answer the charge
that he was not serving the black constituency." Leid attended for
the *City Sun* and reported back that Dinkins said, in effect, "Help
me." "He sounded like a human being," she told Cooper, especially
after Harry Belafonte came in and, according to Leid, told Dinkins,
"It's your fault."

Yet black papers continued to find Dinkins hard to reach; he did
not speak with groups of activists in Brooklyn. As late as October 29,
when he had won the primary and was in the heat of battle with
Rudolph Giuliani, *New York Newsday* reported that the rift was
wider than ever: "We are certainly concerned about the role Brooklyn blacks will play in the administration . . .," Sharpton said. "If he
doesn't address the black community and its concerns, what we
thought was a hero may turn out to be, in fact, an Uncle Tom."
Added Alton Maddox, "We are concerned that we may have an Ed
Koch in blackface." They challenged Dinkins to show up at a November 2 meeting of activists at Bedford-Stuyvesant's Slave Theater,
which serves as a staging point for Sharpton's demonstrations.

Not surprisingly, Dinkins did not attend the meeting. I did, and
listened as Sharpton voiced the militants' dissatisfaction to an audience of two hundred:

We have not asked anybody not to vote for David Dinkins. We have
asked him whether he's on our side. We know Dave's positions on the Jews,
on gays, on big business, on the homeless. What is his program to build the
community he was born in? In 1986, Dave proclaimed Al Sharpton Day.
Now we got to pretend like we don't know each other? It's like being asked
to go on a blind date with an old lover.

Why is it always that when the union leaders come forward, they speak
for unions, and when the Jewish leaders come forward, they speak for the
Jews, but when the black leaders come forward, they say, "I'm for everybody!"?

Dave, we say, come home. We know you had to go to the union hall. We know you had to go to the synagogue. We know you had to make deals. But don't deal us out!

Sharpton stirred his listeners, but even as I sat listening in the dim light of the colorfully painted and muraled theater with my *New York Newsday* colleague Merle English, I knew that Caldwell and Tatum were right: contrary to everything the *City Sun* and Sharpton were saying and what the audience in the theater believed, Dinkins needed to follow Chapin's law; he had to reach out successfully to whites not just to win their votes but, precisely if counterintuitively, to win the support of more back voters than he would get simply by "coming home." The holdouts at the Slave had not grasped this imperative, not even when, in the wake of Yusuf Hawkins's violent death at the hands of Bensonhurst whites on August 23, many in the city had turned to the ecumenical Dinkins as a healer. Perhaps Sharpton finally understood it when, in defiance of the militants' raillery, Dinkins brought in 97 percent of the black vote—more than even Tatum had anticipated.

Nor was Sharpton right when he asserted, to hearty applause, that labor and Jewish leaders speak only for their own groups when they come to the public arena and that therefore African-Americans should do the same. Labor seldom fails to cast its demands upon the public in terms of what's good for America. Jewish leaders, too, as we have seen, are almost notorious for selling their interests in terms of others' needs: not many years earlier, Sharpton would probably have complained that they were casting their interests in terms of what was supposedly best for blacks.

Sharpton was trying to fight his way out of a paradox inherent in American politics: while every group that has assumed a measure of public power has provided first for its own, even the most cynical Irish Tammany sachem has also paid an all-important lip service to working for all citizens. Even when public-sector retrenchments forced ethnic political leaders to act parochially, serving their own groups above all, the maintenance of public power also required that they invoke the interests of a broader community. They did so because they understood that, ultimately, there is no specifically "Irish," "Jewish," or "black" way to expand the number of jobs or build low-income housing. If Sharpton's followers wanted a bigger piece of the action, then, like ethnic leaders in the past, they would have to speak not of reparations to their own group but of interracial strategies to expand the size of the pie—of battles for an economic justice that knows no racial bounds.

But Sharpton never spoke that way, and his reasons were the same as those of Vander Beatty, whom he'd supported against Owens for Congress: any truly broad, vital coalition for systemic change would have outgrown his histrionics, his massaging of old wounds. Even if Sharpton just wanted more city government jobs for blacks, as he said at one point in his speech, he and the insurgents would have to prove that they understood just how David Dinkins had to get elected and to contribute to that effort—on Dinkins's terms.

I asked the *City Sun*'s publisher, Andrew Cooper, what was behind the paper's scathing campaign editorials, which echoed Sharpton's line yet never offered specifics. "I want to know what legislative plans he has for the black community in this city," Cooper told me. "What will he do in education? Look, educating black kids really is a special problem. And what about all the pathologies in our community: why are all the statistics disproportionately against blacks? What does he think are the causes, and what would he do to make things more normal? Nobody is being creative. You know the old cliché about how we can send men to the moon, but . . ."

These answers were not very satisfying. I have addressed the question of black education in chapter 8. And even if there are uniquely black solutions to the "pathologies" Cooper mentions, it isn't necessarily a mayor's job to pursue them. A mayor's role remains quintessentially what LaGuardia made it: to make his "home base" proud of him by embodying the New York idea and the larger American promise, fusing the aspirations and strengths of the city's disparate ethnic groups into a common purpose. That Dinkins takes this race-transcendent role seriously was evident in a preelection interview with Phil Donahue for *New York Newsday*. Donahue asked him whether angry young blacks mightn't see him as too accommodating of the establishment, a possible Uncle Tom. "Au contraire," Dinkins replied. "What I do is provide hope."

A Politics beyond Race?

But that leaves unresolved the question of whether one can "provide hope" at this point in the city's history by transcending the politics of race if one cannot also somehow transcend the politics of the establishment. The latter task involves mediating the inherently unequal power relations between labor and capital, neighborhoods and real-estate developers, the service dependent and the bureaucracies—inequities that are more or less enshrined in law. What else is a mayor elected to do, what else was David Dinkins in training to do even when, early in his borough presidency, he was declaring "Al Sharpton Day" in Manhattan?

That Dinkins offers no answer beyond bringing African-Americans into the establishment in the time-honored American way is made plain in a pair of the *New York Times* editorials about him that were noteworthy for their assurances to jittery white readers that Dinkins could be trusted to keep the blacks in line. The editorials were noteworthy, too, for their underestimation of the man's superb training for establishment politics:

[Mayoral candidate Dinkins's] decency can help the city confront its biggest foreseeable problems: a sagging economy and tension between the races. . . . The next mayor will have to ask for, and sell, sacrifice to all New Yorkers, most notably the poor citizens hurt most by reductions in city services. Mr. Dinkins seems better qualified to persuade all New Yorkers to share the burdens ahead. [October 29, 1989, endorsement of Dinkins]

David Dinkins took office just the way he ran for it—politely, quietly, and with a generosity of spirit. . . . But for all his good will, the 62-year-old Mayor did not ignore the city's bleak realities. He made clear that inclusion, Dinkins-style, will require all New Yorkers to share not only the benefits of prosperity but the sacrifices of fiscal austerity.

There was meaning, too, in the presence of so many black New Yorkers who crowded into City Hall Park to celebrate a political coming of age. . . . Now comes the hard part: governing. . . . [January 2, 1990, the day after Dinkins's inauguration]

Perhaps the condescension in the last line is inevitable; for, again, what is Dinkins's function as mayor of a city government virtually hostage to its financial creditors, if not to try to reconcile desperate constituencies to the structures of debt and deprivation he has pledged himself to uphold? Is there a way to build any other kind of city through electoral politics?

Rudolph Giuliani fancied that he had an answer. It was best expressed by the investigative journalists Jack Newfield and Wayne Barrett in their book *City for Sale,* an anatomy of corruption in the Koch administration. Koch, they wrote, had mortgaged portions of his government to influence-peddling Democratic county bosses like Donald Manes and Stanley Friedman in exchange for votes from their boroughs. These pols in effect sold off the city's powers over zoning and franchising, planning, and taxation to the highest bidders, compromising justice and the quality of life, dragging the city down, costing it its independence. Giuliani was a hero because he'd sent some of these power brokers to prison. The way to rise above establishment politics, in this view, was to send the rest of them packing, too. Everything in David Dinkins's history told the muckrakers that he couldn't be trusted to do that. Almost everything in Giuliani's history told them that he could be. And 1989 was the first year in more than twenty that a "Fusion" Republican like Giuliani seemed likely to win.

But while the former U.S. attorney might be honest, even brilliant, was he the kind of political leader who could rally a broad coalition? Not when his liaison to Jews was the comedian Jackie Mason, a one-man cyst in the Jewish body politic, filled with everything retrograde and perverse about the community. Newfield and Barrett ignored Giuliani's obvious liabilities because they'd spent years documenting how Democratic party machines were ruining the city, only to be frustrated by the public's failure to rebel. Often the muckrakers had turned from persuasion to prosecutors for civic rescue, and they had been rewarded, most recently and formidably by Giuliani.

But did their and Giuliani's guiding assumptions about the importance of fighting corruption really offer an alternative to establishment politics? The corruption of the Parking Violations Bureau and even of decisions about zoning and discretionary tax abatements hasn't much to do with the plagues confronting the city—crime, crack, AIDS, family disintegration. Might corruption fighting root out other systemic injustices, then, like capital flight and unemployment? Not if one considers, as the writer and economic consultant Robert Fitch did in a perceptive essay for *New York Newsday* during the campaign, that anticorruption crusades come around reliably every twenty-five years or so and are led by—the establishment!

Across the decades, the tactics have been wearyingly the same: Select a blue-ribbon commission of academic mandarins and white-shoe lawyers. Appoint a fearless prosecutor—former Manhattan D.A. Tom Dewey; former state special prosecutor Maurice Nadjari; Giuliani. Loose the faithful investigative bloodhounds of the crusading press who bay deafeningly when they discover clues, some of which have been left for them to find. Send the little crooks to jail and the big ones to Mexico City. New York City's banking and property-owning establishment knows how much we love this dog-and-pony show. But what determines when they schedule it, and what do the sponsors get for their efforts?

Fitch's answer is that members of the "banking and property-owning establishment"—finance and real estate are to New York City what big oil has been to Houston—don't want to be bothered with the politics of zoning and planning; when times are flush and they are very busy, they're perfectly willing to pay off the machine to manipulate public decisions for their benefit while they concentrate on selling and accumulating bonds, selling and developing real estate.

But when a collapse comes and office-building construction stops dead, . . . real estate is caught in a squeeze of falling income and rising taxes. Bonds are dragged down by falling municipal revenues and falling real estate values. Bankers and real estate men demand that the city's budget be cut. . . . The whole creaky Fusionist machinery of cyclical reform, with its commissions, prosecutors and journalists, is necessary because New York City's wealthy interests prefer using this apparatus to taking up political vocations themselves. There are exceptions like the [Richard] Ravitches and the [David] Rockefellers. But generally this class alternates between paying baksheesh to the political machine when times are good and indicting it when the Democratic Party's bite begins to cause them real pain.

Fitch's way out of this endless cycle is to create an alternative to the Democratic party. He cites examples—from Henry George's labor-backed single-tax movement of the 1880s to New York City's American Labor party of the 1940s—political coalitions of activist intellectuals, tenants, and workers which challenged the assumptions of both the machine and the Fusionist and muckraking dupes of established power. But, for reasons neither he nor anyone else adequately explained, as the 1989 election approached, there was simply no momentum in those directions outside of the usual impotent thrashings of some on the left.

Political Moderates to the Rescue?

There was, however, another alternative developing in the city's four largest boroughs, one mentioned in earlier chapters—the confederation of four interracial, interdenominational, church-based "power organizations" consisting of nearly two hundred congregations with more than 60,000 dues-paying members, trained by the Industrial Areas Foundation. Organizing civil society's most important institutions—families, churches, voluntary organizations—to wrest power over housing development and school reform from the corrupted bureaucracies, the IAF-affiliated groups had developed cadres of trained clerical and lay leaders. East Brooklyn Congregations' 1,500 Nehemiah homes in Brownsville had transformed a part of the turf where muckrakers and black Brooklyn insurgents had struggled for so many years to so little avail. In fact, one of the first things Major Owens had done after winning the 1982 congressional race described at the beginning of chapter 10 was pack himself off to a ten-day IAF training session, so impressed was he by the group's achievements and growing clout.

Because they work with political moderates—ordinary, churchgoing New Yorkers who are subway conductors, nurses, elementary school teachers—the organizations do not present themselves as political movements or parties. And because, while predominantly black and Hispanic, they include congregations of all races, they refuse to speak, as do the *City Sun* and so many of the Brooklyn insurgents, about a "black agenda" or "black power," the shib-

boleths of impotence. Ironically, through the learning process em-
bedded in their organizing, the IAF groups have developed a critique
of establishment power that comes remarkably close to that of Newfield, Barrett, and Fitch. As Father Leo Penta, an EBC staff member,
told an audience at St. John's Law School in 1987,

We no longer live in a city, in any classic sense of the polis, but in a
municipal marketplace. . . . The "producer" is the rusted but still functioning political machine—that corrupt trading network of contracts, jobs, re-
ceiverships, references, favors, etc. Its customers, aside from itself, are its
major campaign contributors—corporate leaders who have flooded the public arena with money, shopping for favorable decisions and speedy action on
matters which, by the very nature of their enterprise, must be conceived as
profit ventures.
. . . Virtually all [housing] development in New York is now "cost plus"
development—the actual cost of material, labor, etc. plus the additional
sums necessary to legally or illegally "purchase" the requisite "political
commodities" like land-use votes, the cutting of bureaucratic red tape, labor
peace and community acceptance.

But where Newfield and Barrett would call agents of law enforcement like Giuliani to the rescue and Fitch would call for the creation
of new political parties, the IAF groups try to build power through
the families, churches, and voluntary organizations of civil society
itself. They are nonpartisan, though they do register thousands of
voters. It is mainly through proposals presented to elected officials
and bureaucrats by delegations from the groups, backed by the
power of their research and their ability to turn out thousands of
people at rallies and demonstrations, that they have sometimes
forced the city government to serve the real city, not the special
interests.

That the IAF-affiliated groups got more interest and support from
Giuliani than from Dinkins during the 1989 mayoral race wasn't
surprising. Giuliani had no connections to the Democratic party establishment, on whose toes the IAF groups had so often stepped
during their ten years of organizing in New York. Giuliani even
talked with I. D. Robbins, the visionary developer who works with
IAF to produce the Nehemiah homes, about the possibility of

becoming the city's housing commissioner. But if some members of the IAF affiliates were more than ready to upset politics-as-usual by electing Giuliani, many more felt a natural affinity with Dinkins. Even as he embodied their pride in themselves as people of color, he, like they, transcended the politics of race.

How would such conflicting loyalties play out? Without explanation, Giuliani failed to show up at a preelection meeting of a thousand members of IAF community organizations in the basement hall of a cavernous church on Manhattan's West Side, at which part of the agenda was to hear from the candidates. Dinkins did come, and the encounter was revealing.

The meeting opened with the singing of "America the Beautiful" by all assembled. Watching a thousand Hispanic mothers in imitation leather coats, middle-aged black men in cheap suits, rumpled white ethnics in polyester shirts, and ghetto teenagers in army jackets and high-tops rise to render an anthem at an IAF-group assembly could reduce any white middle-class observer to putty as he ponders how these hard-pressed people have kept faith. After the invocation and wildly applauded introductions of the various congregations in attendance came warm-up speeches by a few of the clerics and lay leaders on the dais. The developer Robbins described the South Bronx Churches' proposed new apartment buildings for a site the group had been demanding from the city. Several congregants, unaccustomed though they were to public speaking, spoke beautifully about their organizations' agendas in health care, education, and public safety. The room fairly vibrated, the crowd disciplined yet buoyant.

Now it was time to hear from the political candidates under IAF rules designed to remind them who, in a democracy, is boss. The politicians would be posed brief questions by a member of the group—"Do you endorse the agendas we have presented, and will you work with us to implement them . . . ?" "Will you agree to meet with us for one hour in December and monthly after that?" The candidates, of course, would give the predictable answers before they were allowed just a couple of minutes to speak. Councilwoman Ruth Messinger, running to succeed Dinkins as Manhattan borough president, proudly endorsed the group's work, as did Brooklyn DA Elizabeth Holtzman, running for city comptroller. When Assemblyman

Jose Serrano of the South Bronx said, "No longer will we be divided along racial or ethnic lines, we are one people," the room erupted into thunderous cheering and applause.

Dinkins, it was announced, had been delayed in traffic, so the Reverend Johnny Ray Youngblood of St. Paul's Community Baptist Church in East New York rose to deliver the keynote address. As he had done at the Nehemiah ground-breaking rally described in chapter 5, Youngblood preached in loving, yearning cadences, offering simple, incontrovertible observations, punctuated by amens and applause that piled upon one another, reaching a crescendo that burst like a fireworks display in the energy it released in the crowd. Noting that their meeting place that day was a block from Lincoln Center, he began,

We are not at Lincoln Center, but we are a symphony of beautiful people! All around us here in midtown Manhattan are people of power. But they need us to tell them what they don't know! . . . In the Book of Nehemiah, it says, "The people had a mind to work." We have a mind to work! We're not gonna let a river divide us. Ain't no river wide enough! We are working to be rid of the reproach of poor health care, of poor education, of poor security. We work every day in this city; we have a will; we are a working people! We are a worthy people!

This city is known for celebrities. We're not celebrities. All we want is decent educations [applause], decent places to live, decent health care [roaring applause and cheers]. Because we are a decent people! [pandemonium]

. . . I've been trying to figure out why they won't accept our hands to work. And I think it may be that our hands are attached to the wrong bodies! If these hands were attached to Andrew Cuomo [laughter], David ROCK-a-feller, David Ga-a-arth [mounting, roaring laughter], Roger Ailes, they would be accepted more readily.

We want to build! What do they mean, there's no land to build on? Everywhere I go, I see la-a-and! [roaring laughter and applause] And this land is OUR land! WE ride the subways! WE walk these streets! WE live in these communities! WE elect THEM to office! WE pay their salaries! This land is our land! Thank God for this land! And We Love New York! We Love New York! [the crowd joining him now, on its feet, thundering] WE LOVE NEW YORK!

Midway through Youngblood's rousing speech, Dinkins arrived through a side door and stood waiting in a room off the stage, invisible to all but those on the dais. The candidate was not in a festive mood. He looked tired, irritable. Instead of listening to Youngblood, he dispatched an aide to the dais to request that the minister terminate his remarks to allow him to speak. But Youngblood's speech had its own role to play in the meeting, and the organizers would not interrupt him. Dinkins looked particularly annoyed as the crowd delighted in Youngblood's references to Andrew Cuomo and the other political celebrities.

As borough president, Dinkins had already had some less than satisfactory encounters with tightly organized IAF delegations. At the first, get-acquainted meeting—always an important part of the group's strategy—he'd insisted on eating his lunch and taking phone calls instead of giving them his full attention. The church people, who had traveled some distance and prepared carefully, had been insulted. Dinkins had been "hammered good," too, according to one organizer, at a South Bronx Churches rally, for his collegial support of Bronx Borough President Fernando Ferrer's opposition to an SBC housing initiative on a contested site. Knowing the politics of the Board of Estimate, the IAF people were also acquainted with Dinkins's accommodations to the kinds of developers who'd beaten them in getting other sites from the Koch administration. The organizers had never received from Dinkins the kind of assurances they'd just gotten from Messinger and Holtzman—that he was open to them, that he could be on their side. Their sense was that they made him nervous, as they made the rest of the establishment nervous.

But most of the crowd at the rally knew nothing of these tensions, and as the man who would be the city's first African-American mayor walked onto the stage at the conclusion of Youngblood's speech, the already tumultuous assemblage erupted wildly into foot stomping and cheering. Black people, especially, seemed to burst with pride. When all had been seated, Dinkins took his place by the side of the podium for the few brief questions.

"Mr. Dinkins, will we have land for more Nehemiah housing?"

"Yes." Dinkins said it firmly, clearly, yet almost sullenly, as if he resented being asked in front of a thousand people who would have permitted him no other answer. Many in the crowd sensed his resistance, but they hung on the answer itself and applauded it vigorously.

"Mr. Dinkins, if you are elected mayor, may we have a commitment from you to meet with us for one hour during the transition between the election and the inauguration, to discuss our agenda?"

"Well, I may want greater flexibility. I may meet with you for twenty minutes and have my staff meet with you for three hours. But we can work something out, so the answer to your question is yes." That was a prickly response, resistant to the question and the format, and, this time, everyone in the audience felt it. Dinkins's campaign manager, Bill Lynch, had spoken with the meeting's organizers the day before and asked them not to pose specific questions, but they had refused to alter their plans. "Let's talk tomorrow," Lynch had said, but he hadn't called back, hoping, perhaps, that the leaders would pull their punches at the rally.

Now Dinkins began to read, in a droning voice, a prepared campaign speech on housing that blasted the Republicans for cutting federal aid, talked about reforming the housing court, and defended public housing. Worthy positions all, but the audience was listening for something to amplify the commitment he'd just made to provide their Nehemiah program with the land Youngblood had so compellingly invoked. As Dinkins read on, it became clear that nothing in his canned speech would touch on IAF's readiness to build five thousand homes a year if only the city would give it sites.

The crowd became restless. The speech was a mistake—somebody hadn't done his advance work properly—and Dinkins's soporific delivery was a comedown from Youngblood and the buoyant spirit of the meeting. The assembly, which prided itself on being "clear, specific, and strong" in all its communications, was offended at the lack of any reference to its housing agenda. Finally, the dam burst. A man toward the back rose to his feet and shouted, "What about Nehemiah?" Others joined him as Dinkins read on, then stumbled and stopped, taken aback by the interruption. Here were people who should be "his," on their feet, shouting in unison, "Nehemiah now!" Onstage, Robbins leapt to his feet and shouted, "Why don't you promise us land!" Dinkins tried to parry the cries with assurances that they could discuss Nehemiah housing when he became mayor.

Perhaps the crowd, too, was making a mistake: was this confrontation truly necessary, appropriate? There were second thoughts as some people began shushing the noisemakers. The crowd began to quiet down, though one man wouldn't stop yelling and had to be pulled back into his seat by his neighbors so Dinkins could continue. "When we build new housing, we'll be building new communities," Dinkins continued, departing from his text to look up and say, angrily, "And you oughta like that!" He resumed reading, "I want to lead us into the future . . . ," concluding testily, with a trace of sarcasm, "And thank you for listening."

In fairness to Dinkins, a lesser politician like Vander Beatty might have tried to play the race card with this audience by railing at "big [i.e., white] developers." It wasn't in Dinkins to do that, and it certainly wasn't in this assembly to allow it. Still, stripped now of the mythic sheen imparted by race pride, Dinkins looked like just another big-city pol—distracted, slightly out of touch with his immediate surroundings, stuck behind a canned speech, thinking about his next appointment. Having entered to a tumultuous reception, Dinkins strode out to moderate applause punctuated by a few catcalls. The disillusionment in the room was palpable. But perhaps it had clarified some important truths about establishment politics in New York.

Sobering Lessons

Reflecting on IAF's experience with Dinkins at the rally, an organizer said, "We saw the depth of race and the superficiality of race— all in ten minutes." Whatever the allure of racial solidarity for these minority New Yorkers, it evaporated in the face of a perceived affront to their commitment to a specific, material agenda whose realization requires genuine power. Once again, the politics of race was shown to be a snare and a delusion. To his credit, Dinkins has always fought against the worst of that politics.

But the election showed that the black-militant and white-leftist practitioners of that politics—and the many whites who fear them— could still inflame racial grievances, diverting the city's attention from the real challenge: to reorder municipal priorities on behalf of those with "a mind to work." On November 7, Dinkins defeated Giuliani by approximately two points, a mere 47,080 votes out of more than 1.7 million cast.

As D. D. Guttenplan noted in *New York Newsday,* Dinkins was the first mayor in generations to win without carrying a majority of Jews, Irish, or Italians; he took just 39 percent of the Jewish and 23 percent of the white Catholic vote. Blacks, Hispanics, and women were the only groups of voters, categorized by ethnicity and gender, which gave him better than his 52 percent overall. Although his strong pro-choice stance accounted for a 55 percent win among women and although his tax problems undoubtedly cut into his support among whites, there could be no question that race had dominated the election; for example, the revelation, after the September primary, that Jitu Weusi and Sonny Carson had been put on the campaign payroll by Bill Lynch in response to the militants' complaints surely cost Dinkins several points among Jews, particularly those who had lived through the Ocean Hill–Brownsville conflict as teachers. This, notwithstanding the fact that Sandra Feldman's UFT strongly supported him. Old wounds, once reopened, could not be closed by rational debate.

Dinkins's chillingly narrow victory despite his 97 percent support among blacks ought to have taught him, for once and for all, how needlessly those old wounds had been reopened. Whatever support the militants had lined up for him was alienated when Weusi and Carson were expelled from the campaign, yet it made no difference in his black vote. It did cost him measurably among whites, however, and that forced him, once again, to concentrate on healing racial wounds rather than on addressing the more fundamental challenges posed by angry people of color at the IAF rally—blacks and Hispanics who would have nothing to do with Weusi and Carson, because they want housing, health care, education, and jobs, not rhetoric. Though IAF leaders called Dinkins several times after the election, the promised transition meeting never took place.

Then, on January 2, the day after the inauguration, Dinkins's staff awoke to find that the only important meeting listed on his public schedule was one with the financier Felix Rohatyn and other members of his fiscal brain trust. Frantic calls went out from City Hall to the Nehemiah champion Bishop Mugavero and to the Community Service Society general director David Jones, requesting their presence at a 4:30 P.M. meeting with the mayor. Told that the agenda was unspecified and that he should just show up, Mugavero declined, perhaps sensing a public relations ploy designed to express the new

mayor's social concern. That such suspicions weren't far off the mark
is suggested by the fact that the *New York Times,* presumably relying
on the mayor's staff, reported on January 3 that Mugavero had attended the meeting. He hadn't. Not until May would there be signs
that Dinkins bore IAF no grudge and was willing to help the group
find building sites.

Since the politics of race had handed Dinkins a victory far nar-
rower and supporters far more ambivalent than anyone had anticipated, he would have to exhibit a visionary leadership, rare in mayors. Could he do it? The signals by the spring of 1990 were mixed,
and not only in regard to the Nehemiah program. Early in May, as
Sonny Carson's intimidating, racist "boycott" of Korean grocery
store owners dragged on, deforming the life of a neighborhood not
even Carson's own, Dinkins hesitated to exercise LaGuardian leadership and bring the full moral weight of his office to bear against
Carson. The mayor claimed instead that "quiet negotiation" was
working, even though Carson explicitly rejected all mediation. The
columnist Joe Klein urged Dinkins to shop in the boycotted Korean
stores, leading the majority of blacks in Flatbush and, through them,
the whole city in condemning the self-proclaimed "anti-white" and,
apparently, "anti-yellow" Carson. In a televised address to the city
on May 11, Dinkins condemned the boycotters; not until September
did he go to the store and shop.

Ironically, when a few black demonstrators, egged on by the Revolutionary Communist party, stormed a conference on May 2 at Long
Island University's Brooklyn campus to try to prevent the City College philosophy professor Michael Levin from expressing his anti-
black views, Dinkins lost no time condemning not the demonstrators
but Levin. So doing, the mayor let down the hundred-odd black and
Hispanic LIU students who were in Levin's audience, having voted
overwhelmingly to listen to him and ask him questions—just as the
mayor had let down the black residents of Flatbush who wanted to
shop in the boycotted Korean stores. Taken together, these two failures of leadership were unnerving; as summer approached, New
Yorkers of goodwill awaited a midcourse correction from City Hall.
Nor did Dinkins challenge the people of Bensonhurst to condemn
several witnesses to the Hawkins killing who developed a mysterious
amnesia between the time they told police what they'd seen and the
time they took the witness stand in court.

What accounted for Dinkins's bizarre indulgence of Carson and his crowd? The answer may lie, paradoxically, in the mayor's determination to transcend the politics of race without transcending the politics of the establishment. It may be that his embrace of the permanent government's fiscal-crisis politics left him feeling morally vulnerable to the militants' attacks. A few months into the new administration, Robert Fitch, in a provocative analysis for *New York Newsday,* found that one-third of Dinkins's top appointments had worked for Koch and that the key policy-making positions (first deputy mayor, budget chief, and planning commission chairman) were held by "permanent government" whites, while minorities headed most of the "flak catching" agencies, such as police, welfare, health, and mental health, which bear the brunt of the poor's suffering and anger. Moreover, some of the new administration's first significant decisions, such as granting a huge tax abatement to Chemical Bank, mirrored those of the Koch administration. What did this have to do with indulging the militants? Out of some combination of personal decency and guilt, Dinkins might be finding it difficult to face down Carson and others who marshaled black anger, because the mayor knew that his fiscally strapped government could not deliver on his campaign promises to the poor. As Fitch posed the problem,

Seventy-five years ago, the Irish politicos used the permanent government to obtain construction contracts and transit franchises. Now, African-Americans are using the same techniques in broadcasting and cable TV. But few have asked how the members of the Harlem coterie led by Sutton, whose wealth *Forbes* estimates at over $200 million, achieved such political and financial success while Harlem itself sank to depths of immiseration comparable to those of Bangladesh. The prevailing sentiment has been that we need Dinkins to bring us together. But who is "us'"?

Of course, indulging the militants is the wrong way to fend off Fitch's question. As the city's juxtapositions of private affluence and public destitution become more pronounced, the challenge Youngblood put to the IAF rally is clear: the power to reorder and rebuild cities will have to be wrested from irresponsible elites, who have redistributed incomes and wealth upward and compromised the economic independence and productive capacity of the country, by organizations of people who ride the subways, walk the neighborhood streets, pull the levers in voting booths. True, increasingly, such people are of color; but if Dinkins is to build a new civic consensus, he can do it only by taking his cues from the broadest possible mix of minority and other supporters, people who are united, enthusiastic, and informed about the tasks ahead. They cannot be united if they are absorbed in reopening their racial and ethnic wounds.

To lead them convincingly toward a future beyond tribal recriminations, Dinkins would need a new kind of political instruction, drawn from the history we have reviewed in these pages and articulated by dozens of leaders who help the city's dispossessed to shout, even among the ruins, "We love New York!" Here is a challenge beyond any anticipated by J. Raymond Jones, the Brooklyn insurgents, the white left, defensive middle-class Jews, or beleaguered white ethnics. It is the challenge to all of us, the closest of strangers, to think of ourselves as bearers of the wisdom of that great history—to see ourselves, that is, as New Yorkers.

Epilogue

This book has abounded in dispiriting images of black leaders behaving badly, but it must be clear by now that I have taken this tour of folly because I am haunted by other images, diametrically opposed, which also appear in these pages. The Nehemiah rallies depicted in chapters 5 and 11 come vividly to mind again, as does my visit to the East that hot summer day in 1982; so do the Brooklyn insurgents' many boisterous campaigns and David Dinkins's many moments of quiet courage. Yet, if I were forced to choose a single image of the city's black residents to leave with readers, it would be one that captures the haplessness as well as the hopefulness of ordinary blacks who stand, leaderless, looking for work.

The image I have in mind is drawn from two accounts. The first is from Francesco Cantarella, a senior vice-president of the Abraham & Straus department stores, describing to a congressional committee in 1983 the firm's experience in hiring temporary help for that year's Christmas season in Brooklyn:

I'd like to take you back to 12:30 A.M. on the morning of October 17. The weather was mild as people began lining up on a street outside a door of an office A&S had established for [job interviewing]. By 2 A.M., two hundred people were lined up outside the locked doors. By 9:45 A.M., when the doors opened, there were close to 1,000 men, women and youths lining the sidewalks.

A&S had geared up to hire eighty people a day until the store reached its full complement of 1,200 temporary hires. No advertisements had been placed in newspapers. People heard about job possibilities by word of mouth. The jobs pay $3.35 an hour.

Who are these people? Ninety percent of the 11,000 people who showed up during the hiring period were black. A majority of them had college degrees, were in college or had a high school degree. A "substantial number," said one interviewer, were well dressed, had good communicative abilities and previous sales or business experience. Do you want to know what troubles us most deeply at A&S? It is what happens to those 10,000 people who came to us in hopes of work and who, despite their qualifications, motivation and job-readiness, did not get a job.

The second account comes from the *New York Newsday* columnist Sheryl McCarthy, describing in March 1990, on the other side of the decade's boom, the *Daily News*'s hiring of non-union workers in anticipation of a major strike:

On Monday, 2,500 people turned up to apply for what, at most, will be 116 jobs. Tuesday, at least another thousand showed up. . . . It was an unhappy sight, a bitter reminder of how many New Yorkers need jobs, and of how many others need better jobs than they've got. It was sad for another reason, too. . . . Most of the people waiting on line were blacks and Hispanics. The union members the *News* is trying to replace are almost all white males. The job-seekers come from exactly the same minorities that unions and management have kept out of the *News* building for decades.

Craig Williams, 23, an electrical technician from Brooklyn, was one of those on line. Craig, who is black, is married and his wife is expecting a baby. He read the *Daily News* ad and was hoping he could get a job that would improve on his current $14-an-hour salary. . . . He said he felt no remorse about taking a union job. "It's a shame to say it, but everyone has to go for himself."

Two lessons are inescapable. First, through all the racial vitriol and recrimination recounted in these pages, countless black New

Yorkers have kept faith with the larger society. Second, for all the damage done by black and white-left demagogues who have played the race card since the late 1960s, white racism, deepened by economic undertows, has continued to play an evil role in eroding the promise of the New York liberal tradition.

But these truths point us toward a third presented at the beginning of this book: we cannot respond to the people on these job lines, nor can we hope to overcome economic injustice, if we tolerate a racial politics that resorts to lies, grandiose distortions, vilification of innocent parties, intimidation of independents with legitimate differences of opinion, or dehumanization of opponents. I have taken a loose inventory of such mistakes in the city's postwar politics because I am certain that if we cannot learn from it, we are lost.

The Media

What can we do to prevent such mistakes in the future? The answer depends upon who each of us is. I am a journalist, yet I have said next to nothing in this book about the role and responsibility of the media in the tragedies of miscommunication and mistrust we have surveyed. On November 15, 1989, I attended a forum on the topic "Youth, Media, and Race Relations," sponsored by New York University's Urban Research Center. There Kevin Bernard and Jason Garel, black students at FDR High School in Bensonhurst, shocked many in the audience by joining white fellow students in complaining that, following Yusuf Hawkins's murder the previous summer, the media had presented a picture of Bensonhurst so grotesque that none of them, black or white, could recognize it.

These two black students challenged a panel of journalists to "conciliate, not divide people," by showing "the truth about how most people get along" in interracial school clubs and friendships. "Why don't you take more time to see what's really going on?" asked Garel. Bernard, a wiry eighteen-year-old, was infuriated by a columnist's comparison of Hawkins's murder to the 1955 lynching of Emmett Till, who was coldly stripped, shot, tied to an industrial fan, and dropped into a river in Mississippi. After reading aloud from the column, Bernard commented,

Anyone who writes that doesn't really care what he's doing. I mean, think about it—"one was lynched in Tallahatchie County, the other in Bensonhurst." Give me a break! Up here, African-Americans are victims much more often in their own neighborhoods. You people in the media influence a lot of people. You don't realize that you have great power. I go to Bensonhurst every day to school, and my mom expresses a lot of fear now.

When the black youths had finished speaking, a grimly amusing reversal of roles ensued. White journalists accustomed to being accused of racism in their coverage—that is, of ignoring blacks' suffering at the hands of whites—were caught off balance. Paul Sagan, director of Channel 2 News, actually grew testy with a female student on the panel, practically informing her that, whether she wanted to admit it or not, racism was endemic in Bensonhurst. But then he showed a tape of a broadcast in which a black reporter emphasized the community's better side.

A journalism professor in the audience suggested that since the media's role is to report the unusual and unexpected, it is hardly surprising that reporters who barely knew where Bensonhurst is descended upon it after Hawkins's murder, looking for causes and ramifications, ignoring the many ways in which life somehow goes on for people like Bernard and Jarel. But as the professor spoke, it occurred to me that what has become unusual and unexpected under the pressure of daily stories about mayhem and recrimination is racial comity. If journalists really want to report on the unexpected, perhaps they should try describing the extensive interracial dating that has been flowering, usually without incident, in communities where it would have been unthinkable just ten or fifteen years ago.

After the discussion, Bernard insisted to me that he has never had any trouble in three years of commuting from his home in Flatbush to FDR. I wondered, but did not ask him, whether his very vulnerability as an outsider to the community made him deny its dangers; perhaps the possibility of a "lynching" was just too awful to contemplate. Just a week before Hawkins's killing, ironically, the *City Sun* had profiled three of the first black students at FDR in the 1960s; now established professionals, they recalled running gauntlets of whites after school on their way to the subway. Yet everything about the feisty, clear-eyed Bernard told me that he was not given to self-deception in such matters; he was insisting that conditions had improved. Bernard and Garel even said that they thought the Hawkins killing was more about "turf" and the psychology of "packs" than about color—precisely what the black attorney Charles Simpson had told me in defending Jon Lester in Howard Beach.

I remain conflicted about such perceptions, but this much I have learned: like everyone else, we in the media do carry "scripts" in our heads, storytelling devices that help us make sense of conflicts into which we are thrown, on deadline, with only fragmentary evidence to guide us. The more seasoned we become through diverse encounters with the people we write about, the more refined are our scripts. But they can also remain tainted by the private guilt, anger, cynicism, or hope we carry with us. Above all, we know that the greater the horror, the "better" the story; journalists, too, operate within a "pack" psychology. Since nothing could have been more horrible than the Hawkins story, it was doubly hard for reporters not to find the tragedy in embryo again and again, in every grimace and stray remark. And find it we did.

How many of us are seasoned enough to explore Gasper Signorelli's suggestion, cited in chapter 4, that some of the white Bensonhurst counterdemonstrators, waving watermelons and shouting epithets, were engaged in a vicious self-parody, a half-conscious attempt to exorcise "the terrible judgment that is, at bottom, their own"? Do we take time to pull such people aside when they are calm and hear the words that confirm what Signorelli has seen? Or do we follow a familiar script and write about which wise guys are relatives or neighbors of certain defendants? Why did only one reporter besides me ask Charles Simpson, Jon Lester's black lawyer in the gun possession case, about him? By the same token, while we field teams of reporters to expose—and then, in editorials, rightly condemn—the vicious histrionics of the Brawley hucksters, do we take time to examine what drives these men and to ask whether they and their followers represent black opinion? To understand is not to pardon, in Howard Beach, Bensonhurst, or Dutchess County. But understand we must.

I will not belabor the point that the black media pay an even higher price for not learning this lesson. By all means, examine and assail unions whose racism has forced blacks to "scab." Encourage boycotts of institutions whose practices reduce educated blacks to "temping" at A&S. But avoid the fantastical conspiracy theories that so often pass for reportage; print no "news analyses" that only deepen the feelings of impotence, despair, and hatred that make it harder for blacks to present themselves to society on terms it has to respect.

White Liberals

"There's no question that the black fight for equality has been poorly served by Sharpton, Sonny Carson, and the others," says Mario Cuomo. "But Italians, who are anguished and enraged by the organized-crime stereotype, have also sometimes been fooled into supporting protest leaders who turned out to be organized-crime associates themselves. We lost a great deal of credibility when that happened. But this kind of thing happens all the time. . . . There's nothing unique about race. I'm insisting on this."

As I spoke with him shortly before Christmas in 1989, I was taken aback by Cuomo's determination to downplay the dangers which racial politics pose for New York. I insisted that with rights come responsibilities, that we pay an enormous price for upholding the former without demanding the latter. Cuomo preferred to emphasize that in real life, and certainly in the rough-and-tumble politics of the state, it isn't only blacks who behave irresponsibly. He painted a vivid portrait of a society filled with special-interest groups, from rebellious taxpayers to large corporations, whose members care little for the good of the whole:

When we invented the public schools, that cost everybody, including the people who sent their kids to parochial school. They said, "I can't use your school, why should you take my tax dollars and raise up a system which even serves rich people?" Or what do you say when we save Chrysler, and little companies that pay taxes for that are going down the tubes? Or when public employees, the Civil Service Employees Association, come in here and bang on the doors and get themselves cost-of-living increases on their pensions, which I give them, when my mother and father had no pensions, because they had a little grocery store? I can show you this in government all the time.

[In talking about blacks' demands,] you haven't given me a difference that's worth a distinction. . . . If you leave [race] isolated, you give people a perverted view on this subject, and it'll be negative, that we've done it uniquely wrong here, and only here, that elsewhere we don't make these mistakes. People will attribute it all to race.

Are there some [racial] initiatives that are wrong? Of course there are. Quotas . . ., busing. . . . A given case [of affirmative action] where an incompetent person drives out a competent one. Of course you can do it clumsily. The one that got me involved most notably in public life was housing. What I said [in *Forest Hills Diary*] was, look, the housing policy of the United States for poor people is an excellent illustration of how we can do things badly. . . .

But Cuomo believes that while we ought to correct such clumsy, unjust policies where we can, whites who complain too sweepingly of being oppressed by them are forgetting the overriding injustice which the race-based initiatives are meant to correct. "You inherited the corporate existence [of the United States]," Cuomo admonishes me and whites generally; "you're taking advantage of every part of that Constitution; so you live with the corporation's debt."

There is, I believe, an evasion running through Cuomo's argument. With justice, he says that because blacks have been oppressed by a racist society, the debt we owe them is deeper than anything we owe Chrysler or public employees. Blacks who demand preferments on the basis of past oppressions have more right behind them than do other interest groups, whose justifications are far more specious. Therefore it is hypocritical of us to hold blacks, even those who trade irresponsibly on their status as special creditors, to standards of social reciprocity we certainly don't apply to savings-and-loan sharpies who come to us for bailouts and civil servants who demand pension increases. Cuomo knows well that government barely holds its special-interest-group plunderers, white or black, to any standards at all. He admits that, in the pulling and hauling of politics, government ends up accommodating them all, regardless of merit, and he notes that the state rewards white special-interest groups far more handsomely than black. It is almost as if he were saying that tax deductions on luxury vacation homes for the rich somehow justify promotions of minority police officers who failed a test or toleration of

Glenda Brawley's refusal to answer a subpoena.

But there is something missing here: an acknowledgment from Cuomo of the truth that two wrongs don't make a right, that one kind of irresponsibility does not justify another, that, in fact, neither kind of irresponsibility is tolerable. Cuomo admits candidly that he tolerates special provisions for white, often wealthy, interest groups. He knows, too, that he is not doing enough to sustain real opportunities for poor blacks; the state school-aid formula, for example, is scandalously unfair to poor communities. And here, I suspect, he finds himself paralyzed morally: since whites get away with murder, how can I come down on blacks who occasionally get away with it, too? Since public employees force pension increases out of me simply by a show of muscle and greed, how can I bear down on those blacks who also abuse the principles of social reciprocity—of honesty, accountability, and trust? Society cannot survive without such principles, of course; yet, instead of insisting on them, Cuomo lets everyone drag everyone else down, each group pointing an accusing finger at the others instead of examining its own motives and behavior. One double standard somehow justifies another. Cuomo is acting as if we will have to bear this sickness because we cannot bear its cure.

If we narrow our focus to only those groups that truly deserve public aid and redress on the basis of past injustices, we can see more clearly why race-based public initiatives that ignore reciprocity are so dangerous and so charged. Consider a comparison between the black movement and the women's movement. Like blacks fighting racism, feminists litigate, boycott, and protest against official and consensual sexism. Like blacks, they often shock and affront social conservatives. But even the most militant feminists do not demand reparations, as Sonny Carson does in demanding that Korean grocery stores be handed over to blacks; nor do feminists demand that public schools allow them to set up "girls schools" at taxpayers' expense, as Carson and other black militants did in the 1960s.

Indeed, women's tremendous strides toward self-sufficiency have mitigated their automatic custody rights and the amount of alimony they receive in divorce settlements. That is because, to an extraordinary degree, women's demands for equality are backed up by prodigious displays of hard work and by private struggles to overcome fears of success and to prove they are truly men's equals. Such demonstrations of internal discipline and social reciprocity are precisely what have been lacking in too much of the black militancy we have seen. Nor are they seriously expected by many of those who govern our public institutions and professional associations.

By the spring of 1990, for example, as lawyers' grievance committees wrestled with the questions of whether Maddox and Mason had obstructed justice and knowingly made false statements in the Brawley case, the committees reportedly had no stomach for censure or disbarment. This, despite noncooperation by Maddox that virtually forced the committee considering his case to recommend, and a court to order on May 21, his suspension from the practice of law. Membership in the bar is a privilege, not a right; disbarment in no way infringes on an individual's First Amendment right to go on saying what he wants. Failure to disbar the lawyers for their conduct in the Brawley case would give most of us reason to think even less of lawyers than we already do, for it would show that the standards of that profession are so flaccid and self-serving that character counts for nothing in a lawyer.

Cuomo knows what a toll such liberal spinelessness has taken. In 1974, in his first speech as a political candidate, he eloquently told the state's New Democratic Coalition that liberals need to understand and respect white-ethnic resistance to the kinds of social engineering he had just tried to curb in Forest Hills. He warned that the Democratic party was losing the white worker because it refused to nail its ideals of social justice to the "procrustean bed of political reality" and find ways to implement them without gratuitously affronting those who must share in the sacrifice. Similarly, Cuomo's observations on tenant screening, scatter-site housing, and crime, cited in these pages, reflect his understanding that irresponsibility does not justify more irresponsibility, that even one's status as a unique kind of social creditor does not exempt one from traditional social obligations.

Yet now he seems to accept as inevitable the social-policy abuses, the badly designed "relief" packages that go not only to blacks but also to Chrysler, public employees, and the rich. There must be something which Cuomo and other liberals like the education commissioner Thomas Sobol are willing to demand of the recipients in return. What is it? Why don't they ever articulate it?

Black Leadership

Black leaders in the city have had their own reasons for not talking much in public about social responsibility. To criticize other blacks within whites' hearing is to aid and comfort the enemy. Yet, as Herbert Daughtry said, "If all whites are wrong, then you have no check on your own leadership. [The Brawley advisers] skillfully made it a black/white battle: everything my enemy says is wrong." Believing that lie relieves one of the moral obligation to trust. One stoops to victimology, casting every setback as a conspiracy and so relieving oneself of the moral obligation to act in one's own behalf. This is a point well enough developed, I hope, in chapter 7; it poses two challenges for the city's black leaders in the years ahead.

The first is to follow more boldly in the footsteps of Assemblyman Roger Green, who was willing to be called a Tom, a coon, and a stooge of Cuomo for denouncing the Brawley advisers' scurrilous attacks on officials like Attorney General Abrams. It was Green who told me, "Efforts to stop the polarization in the city can't be geared totally toward race anymore. It's a point I have to argue, but folks do realize it." Young blacks like Kevin Bernard and Jason Garel are counting on people like Green to keep on speaking such truths. These youngsters and blacks of all ages, interacting daily on a footing of rough equality with white peers, enjoy none of the rhetorical and moral exemptions granted to black leaders by the media, liberals, and the left. Black leaders should consider that every time they fail to challenge militants who equate Bensonhurst with Johannesburg, they make the lives of people like Bernard and Garel much harder. By what right? Are these youngsters Toms for doubting them? Why isn't it possible for self-respecting blacks like Spike Lee to ridicule, through guerrilla theater and political satire, those who have made careers of lying to and exploiting fellow blacks? Why can't there be a "truth squad" within the community? Why in heaven's name aren't the *City Sun* and the *Amsterdam News* arraigning the clowns and conspiracy theorists among blacks? Mightn't that increase the circulation of these two papers, which currently sell a grand total of

80,000 copies a week in a city with nearly two million African-Americans?

The second challenge is to distinguish that part of the black agenda which is internal to the community—in that it is primarily cultural and spiritual—from that which is political and therefore appropriate to pursue in the pluralist public arena, in liberal institutions and the news media.

From Emancipation through the triumphs of the civil rights movement of the 1960s, blacks' greatest political strength lay in their ability to blur the distinction I have just drawn, to invoke for all Americans the wellsprings of yearning and faith that nourished our national experiment. As we saw in chapter 1, blacks preceded the liberal Constitution on these shores, and they remained marginal to it after it had been framed. Yet, because they had also been denied a fully viable culture of their own, they were the most profoundly dependent of all Americans upon the country's commitment to realize its stated creed. Time and again, from out of the depths of that dependency, black leaders have called the rest of us to account and redeemed us. When David Dinkins said, on winning the mayoral primary, "Tonight, we have forged another link in the chain of memory"; when, at his inauguration four months later, the Reverend Gardner Taylor began his benediction with the words "God of our weary years, God of our silent tears," who could fail to hear the ancient summons?

And yet that ability to fuse the spiritual and the political which has been blacks' greatest strength may now have become their greatest weakness. Increasingly, the complex liberal political arena can be entered only on its own terms. The Brawley psychodrama, the theories of white genocidal conspiracy, the intimations of racism in every leaf that falls, all violate the transracial truth-making of the pluralist consensus. They are ghosts on the walls of a people's innermost chamber. While these shadows have been cast by real historical events, they cannot easily be imposed upon present transactions in workplaces and streets, in courtrooms and legislatures. They have to be confronted and worked through by blacks among themselves. That is why the same David Dinkins who invoked the mystic chain of memory could teach black youngsters on the campaign trail the cold, hard truths of the liberal credo: "I want a pledge . . . that you will never use obstacles and barriers as an excuse. I know that life is not always fair, but your obligation is to work hard, to respect the law, to be disciplined and strong—and take responsibility for your actions."

There is, I believe, a legitimate if quite limited analogy here to personal growth in therapy or analysis. In private encounters with past hurts, there is a time for painful, angry recognition of terrible damage suffered when one was small and vulnerable. But feeling that pain and anger opens wellsprings of fresh insight and energy, energy to be used not against one's parents and other past tormenters, if they are still alive, but against daily obstacles which have seemed insurmountable because of the ancient hurts they recalled. At some point, a person decides, existentially, courageously, to say, "Yes, I have been damaged. But I'm well enough now. I can walk on." That is what Jesse Jackson means when he leads his listeners in affirming, even in their destitution, "I am somebody!" reminding them that whites' past denials of basic civil rights are no excuse to commit "civil wrongs" against them now.

Perhaps the current inhospitality of our political culture to negative black preaching about white guilt and moral obligations reflects a fragmented, contractual America, one no longer worthy of the old spiritual invocations. Perhaps it is a symptom of the broader disenchantment of the world. Perhaps it is the inevitable result of blacks' own political coming-of-age with the winning of basic civil rights, which carry with them responsibilities. Then again, perhaps the waning of black moral influence upon the larger society reflects whites' perception that black social preaching, like that of white televangelists, has too often coexisted with the most flamboyant refusal to take responsibility for one's actions.

There is, in short, a white weariness with black communal seizures masquerading as struggles for social justice. Whatever the reason, the long, tortuous spiritual pilgrimage of the race must henceforth be its own. There is great work to do on that journey, and the cultural and spiritual ferment under way among American blacks shows that it is being done. It may yet rejuvenate all American culture. But, for now, internal dramatizations of victimhood and redemption, however irresistible, however necessary in their own terms, cannot substitute for intelligent politics. Yet, too many black activist leaders, from the Reverend Calvin Butts to the *City Sun*'s Utrice Leid, from Al Sharpton to Adelaide Sanford, continue to rail against whites for refusing to confront their racism. Haven't they figured out by now that only real, interracial work toward shared economic and political goals stands the slightest chance of gaining whites' attention and providing a basis for equality? Don't they see that, in a city full of rising new ethnic and racial communities besides their own, the successful leaders of the 1990s will be not those who rally only their own home bases but those who know how to touch others across lines of color and culture? Or do black leaders fear, perhaps correctly, that there would be no place for their histrionics in such undertakings?

Communal paroxysms and tribal truths are certainly appropriate in religious and cultural mournings and celebrations. They are inappropriate in those public arenas where people of vastly different backgrounds make progress only by interacting through consensual norms that balance and orchestrate power. Liberal institutions must always make room for disciplined confrontation, civil disobedience, power politics. But a frenzied, purely symbolic politics of communal and personal posturing only dooms its practitioners to impotence and to others' condescension. Or it destroys liberal institutions and paralyzes society itself.

A bit of both happened in the Tawana Brawley case. Maddox and Mason made it easy to forget that they weren't actually defending the Brawley family against the state, that, indeed, the state presumed Tawana Brawley's victimization and was expending hundreds of thousands of dollars trying to find the perpetrator of her ordeal. As usual, Mason and Maddox found the prospect of collaboration with "white" authority so disorienting, so counterintuitive, that they contrived to make the state the enemy anyway, as Mason did by assisting Glenda Brawley in defying a subpoena.

The irony, as my former *North Brooklyn Mercury* colleague Jim Miskiewicz has noted, is that Maddox and Mason, "swept into the maelstrom of racial hate, had already let down their lawyerly guard and been blindsided by the seemingly most harmless character of all: a little girl with a big lie." That they were able to carry so much of the black community with them for so long—that so few felt strong enough, at any rate, to stand up and say what they knew to be true—

is a part of a continuing tragedy. If our discussion in these pages has established anything, it is that the failure of the New York liberal tradition to bear the fruits of black progress reflects not only the intransigence of white racism and the ravages of economic change but also the derelictions of those who have stepped forward to make history. The costly black communal silence in the Brawley case was the product not only of white racism but also of years of radically self-indulgent demagoguery, supported blindly at almost every turn by the white left, indulged by guilt-ridden liberal elites, and enforced upon blacks by the militants themselves.

The bitter legacy of that politics was evident in the *Daily News* strike of 1990–91, when some black writers sided with management on the grounds that since some *News* unions had engaged in racist practices, the strike was not their fight. It took Jesse Jackson to remind them, at a tumultuous rally on September 10, 1990, of the principle affirmed so long ago in Harlem's "Don't Buy Where You Can't Work" campaign: Union-busting is an overriding issue; racial "divide-and-conquer" strategies must not succeed; and, when blacks and whites fight them together, racism itself is weakened. Even as most black workers heeded Jackson's advice, Sharpton, Maddox, Mason, and others of the city's militant black leaders were conspicuously absent from this real, bread-and-butter battle.

It is long past time for the ordinary black people who are standing in job lines, ready to share society's burdens as well as its rewards, to demand of their leaders such a change in course; for the politics of paroxysm, grievance, and conspiracy is clearly not working. Surely it is time for the rest of us to demand it, too. But, for whites, fair warning: as we make such demands upon our black neighbors, the closest of strangers, we also obligate ourselves. We have to be sure that Yusuf Hawkins's family would have found justice without Sharpton and that justice would have been done in Howard Beach without Maddox and Mason. We have to be certain that we are offering to all those "with a mind to work" our hands and our hearts. That has always been the point and promise of the liberal tradition in New York, and it is all that awaits us on the other side of despair.

Notes

ABBREVIATIONS

JS   Jim Sleeper
NYN   *New York Newsday*
NYRB   *New York Review of Books*
NYT   *New York Times*

INTRODUCTION

Pages 1–2. Goldin's remarks are from the transcript of the Democratic mayoral candidates' debate of Aug. 1, 1989, sponsored by *NYN* and Channel 2 News. The classic New York paradigm of ethnic upward mobility is described in Nathan Glazer and Daniel Patrick Moynihan, *Beyond the Melting Pot: The Negroes, Puerto Ricans, Jews, Italians, and Irish of New York City,* 2d ed. (Cambridge: MIT Press, 1970), introd.

Page 19. Alton Maddox's remarks were made on Gary Byrd's morning talk show, radio station WLIB, Dec. 4, 1989. Maddox and the attorney Colin Moore viewed police videotape in the Central Park case, according to the *NYN* reporter Tim Clifford, who covered the case. Blacks' reaction to militant's leadership is reflected in the *NYN* telephone poll of 759 black New Yorkers conducted in Feb. 1988 and published on April 7, 1988. While 45 percent rated mainstream civil rights organizations like the NAACP as very effective in leading blacks, militants were so rated by 12 percent. Among individual leaders, Jesse Jackson was viewed very favorably by 76 percent; Cuomo, by 57 percent; Dinkins, 50; C. Vernon Mason, 39; Koch, 33; and Sharpton, 27. Thirty-six percent viewed Koch highly unfavorably; 35 percent viewed Sharpton that way.

Page 20. A comprehensive profile of Maddox by Alexander Stille in the Feb. 16, 1987, issue of the *National Law Journal* describes the genesis of the strategy to frustrate prosecutions, beginning with a 1981 case against Black Liberation Army members. Of the Michael Stewart case, the civil rights attorney Richard Emery told

Stille, "[Maddox and Mason] put all their energies into trying to sabotage what I thought was a vigorous prosecution." Stille reports that Maddox and Mason objected to Hynes's appointment in the Howard Beach case. That Cuomo had outsmarted black leaders in appointing Hynes over Maddox's and Mason's objections is reported at length in The *City Sun*'s weekly issues in Jan. and Feb. 1987. See especially "How Black Leaders Turned Down the Heat on Cuomo," by Utrice Leid, Feb. 4–10.

Page 20. A list of some of the many murders of young blacks, allegedly by other young blacks, appears on pp. 195–97. Population statistics and trends from the New York City Department of City Planning and from Roger Waldinger's essay, "Race and Ethnicity," in Ray Horton and Charles Brecher, eds., *Setting Municipal Priorities 1990* (New York: New York University Press, 1990).

Page 29. Black boycotts and demonstrations against merchants, utility companies, and restaurants are described in Cheryl Greenberg's forthcoming *Or Does It Explode? Black Harlem in the Great Depression* (New York: Oxford University Press).

Page 31. E.B. White *Here Is New York* (New York: Harper, 1949), 26. Liff's comments are from an interview with JS, Oct. 1989.

Pages 39–41. Steele, *The Content of Our Character: A New Vision of Race in America* (New York: St. Martin's Press, forthcoming in 1990). IAF's philosophy and organizing strategies are the subjects of "Organizing the South Bronx," a beautifully written doctoral dissertation by James Rooney, Harvard Graduate School of Education. See also JS, "East Brooklyn Rising," *City Limits*, a New York City neighborhood monthly, Dec. 1982, and "Nehemiah Opens Its Doors and Answers Its Critics," June 1984; JS, "In Brooklyn, New Political Clout," *City Sun*, Nov. 21–27, 1984; JS, "Two Tactics to Get People Housing," *NYN*, Sept. 4, 1985.

1: THE BLACK POLITICAL ODYSSEY IN NEW YORK

Little has been published on the history of race relations in New York City before World War II. The best-known books are Gilbert Osofsky's *Harlem: The Making of a Ghetto* (New York: Harper Torchbooks, 1963) and James Weldon Johnson's *Black Manhattan* (New York: Atheneum, 1968; originally published 1930). I am indebted to the Columbia University historian Eric Foner for directing me to Herman D. Bloch's *Circle of Discrimination: An Economic and Social Study of the Black Man in New York* (New York: New York University Press, 1969), which emphasizes discrimination in employment since colonial times, and to Cheryl Greenberg's forthcoming *Or Does It Explode? Black Harlem in the Great Depression*, which includes an extensive list of sources. References to Greenberg are drawn from the prepublication manuscript and so provide chapter but not page numbers.

Pages 43–44. Johnson's descriptions of slavery in New York are in *Black Manhattan*, chap. 1. Glazer and Moynihan note in *Beyond the Melting Pot*, xxix, that after the draft riots of 1863, New York had never experienced a "race riot"—as that term was widely understood, that is, mass violence by whites against blacks—on the scale of Chicago's in 1919 or Detroit's in 1943. The closest thing to it was a police riot, with vigorous white citizen participation, in the Hell's Kitchen area in 1900, described in Johnson, *Black Manhattan*, 126–29. The most famous New York City riots in the twentieth century—those in 1935, 1943, and 1964 and the extensive looting during the power failure of 1977—were primarily black ghetto explosions, not attacks by white citizens upon blacks. That grievances against white racism figured in these violent outbursts is beyond question, but widespread white mass violence against blacks has been virtually unknown in New York City. Police brutality is another story; so are the Howard Beach, Bensonhurst, and other assaults of the 1980s, which are primarily the work of teenagers and are addressed here in chapter 7. Northrup's *Slavery in New York* is quoted in Bloch, *Discrimination,* 244. Slavery as a function of dispassionate, economic calculation is described by Carey McWilliams, *Brothers under the Skin* (Boston: Little, Brown, 1964; originally published 1942), 250–56. The incident with Abigail Adams and "neighbor Faxon" is cited in Bloch, *Discrimination,* 21–23. The African Free School is described in Johnson, *Black Manhattan,* 21–24.

Pages 45–46. The draft riots and elite white reaction are described in Johnson, *Black Manhattan,* 51–53, and in Osofsky, *Harlem,* 46, 83, and 191. For Ovington's remarkable career of fighting for black improvement, see Osofsky, *Harlem,* 54–65. Blacks' exclusion from trades under the impact of white immigration in the late nineteenth and early twentieth centuries is described in Block, *Discrimination,* chaps. 5 and 6.

Page 46. The population figures are from Diane Ravitch, *The Great School Wars: A History of the New York City Public Schools* (New York: Basic Books, 1988), 241–42. The development of real-estate segregation and exploitation is described in Osofsky, *Harlem,* chap. 9. Conditions in segregated Harlem in the 1920s and 1930s are described by Greenberg, *Or Does It Explode?* chaps. 1, 3, and 8. Greenberg notes in chap. 1 that as early as 1925 the infant mortality rate for blacks (118.4 per 1,000 live births) was nearly twice that for whites (64.6). She reports that as the Depression set in, in 1930, public school teachers and administrators (virtually all white) donated 1 percent of their monthly salaries to provide lunches, shoes, clothing, and funds to needy children; in 1930, they gave away 100,000 pairs of shoes.

Pages 46–51. The 1935 Harlem riot and the Commission on Conditions in Harlem, whose research was directed by E. Franklin Frazier, are described at length by Greenberg, *Or Does It Explode?* chaps. 5–7, and briefly in Thomas Kessner, *Fiorello H. La Guardia and the Making of Modern New York* (New York: McGraw-Hill, 1989), 374–75. A fascinating account of the "Don't Buy" campaign, with the quotation from Adam Clayton Powell, Sr., is in Greenberg, *Or Does It Explode?* chap. 5. The IBEW newsletter, *Electrical World,* is cited ibid. An analysis of Randolph's dilemmas is in Bloch, *Discrimination,* 101–2. The threatened march on Washington and Roosevelt's executive order are described in Greenberg, *Or Does It Explode?* chap. 8. For European fascism's impact on Americans' changing attitudes toward race, see ibid.

Page 52. Starr's stand was reported in *PM,* July 24, 1941. His views on race are reported in JS, "The Apple Polisher," a review of Starr's *The Rise and Fall of New York City* (New York: Basic Books, 1985) in the *Nation,* June 15, 1985. Canarsie residents' comments to Jonathan Rieder are in his *Canarsie: The Jews and Italians of Brooklyn against Liberalism* (Cambridge: Harvard University Press, 1985), 57–59.

Page 53. The role of the Communist party in black organizing in the 1930s and 1940s is described in Mark Naison, *Communists in Harlem during the Depression*

(Urbana: University of Illinois Press, 1983), and in Greenberg, *Or Does It Explode?* chap. 4. Street-corner speakers' antiwar comments are described in Greenberg, *Or Does It Explode?* chap. 8. The immediate postwar white backlash against blacks is described in McWilliams, *Brothers,* 29–35; the court case in Elizabethtown, ibid., 41.

Pages 53–55. Benjamin Davis and Adam Clayton Powell, Jr., in the 1940s are described in Greenberg, *Or Does It Explode?* chap. 8. J. Raymond Jones's background is described in *The Harlem Fox: J. Raymond Jones and Tammany, 1920–1970,* by Jones as told to John C. Walter (Albany: State University of New York Press, 1989), chap. 1. For Jones's views on Davis, see ibid., 110–14. Dinkins has repeated his comment about Sutton, with variations; the version here is as recalled by JS; another is cited by Joe Klein in *New York* magazine, Oct. 30, 1989.

Pages 55–57. The comments about Jones are in a comprehensive profile of Dinkins by Flynn and Henican, "David Dinkins' Steady Climb," *NYN,* Oct. 29, 1989. The Basil Paterson interview with Liff is in *NYN,* Nov. 22, 1989. Early black settlement in Brooklyn is described in Harold X. Connolly, *A Ghetto Grows in Brooklyn* (New York: New York University Press, 1977), 3–7. Connolly is an academic-turned-account executive at the J. Walter Thompson Company. The most comprehensive study of West Indians in New York politics is Philip Kasinitz's unpublished 1987 doctoral dissertation for New York University's Department of Sociology, "West Indian Diaspora: Race, Ethnicity and Politics in New York City." See also JS, "Will These Men Change New York?" *Village Voice,* Dec. 9–15, 1981. The NAACP's protest against police brutality is described in Connolly, *Ghetto,* 150–51.

Pages 58–61. Cooper's comment is from an interview with JS, Oct. 1989. The Brooklyn insurgents' early economic boycotts and protests are described in Connolly, *Ghetto,* 188–92. School integration efforts in the late 1950s are described in Ravitch, *Wars,* 267–80. The confrontation over the Mississippi Freedom Democratic party in Atlantic City is described in Nicolaus Mills's unpublished manuscript "Mississippi, 1964," and in Richard Cummings, *The Pied Piper: Allard K. Lowenstein and the Liberal Dream* (New York: Grove Press, 1985), 263–74.

Pages 61–62. The white reformers' relations with Dinkins and other blacks were described by Dinkins's chief of staff (now deputy mayor), Barbara Fife, in an interview with JS, Dec. 1989. Starr's seminal, contemporary assessment of Lindsay's mayoralty appeared in his "John V. Lindsay: A Political Portrait," *Commentary,* Feb. 1970. This extraordinarily insightful profile is one of the first and most eloquent expressions of the neoconservative political sensibility then beginning to emerge in the city.

Page 66. McPherson, "Hab Rachmones," *Tikkun* magazine, Sept.–Oct. 1989, 15.

2: THE LIBERAL NIGHTMARE

Pages 70–71. Lester's black attorney, Charles Simpson, was interviewed by JS in April 1990; more of his comments appear on pp. 000–00. More Mississippi Freedom Summer volunteers were from New York than from any other state; New Yorkers composed between one-quarter and one-third of the one thousand volunteers, according to Professor Douglas McAdam, of the University of Arizona at Tucson, who has the original applications and is the author of *Freedom Summer* (New York: Oxford University Press, 1988). Rieder, *Canarsie,* 37. Rieder's book is one of the most important on race relations in New York City in the past twenty years because of its compelling evocation of the experiences, strengths, and foibles of Brooklyn white ethnics; it ought to be required reading for anyone presuming to discuss race relations. Liff's comments were made in an interview with JS, Oct. 1989.

Pages 73–74. On Guinier, see his obituary in *NYT,* Feb. 7, 1990. Glazer and Moynihan, in *Beyond the Melting Pot,* note that in the late 1950s and early 1960s, before race became an emotionally charged issue in the city's civic culture, blacks were routinely nominated for high public offices on Democratic party tickets, for example, Edward Dudley for state attorney general in 1962; this was the period when Massachusetts, too, elected the first black U.S. senator since Reconstruction, Edward Brooke. Cuomo's comments come from an interview with JS, Nov. 1989. Podhoretz, "My Negro Problem—and Ours," *Commentary,* Feb. 1963.

Pages 75–78. The "civic unity" movement is described in McWilliams, *Brothers,* 17–29. Starr's comments in JS, unpublished MS for Charles Revson Fellowship, Columbia University, 1982–83. Cooper's comments in JS, "Will These Men Change New York?" *Village Voice,* Dec. 9–15, 1981. George Meany's failure to reform his plumbers' local are discussed in Bloch, *Discrimination,* 119; blacks' underemployment and on-the-job experiences, in Greenberg, *Or Does It Explode?* chap. 3; the failure to cancel construction contracts, in Bloch, *Discrimination,* 130–31. The characterizations of Jewish attitudes are from Levine's interview with JS, Oct. 1989. See also Hasia Diner, *In the Almost Promised Land: American Jews and Blacks, 1915–1935* (Westport, Conn.: Greenwood Press, 1977).

Pages 78–80. Kallen's work celebrating diversity and challenging the melting-pot concept is described in Orlando Patterson, *Ethnic Chauvinism: The Reactionary Impulse* (New York: Stein & Day, 1977), chap. 6. The role of Jewish organizations in promoting fair-housing and other antidiscrimination efforts are described in Glazer and Moynihan, *Beyond the Melting Pot,* 71. The 1958 incident involving King is described in Alfred J. Marrow, *Changing Patterns of Prejudice* (Philadelphia: Chilton, 1962), 9–10. Barbara Grizzuti Harrison, "Women, Blacks and Bensonhurst," *Harper's,* March 1990. Levine's and others' role in pioneering intergroup relations through the Brownsville Boys Club in the 1940s is described in Gerald Sorin, *The Nurturing Neighborhood: Jewish Community and the Brownsville Boys Club, 1940–1990* (New York: New York University Press, 1990). Greenberg's instructive career in civil rights work is profiled in Jonathan Kaufman, *Broken Alliance: The Turbulent Times between Blacks and Jews in America* (New York: Scribner's, 1988), chap. 3.

Pages 80–85. Early antidiscrimination efforts in housing are described in Ira S. Robbins with Gus Tyler, *Reminiscences of a Housing Advocate* (New York: Citizens Housing and Planning Council, 1984), chaps. 2 and 4, and in Marrow, *Prejudice,* 97–130. Marrow chaired the city's Commission on Intergroup Relations from 1955 to 1960. Starr's comments are from a 1959 CHPC newsletter and an interview with the author, Nov. 1989. On housing-project screening, see also Starr, "Twenty Years of Housing Programs," *Public Interest,* fall 1985. The Housing Authority integration plan is described in Marrow, *Prejudice,* 124–25. Cuomo's comment on screening is in his *Forest Hills Diary* (New York: Vintage Books, 1983; originally published 1974), 55–59.

Pages 86–87. For Clark's role, see Ravitch, *Wars,* 306. The accounts of early busing disputes are from Irving Levine's interview with JS, Oct. 1989; Marrow, *Prejudice,* 147–60; and Ravitch, *Wars,* 270–78. Galamison's role comes from Jitu Weusi's interview with JS, Oct. 1989, and from Ravitch, *Wars,* 257, 269. Arricale's comments were made in an interview with JS, Sept. 1989.

Pages 87–90. The school dropout rate from the turn of the century through the 1940s was nearly 50 percent for youths fourteen and over, according to Ravitch, *Wars,* 190. Levine's comments are from an interview with JS, Oct. 1989. The *Pittsburgh Courier* editorial is reported in Marrow, *Prejudice,* 158–59. Garrity is profiled in J. Anthony Lukas, *Common Ground: A Turbulent Decade in the Lives of Three American Families* (New York: Knopf, 1985), 222–51. Daughtry, interview with JS, Nov. 1989. Levine, interview with JS, Oct. 1989. For comments on Jewish-black violence, see pp. 100–02 and notes to those pages below.

3: THE POLITICS OF POLARIZATION

Pages 91–94. Piven and Cloward prescribe racial polarization in *The Politics of Turmoil: Essays on Poverty, Race and the Urban Crisis* (New York: Pantheon Books, 1974): "A series of welfare drives in large cities would, we believe, impel action on a new federal program to distribute income. . . . These disruptions would generate severe political strains and deepen existing divisions among elements in the big-city Democratic coalition: The remaining white middle class, the white working-class ethnic groups and the growing minority poor. . . . To avoid a further weakening of that historic coalition, a national Democratic administration would be constrained to advance a federal solution to poverty . . ." (p. 90). On voting, Piven and Cloward conclude, "The chief point that emerges from this analysis [of electoral politics] is that low-income people have no regular resources for influencing public policy" (p. 85). On unions, see below, p. 000. See also a brisk, critical summary of the welfare-rights strategy by the former city welfare director Charles Morris, in *The Cost of Good Intentions: New York City and the Liberal Experiment, 1960–1975* (New York: W. W. Norton, 1980), 67–71. Morris's notes provide a valuable listing of additional sources.

Pages 94–95. A review of the argument that black ghettos are "colonies" is in Theodore Draper, *The Rediscovery of Black Nationalism* (New York: Viking, 1969), 120–25. For an example of the conquest of antipoverty boards by political mercenaries, see JS, "The Battle for Black Brooklyn," *Village Voice,* Aug. 31, 1982. Murray's comments are from a roundtable discussion organized by the Manhattan Institute and transcribed in "Losing Ground: Why the War on Poverty Failed," 1985. Other participants included Nathan Glazer, Gertrude Himmelfarb, Ken Auletta, and Charles Peters.

Pages 96–97. Starr's comments were made in an interview with JS, Nov. 1989. The comment about the traditional, middle-class family roots of many radicals is based on my personal observations of community organizers in New York City. The comment by Jencks appeared in "Deadly Neighborhoods," a review of William Julius Wilson's *The Truly Disadvantaged,* in the *New Republic,* June 13, 1988.

Pages 97–98. The Harlem neighbors' calls for caseworkers is in Nina Bernstein, "Needles in Angry Hands," *NYN,* Dec. 20, 1989. In addition to Kaufman, *Alliance,* and Ravitch, *Wars,* see Martin Mayer, *The Teachers Strike, New York, 1968* (New

York: Harper & Row, 1969), and comments and responses to Mayer by Jason Epstein and others in *NYRB,* March 13, 1969. See also Epstein, *NYRB,* Nov. 21, 1968, and Dwight Macdonald, *NYRB,* Dec. 5, 1968.

Pages 100–02. McCoy's association with Carson and Malcolm X is described in Kaufman, *Alliance,* 147. Kaufman also cites McCoy's apothegm "It's better to be free without any power than to be a slave and have it all" (p. 131)—a rather narrow characterization of the choices facing blacks in the 1960s. McCoy's comment on a "predetermined script" comes from his Ph.D. dissertation on the Ocean Hill–Brownsville experiment, for the University of Massachusetts at Amherst, cited by Steve Mufson, "A Dream Deferred," *Village Voice,* June 6, 1989. Regarding Jewish-black violence, see Robert I. Friedman, *The False Prophet: Rabbi Meir Kahane— From FBI Informant to Knesset Member* (Brooklyn: Lawrence Hill Books, 1990). In an advance excerpt published in the April 10, 1990, *Village Voice,* Friedman reports that the FBI deliberately incited Kahane's Jewish Defense League against black militants, but he shows that the JDL, even at fever pitch, was always a pathetically small outfit with little more than a dozen hardened "chayas" ("animals") who postured more often than they fought. The incident involving Al Ungar is recounted by Unger in an interview with JS, May 1990. For a profile of Carson, see Dena Kleiman, "Limelight Shines Again on Sonny Carson," *NYT,* July 6, 1987.

Pages 103–08. These pages are adapted from JS, "Will These Men Change New York?" *Village Voice,* Dec. 9–15, 1981.

Pages 108–15. These pages are adapted from JS, "Ed Koch and the Spirit of the Times," *Dissent,* spring 1981. See the studies by Walter Stafford, "Employment Segmentation in New York City Municipal Agencies" (Community Service Society, 1989), and Thomas Bailey, "Black Employment Opportunities," in Horton and Brecher, eds., *Priorities 1990.*

4: WHITE ETHNICS ON THE BLOCK

Page 117. The area of Park Slope which I am describing from personal experience has also been studied formally. The behavior of absentee owners is described in Francine Justa's doctoral dissertation for CUNY's graduate program in Environmental Psychology, "Effects of Housing Abandonment, Resettlement and Displacement on the Evolution of Voluntary Community Organizations in Park Slope, Brooklyn, New York" (1984). See also Timothy O'Hanlon, "Neighborhood Change in New York City: A Case Study of Park Slope, 1850–1980," a 1982 doctoral dissertation for the same program. Both Justa and O'Hanlon lived on my block of Carroll Street; I am especially indebted to Justa and her husband, Morris Kornbluth, for introducing me to its residents and setting an extraordinary example of neighborhood leadership as leaders of the United Block Associations and the Fifth Avenue Committee in the 1970s.

Pages 121–22. The comments on visiting the old neighborhood are from Rieder, *Canarsie,* 90–91. "Grieving for a Lost Home" is the title of a chapter as well as the name of a syndrome identified by Marc Fried in L. J. Duhl, ed., *The Urban Condition* (New York: Basic Books, 1963). Alinsky's "hara-kiri" comment is in Arnold R. Hirsch, *Making the Second Ghetto: Race and Housing in Chicago, 1940–1960* (New York: Cambridge University Press, 1983), 209.

Pages 129–32. Arricale's comments are from an interview with JS, Sept. 1989.

Signorelli, "Bensonhurst's Broken Mirror," *NYN,* Aug. 31, 1989, 83. See also J. Anthony Lukas, "Their Fate Is on the Block," *NYN,* Aug. 30, 1989. Papa's experience was reported in *NYN* by T. J. Collins and Ji-Yeon Yah, March 8 and 9, 1990; his comments on racism are in "They Smashed His Body and His Dreams," an interview with Alexis Jetter, *NYN,* March 14, 1990.

5: THE SPECTER OF NEIGHBORHOOD DECAY

Pages 133–38. The citations and date in these pages come from Connolly, *Ghetto,* 136–39. Zwerman's comments are from an interview with JS, July 1989. Levine, interview with JS, Oct. 1989. See also Sharon Zukin and Gilda Zwerman, "Housing for the Working Poor: A Historical View of Jews and Blacks in Brownsville," *New York Affairs,* summer 1985. Sorin, *Nurturing Neighborhood.* Reports of laundromat and housing-project muggings are in Rieder, *Canarsie,* 68–79.

Pages 138–40. Scherma, interview with JS, June 1989. Not until a year after the Howard Beach trials of 1987 did I recall, in conversation with a friend, the 1982 robbery spree. I looked up the old *NYT* accounts and, with the help of addresses from the news clips, telephone books, and a Hagstrom atlas, traced the routes of 1982 and 1986. I then spoke with half a dozen victims of the 1982 robbery spree. To the best of my knowledge, no account of the 1986 Howard Beach incident made these connections, nor did any reporters investigate the history of robberies by blacks in the community. The police "system" for catching robbers was described to me by Lieutenant Eugene Dunbar, currently of the 106th Precinct, Queens. I also visited the convicted 1982 robber Larry Jeffries in the summer of 1989, at Sing Sing prison, where he is serving seven to twelve years for the robberies; parole was denied shortly after my visit. Jeffries, a former resident of the Brownsville Houses, which had been integrated at the insistence of liberal Jews there years before his birth, seemed healthy and confident; he insisted to me, not very credibly, that he had never been in Howard Beach and had been framed, thereby foreclosing my intended questions about his motives and experiences in the community.

Pages 140–45. Signorelli's comments come from an interview with JS, July 1989. Glazer's comments are from his "Negroes and Jews: The New Challenge to Pluralism," *Commentary,* Dec. 1964. Wilson, *The Truly Disadvantaged* (Chicago: University of Chicago Press, 1987). The West Side Urban Renewal Plan is described in an unpublished manuscript on the life and works of Roger Starr, written for a Charles Revson Fellowship at Columbia University by JS, 1983.

Pages 146–47. Price's comments were originally published in a community newsletter distributed in the West Side Urban Renewal Area, 1975; see also JS, " 'Tipping' in Housing: A Hard Case," *Dissent,* winter 1985. For Saul Alinsky's "5 percent" proposal, see Hirsch, *Second Ghetto,* 209.

Page 148. *The Kerner Report: The 1968 Report of the National Advisory Commission on Civil Disorders* (reprinted New York: Pantheon Books, 1988) helped shape a generation of journalists' and public officials' conceptions of the role of racism in American life. According to the former city welfare director Charles Morris, Lindsay presented each of his commissioners with a copy of the report and made it required reading.

Page 148. Bushwick's story, told by Martin Gottlieb in a fall 1977 *Daily News* series, "Our Dying Neighborhoods," and to JS in 1978 interviews for the *North Brooklyn News* (Jan. 5–11, 1979) with John Dereszewski, former city district manager for Bushwick, the Reverend James Kelly of St. Brigid's Church, and others. Pages 148–57. The dynamics of disinvestment are explained in Geoffrey Stokes and Gary Tilzer, "The Lords of Flatbush," *Village Voice,* Sept. 3–9 and 10–16, 1980, and in JS, "Neighborhood Gentrification: More Inequity than Meets the Eye," *Dissent,* spring 1982. Lindsay's comment is in Robbins, *Reminiscences,* 118. Cuomo, *Diary,* 86. Cuomo, interview with JS, Nov. 28, 1989. Benjamin, "The Continuing American Tragedy," *Emerge* magazine, Nov. 1989. Hynes, interview with JS, Oct. 1989. JS's observations of the Nehemiah program and rally are reported in *City Limits,* a New York City housing monthly, Nov. 1982.

6: RIGHTS AND RECIPROCITY

Pages 162–64. Gilder, *Wealth and Poverty* (New York: Basic Books, 1980); Murray, *Losing Ground: American Social Policy, 1950–1980* (New York: Basic Books, 1984); Mead, *Beyond Entitlement: The Social Obligations of Citizenship* (New York: Free Press, 1986). On the police sergeants' exam, see *NYN,* Nov. 19 and 30, 1985; Dec. 8, 1986; Dec. 1, 1987. For whites who reclassified themselves, see Leonard Levitt, " 'Race Change' Helps Out Cop," *NYN,* Dec. 6, 1985.

Pages 165–67. Siegel, a professor of history at the Cooper Union, in New York City, is at work on a book about liberalism and the judiciary. See his "Nothing in Moderation," *Atlantic,* May 1990, and "What Liberals Haven't Learned, and Why," *Commonweal,* Jan. 12, 1990. Siegel's comments on judicial liberalism are reported in JS, "Has Liberalism Self-Destructed?" *Prospect Press,* Dec. 5–18, 1985. On housing project screening, see Starr, "Twenty Years of Housing Programs," *Public Interest,* fall 1975. Siegel's comments on liberals and government are in "What Liberals Haven't Learned."

Pages 168–69. The NYCLU's conduct in 1968 is described and debated in Joseph W. Bishop, "Politics & ACLU," *Commentary,* Dec. 1971, and in letters from readers, ibid., March 1972; Mayer, *Strike,* 48; and Ravitch, *Wars,* 357–66. For the NYCLU's indecision about the post–Howard Beach high school meeting, see Nat Hentoff, "All Because of the Color of Their Skin," *Washington Post,* Jan. 24, 1987: "As a reporter who had covered the civil rights movement in the South during the 1960s later said, 'The only thing that was missing was a sign on the door, "For Colored Only." ' . . . 'Look at it this way,' [Mayor Koch told the WCBS radio reporter Irene Cornell]. 'What if a white community group had a meeting in a public place and excluded black reporters. All you journalists would have called that a vile act.' I wondered at the silence of the NYCLU. The executive director told me they had no policy on the matter. . . . An extended internal debate then took place among some NYCLU staff, with some of the attorneys arguing that the privacy rights of free association were paramount in this case. . . . Getting a copy of the state education law, the NYCLU discovered that the law declares unequivocally that any use of a school building for social and civic meetings 'shall be nonexclusive and open to the general public." LaMarche, "Don't Scapegoat Civil Liberties," *NYN,* Nov. 3, 1988.

Pages 172–74. Kevin Flynn, "State Probes 'Racist' Manual," *NYN,* May 4, 1987. Paul Moses, "Lawmakers Angrily Debate 'Racist' Manual," *NYN,* May 7, 1987.

Robert D. McFadden, "Manual Says Whites Are Racists," *NYT,* May 16, 1987. Steinberg's comments on institutional racism are from his *The Ethnic Myth: Race, Ethnicity and Class in America* (Boston: Beacon Press, 1989), 288. Steele's comments on "race fatigue" are in *his Content of Our Character.*

Page 175. For the turnover in New York City public schools and the low availability of minority candidates, see Michael Powell, "The Front Lines," *NYN,* Dec. 12, 1989. According to the American Council on Education, 85 percent of whites and only 50 percent of blacks passed teacher competency examinations in New York State in 1985; reported by Andrew Hacker in *NYRB,* Oct. 12, 1989.

Pages 175–77. Chavis's charges and the environmentalists' responses are reported in *NYT,* Feb. 1, 1990. For Pitts's termination, see Rex Smith, " 'Racist' Manual + False Resumé = No Job," *NYN,* June 20, 1987. Steele's comments on "integration shock" are from his *Content of our Character.*

Pages 177–82. These pages are adapted from JS, " 'Tipping' in Housing." See also Jefferson Morley, "Double Reverse Discrimination," *New Republic,* July 9, 1984, and Elise Rosen, "Starrett Optimistic a Year after Quotas Were Dropped," *City Sun,* Nov. 29–Dec. 5, 1989.

7: BLACK MILITANTS' NEW END GAME

Pages 184–87. JS, "Maddox Maneuver No Help to Black Cause," *New York Post,* Jan. 3, 1987. Charles J. Hynes with Bob Drury, *Incident at Howard Beach* New York: (G.P. Putnam, 1989). Simpson's comments are from an interview with JS, March 1990.

Page 191. Lasch's comments on E. Franklin Frazier are in his *The Agony of the American Left* (New York: Vintage Books, 1968), 120. Chap. 4 of this book, "Black Power: Cultural Nationalism as Politics," is valuable reading. Cuomo, *Diary,* 137.

Pages 194–97. McWhite, president of the Marlboro Houses Roving Patrol, was honored by the Bensonhurst West End Community Council for her defense of the community against Sharpton during the march of Jan. 2, 1988; see Rita Giordano's report in *NYN,* Jan. 25, 1988. For a brief profile of Sharpton, see E. R. Shipp, "A Flamboyant Civil Rights Leader," *NYT,* Jan. 21, 1988. The murders are described in *NYN* accounts, each published the day after the date indicated for the murder. Crime statistics provided by New York State Division of Criminal Justice show that, in 1988, perpetrators were identified for 904 of the 1,913 murders in New York City. Among the 904 victims whose killers were known, 87 blacks were killed by whites and 88 whites were killed by blacks.

Pages 197–98. Sharpton's comments were reported by Douglas and Haberman, in *NYN,* Dec. 3, 1989. McCarthy, "Black Men's Crisis Still Allows Choice," *NYN,* Jan. 10, 1990. O'Gorman's comments are reported in Michel Marriott, "This Wasn't the Boy East Harlem Knew," *NYT,* Feb. 7, 1990. See also Ned O'Gorman, *The Children Are Dying* (New York: Signet Books, 1978). An exchange between Daughtry and Bensonhurst's Reverend Charles Fermeglia is in *NYT,* Sept. 6, 1989. Daughtry, interview with JS, Nov. 1989.

Pages 199–201. For the Strianese murder, see Patricia Hurtado, "Man, 19, Acquitted of Murder," *NYN,* Feb. 5, 1987. Hynes's comments are from an interview with JS, Oct. 1989. For the Hanson-slashing trial, see Patricia Hurtado, "Maddox

Faces Misconduct Complaints," *NYN,* May 12, 1988. For Maddox's 1967 beating, see Jill Nelson, "Up Against the System," *Washington Post Magazine,* May 10, 1987. Steele, *Content of Our Character.*

Pages 202–04. Hudson, interview with JS, Sept. 1989. For Carson's comment, see Ron Howell, "A Call for Black Action," *NYN,* Jan. 4, 1987. JS, "Black Howard Beach Response Feeds Racism," *In These Times,* Jan. 21–27, 1987. Emery, in Alexander Stille's *National Law Journal* profile of Maddox, Feb. 16, 1987. Lasch's observations on Martin Luther King, Jr., are in *Harper's,* March 1987. For Green's criticism of Sharpton and the latter's response, see James Barron, "Black Official Faults Tactics of Sharpton," *NYT,* March 2, 1988. For Montgomery's comment, see James Barron, "Legislator Seeks to Oust Leader of Black Caucus," *NYT,* March 3, 1988.

Pages 204–07. Green's comment is from an interview with JS, Oct. 1989. Butts's comment is from the Associated Press, May 20, 1989. Jackson's comment was reported to JS by Youngblood and confirmed by *NYN*'s Curtis Taylor. Daughtry's "ambivalence about IAF" was expressed to JS in an interview, Nov. 1989. Youngblood's comments on IAF training are from an interview with JS, Nov. 1989. Dinkins's comment to high school students is cited in Joe Klein, "The Sorrow and the City," *New Republic,* Nov. 13, 1989.

Pages 207–09. For Carson's and Chimurenga's comments, see *NYN,* Sept. 22, 1988. The Slave Theater mural was viewed by JS. Wieseltier, "Scar Tissue," *New Republic,* June 5, 1989.

8: Militants, "Professional Blacks," and
the Culture of Schools

Pages 211–16. Weusi's and Barkar's comments are from interviews with JS, Sept. 1989. Johnson, interview with JS, Dec. 1989. The Liberal party chief Raymond Harding attacked Jitu Weusi, as reported in "Liberal Chief: Dinkins Aide Is a Jew-Baiter," *New York Post,* Oct. 6, 1989. Meier, interview with JS, Dec. 1989. Cruse, "The Fire This Time?" *NYRB,* May 8, 1969. Remarks of Youngblood, undated paper on education issued by EBC. Other EBC comments on education in an Industrial Areas Foundation paper, "Nehemiah II: Schools/Work," Oct. 1985.

Pages 217–20. Bernstein, "Two Schools: One Works, the Other Doesn't," *NYN,* Dec. 11, 1989, and "Foes: Carson Is School Bully," *NYN,* Oct. 18, 1989. Vann's comments on community control are from an interview with Alex Poinsett, in *Ebony,* May 1969. Nathan Glazer took a benign view of community control in *NYT Magazine,* April 27, 1969; Weusi, in an interview with JS, Sept. 1989; Carson, in Bernstein, "Foes."

Pages 221–23. For Sanford on cultural learning styles, see John Hildebrand, "Panel: Book Should Drop Ethnic Slants," *NYN,* Oct. 20, 1988. Sanford commented that because black children's needs were so great, white children were not on his agenda; see "Regent Is Asked to Quit Board," UPI, in *NYN,* Jan. 24, 1988. Julius Lester's comments are cited in Draper, *Rediscovery,* 126–27. Fordham and Ogbu, "Black Students' School Success: Coping with the 'Burden of "Acting White,"" *Urban Review* 18 (1986): 176–206.

Pages 224–26. Sharpton's declaration is in JS, "Schools Chancellorship: Would

Gifford Get an Impossible Job?" *New York Observer,* Oct. 12, 1987. Sanford's statement on not challenging a black male chancellor is from the transcript of WABC's
"Like It Is," June 25, 1989. For the search panel's finding on Sanford's experience
and ability, see Emily Sachar, *NYN,* Dec. 24, 1987. On Dec. 31, 1987, Sanford
charged that racism and sexism had prevented her from becoming a finalist in the
search; see Barbara Whitaker, "Green Leaves Cool Success for NYC Hot Spot,"
NYN, Jan. 4, 1989. Gifford's words on the race question are from Preston Wilcox,
"The Right to Emphasize Race," *NYN,* Oct. 13, 1987. Mason's comment about
Green and the latter's response are from Whitaker, "Green Leaves Cool Success."
Weusi's comment is from an interview with JS, Sept. 1989.

Pages 227–31. For Hacker on the SAT, see his "Affirmative Action: The New
Look," *NYRB,* Oct. 12, 1989. The quoted *NYN* editorial dates from Feb. 13, 1990.
See also the *NYT* editorial "A Tough Test for the Regents," April 27, 1990. For
Assemblyman Eve's comments on "genocide," see "Regents Consider Changes,"
City Sun, Aug. 9–15, 1989. The comments to Noble by Clarke and Jeffries are from
the transcript of "Like It Is," Feb. 26, 1989. See Hacker, "How Much Bias Is Too
Much?" *NYN,* Sept. 17, 1989.

Pages 231–38. Sobol, letter to newspaper editors, Feb. 5, 1990. *NYN* editorial,
Feb. 13, 1990. Patterson, *Ethnic Chauvinism,* chap. 6. Johnson, interview with JS,
Dec. 1989. Harris, interview with JS, "Can the City Schools Afford to Lose Him?"
NYN, March 10, 1988. Pierre sent a copy of his letter to Chancellor Richard Green,
written April 4, 1989, to JS. JS has a copy of Schwartz's letter as it appeared in the
Daily News, but the date is missing from the clip. For Lucas's comments about Jews
at a rally for Adelaide Sanford, see Clem Richardson, "Racial Tensions Usher In
New Year," *NYN,* Dec. 28, 1987.

9: FOLLY ON THE LEFT

Pages 239–44. Naison, *Communists in Harlem,* 216–17. Siegel, *Troubled Jour-
ney: From Pearl Harbor to Ronald Reagan* (New York: Hill and Wang, 1984).
McWilliams, "Muhammad Ali for Congress," *Nation,* July 22–29, 1978. Kopkind,
"Jackson Action: Strategies for Now—and Next Time," *Nation,* Sept. 25, 1989.
Kopkind's dismal oeuvre on race relations stretches back to his "Soul Power,"
NYRB, Aug. 24, 1967. For Jackson's remarks, see Cowan, *The Tribes of America*
(Garden City, N.Y.: Doubleday, 1979), 93.

Pages 244–47. Fink and Brian Greenberg, *Upheaval in the Quiet Zone: A History
of Hospital Workers' Union Local 1199* (Urbana: University of Illinois Press, 1989),
chap. 10. Weusi and Daughtry, interviews with JS, Sept. and Oct. 1989. Weusi's
comments about youths demonstrating with posters of Mao Zedong are from an
interview with *Forward March,* a radical journal, March–April 1987.

Pages 248–50. Naison, "A Corps of Last Resort," *NYN,* Oct. 3, 1989. Currie,
"Crime and Drugs: Reclaiming a Liberal Issue" (Paper for a conference on FDR
and the Future of Liberalism, Oct. 1989). See also the letters by Currie, Richard
Herrnstein, and Christopher Jencks in "Genes and Crime: An Exchange," *NYRB,*
June 11, 1987. Morris, *A Time of Passion* (New York: Harper & Row, 1984), 188–
89.

Pages 250–54. Steinberg, *Ethnic Myth,* 288–99. Glasgow's comment, cited by

Steinberg, is from Glasgow's *The Black Underclass* (New York: Vintage Books, 1981), 25. Kunstler on Pang Ching Lam is from Stanley Pinsley, "Kunstler Still Making the Left's Case," *Manhattan Lawyer*, Aug. 1, 1989. For an interesting defense of Kunstler's contention that police in the Bronx could not be trusted in the Larry Davis case, see Francis Wilkinson, "Davis 2, Cops 0," *7 Days*, Nov. 30, 1988. Naison's comments are from an interview with JS, Oct. 1989. The *Nation*'s editorial on Goetz, "Subway Catharsis," appeared on Jan. 19, 1985; JS, letter to the editor, Feb. 15, 1985.

Pages 254–56. Jones, "Brawley and Others: Justice in the Hudson Valley," *Nation*, March 19, 1988. Diamond, "Reversing Brawley," *Nation*, Oct. 31, 1988. Kunstler, interview with Jon Kalish in *NYN*, June 23, 1988. The *New Republic*'s stories on Brawley case: Tucker, "Mystery at Wappinger's Falls," March 21, 1988, and Stanley Crouch, "Three Buckets of Jive," July 11, 1988.

Pages 256–59. Miskiewicz, "They'd Practice, Not Preach," *NYN*, Aug. 12, 1988. The *Nation*'s editorial on the Central Park jogger case, "The Rape in Central Park," May 29, 1989. Monteiro, "African-American Equality and the Struggle against Racism," *Political Affairs*, Aug. 1989. Mayer, *Strike*, 116–17. Kunstler, interview with Jon Kalish in *NYN*, June 23, 1988. Greenman, "Kunstler's Reverse Racism," *NYN*, July 8, 1988.

10: "VOTE YOUR HOPES—AND YOUR FEARS"

Pages 261–62. These pages are from JS, "Will These Men Change New York?" *Village Voice*, Dec. 9–15, 1981.

Pages 262–72. These pages are adapted from JS, "Black Politics in Brooklyn: Starker Choices, Higher Risks," *Dissent*, spring 1983. JS, "The Battle for Black Brooklyn: A Heated Race for Chisholm's Seat," *Village Voice*, Aug. 31, 1982, and "Vander Beatty's Desperate Gamble," ibid., Oct. 26, 1982. Sydney Schanberg, "Stealing an Election," *NYT*, Oct. 23, 1982. The *NYT* endorsement of Owens came on Sept. 20, 1982. For the "nigger-breaker" accusations, see *Big Red*, Sept. 11, 1982.

Pages 272–78. The pattern of appointment to the Manhattan borough presidency was described by Barbara Fife in an interview with JS, Nov. 1989. The description of Jackson's 1984 campaign is in JS, "Black Empowerment Blues," *In These Times*, Jan. 16–22, 1985. JS, "A Message from New York City's Black Voters," *NYT*, Sept. 22, 1984. Kilson, "Blacks: Ready for the Rainbow?" *NYN*, Aug. 22, 1989. Chapin, "United They Stand a Chance," *NYN*, Aug. 11, 1989, and "A Tabernacle for Dinkins?" May 3, 1989. For Dinkins and Farrakhan, see Jeffrey Schmaltz, "Dinkins Gets a Police Guard after Remarks by Farrakhan," *NYT*, Oct. 10, 1985.

11: A POLITICS BEYOND RACE?

Pages 280–84. Arrests at the Board of Education were reported by Joyce Purnick in *NYT*, April 26, 1983. Weusi, interview with JS, Sept. 1989. For Jack Newfield's comments on the coalition and Vann's comments on Hispanic reaction, see JS, "Something Rotten in the Big Apple," *In These Times*, March 20–26, 1985. Of the Coalition for a Just New York's surrender to Farrell, Newfield wrote, "No one who was an accomplice to this act of perfidy should be rewarded for it. We are all responsible." Cooper's remarks on Dinkins are from an interview with JS, Nov. 1989. Jones's comment is in *NYN,* Oct. 29, 1989.

Pages 284–87. Chapin's dictum is in *NYN,* Sept. 30, 1988. The account of the meetings with Lynch was given by Cooper in an interview with JS, Nov. 1989. Curtis Taylor with George E. Jordan, "Activists Miffed at Dinkins," *NYN,* Oct. 30, 1989. Sharpton's comments were heard by JS on Nov. 2, 1989.

Pages 289–92. For an analysis of earlier ethnic machines, see Steven P. Erie, *Rainbow's End: Irish-Americans and the Dilemmas of Urban Machine Politics, 1840–1985* (Berkeley: University of California Press, 1988). Cooper's comments are from an interview with JS, Nov. 1989. Dinkins's interview with Phil Donahue is in *NYN,* Sept. 5, 1989. Newfield and Barrett, *City for Sale: Ed Koch and the Betrayal of New York* (New York: Harper & Row, 1989). "Journalist Jack Newfield, whose book *City for Sale* lionizes Giuliani, was whispering into the prosecutor's ear that the city wanted and needed him. . . . Robert Hayes of the Coalition of the Homeless . . . arranged [a tour for Giuliani of shelters] at the request of a mutual friend and Jack Newfield," reported James Ledbetter in "Making Mr. Right," *7 Days,* May 31, 1989. Fitch, "Koch's Karma—and Ours," *NYN,* March 2, 1989. See also Fitch, "Did Dinkins Really Win?" *NYN,* April 20, 1990.

Pages 293–98. Penta, "New York City's Political Culture: A Bigger Rotten Barrel" (Speech to St. John's Law School faculty, Nov. 17, 1987). JS attended the IAF at St. Paul the Apostle Church auditorium, Ninth Avenue and fifty-ninth Street, Oct. 29, 1989.

Pages 298–302. Guttenplan, in *NYN,* Nov. 8, 1989. Klein, in his *New York* magazine column, May 7, 1990. Dinkins's address was reported in *NYN,* May 12, 1990. The Levin fracas was reported in *NYN,* May 3, 1990.

EPILOGUE

Pages 303–04. Cantarella's testimony of Dec. 19, 1983, before a House Subcommittee on Domestic Monetary Policy, was reprinted in the *Amsterdam News,* Dec. 31, 1983. McCarthy, "Minority Pawns in a Power Play," *NYN,* March 28, 1990.

Pages 305–06. Bernard was reading from an Aug. 27, 1989, *Daily News* column by Bob Herbert which likened Hawkins's murder to the elaborate, protracted lynching of Emmett Till in Mississippi in 1955. Jesse Jackson is seen drawing an analogy to the Till murder while speaking with reporters at Hawkins's funeral in the documentary *Seven Days in Bensonhurst* (Tom Lennon Productions), which aired on May 15 on Channel 13 in New York. But Shelby Steele, the film's narrator, says that the crowds mourning Hawkins were enacting a "ritual" that glossed the differences between the two events.

Pages 306–16. The *City Sun* reported reminiscences of FDR alumnae of the 1960s on Aug. 23–29, 1989. Cuomo, interview with JS, Nov. 28, 1989. Maddox's suspension was ordered by Appellate Division, Second Judicial Dept., Supreme Court, State of New York, Motion No. 624 Attny., May 21, 1990. Cuomo spoke to the New Democratic Coalition, May 11, 1974, while running for lieutenant governor. He lost, and Governor Hugh Carey appointed him secretary of state. He lost a mayoral race to Koch in 1977 and was elected lieutenant governor in 1978.

Index